West Africa and Christianity

Peter B. Clarke

Edward Arnold

© Peter B. Clarke 1986

First published in 1986 by
Edward Arnold (Publishers) Ltd
41 Bedford Square, London WC1B 3DQ

British Library Cataloguing in Publication Data

Clarke, Peter B. (Peter Bernard)
　　West Africa and Christianity.
　　1. Africa, West—Church history
　　I. Title
　　209′.66　　　　BR1460

ISBN 0 7131 8263 6

Typeset in Great Britain by The Castlefield Press, Moulton, Northampton
Printed in Great Britain by Whitstable Litho Ltd., Whitstable, Kent

Contents.

Maps and plates   v

Acknowledgements   vi

Introduction   1

1 The first phase: 1445–1790   7
*Cape Verde, Sierra Leone
and Senegambia*   9
*São Tomé, Elmina, Benin
and Warri*   17
Protestant missionary efforts   23

2 The emergence of the
modern Christian missionary
movement and its impact on
West Africa 1790–1840   30
Sierra Leone   32
Liberia   37
Ghana   41
Senegambia   43

3 Towards the establishment
of 'self-governing,
self-supporting, self-
propagating' African
Churches 1840–1890   47
Sierra Leone   48
Liberia   51
Ghana   57
Benin and Togo   60
Nigeria   62
Senegambia   70
*Cape Verde, Guinea Bissau,
São Tomé e Principe*   80

4 The Christian missionary
movement during the
colonial era 1890–1960 in
former British West Africa
and Liberia   86
Sierra Leone   87
Liberia   92
Ghana   96
Nigeria   99

5 The Christian missionary
movement during the
colonial era 1890–1960 in
former French West and
Equatorial and Portuguese
West Africa   121
Senegambia   122

Mauritania   126
Guinea   126
Mali   130
Burkina Faso (Upper Volta)   133
Niger   137
Benin   138
Togo   140
Ivory Coast   143
Cameroon   148
Chad   150
*Cape Verde, Guinea Bissau,
São Tomé e Principe*   150

6 The rise, expansion and
impact of independent
Churches, 1890–1960   157
Nigeria   160
Ivory Coast   179
Ghana   187

7 Christianity since
independence, 1960 to
the present: growth and
change   195
*Anglophone West Africa:
Sierra Leone, Liberia, Ghana,
Nigeria*   195
*Francophone West Africa:
Ivory Coast, Guinea, Senegal,
Burkina Faso*   202
*Transfer of ecclesiastical
authority*   207
*Growth of interdenominational
organisations*   209

8 Developments in Christian
relations with Islam and
African traditional
religions   215

9 Christianity, nation
building, nationalism
and the State   227

10 Conclusions: Christianity
and religious change in
West Africa   244

Select bibliography   250

Essay questions/Topics
for discussion   256

Index   259

Maps and plates.

Maps
I   Christian missions in West Africa, 1792–1914   30
II   British influence in West Africa, 1914   86
III   French and Portuguese influence in West Africa, 1914   121
IV   Contemporary West Africa   227

Plates
I   Elmina castle   18
II   Church made of mud, Wusasa, Zaria, Nigeria   116
III   The altar in the church at Wusasa   116
IV   Garrick Sokari Braide   165
V   Members of the Cherubim and Seraphim Society   172
VI   Prophet Harris   180
VII   A woman Presbyterian minister in Ghana officiating at the
communion service   199
VIII A modern-day missionary going about her work in
northern Nigeria   202

Acknowledgements.

Many people have helped to make this book possible and to all of them I say a sincere thank you. Archivists at mission archives in Nigeria, Senegal, London and Paris, and in particular Père Bernard Noël, archivist at the Holy Ghost Fathers at Chevilly, Paris, gave me every help and encouragement.

My former colleagues in the Departments of History, and Religious Studies at the University of Ibadan, also deserve a special mention for their encouragement and friendship. And the same applies to my colleagues in the Department of the History and Philosophy of Religion at King's College, University of London.

Mr. Christopher Fyfe, Professor Richard Gray, Professor Bengt Sundkler and Dr. Antonio Barbossa da Silva read an earlier draft of this work and provided me with many valuable comments and insights both with regard to form and content. And while they may still have certain reservations about the final product I can only say in thanking them that without their help even less would have been accomplished.

Pa David Adeniji of Ibadan, a friend, interpreter and guide through towns and villages in Western Nigeria deserves special mention and thanks as do the many clergy, catechists and lay Christians in Nigeria and Senegal who gave me their time and hospitality.

I also wish to thank Professor Harold Turner for supplying me with the photograph of Garrick Sokari Braide and that of the Aladura church members.

Finally I thank my family and friends and the editors at Edward Arnold (Publishers) for their patience and understanding during the years spent writing this book.

The publishers would like to thank the following for permission to reproduce photographs in this book:

The Bodleian Library, Oxford (ref: Ms Afr. s. 1530 1. p. 43 No. 11): plate I;
Professor Harold Turner: plates IV and V;
The Methodist Church: plate VI;
Kyrkans Internationalla: plate VII;
John Hare: plates II, III and VIII.

Thanks are also due to J.D. Fage and Maureen Verity for the maps reproduced in this book which are taken from *An Atlas of African History*, 2nd edition (Edward Arnold, 1978).

Introduction.

The West African setting

West Africa, like other regions of Africa has a long, intricate and complex history behind it. Not only have empires such as Ancient Ghana, Mali and Songhai come and gone, but there have also been significant changes in every aspect of life and culture including religion. Religion in Africa – and as far as this study is concerned that means Christianity in particular – has both influenced and been influenced by economic, political, social and cultural developments. However, before moving on to the subject of Christianity we will first of all consider the overall setting in which this religion began to develop in the second half of the fifteenth century. Of course, the following account of the West African setting in the fifteenth century presents a rather static picture of what was a changing society.

Land and people[1]

West Africa can be divided geographically into three main regions: the Coastal, Forest and Savanna regions. The Coastal region extends from Mauritania in the north to the Niger Delta in the south and stretches inland for a distance of between 40 and 120 kilometres; the Forest region stretches across West Africa from Sierra Leone to Cameroon, a distance of some 480 kilometres, and varies in width from a few to over 100 kilometres; and the Savanna region is situated between the Forest region in the south and the Sahara desert to the north.

Among the oldest of the many inhabitants of the Coastal region are the Wolof and Serer, the Bullom and Sherbo, the Guan and the Ijaw. In the Forest region there are also numerous peoples including the Fon, the Ashanti, the Baule, the Mende and Temne, the Kru, the Yoruba, Edo and Ibo. The Savanna region includes the Tokolor, Fulani, Mandinka, Songhai, Hausa, Kanuri and Tiv. These are but a few of the peoples of these regions. Those inhabiting the Coastal and Forest zones speak what are classified as West Atlantic languages, with the exception of the Mende and Temne who are Mande-speaking. A number of those in the Savanna region are also Mande-speaking, for example the Bambara, Malinke and Soninke who are all Mandinka, while others such as the Kanuri and Songhai speak a Nilo-Saharan language and the Hausa, an Afro-Asiatic language.

Political and social organisation

Throughout West Africa and even within the three zones mentioned above, political and social organisation differed. In some parts of the Coastal region, for example, along the coast of northern Senegal there were fairly compact, centralised chiefdoms, while further south in Sierra Leone and Liberia political units were much smaller and were sometimes village based. This, however, did not prevent the development of a fairly wide trading network along the coast and into the interior. But most people would have been engaged in such occupations as animal husbandry, agriculture and fishing.

The pattern of political and social organisation was not that dissimilar in the Forest region where chiefdoms and states could be found alongside much smaller independent communities consisting of no more than a handful of villages. Urban settlements were more common among the Yoruba than most other peoples, and in Oyo and Benin, both in Nigeria, large centralised states had either begun to emerge or were already in existence by the time the first Christian missionaries arrived in West Africa in the second half of the fifteenth century. This development was assisted by the fact that these two states with their iron deposits had established wide trading networks with commercial centres in the Savanna region and elsewhere.

Some of the largest kingdoms established in the Savanna region have already been mentioned, and in general the kingdom was the most common form of political organisation in this part of West Africa. One reason for this lay in the fact that communication and travel were much easier in the Savanna and this facilitated the establishment of relatively large political entities. Of course, there were also to be found in this region, as elsewhere, highly decentralised societies, even stateless societies with no central authority, for example in areas inhabited by the Bobo, Dogon, Lodagaa and Tiv.[2]

While some people engaged in such occupations as the mining, smelting and forging of iron, the making of agricultural implements, domestic utensils and weapons, the weaving and dyeing of cloth, or leather work, others were involved in agriculture, fishing or in administration. But it is important to remember when we come to discuss Christian missionary expansion in this region, for example among groups of Bambara in present-day Mali, that there were small-scale societies and scattered, isolated settlements even in the Savanna. This made missionary activity difficult and accounts to some extent for the somewhat slower pace of development of Christianity in these areas (see Chapter 4 pp. 107 ff. and Chapter 5 especially pp. 131 ff.

Religion

Several centuries before the arrival of Christianity in West Africa Islam had already established a presence there.[3] However, Islam at this time was for the most part confined to a limited number of areas in the Savanna region while traditional African religions remained, as far as we know, the religion of the vast majority. The use of the term 'traditional' here to describe African religions is not intended, it should be noted, to convey the impression that these religions were static, unchanging systems of belief and practice, but is simply a convenient and appropriate way of referring to the oldest of West Africa's 'living religions'.[4] Although traditional religions were once regarded as nothing more than fetishism or a bunch of superstitions by social scientists, historians and missionaries alike, they are now studied with greater sympathy, objectivity and understanding.[5]

It is not our purpose in this study to describe in any detail the 'nature' of African traditional religions but simply to point out that they were often a very important force in society, exercising a strong influence on the educational, medical, cultural, economic, social and political spheres. Indeed it is sometimes difficult to draw a line between the religious and these other areas of life. There is, of course, a personal as well as a social dimension to traditional religions.

While recognising that there were differences in beliefs and practices many African traditional religions not only shared a belief in a Supreme Being but also similar views on such matters as the nature of the person, the relationship between the individual and the wider society, and the role of religion in society. While it was stressed that the individual was unique, with his or her own personality, talents and 'destiny', the individual was not thought of in isolation from the cosmos as a whole or the rest of society.

Dogon ideas on the 'self' or 'soul' demonstrate this point. Among the Dogon of Mali, while a person at birth is regarded as a human being, that is not the end of the matter. Society also confers on that person its own form of a 'spiritual', 'sexual', 'social' and 'intellectual' identity. The community, for example, in one of its naming ceremonies which the newborn person must undergo, confers upon the child both an 'intelligent' soul and all that is necessary to link the person with the laws of the cosmos.

Thus, in a sense, one is a person by virtue of one's membership of the community, and this establishes an inextricable bond between the individual and society. Moreover, individual freedom and maturity consist in large measure in being socially responsible and in adapting one's thoughts and actions to the needs and requirements of the society of which one is a member. It was the role of religion to sustain and maintain this relationship between individual and society, and in the course of doing so it would inevitably tend to uphold and reinforce the existing norms and values of society at large. This to some extent explains the close relationship between the religious and political spheres (see Chapter 8, p. 214).

Religion, as we have already pointed out, influenced every sphere of life, including art. In western Nigeria, to take but one example, the well-known terra cottas and bronzes from Ife which date back many centuries are among other things representations of sacred kings, while others are of gods including Oduduwa, the founder of the Yoruba people. In other places such as Benin, bronze casting was done on a prolific scale, as was wood carving. This art, which often had some religious significance, was intended like religion itself to give cohesion and unity to the community.

Christianity

To treat Christianity as if it were a unified system of beliefs and practices would be to distort the reality, as the history of Christianity in West Africa and elsewhere demonstrates very clearly. There is a vast variety of Christian Churches and movements and these have emerged at different times in history. One important historical landmark, as far as the diversity of Christian missionary bodies and societies in West Africa and elsewhere is concerned, was the Reformation that took place in Europe in the sixteenth century. Until then the Western part of the Christian Church was under the authority of Rome. The distinct Eastern Church, which had separated from Rome in 1054, was centred on Constantinople (Istanbul). In the first half of the sixteenth century, under the inspiration and leadership of Martin Luther, and later of John Calvin, the Protestant Reformation took shape and gave a new direction to Christianity in the West. It gave rise to several new Church organisations which rejected the authority of the Pope of Rome and insisted that Scripture alone was the only source of guidance and authority.

The Roman Catholic Church which accepted the authority of the Pope remained a very large body, but Protestant Churches became prominent in a number of European countries. The Lutheran Church, for example, spread throughout Germany, Denmark, Norway and Sweden; the Calvinist or 'Reformed' Churches in Switzerland, Holland, France and Scotland; and the Anglican Church in England. These Protestant Churches gave rise to other Christian groups and Churches, for example the Baptists, Presbyterians, Quakers, Methodists and many more.

The divisions within the Christian Church were later reflected in the development of Christianity in West Africa, and indeed in the pattern of worldwide Christian missionary expansion as it got underway in earnest in the eighteenth and nineteenth centuries (see Chapters 2 and 3). Moreover, in West Africa itself and in other parts of Africa such as Southern Africa, independent, African Christian Churches were established in the nineteenth century, creating even greater diversity within the Christian Church (see Chapter 5).

Christianity, therefore, is a very general term covering a great variety of religious beliefs, practices and organisations. Furthermore, disagreement, rivalry, competition and conflict characterised relations between the various Christian traditions for a long time after the Reformation and this was once again reflected in the West African context. In more recent times efforts have been made to bring about closer co-operation between the Christian Churches and to promote greater tolerance and understanding not only between themselves but also between

Christianity and other religions (see Chapters 6 and 7).

While disagreements have loomed large, it is possible, none the less, to point to some overall agreement on a limited number of fundamentals which all Christian traditions have accepted in the past and accept today. For example, although the way they interpret this may differ, all agree that because of 'Original sin' all men need to be saved, and that Jesus Christ is the Saviour. This is given as a central reason for missionary activity. There is also general agreement that the Old and New Testaments are the two most important, revealed sources of Christian belief, and that the fulfilment of human existence is to be found in an after-life beyond death. While the emphasis and interpretation have varied from one tradition to another, all Christian traditions appear to have accepted these three fundamental beliefs, the first of which, supported by other scriptural passages, is used to explain the universal, missionary role of Christianity.

Christianity arrived in West Africa in the middle years of the fifteenth century (see Chapter 1, pp. 9 ff.), but this was not its first appearance on the African continent. The first Christian Churches to be established in Africa were in Egypt, Tunisia, Ethiopia and Nubia (Sudan). In fact the founder of Christianity, Jesus, is said to have visited Egypt as an infant, and the foundation of the Christian Church at Alexandria in Egypt in the first century of the Christian era is attributed to St Mark, author of one of the four Christian gospels. The Christian New Testament suggests that the first African to be converted to Christianity was an Ethiopian from the ancient Kingdom of Meroé, between Aswan and Khartoum.[6] However, the Christian Church in Ethiopia was probably not established until the middle of the fourth century AD, and was dependent on the Church in Egypt.

A number of distinguished African Christian thinkers and writers emerged in this early period of Christianity in North Africa and Ethiopia, and their work has had a profound influence on the subsequent development of Christianity worldwide. According to one writer 'It was perhaps African missionaries who made the first translation of the Bible into Latin', and this Latin Bible had become established, by the year 400, as the authorised version.[7] The best known and perhaps most influential of the early North African Christian writers is Augustine, born in 354 AD at Thagaste, a small Numidian town now known as Souk-Arrhas in modern-day Algeria. Augustine, Bishop of the North African diocese of Hippo (395–430) not only wrote on specifically doctrinal matters but also on matters such as Church-state relations (see Chapter 8), and one of his books *The City of God* is still widely used today by, among others, students of history and political theory.

The impact of sub-Saharan African Christianity on Christianity generally is not likely to be any less profound than that of early Christianity in North Africa. As one writer points out, African Christianity is not a marginal curiosity, nor 'a mere exotic appendage' to Christianity in the wider world, but of central importance to its development. The study of the development of West African Christianity is not only of great interest in itself and to West Africans. It is also of interest and importance to students of Christianity in the rest of Africa and beyond its boundaries, because although increasingly grounded in its own culture, it is global none the less, ranging from the era of the trans-Atlantic slave trade through to the era of colonialism, industrialisation and nationalism.[8]

Notes

1   A.L. Mabogunje, The Land and Peoples of West Africa. In J.F.A. Ajayi and M. Crowder (eds), *The History of West Africa*, Vol. 1 (2nd ed.). Harlow: Longman, 1976: 1ff.
2   R. Horton, Stateless Societies in the History of West Africa. In J.F.A. Ajayi and M. Crowder (eds), op. cit., pp. 72 ff.
3   P.B. Clarke, *West Africa and Islam*. London: Edward Arnold, 1982.
4   G. Parrinder, *Africa's Three Religions* (2nd ed.), London: Longman, 1976, p. 8
5   J.O. Awolalu, *Yoruba Beliefs and Practices*, London: Sheldon Press, 1979.
6   Parrinder, *Africa's Three Religions*, p. 107.
7   H. Chadwick, *The Early Church*. Harmondsworth: Penguin, 1967: 65.
8   R. Gray, Christianity and Religious Change in Africa, *African Affairs* 77(306), January 1978: 89 ff.

1
The first phase: c. 1445–c. 1790.

Background

The arrival of the Portuguese at Cape Verde and the mouth of the River Senegal in 1444–5 began the first phase of the history of Christianity in West Africa. During this first phase, which was to last some 350 years, very little was achieved. For some time prior to 1444–5 the Portuguese prince, known to history as Henry the Navigator (1394–1460), had been systematically planning his country's exploration of the West African coast. One of his main objectives was the acquisition of sufficient knowledge to enable Portuguese ships to sail along the West African coast, around the Cape of Good Hope, and up along the east coast of Africa to the Christian state of Ethiopia. This would enable the Portuguese to avoid having to cross the Muslim states of the Middle East and North Africa in pursuit of their trading interests.

The forging of alliances with African states in order to combat more effectively any Muslim expansion was an important part of Portuguese political and economic policy at the time. The realisation that gold and slaves could be obtained in plenty from West Africa – though not the only reason, particularly at the outset – was eventually to play a very important part in Portugal's decision to try to establish Christian kingdoms there. These kingdoms would in theory be allies and trading partners of Portugal – in reality they would be client states – and enable Portugal to limit the political, economic and religious influence of the Muslim world while at the same time ensuring that she enjoyed a monopoly over the trade in gold and slaves. During the period c. 1450–c. 1550 alone the Portuguese carried a large number of African captives, sometimes as many as 2,000 a year, to Portugal. About half were re-exported to Castile (Spain) and the Americas, while half remained in Lisbon, Portugal's capital, creating the impression by the 1550s 'that in Lisbon there are more men and women slaves than free Portuguese'.[1] At this date slaves in fact accounted for some 10 per cent of Lisbon's population. Many worked as domestic servants, boatmen, water sellers, refuse collectors, and street vendors of snacks and refreshments. Others spent their life as agricultural labourers in the southern provinces of Alentejo and Algarve.[2]

The slave trade was to intensify, and in the opinion of one scholar the number of enslaved Africans from sub-Saharan Africa that were transported across the Sahara to the Muslim world along with those transported to Christian Europe and its colonies 'could not have been less than thirty million during the whole period of the trade'.[3] Some have suggested that there were many more than this,[4] while others put the figure much lower.[5] The thirty million figure, however, seems well founded.

Scholars have disagreed about the impact on Africa of the trans-Saharan and trans-Atlantic slave trades. Some maintain that the trade in slaves was not a new development in Africa and that in some respects, leaving moral issues to one side, it contributed in a positive way to political and economic development there.[6] Others maintain that, at least in certain areas of sub-Saharan Africa, the type of slavery that was carried on across the Sahara and the Atlantic did represent something new, and that its consequences for Africa were entirely negative.[7] Inikori convincingly argues that the trans-Saharan and trans-Atlantic slave trades had profound adverse consequences for the political, social, demographic, cultural and economic development of sub-Saharan Africa, to say nothing of the human misery and degradation endured by so many.

For about 100 years after the arrival of the Portuguese on the West Coast of Africa in the 1440s, West African gold was just as important as slaves, in fact even more so. Before the advent of the Europeans on the west coast the gold-producing regions of West Africa had been linked via the great empires such as Ancient Ghana and Mali to the Islamic world by means of trade routes across the Sahara. With the coming of the Europeans this situation began to change. More trading centres sprang into existence along the coast and gold from the Bambuk and Bure goldfields was directed along the rivers Senegal and Gambia to these centres. The Portuguese attempted to settle in Bambuk in order to acquire direct control over the gold supplies, but were expelled. Nevertheless, until the middle years of the sixteen century the quantities of gold that poured into Europe from West Africa were on the same scale as those from the Americas.[8]

Christian Europe, like parts of the Muslim world, was attracted to West Africa for commercial reasons as much as anything else. Making little distinction between religion and politics the Portuguese ultimately explained and justified their designs for and activities in West Africa in terms of the advance of religion. Prince Henry the Navigator, who was genuinely interested in expanding his geographical knowledge, spoke of his desire to discover the strength of his national and religious enemy, the Moors, and to advance the Christian faith. Moreover, a papal document commended his expeditions on the grounds that they were undertaken 'for the destruction and confusion of the Moors and the enemies of Christ and for the exaltation of the Catholic faith'.[9]

During this first phase of Christianity in West Africa (*c.* 1445–*c.* 1790), the Roman Catholic Church provided the vast majority of the missionaries. Missionary activity was not, however, continuous during this period, nor was the number of missionaries large. Mission centres in many parts of West Africa were left without a missionary for long periods of time. And difficulties arising from the climate, lack of interest in spreading Christianity, rivalry between those European countries competing for commercial supremacy in the region, and opposition from local rulers and people, though this was not general or widespread, go some way towards explaining the haphazard, intermittent nature of Christian missionary activity in West Africa during the period. Other factors include a lack of resources and the failure to build up an indiginous Church run by local clergy. It was not until 1975, over five hundred years after the arrival of the Portuguese, that the first Cape Verdean was consecrated a bishop in his own country. Generating sufficient resources and building a local church were not easy in the circumstances. In the case of the Portuguese missions, for example, the Portuguese Crown not only had control over the appointment of missionaries but also over the appointment of bishops to Africa. In the eighteenth century the French monarchy gained control over the appointment of clergy to Senegal. This meant that the missions were very much dependent on and controlled by the politics, directives and financial support of the state.[10] For the most part the clergy were little more than the equivalent in today's terms of rather poorly paid civil servants, hemmed in by numerous restrictions. It is against this background that the first phase of Christianity in West Africa needs to be considered.

The spread of Christianity c. 1445–c. 1790: a general outline

Before going on to consider the Portuguese attempts to establish Christian kingdoms at Benin and Warri, both in Bendel State in modern-day Nigeria, it is necessary first to provide a general outline of the spread of Christianity in West Africa in what might be called its first abortive phase.

The Cape Verde islands, Sierra Leone and the Senegambia

The Cape Verde islands, discovered by the Portuguese in 1458, are situated some 600 kilometres to the west of Dakar, capital of Senegal. These islands, fifteen in all, regained their independence from Portugal after a war of liberation in 1975, and are known today as the Republic of Cape Verde. The population is nearly 300,000, but there are many Cape Verdeans in Portugal and the United States, and smaller numbers in Senegal, Guinea Bissau and other West African countries.[11]

A Christian mission was established on the Cape Verde island of Santiago in 1462, and from 1533 this mission became the headquarters of Christian missionary activity not only for Cape Verde, but also for that stretch of the West African mainland which runs from the River Senegal in the north, southwards to Cape Palmas in present-day Liberia. In Cape Verde itself, missionary activity was not only lacking in continuity but was also narrow in scope. Religious authorities in Europe were slow or unable to replace missionaries whose assignment had ended or who had died. An attempt was made in the 1570s to train indigenous priests but this had little success, largely due to a shortage of personnel and resources. The school established at Santiago in the 1650s provided a basic education for a few but had little influence on the vast majority of the people. However, what little education there was at this time laid the foundations, in the opinion of one scholar, for the emergence of an intellectual, economic and social élite, many of them clerics, who became known locally as the *padri di terra*.[12]

One of the better-known missionaries who worked in Cape Verde and in other parts of West Africa in this period was the Jesuit Father Barreira. This missionary's career illustrates as well as that of any other the aims, aspirations, frustrations, moral dilemmas and problems facing most missionaries in this period. Barreira set out for the Cape Verde islands in June 1604. He believed, along with other members of his society, that the Cape Verdeans, and indeed the peoples all along the coast and in the interior of Africa south of the Sahara would, immediately on encountering a missionary, turn to Christianity.[13] This clearly overlooked the close connection between religion and the political, economic and social organisation of African societies. In fact, it also overlooked the close connection between the Christianity the missionaries wanted to spread in Africa and the cultural values and way of life of the Portuguese. Moreover, since they were funded, appointed and controlled in large measure by the Portuguese Crown, Barreira and his colleagues had little choice but to preach a Christianity that was not only anti-Muslim but also intensely nationalistic and closely linked to the political and economic interests of Portugal.[14]

While the government provided the finances and the transport and thereby made missionary activity possible, its control over these matters and over appointments posed serious problems for the missionaries. Moreover, as Barreira and others also found, the funds provided by the state were inadequate and this meant that missionaries had to become involved in trade to support themselves and their work. Some missionaries who were without too much scruple took to the buying and selling of slaves for the upkeep of the mission.[15] For others, slave trading constituted a serious moral problem.

Barreira, for instance, was of the opinion that it was neither easy nor even possible to justify the buying and selling of slaves. This practice, however, would have to be tolerated until some other means of financing missionary activity was discovered. He wrote:

> Experience has shown me . . . that we cannot live without slaves. I am also constrained to buy some. But I am of the opinion . . . that we ought to limit the service of those whom we will buy to a few years. We will declare that they are free if they have served us well, but if they do not serve us well . . . we will sell them.[16]

This compromise proposed by Barreira, while it satisfied some, was totally rejected by other missionaries. One Jesuit told Barreira that they should have no part in creating in West Africa a supply of Christians destined to go to their death in the mines of Peru. He stated 'If we understood correctly what was prohibited in this traffic (in slaves) that would be a great step forward for the Africans and for us who commit such a sin by this commerce'.[17] Despite this sort of absolute condemnation of the slave trade, missionary participation in it continued.

While tolerance of the slave trade no doubt provided the missions with very necessary funds and labour, in the long term it proved to be both short-sighted and misguided. The slave trade, by giving rise to political and social instability and by holding back economic development, undermined the conditions necessary for missionary success.[18] Moreover, from the perspective of the African there was probably not a great deal of difference between the missionary and the European, Christian layman in West Africa, many of whom showed very little or no interest at all in Christianity.

Missionaries not only engaged in trade and commerce, but were also active in politics. In 1608 in Sierra Leone, for example, missionaries were involved in the war for the kingship of the Temne, backing the claimant educated by them against a lapsed Christian.[19] Against this, it should be noted that some missionaries, like Barreira, were also engaged in confrontation from time to time with the Portuguese authorities. The Portuguese governor of Cape Verde is said to have commented on the death of Barreira in 1612 'that now his greatest enemy had gone'.[20]

Dedicated to the establishment and success of his Jesuit mission in Cape Verde and West Africa, Barreira accomplished a great deal despite the difficulties and problems outlined above. In Sierra Leone, where he worked (apart from a brief interval) from 1605 to 1608, Barreira converted two rulers, the King of the Temne and the King of Sierra Leone, and built a church on the south bank of the Sierra Leone River near Kru Bay. He believed like many of his contemporaries and many missionaries in West Africa in the second half of the nineteenth century that the best strategy was to go all out to convert the local rulers, and that once they had been converted all their subjects would follow their example. This, however, was to misunderstand the nature of the authority and power exercised by African chiefs. They were not dictators exercising absolute control over their people, but subject to a great many checks and balances. Moreover, though some were genuinely interested in Christianity as a religion and for its own sake, others adopted a highly pragmatic attitude towards it. In return for becoming Christians they expected the Portuguese to supply them with arms and ammunition.

What puzzled many missionaries was the fact that while African chiefs would listen with interest to what they had to say about Christianity, and express some agreement with what was said, they did not become Christians. Here the missionaries tended to mistake tolerance and openness for assent. They also did not realise that for an African ruler, like any other, a complete and total change in religious allegiance could have profound political and social consequences.

Some African rulers did convert to Christianity, but for many it was never going to be a straightforward, easy decision. The Jolof Prince

Bemoy is a case in point. Pressed by the Portuguese to become a Christian, this Senegalese ruler only began to contemplate the idea seriously when a section of his people rebelled against his authority. In need of arms, horses and men, Bemoy approached the Portuguese authorities and was informed that these would be supplied provided he gave serious thought to becoming a Christian.[21] Bemoy maintained all along that if he took this step his followers would desert him, and it was only after he had been defeated by his political rivals that he took the decision to convert to Christianity.

Conversion to Islam posed similar problems at this time for African rulers. This is well illustrated in the case of Moro Naba, ruler of the Mossi of Upper Volta (now Burkina Faso), who even under threat of *jihad* (holy war) from the Muslim ruler Askiya Muhammad Ture I of Songhay, refused to convert to Islam. The Moro Naba explained to a delegation from Songhay that before replying to Askiya Muhammad's request that he should convert to Islam, he must first of all consult his ancestors. This he did and was told by an old man in the temple who called upon the ancestors on his behalf: 'I will never agree to this step for you. On the contrary you must fight until you or they die to the last man.' Thereupon the Songhay delegation was reportedly told by the Moro Naba to 'Return to your master and tell him that between him and us there will only be war and combat.'[22]

This account may not be factually correct in every detail but it does make clear that conversion to another religion, whether it was Christianity or Islam, was not for many West African rulers a private, individual decision, but closely linked to the religious, political and cultural norms and interests of society as a whole.

The historian Ayandele divides the traditional rulers of West Africa into two broad categories on the basis of their response to Christian missionaries. There were those who, 'instinctively alarmed at the appearance of a people who had not been invited and whose presence, it was feared, might disturb traditional political and social life', rejected the missionaries.[23] The other group at first welcomed 'or even hankered after missionaries in the hope that these foreigners would prove a political and economic asset'.[24] These are broad categories, and though they do not allow for the genuinely disinterested response to Christianity based on conviction – and it seems there were cases of this[25] – they do nevertheless highlight two types of response that were fairly common in the pre-colonial period. The response of West African rulers to Christianity will be touched upon again, but it is worth noting here that in West Africa religious ritual and worship emphasised the unity of society as well as its social divisions. Religion was a collective act, an affirmation of social cohesion and solidarity, highlighting the common concerns which all of society showed.

In their efforts to convert African rulers Christian missionaries also occasionally came up against competition from Islam. For example, Barreira had high hopes in 1607 of converting the ruler of the Kingdom of Bena but on arrival there found that the king, at one time very anxious to become a Christian, 'had become very reticent under the influence of a Muslim preacher'.[26] This ruler was also unprepared to abandon aspects of his traditional religion such as ancestor worship. This whole affair obviously increased Barreira's detestation of Islam which, when he assumed responsibility for the Cape Verde mission in 1604, he was determined to defeat. He wrote then:

> the more I discover about Guinea the more I am afflicted by the abandonment of so many thousands of souls who rest without any knowledge of the inestimable grace of their redemption . . . while in these regions the accursed sect of Muhammad spreads increasingly further and further afield.[27]

This view of Islam and the efforts to limit its expansion were to persist in Christian missionary circles for a long time to come (see Chapters 4 and 7).

After Barreira's departure from Sierra Leone in 1608 Christian missionary activity there, though it did not completely grind to a halt, was very sporadic and intermittent. The Jesuits stayed on till 1617 and built a number of churches, one of them on the Bullom shore and another on the island of Tombo. The longest uninterrupted period of Christian missionary activity in the seventeenth century in Sierra Leone, as we shall see below, came between 1647 and 1669.

In December 1646 fourteen Spanish missionaries arrived at Portudal in Senegal. They were in fact probably heading for The Gambia to preach to the 'Mandingo people, followers of Muhammad'.[28] While some of the missionaries remained in Senegal, others travelled towards The Gambia. After their arrival in The Gambia in 1647 three departed for Guinea Bissau to inform the Portuguese authorities there of their arrival, only to be arrested by the Portuguese and charged with spying for Spain. This illustrates an aspect of the political problem in the way of missionary activity during this period. Of course the case for these missionaries was not helped by the fact that they were disguised as soldiers. Their purpose, they explained, in disguising themselves in this way was to convert to Catholicism the English and Dutch Protestants engaged in commerce on the West African coast.[29] The missionaries were later deported to Lisbon with the approval of the Portuguese religious authorities in West Africa.

The remaining Spanish missionaries continued their work in the Senegambia and even extended their activity to Sierra Leone. Father Seraphim undertook the work in Sierra Leone and apparently on his arrival there in 1649 was asked by several local rulers if he would baptise them and their families. He also met one of the rulers baptised by Barriera in the first decade of the seventeenth century, 'who no longer knew how to make even the sign of the cross', but who was anxious to relearn the teachings, practices and duties of the Christian faith.[30] Seraphim himself converted several important kings, one of whom ruled over as many as nine kingdoms. Moreover, he looked after four Christian villages, built several churches and restored some that he had found in ruins. He died in Cacheo, Guinea Bissau, soon after leaving Sierra Leone in 1657.

The Sierra Leone mission was effectively abandoned between 1669 and 1678. Another team of Spanish priests left for Sierra Leone in 1678 and some of them worked there until 1688, despite the opposition from the Portuguese authorities who made their task extremely difficult. For the rest of the century and until 1715 there was no resident missionary in Sierra Leone until the arrival of Father Joseph, a missionary of African descent, who had lived in North America, had been educated in Britain, and was ordained in Portugal. He established a mission in what later became Granville Town before moving to Kissy.[31] Elsewhere, for example in Cape Verde, Sao Tomé and much further south in Angola, a number of Africans were trained as priests in the seventeenth and eighteenth centuries and were given responsibility for Christian missionary work in the areas outside the Portuguese settlements.[32]

Christian missionary activity continued in the Senegambia in commercial centres such as St Louis, Gorée, Refisque, Portudal and Joal. By the middle of the seventeenth century there were about 300 Catholics in Rufisque, and about 100 in Joal. By 1750 Gorée had a Catholic population of 1,200.[33] The French government took a keen interest for a time in ensuring the maintainance of a Christian presence along the West African coast. By an edict of 1664 this government laid down that the Compagnie des Indes was to make sure that priests were present in territories to care for the spiritual needs of its personnel, to evangelise the indigenous and to build churches.[34] In addition to the chaplain the Company was to carry priests whose sole task was to be missionary work.

A number of accounts, for example, that by Chambonneau, written in the 1670s, contain interesting descriptions of the religious situation in the Senegambia in the second half of the seventeenth century and provide some idea of the task that faced the Christian missionary. According to Chambonneau the Senegalese were in principle Muslim. He wrote, 'they are Muslims and obey the precepts of the Qur'an (though) they retain a number of beliefs and customs that are purely African.'[35] Chambonneau adds, interestingly, that the French expatriate community were also profoundly interested by African customs and traditions. He observed, 'They (the French) have begun to believe in witchcraft and are convinced that African sorcerers can prevent their firearms from working or kill them by placing charms in their drinking water.' Furthermore, the French Christians, according to Chambonneau, converted in greater numbers to the traditional religion than traditional religionists to Christianity. 'It is more frequent to see', he wrote, 'the French embrace the traditional religion than to see them convert the indigenous people to their own.'[36]

The missionary's task was made extremely difficult not only by the fact that many Senegambians were Muslims and by the behaviour and attitude of European Christians, but also by the behaviour and attitudes of the indigenous Christians themselves. For example, some of the latter in Joal and Gorée, convinced that Christianity gave them a higher status and greater prestige than membership of the Islamic or the traditional religion, refused to allow that status and prestige to be eroded by the wider expansion and dissemination of Christianity.[37] This, however, did not prevent indigenous Christians from incorporating elements of traditional ritual and belief into the Christian religion and this was particularly so with regard to rites of passage such as marriages, funerals and baptism.

Throughout the period under review the Christian missions in the Senegambia suffered from their close association with the expatriate community on the spot and with European rulers. Most of the priests came with the commercial companies, lived with them in the *comptoirs* (European commercial centres) and eventually left with them. The commercial companies in turn made it clear to the Senegambian rulers and traders that they represented the interests of their own governments in Europe. On occasion company ceremonial display was the exact replica of that which took place in the metropolis. In St Louis in 1674 the ceremonial at the funeral of the director of the French West Africa Company resembled in the most minute detail that performed at Versailles on the death of the King of France.

The fact that there were so many rival European interests in the Senegambia also hindered the work of the Catholic missions. The commercial centres changed hands relatively frequently between the Portuguese, Dutch, English and Spanish and this led to impermanence and instability, each government pursuing its own strategy with regard to missionary activity.

The Catholic missions in the Senegambia, moreover, were adversely affected by the shortage of manpower. There were very few missionaries and of the few who did work in the Senegambia many died after a relatively short stay there and more often than not were never replaced. When the Jesuit missionaries visited Joal in the first decade of the seventeenth century they found that the Christian community had not seen a priest for several years. Though there were plans for training indigenous clergy by 1600, only one, Joao Pinto, a Wolof, from Cayor (or possibly Baol) had been ordained.

The reaction of the Senegambian rulers to Christianity was to an extent determined by the local political situation and their perception of the political ambitions of the commercial companies. In the 1670s the Senegal Company, assisted by local traders, became involved in the Muslim reform movement in Futa Toro led by Nasr al-Din. The Company was attacked and a number of its supporters massacred. The Company commander, De Muchins, had interfered in local politics and had convinced this Muslim reform movement that the Company had territorial ambitions in Senegal. On occasion, moreover, 'foreign' companies refused to pay the local customs duties and attempted to impress upon the indigenous that as subjects of more powerful and esteemed rulers than the local Brak or Bour (king) – Louis XIV was given the title Emperor by the Senegal Company – they could not be obliged to pay taxes or custom duties. The commercial companies were normally requested to pay customs duties of around 10 per cent on their imports. A number of local rulers, as a consequence, felt a certain hostility towards Europeans including the missionaries, whose role and function appeared to consist in justifying the economic and expansionist aims of the commercial companies.

Senegambian rulers, moreover, sometimes exploited to their own advantage the rivalry between the Europeans. At Portudal, for example, about forty English traders who were attempting to break the Portuguese monopoly in the area were massacred by the latter with the assistance of the local ruler. In contrast the ruler of a province close to Portudal and Joal where the massacre took place welcomed the English and requested their support against a neighbouring state which was backed by the Portuguese. It was in this situation of rivalry that the missionaries carried on their work. Not only were the missionaries caught between the rivalries of local rulers and commercial companies on the spot, they were also affected by the international political situation in Europe. The establishment of the Jesuit mission in Cape Verde in the sixteenth century is a case in point. Because missionary work was under the control and jurisdiction of the government and because of the political tension between Portugal and Spain, it took some twenty years to decide whether or not this Jesuit mission should be established.

None the less, in the eighteenth century Catholic missionary activity in parts of the Upper Guinea coast acquired a certain permanence and stability. From 1763 the French government took over from the commercial companies direct control of the colonies. From this time onwards a governor dependent on the Ministry of the Marines became the representative in the overseas territories of the French government, in civil as well as religious affairs. A resident Prefect Apostolic was appointed to the Senegambia who depended on both the French government and the Congregation of Propoganda of the Roman Catholic Church for his authority and powers. In 1779 by common agreement between Rome and the French government missionary work in the Senegambia was entrusted to French priests trained by the Congregation of the Holy Ghost. Thus the Senegambia was assured, for the first time, of a permanent missionary presence, albeit a presence fettered by government control. Each Governor of Senegal, for example, was on appointment instructed to safeguard and defend religion and to exercise authority over the missionaries and their superiors, since they were paid and sent by the state and were government functionaries like any other government functionary.

A Senegalese priest, Boilat, writing in the mid-nineteenth century states that differences frequently occurred between the government and the missionaries and that the latter had to obey the former or be deported.[38] The governors certainly exercised their authority, interfering continually in the missionary work. Father Démanet and several of his missionary colleagues were 'deported' from Senegal by the governor in 1775 leaving the mission stations at Gorée, Joal and Portudal with little or no personnel.[39] And those who remained had to operate in very unfavourable circumstances occasioned by the slave trade. In St Louis in 1786 out of about 6,000 inhabitants, 700 were Europeans, about 2,000 were freed slaves and the rest were slaves. And here, as was the case in the West Indies and elsewhere, missionaries were either prevented by commercial interests or by their own theories and beliefs from preaching emancipation and reform.

The problems of evangelisation were compounded by the changing political situation in the region. Gorée, for example, was seized by the English in 1774, returned to the French in 1783, and became English territory again from 1800 to 1817. Catholic missionaries, always few in number, came to Gorée, stayed a few months – Chardonnier was an exception, staying three years (1787–90) – and returned to France. It was the lay community, in particular the military, who kept Catholicism alive. The 1789 Revolution and its decree against the clergy, though it did not apply to the colonies, had a further negative impact on missionary activity. Some missionaries, like Chardonnier, made no attempt to resist these decrees, and abandoned missionary activity to become a clerk to the court at St Louis.

São Tomé, Elmina and the surrounding coast (Ghana), and Benin and Warri (Nigeria)

São Tomé, in union with Il Principe, became the Republic of São Tomé e Principe in 1975. In terms of Christian missionary work, it played the same strategic role for the Lower Guinea Coast as did the Cape Verde island of Santiago for the Upper Guinea Coast. In the late fifteenth century, Portuguese outcasts, adventurers and convicts were settled on the island of São Tomé and, along with slaves imported from the mainland, worked the plantations. This island, in fact, which was the springboard for much missionary activity on the West African mainland became the only permanent Christian settlement in West Africa until the nineteenth century.

For considerable periods of time the Christian community on São Tomé was administered and supervised by bishops who resided in Portugal or elsewhere. Moreover, when a bishop did take up residence on the island, relations between the Church and the state often proved to be hostile. Bishop Gaspar Cão, for example, who took up residence on São Tomé in 1554 had numerous disputes with the governor and was brought to trial before an ecclesiastical court in 1571.

The bishop was acquitted, and in the early 1570s, in addition to sending missionaries from São Tomé to Benin (Nigeria), he also established a college for the training of African priests. This attempt to form an indigenous clergy failed, largely because of the poor relations between the Portuguese and the Africans on the island. Many of the latter, embittered by the treatment they received at the hands of the Portuguese, refused to allow their sons to enter the college. Moreover they staged in 1584, 1593 and 1595 a revolt in protest against their servile condition. The Portuguese response came in 1598 when they waged a war of extermination against the black inhabitants of the interior. However, the Portuguese themselves suffered a setback when the Dutch invaded the island in 1599. The former regained control over São Tomé in the early years of the seventeenth century only to lose it again to the Dutch from 1641 to 1649.

The situation of the Christian Church in São Tomé in the seventeenth and eighteenth centuries differed little from that of the sixteenth century. Some bishops administered the diocese from Portugal or some other remote place while others who took up residence on São Tomé found themselves in dispute either with the governor or the local Christian community. Bishop Domingos da Ascencão who died in 1632 was allegedly poisoned by the 'new' Christians, that is, converted Jews and Muslims from Spain who had been settled on the island. The black population of the island, moreover, remained indifferent and even hostile to the formation of a local clergy. Further, by the 1790s, largely because of Portuguese restrictions on non-Portuguese priests residing on the island, missionary work there had come to a standstill.

I   Elmina castle

Elmina and the surrounding coast

Overcoming opposition from the Akan people of the area, the Portuguese in 1482 built a stone fort which housed a church and named the settlement São Jorge da Mina (St George of Mina), now known as Elmina. In an attempt to persuade the Akan to accept their presence the leader of this group of Portuguese settlers, Diego d'Azambuja, is believed to have told them of the commercial benefits they would derive from an alliance with Portugal, and of the values of the Christian faith.[40] Later, other Portuguese forts were built, for example at Shama at the mouth of the Pra River, at Axim to the west and Accra to the east of Elmina and all situated in what is now Ghana.

The priests who acted as chaplains in these forts also did a limited amount of teaching and preaching outside their walls. This resulted in a number of conversions to Christianity among the local rulers and their people. For example Xerele, the ruler of Komenda to the west of Elmina, and many of his people accepted Christianity in 1503, and some ten years later, King Nana Sasaxy of the Efutu and some of his subjects who lived north-west of Elmina embraced Christianity.

However, it appears that it was not until the 1570s that any sustained or concerted effort was made to evangelise the people outside the forts. One of the main reasons for this slow start was the far greater importance attached by the Portuguese, priests as well as people, to trade and commerce than to the spreading of Christianity. An Englishman called Frobisher, who was brought to Elmina in 1555 as a captive, made the point that no attempts were being made to convert the African population to Christianity.

By the 1570s the situation had altered somewhat. The four priests then at Elmina worked out a strategy for looking after the interests of the fort and at the same time working among the local people outside its walls. While two of the priests stayed at the fort, the other two worked among the Komenda, and on the return of the latter to the fort those who had stayed behind went out among the Efutu.

This strategy, however, had to be abandoned because of a conflict between the Portuguese and the local people in which three of the four priests died. Moreover, in the late sixteenth century and the first half of the seventeenth century Portuguese, English and Dutch rivalry over West African trade, which often resulted in conflict, made Portuguese missionary activity extremely difficult in this region. There were Dutch raids on Axim and Elmina in 1607, and in 1615 Elmina was stormed on three occasions by the Dutch. Again in 1625 a combined force of 2,000 Dutch and African soldiers attacked Elmina. It was not, however, until 1637 that Elmina finally fell to the Dutch who also gained control of Shama in 1640 and Axim in 1642. The Danes, the French and the English were to follow the Dutch and to vie with the latter and with one another for trade advantages in this and other areas of Africa. The spread of Christianity was the least of their concerns. As Barbot, an eyewitness, wrote in 1680, 'The great concern of the Dutch on this coast, as well as of other Europeans, settled or trading here, is the gold and not the welfare of souls.'[41]

Seventeenth and eighteenth century attempts to establish Christianity elsewhere along the coast – for example at Assinie (Ivory Coast), and Whydah and Arda (Republic of Benin) – were no more successful than those made in and around Elmina. One of the only surviving traces of Christianity at Elmina from this period is the cult of St Anthony known as Nana Ntona.

Benin (Nigeria)

Although they were aware of the existence of Benin from around 1472, it was not until 1486 that the Portuguese made their first contacts with this kingdom. The then Oba (King) of Benin, Uzulua, opened up negotiations with the Portuguese with a view to the formation of a Benin-Portuguese alliance. Uzulua was anxious to forge an alliance with the Portuguese mainly (if not solely) for reasons of trade in weapons and sent an ambassador to Portugal for this purpose. The Oba also requested that Christian missionaries be sent to his kingdom, thus creating the impression in Portugal that he was seriously interested in establishing the Christian faith in Benin. Uzulua was no doubt aware that Portugal, a Christian kingdom, could not in principle (because of papal decrees forbidding this) sell arms to non-Christian kingdoms.

The Portuguese, encouraged by the request for missionaries and by the fact that the people of Benin already believed in a Supreme Being which, they thought, would facilitate the work of the missionaries, responded positively to the Oba's request. A trading post was opened at Benin's port of Gwato. Trade between the two states began in pepper, and later extended to ivory and slaves. But the Oba did not convert to Christianity, and this partly explains why when a request was made for arms in 1514 it was turned down.

Despite this rebuff the Oba of Benin, at war with Idah at the time and in need of arms, welcomed the Portuguese missionaries who arrived in his kingdom with the Portuguese representative Duarte Pires in 1515. The priests – and this was most unusual – were allowed to visit every part of the Oba's palace and were invited to dine with his son. The Oba even allowed a church to be built and permitted his son and some of the more influential and prominent members of Benin society to become Christians. He himself, however, drew back from taking such a step claiming that he needed more time to think about such a 'deep mystery' as Christianity. But by 1517 Oba Uzulua was dead, and in 1532 the Portuguese station at Gwato was closed.

On several other occasions in the sixteenth century Portuguese missionaries attempted to convert the rulers of Benin but to no avail. In 1538 two such missionaries were put under house arrest, and another, a Bini, Gregorio Lourenço, who had become a Christian in 1516, was prevented from bringing up his children as Christians. Obas were ready to trade, learn Portuguese and wore Christian dress as a form of ceremonial robe, but none the less were not prepared to become Christians.

In the 1640s Spanish rather than Portuguese missionaries were assigned to the Benin mission by Rome and arrived at Benin City in August 1651. But after a cordial reception by the Oba the missionaries encountered difficulties in their dealings with the chief minister – Uwangue – who sought to restrict their activities and keep them away from the palace. From this point onwards Rome decided to attempt the conversion of Benin indirectly through Warri and the Itsekiris, though one more attempt was made at direct conversion with the establishment of a mission in Benin City in 1710. This mission was abandoned in 1713, mainly because of lack of material support from Europe.

Warri (Itsekiri)

In terms of introducing Christianity and establishing a relatively permanent Christian presence, the missionaries were far more successful in Warri (Itsekiri), situated in the Forcados River area of mid-western Nigeria in present-day Bendel State than in Benin, the capital. Warri probably came into existence as a state independent of Benin in the middle years of the sixteenth century, and support in the form of firearms from the Portuguese may well have assisted this development.

Christianity was introduced into Warri from São Tomé in the second half of the sixteenth century, probably some time between 1571 and 1574 when Gaspar Cão was the bishop of São Tomé.[42] The first major breakthrough for the mission came with the baptism of the son of the Olu (king) of Itsekiri, who was named Sebastian after the King of Portugal. Sebastian became Olu sometime before 1597. He remained a Christian even though the circumstances did not favour this. There were, for example, no missionaries in Warri between 1584 and 1593 mainly because of the difficult climate and the lack of finance. And after enjoying the luxury of a resident missionary again from 1593 to 1597 Warri was once again left without a permanent missionary presence.

The problem of a permanent missionary presence was partly solved when on being requested by the Bishop of São Tomé to supply priests for the kingdom King Philip II of Spain ordered that merchant ships trading for ivory in Warri take with them a missionary from São Tomé. These missionaries would stay in Warri until the merchant ship was ready to sail with its cargo, that is, for about three months. And the problem of paying for the upkeep of these missionaries was also partly solved when King Philip on the suggestion of the Bishop of São Tomé decided that 'those who visited the kingdom of Warri in merchant ships should be allowed to buy slaves in Warri and sell them anywhere in Portuguese territories on payment of nominal fees.'[43] Obviously, those in authority in Church and State were prepared to make a clear distinction between the spiritual and the human needs and rights of an individual.

The outcome of the Bishop of São Tomé's efforts to find missionaries for Warri resulted in the stationing of a resident missionary there until 1616, when once again it was necessary to resort to the practice of a missionary accompanying a trading ship and leaving when the ship left. Much of the work of the missionary was in fact carried on by the Olu, Sebastian. His activities were confined however to a narrow circle of people, and by 1620 only a few people in the small town of Santo Agostino, together with the Olu and some of his courtiers, had become Christians. Though Portuguese and Spanish Catholic influence in West Africa was on the decline from this moment (1620) and missionary contact between São Tomé and Warri became even less frequent, the situation began to change again in the 1650s.

The 1650s in fact saw a revival of Christianity in Warri, a revival brought about by the Olu, Antonio Domingos, and Spanish missionaries. The fact that the missionaries were Spanish caused problems, since the governors

of São Tomé e Principe, the embarcation points for Warri for the
missionaries, were Portuguese and relations between Portugal and Spain
were hostile at this point. The Olu of Warri, however, wrote to the Pope
requesting him to send the same Spanish missionaries expelled from
Benin in 1651 to his kingdom. An extract from the Olu's letter written in
November 1652 reads, 'such is my need of disinterested ministers to
spread the faith in my kingdom that it is almost gone to perdition, since it
is more than seven years that a priest has been here . . . I leave it to your
Holiness to imagine how many are falling away from the Faith.'[44]

The missionaries requested by the Olu did not arrive till 1656, and this
time they were Italian. Despite some Portuguese harassment and
opposition these missionaries appear to have made a considerable impact
on the Itsekiri, many of whom, together with their chiefs, embraced
Christianity. But after the departure of the last of this contingenent of
Italian missionaries from Warri in 1660 very little was accomplished in the
way of missionary work in that kingdom during the remaining decades of
the seventeenth century. Between 1660 and 1700, it was only very rarely
that a missionary spent as long as a year in Warri. More usually, the few
missionaries who did visit Warri remained there for only a matter of
months, despite attempts by the Olu to keep them longer. While some of
these missionaries worked hard to spread Christianity others devoted
most of their time to trade and related matters. It should be understood
though that in order to maintain themselves the missionaries felt they had
no choice but to trade, and at first this included trading not only in
earthenware pots and cloth, but also in slaves. By the early years of the
eighteenth century, however, though they still maintained that trading in
slaves was indispensable to the survival of the mission, a decision was
taken to abandon such activity on the grounds that it was both 'unworthy'
and 'absolutely contrary to our condition'.[45]

Nevertheless the mission in Warri survived for some time, and the level
of activity increased in the period 1710–1730. The missionaries were
promised supplies by the Portuguese government, and these sometimes
arrived via Brazil. In the mid 1730s, however, missionary activity was to
come virtually to a standstill for almost forty years. One of the Olus at the
time adopted an anti-mission, anti-Christian stance, which resulted in the
official reinstatement of the traditional gods and Warri's only church, St
Anthony's, fell into disuse.

Though it had never made much impact beyond the walls of the royal
palace, when Christianity lost the support of the Olu, it lost its main prop
within the Itsekiri state. Rulers continued to be baptised but their interest
in promoting Christian teachings and practices waned. Thus by the end
of the eighteenth century Catholic missionary activity in Warri had in
effect come to an end and was not effectively resumed until the closing
years of the nineteenth century.

Borno (north-eastern Nigeria)

There is some evidence to suggest that a Catholic missionary passed

through northern Nigeria in the 1680s.[46] But it was during the early years
of the eighteenth century that the Catholic Church attempted, without
much success, to establish a mission in the north of Nigeria. The plan was
for priests to set out from Tripoli, cross the Sahara desert and continue
south as far as Borno and there establish a mission. One such abortive
attempt was made in 1703. Another followed in 1710 and this time two
missionaries succeeded in crossing the desert and entered Nigeria via
Agades in Niger. However, because of the great dangers of the route they
were unable to continue their journey to Borno and instead made their
way to Katsina in northern Nigeria. Both missionaries died soon after
their arrival in Katsina in August 1711,[47] and the first Catholic missionary
was not to reach Borno until 1850.

Protestant missionary efforts

So far we have been outlining the course of Catholic missionary
endeavour in West Africa during the period from 1450 to 1790. There
were, however, a small number of Protestant missionary societies
involved in missionary work in West Africa in the eighteenth century. For
example, in 1737, the United Brethren or Moravian Church founded in
Denmark by Nikolaus Zinzendorf sent Christian Protten, born in Accra
(Ghana) of a Danish father and African mother, to undertake missionary
work in Accra. However, Protten, who worked on and off in Accra for
some eighteen years in all, confined his activities for the most part to the
Danish settlement, thus making virtually no impact at all on the
indigenous people of the area. Another Moravian missionary, Capitain,
an ex-slave from the Ivory Coast, after successfully completing his studies
at Leyden University in Holland, was posted to Elmina (Ghana) in 1742.
He taught in a school there from 1742 until his death in 1747.

Frederick Svane, like Christian Protten mentioned above, was also
born of a Danish father and African mother, and after studying in
Copenhagen returned to Accra as a missionary in 1735. And like Protten
he concentrated his attention and activities on the Danish fort, claiming
that he could not express Christian ideas and teachings well enough in his
own language, Ga. Philip Quaque, one of many West Africans studying
in England at the time, was ordained a priest of the Anglican Church and
went to work as a missionary in Cape Coast (Ghana) in 1766. No longer
able to speak Fante with any degree of fluency Quaque decided to devote
most of his time to school teaching and to the needs of the English and
mulatto people at Cape Coast.

It was the Englishman Thomas Thompson of The Society for the
Propagation of the Gospel (SPG) who sent Philip Quaque to London for
training as a missionary in the first place. Thompson himself arrived in
Cape Coast in 1751 and remained there until 1756 when he resigned on
grounds of poor health. Thompson left an account of his journey to West
Africa which contains a good deal of information about his activities
there, and his attitudes and outlook. For instance, he writes that on the
Sunday following his arrival at Cape Coast Castle on 13 May 1751:

> I preached in the Chapel of the Castle before the Governor and Officers. There was also present the chief man of Cape Coast Town, Cudjo Cabosheer. I baptised at the same time one white child and one mulatto: and the next Sunday two more children, both of whom were mulattoes.[48]

Thompson first addressed the indigenous inhabitants of the Cape Coast at Cudjo's house preaching to them on 'The Nature and Attributes of God; His Providence, and of a Future State', before specifically mentioning Christianity.

The reaction of the local people to Christianity was mixed. Some did not really want to hear about it, others suggested that it appeared to have little impact on the lives of those Europeans who professed it. Moreover, the local people opposed any suggestion that might allow the preaching and teaching of Christianity on Sundays. This would interfere with their business activities, and if Thompson wanted to instruct them in the Christian faith he should attempt to do so on Tuesdays which was the local holy day and day of rest. Thompson's approach was characteristic of that of many missionaries until recent times. He began by saying very little directly about Christianity, but sought instead to 'strike at their false worship, and endeavour to convince them of their false notions, and expose the folly of their idolatrous and superstitious rites; so that if possible, I might disengage their minds from these, for the reception and entertainment of Divine Truths.'[49]

The mulattoes of Cape Coast, quite a number of whom had been baptised, were at first less enthusiastic about Christianity than the traditional religionists. Thompson wrote: 'they avoided me, and I may truly say of them that they are more heathenish than the Negroes.'[50] The latter, Thompson soon realised, did have a belief in a Supreme Being whom they worshipped regularly. However, despite the lack of enthusiasm for Christianity, Thompson was impressed both by the fact that he could go about his work freely, and at the low level of violence and crime. He commented, 'And I can say there are fewer murders or violences committed among them, as perhaps in any nation or country in the world.' Thompson, however, could still write a treatise justifying the slave trade, and this despite the fact that he considered the 'Blacks of the Coast of Guinea as being a more civilized people than the Nations in general'.[51]

According to Thompson many Africans saw Christianity as the religion of the white man and this made his task very difficult. He also found his lack of knowledge of Fante and of other local languages a great handicap, not fully overcome even with the help of an interpreter. By the time he left the Cape Coast in 1756, Thompson had converted only a handful of Africans to Christianity. But he remained optimistic. The language problem was not insuperable, he believed, and the aversion of the people to Christianity would be overcome when its foundation, 'the Heathen Education System', was replaced.

Conclusions

Christian missionary activity in West Africa achieved very little between 1450 and 1790. Much better results were achieved in China in the eighteenth century and to some extent in the Congo in Central Africa.

One can cite any number of reasons for this relative lack of success in West Africa. There were the problems of climate, the high mortality rate, the paucity of missionary personnel, the lack of success in training sufficient numbers of indigenous clerics, the slave trade, the close association of Christianity with European politics, commerce and culture, and the rivalry between the European nations themselves. These factors all militated against the establishment of a strong and expanding Christian Church in West Africa in this period. Missionary attitudes and strategy were also on occasion part of the problem. Some missionaries were more interested in trade than in preaching Christianity while others confined themselves to the European forts, showing little or no interest in the local people. Moreover, the local people for their part had their own belief system and religious rituals and in many instances were simply not convinced by what was to them a largely alien, unknown and untried faith. There were those, it is true, who were attracted by Christianity as a religion and way of life. But Christianity was often presented and seen as only one part of a package deal, the other part being an agreement on questions of politics, trade and commerce. Consequently, when the latter were not forthcoming or were unsatisfactory, little interest was shown in the former.

The lack of interest shown by leading Christian thinkers and others in high places in the Christian Church in the conversion of Africans, compounded by financial difficulties, also weakened in the early Christian missionary endeavour. For the most part missionaries had to rely on their respective governments – Portugal, Spain and others – for financial support which was often inadequate. Furthermore, little by way of contributions came from the indigenous people, and in this situation missionaries turned to trade, including the slave trade, to support themselves and their work. Although quite early on some missionaries came to see the slave trade as morally wrong, others like Thompson, justified it not only on financial but also on theological and on religious grounds. Then there were those who seemed to see nothing wrong in the Portuguese government turning Warri into a slave market to serve the Brazilian plantations, and indeed even encouraged this.[52] They believed that this would help the spread of Catholicism and obtain from the government financial support for the mission in Warri. It was, it is true, the view of many missionaries that financial constraints constituted one of the main reasons for the lack of success. In the seventeenth century one bishop appealed to the Kings of Portugal and Spain to support one missionary for Warri so that the poverty of the kingdom may not bring so many souls to perdition.[53] The financial difficulties of the missions and their association with the slave trade were, thus, two of the many obstacles to the growth of Christianity in the period *c.* 1450 to *c.* 1790.

Direct involvement in local politics also worked against the missions on occasion. Christianity was rarely, if ever, a real issue in local disputes and conflicts and stood to gain very little by identifying with one or other of the factions engaged in a power struggle. Missionary interference in local ritual and ceremonial, however well-intentioned, could also cause problems. In Benin in the 1650s, priests who intervened in the ceremony in the royal palace where the ritual killing of five men took place were forced to leave the city and were eventually deported to Lisbon. This was not the Oba's doing but that of court officials who no doubt feared that the adoption of the new religion would undermine their authority, rank and influence in the palace.

Some rulers and their subjects often put up strong resistance to the spread of Christianity, regarding it as a subversive element and a danger to political stability. Some examples of this have already been given (see pp. 12 ff.) and there are many more. This in part explains why the Susu in Sierra Leone burned down the mission stations in 1815.

Alongside missionary involvement in local politics and the resistance just mentioned went the political and economic rivalry resulting on occasions in military confrontation between various countries which the missionaries represented (see p. 19). And, additionally, there was the fact that the quality of missionaries sent to West Africa was not always very high. Of course, they did not have a great deal of relevant literature and information from which to obtain guidance, nor were there any female religious orders that could perhaps have influenced wives and mothers and home life in general. Christianity was presented as something new, and to accept it meant in theory at least accepting another way of life that was different, but which on the basis of the evidence was not necessarily better. It demanded a radical break with custom and tradition while the advantages of such a break were by no means obvious to many West Africans.

The two hundred years of missionary endeavour following this first attempt to Christianise West Africa were to be much more productive. The idea once adhered to by some Protestant Churches that Africa had rejected the preaching of the Apostles and that as a consequence God's will was directed against its people – a belief that to some extent explains the reluctance of these churches to engage in missionary work in this early period – was to be abandoned and Protestant Churches were to be at the forefront of missionary interest in Africa in the second half of the eighteenth century.

Notes

1   A.C. de C.M. Sanders, *A Social History of Black Slaves and Freedmen in Portugal, 1441–1555*, Cambridge: Cambridge University Press, 1982.
2   ibid.
3   J.E. Inikori (ed.), *Forced Migration. The Impact of the Export Slave Trade on African*

Societies, London: Hutchinson, 1982, p. 59.
4   ibid., pp. 19 ff. for a critique of various estimates.
5   P. Curtin, *The Atlantic Slave Trade: A Census*, Wisconsin: University of Wisconsin Press, 1969.
6   J.D. Fage, Slavery and the Slave Trade in the Context of West African History. *Journal of African History* (henceforth JAH), **X** (3), 1969, pp. 393–404.
7   J.E. Inikori, *Forced Migration*, pp. 19 ff.
8   J. Suret-Canale and B. Barry, The Western Atlantic Coast to 1800. In J.F.A. Ajayi and M. Crowder (eds), *The History of West Africa*, Vol. 1, Harlow: Longman, 1976: Chapter 12, pp. 456–511.
9   C.P. Groves, *The Planting of Christianity in Africa*, Vol. 1, London: Lutterworth Press, 1948: 119.
10 R. Gray, The Origins and Organization of the Nineteenth-Century Missionary Movement. *Tarikh* **3** (1), 1969, pp. 14–22.
11 C. Fyfe: The Cape Verde Islands, *History Today*, Vol. 31, May 1981, pp. 5–9 incl.
12 N.E. Cabral, *Les Iles de Cap Vert. Cinq Siècles de Contacts Culturels, Mutation et Mélange Ethnique*. Doctoral Thesis, Sorbonne, Paris, 1979.
13 G. Thilmans and N.I. de Moraes, La Description de la Côte de Guinée du Père Baltasar Barreira (1606). Bulletin de l'Institut Fondamental de l'Afrique Noire (henceforth BIFAN) T. XXXIV. sér B. No. 1, 1972, p. 1.
14 A.F.C. Ryder, Portuguese Missions in Western Africa. *Tarikh* **3** (1) 1969: 1.
15 ibid., p. 11.
16 Thilmans and de Moraes 1606: 21.
17 ibid.
18 A.F.C., Ryder, Portuguese Missions in Western Africa. *Tarikh* **3** (1), 1969: 13.
19 ibid., p. 12. See also Ryder's *Benin and the Europeans 1885–1897*, London: 1969.
20 Thilmans and de Moraes, op. cit.: 17.
21 J.D. Hargreaves (ed.), *France and West Africa*. London: Macmillan, 1969: 18–28.
22 E.P. Skinner, *Islam in Mossi Society*. In I.M. Lewis (ed.), *Islam in Tropical Africa*, (2nd ed.), London: Hutchinson, 1980: 176, note g.
23 E.A. Ayandele, Traditional Rulers and Missionaries in Pre-Colonial West Africa. In *Tarikh* 3(1), 1969: 23–7.
24 ibid.
25 See, for example, Thilmans and de Moraes, p. 25.
26 ibid., p. 16.
27 ibid.: 10.
28 P. Lintingre, Le Vénérable Père Seraphim De Leon Apôtre du Sénégal et de la Sierra Leone, Holy Ghost Archives, Paris (henceforth H.G.F. Archives, Paris) Boîte 147, p. 96.
29 ibid., pp. 101–2.
30 ibid., p. 122.
31 A.P. Kup, *The History of Sierra Leone*. Cambridge: Cambridge University Press, 1961: 49.
32 A.F.C. Ryder, Portuguese Missions in Western Africa. *Tarikh* **3** (1), 1969: 10.
33 P. Godefroid Loyer, *Relations du Voyage d'Issinie*, Paris, 1914: 138. See also P. Cultru, *L'Histoire du Sénégal*, Paris 1910 and L'Abbé Boilat, *Esquisses Sénégalaises*, Paris, 1853.
34 A. Ly, La Compagnie du Sénégal, *Présence Africaine*, Paris 1947: 273.
35 Citation from Carson, I.A. Ritchie, Deux Textes sur le Sénégal, BIFAN T. XXX sér. B. No. 1 1968: 313.

36   ibid., p. 318.
37   ibid.
38   L'Abbé Boilat, *Esquisses Sénégalaises*, Paris, 1853: 244.
39   J. Delcourt, *L'Histoire Religieuse du Sénégal*, Daka, 1976: 21 ff.
40   C.P. Groves, *The Planting of Christianity in Africa*, Vol. II, London: Lutterworth Press, 1948–58: 123.
41   J. Barbot, *A Description of the Coast of North and South Guinea*. Translated from the French. Churchill's Collection of Voyages and Travels, Vol. V, London, 1722.
42   A.F.C. Ryder, Missionary Activity in the Kingdom of Warri to the Early Nineteenth Century. In *Journal of the Historical Society of Nigeria* (henceforth JHSN), **2** (1), 1960.
43   ibid., p. 4.
44   ibid., p. 10.
45   ibid., p. 18.
46   R. Gray, Christian Traces and a Franciscan Mission in the Central Sudan. *JAH* **VII**, 1967: 392–3.
47   ibid.
48   T. Thompson, *Two Missionary Voyages, 1745–1756*. London: SPCK, 1937: 33–4.
49   ibid., p. 54.
50   ibid., p. 57.
51   ibid., p. 81.
52   A.F.C. Ryder, Missionary Activity in the Kingdom of Warri to the Early Nineteenth Century. In *JHSN* **2** (1), 1960: 20.
53   ibid., p. 7.

2

The emergence of the modern Christian missionary movement and its impact on West Africa c. 1790 to c. 1840.

The revival of missionary interest in West Africa

During the first period of Christian missionary activity the Catholic Church dominated the scene, but it was the Protestant Churches in the main which were at the forefront of the modern missionary movement in its initial stages in West Africa. Religious, as well as humanitarian, social, economic and political interests, and medical and technological advances combined to make possible this revival of missionary interest in West Africa.[1] The emphasis, for example among the Methodists in Britain, on evangelism and conversion was an important factor in the early development of the modern missionary movement.[2] The zeal to convert all men to the Christian faith (also present in the Roman Catholic Church) was, however, 'never matched by the availability of personnel, especially among Protestants'.[3]

In North America also during the second half of the eighteenth century and the first part of the nineteenth century, Methodists, Baptists and Quakers (The Society of Friends) showed great enthusiasm for preaching the Gospel to people of African descent. Already by the first half of the eighteenth century the Quakers had become persistent opponents of slavery and worked consistently to free, train and provide a Christian education for their own slaves. Some Methodist and Baptist Churches joined the Quakers in their campaign in the second half of the eighteenth century, as did the Catholic Church, whose concern was somewhat more muted given its relative lack of contact with slaves in the pre-Civil War south.[4]

The Atlantic slave trade gave rise to a great deal of soul-searching and remorse among groups of Christians in parts of Europe and North America in the second half of the eighteenth century. The Methodist John Wesley spoke of the slave trade as 'This execrable villainy', and in his 'Thoughts on Slavery', published in 1774, he argued against those who maintained that it was necessary, that 'villainy was never necessary'.[5] In addition to Wesley, Christian philanthropists, business people and politicians, such as Granville Sharp, Thomas Clarkson, William Wilberforce, Hannah Moore, Zachary Macaulay, Henry Thornton, along with members of the Society of Friends and other Christians, many of them very ordinary and unknown, as one historian has noted,[6] engaged

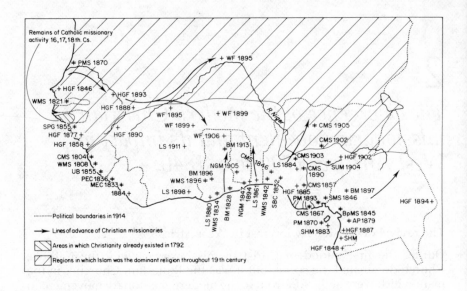

Remains of Catholic missionary activity 16,17,18th. Cs.

+ PMS 1870
+ WF 1895
+ HGF 1846
WMS 1821 +
+ HGF 1893
HGF 1888 +
WF 1895
+ WF 1899
R. Niger
SPG 1855 +
HGF 1877 +
HGF 1858 +
HGF 1890
WF 1899 +
WF 1906 +
+ CMS 1905
CMS 1902
CMS 1804 +
WMS 1808 +
UB 1855 +
PEC 1836 +
MEC 1833 +
1884 +
LS 1911 +
BM 1913
CMS 1846
LS 1884
CMS 1903
+ HGF 1902
SUM 1904
CMS 1890
NGM 1905 +
BM 1896
WMS 1896 +
LS 1898 +
+ CMS 1857
HGF 1885
PM 1893
+ BM 1897
+ SMS 1846
HGF 1894 +
LS 1880
WMS 1834
BM 1828
NGM 1847
1894
LS 1861
WMS 1842
SBC 1852
CMS 1867
PM 1870 +
SHM 1883
BpMS 1845
+ AP 1879
+ HGF 1887
+ SHM
HGF 1848 +

--------- Political boundaries in 1914

——▶ Lines of advance of Christian missionaries

Areas in which Christianity already existed in 1792

Regions in which Islam was the dominant religion throughout 19th century

+ Protestant Missions	SMS Swedish Missionary Society
AP American Presbyterians	SPG Society for the Propagation of the Gospel (C.of E.)
BM Basel Mission	SUM Sudan United Mission
BpMS Baptist Missionary Society	UB United Brethren in Christ (U.S.A.)
CMS Church Missionary Society	WMS Wesleyan Methodist Missionary Society
MEC Methodist Episcopal Church (U.S.A.)	
NGM North German Mission (Bremen)	**+ Roman Catholic Missions**
PEC Protestant Episcopal Church (U.S.A.)	HGF Holy Ghost Fathers
PM Primitive Methodists	LS Lyons Society (Society of African Missions)
PMS Paris Missionary Society (Société des Missions Evangéliques)	SHM Sacred Heart of Mary
SBC Southern Baptist Convention (U.S.A.)	WF White Fathers

I Christian missions in West Africa, 1792–1914
(Note: It is not possible on a map of this scale to show all mission stations nor even all mission societies in the field. What has been attempted is to show the pioneer missions in each area whose work has been continuous since their establishment.)

in a long campaign for the abolition of the Slave Trade. However as the struggle to end slavery in Britain from the early 1770s intensified the already existing social problem of the homeless unemployed, unwanted poor, many of whom were black. In a short period of time, between 20,000 and 30,000 slaves were manumitted in London, Liverpool and Bristol. One solution proposed was to settle these people in a Province of Freedom in Sierra Leone, West Africa (see pp. 32 ff.).

The first missionary society to be founded in Britain in the late eighteenth century was the Baptist Missionary Society in 1792. This was followed by the London Missionary Society (LMS) in 1795, while the Church Missionary Society (CMS), the Wesleyan Missionary Society (WMS) and the Scottish Presbyterian Society (SPS) were formed in 1799. Around the same time missionary societies were established elsewhere in Europe; for example, the Netherlands Missionary Society came into being in 1797 and missionary training centres were set up in Berlin and Basel. In North America the Board of Foreign Missions was established in 1810. The nineteenth and twentieth centuries saw the establishment of many more Protestant missionary societies in Europe and North America. In Britain the Universities Mission to Central Africa was founded in 1859 and The Sudan Pioneer Mission, later the Sudan Interior Mission (SIM) in 1902.

The revival of Catholic missionary activity in West Africa is sometimes dated to the arrival on the island of Gorée, Senegal in 1819 of the French order of nuns called the Sisters of Our Lady of Cluny. The nuns moved to the Senegalese mainland in 1823. This was not a completely new start, for Catholic priests were already working at Gorée before the arrival of the Sisters of Cluny. But it was not until the 1840s that the modern Catholic missionary movement really got under way. In 1842 Catholic missionaries and an American Bishop of Philadelphia, John England, arranged for Fr Edward Barron and a number of other priests to go to Liberia to work among the black American Catholic population that had returned there under the auspices of the Maryland Colonization Society.[7] Then in 1848 the Society of the Immaculate Heart of Mary founded by François Libermann joined with the old French Congregation of the Holy Ghost, established in 1703, to form the Congregation of the Holy Ghost and The Immaculate Heart of Mary. This society, known as the Holy Ghost Fathers or Spiritans has played a prominent role since 1848 in the development of Catholicism in West Africa and other regions of the continent. Another French Catholic missionary order to enter West Africa in the nineteenth century was the Society of African Missions (SMA), followed by the White Fathers towards the very end of the same century.

A number of important changes in the way the Catholic missions were financed, organised and administered helped to make them much more effective than was the case in the earlier period discussed in the previous chapter. Government control over the appointment of mission personnel was then much tighter. The missions were also very heavily dependent for financial support and transport on the government. From the nineteenth century the Catholic missions enjoyed more autonomy and were more financially independent. However, the extent of this freedom from secular control should not be exaggerated. Throughout the region of West Africa colonised by France the French government had for a considerable length of time an important say in the appointment of bishops. Moreover, missionary societies depended to some extent on government financial backing. Nevertheless, on balance, they had more control over their own affairs than was previously the case.

Missionary developments 1790–1840

Sierra Leone: the 'Province of Freedom'

There were three phases in the establishment of Christianity in Sierra Leone in the period from 1790 to 1840. The first phase culminated in the establishment of Granville Sharp's 'Province of Freedom' at Granville Town near present-day Freetown in 1787.[8] For the origins of the settlement we can look back to the anti-slave trade movement in Britain and from there to the Age of Enlightenment and the pursuit of a more perfect society. Granville Sharp, after whom Granville Town was named, was a committed Christian who argued that the slave trade was unnatural because it was not sanctioned by any universal law. This argument, based on natural justice, was strengthened by an economic argument that favoured the abolition of slavery on the grounds that it impeded the natural development of trade.

Sharp, involved with plans to help the black poor of England since the 1770s, welcomed and participated in a scheme launched by Dr H. Smeathman in 1783 to establish a 'perfect society' in West Africa based on free agricultural labour. Further, the 'Committee for Relieving the Black Poor' accepted Smeathman's plan for settling them in Sierra Leone. In addition to the 20,000 to 30,000 already mentioned, there were others among the 'Black Poor', former slaves, who had fought on the side of England during the American War of Independence (1775–83).

It was Sharp who drew up the constitution of this 'perfect' or 'ideal' society which, he intended, would be strictly administered according to Christian principles. Associates of Sharp, Wilberforce, Venn and other members of the evangelical wing of the Church of England known as the Clapham Sect, supported the resettlement proposals, seeing in Sierra Leone a launching pad for the work of 'civilising' and christianising Africa. Moreover the British government agreed to pay the passage to Sierra Leone of those to be resettled there.

In 1787 a convoy of ships with 351 black and sixty white people left England for Sierra Leone. Some eighty-five of the passengers died before reaching Sierra Leone and the rest, accompanied by Mr Fraser, a missionary of the Society for the Propagation of the Gospel (SPG) disembarked at a watering place on the Sierra Leone River in the Temne Kingdom of Koya.

The settlers encountered problems from the outset. On arrival they set about erecting their dwelling places on a hill just above the watering place, named their settlement Granville Town and chose one of their members, Richard Weaver, as governor. But the terrain was poor, the conditions in which they lived appalling, and the heavy rains that began soon after their arrival made their situation intolerable. Some died in the very early days and others moved away in search of better conditions. And as if this were not enough there were political problems. The overall ruler of the kingdom, Naimbaña, had very strong reservations about the settlement as did King Tom, the sub-chief, who gave up his authority over the area in which the settlement was established for goods worth fifty-nine pounds sterling. King Tom's successor, King Jimmy, ordered what remained of the settlement to be razed to the ground in retaliation against the settlers who had taken the side of the Captain of a British ship with whom he was in dispute. This marked the end of the first phase of the settlement. The second phase, from 1792 to 1808, began with the take-over of the settlement by the Sierra Leone Company and the arrival of the Nova Scotians in 1792. From this point in time, religion and philanthropy were to be clearly mixed with business and commerce.

The foundation of the Sierra Leone Company and the arrival of the Nova Scotians

The Sierra Leone Company, set up in 1791, led to the influx of about 1,200 black settlers from Nova Scotia in North America in 1792. The Company, under the directorship of Henry Thornton, set out to replace the slave trade with Africa with 'legitimate' trade. Once in control of the territory obtained by the first settlers, the Company prohibited slave trading within its sphere of influence, encouraged agriculture with a view to ending slave trading, and proposed to build schools which, run by missionaries, would become instruments of evangelisation. A promise was given that any African who came to live within the territory would enjoy the same rights as any European living there. And Granville Town, destroyed by King Jimmy, was rebuilt and renamed Freetown.

The Nova Scotians, like some of the first black settlers at Granville Town, had fought on the British side during the American War of Independence. After the war they had been taken to Nova Scotia, a British colony north of the United States, and today part of Canada. Promised land to farm which they never received, the Nova Scotians sent a representative, Thomas Peters, to London to lodge a complaint with the British government. While in London, Peters met the directors of the Sierra Leone Company and was offered land in Sierra Leone. This offer was accepted by the Nova Scotians who left for Sierra Leone in January 1792.

In several respects the Nova Scotians appeared to be an ideal group of people to help run the settlement. Many of them were Christians, some had received a western education, and almost all were acquainted with English law. However, like the first group of settlers, the Nova Scotians found the climate and the rains in particular very trying and over one hundred of them died very early on. Then came problems over farming land and difficulties with local rulers and the Sierra Leone Company.

King Naimbaña opposed the farming of land by the settlers east of Freetown and King Jimmy refused to allow them to farm west of the watering station on the Sierra Leone River. All that remained were the rocky, infertile slopes, inland behind Freetown.

The disappointment of the Nova Scotians who had dreamt of large, fertile farms in Africa, was made worse when the Sierra Leone Company increased the price of its goods in the Freetown shops. The war in Europe between Britain and France from 1793 to 1815 was in part responsible for this rise in prices since it meant that the Company itself had to pay more for its goods. Further, the situation of the settlers was made virtually impossible when a French naval squadron bombarded Freetown in 1794, looted the homes of the settlers, burnt down the Sierra Leone Company's stores and offices and commandeered a number of its ships which had large cargoes aboard.[9] Freetown was rebuilt after the departure of the French.

The Nova Scotian rebellion, the arrival of the Maroons and British government control of the settlement

The main grievance of the Nova Scotians was the insistence by the Sierra Leone Company that they should pay an annual rent for their land, despite the fact that they had been promised that the land would be provided free of charge. Some of the Nova Scotians, led by Isaac Anderson, responded by insisting on self-government. In September 1800 they proclaimed new laws and declared those of the Sierra Leone Company to be obsolete. The then governor of the settlement, Thomas Ludlam, reacted by attempting to arrest the rebels. Some were captured while others escaped and took up arms. Unfortunately for the rebels a British ship carrying British troops and about 550 Maroons – runaway slaves from Jamaica – entered Freetown harbour. The troops and Maroons joined the governor's forces and the uprising was put down. From this point onwards until 1808 when the British government took control, the settlement was ruled by the Sierra Leone Company directly, the settlers losing even the right to elect their own representatives. In 1808 the third phase began when the settlement became a British Crown Colony ruled by a governor who represented the British Crown. The population was about 2,000 strong and was composed in the main of Nova Scotians and Maroons who lived in separate quarters of Freetown.

The arrival of the Church Missionary Society (CMS)

The settlement in Sierra Leone was, as we have seen, intended to solve the 'black problem' in Britain. It was also the result of humanitarian protest against slavery and the slave trade, which was legally abolished in Britain and in British colonies in 1807. There was also a desire to make a commercial profit, as the activities of the Sierra Leone Company made clear. A most important motive, however, of the founder of the Sierra Leone settlement was the spread of Christianity and 'civilization' across

Africa from this base on the coast.

The Nova Scotian settlers arrived in Sierra Leone according to one account 'convinced and instructed Christians with very firm if not always very consistent beliefs'.[10] Some of the settlers were members of the Baptist Church, others were Methodists, and others members of the Countess of Huntingdon's Connection, a splinter group of the Anglican Church. Church buildings, in addition to being places of worship, were also used for political and social purposes. They were also places where one could acquire status, rise to a position of leadership, gain a following, exercise authority and influence and preserve one's identity and culture. It was through the Churches as *organisations* that Methodists attempted to oppose government taxes or rent increases. Cato Perkins of the Countess of Huntingdon's Connection organised opposition to government policy through his Church, while David George obtained support for that same policy through the Baptist Church. Furthermore, representatives were elected to political office from the Church communities. The Church, then, was an all-purpose institution.

In addition to the few remaining first settlers – the Nova Scotians and the Maroons – numerous others, known as 'recaptives' or 'liberated slaves', were settled in Sierra Leone after the British Anti-Slave Trade Act in 1807. In an attempt to enforce the Act, British naval ships were given power to capture slave ships, and after a trial before a British court, to free the slaves. Hence the term 'recaptive' or 'liberated slaves'. These recaptives, who might have come from anywhere along the West African coast – from Senegal, the Ivory Coast or Ghana or from even further, for example, from Zaire – were settled in what was then the Crown Colony of Sierra Leone. By 1815 an estimated 6,000 recaptives had been settled in the colony.

On landing in Sierra Leone, many were baptised and given European names. This was the first stage in the 'civilising' process pursued by the government. Some remained in Freetown, while others were sent to establish new villages, such as Leicester Village, founded by Wolof and Bambara, recaptives from Senegal and Mali.

One of the principal tasks of the Church Missionary Society (CMS) which began work in Sierra Leone in 1804 and of the Wesleyan Methodist Mission which became involved there in 1811 was to contribute to this 'civilising' process through their schools. The CMS enjoyed close ties with the Sierra Leone Company and the support and patronage of the British upper and ruling classes. The Methodists, regarded as a dissenting Church, did not have the same support. In 1816 Governor MacCarthy divided the colony into sixteen parishes and appointed missionaries of the CMS as administrators, thus bringing the Church directly into politics. MacCarthy maintained that the role of the Church was to create both 'civilised' citizens and Christians, seeing baptism itself as an act of civilisation.

The Church was the school and the school was the Church in these early days or, as one writer has expressed it, 'the school developed not as an institution in itself but as a function of the Church.'[11] In addition to running primary schools, the Church opened the Christian Institute at Fourah Bay in 1827, and by the 1840s a secondary school had been started.

In these schools the settlers were taught the Christian faith and other subjects, in English, and were made to understand that they were Britain's partners in the 'civilising' of Africa. Christianity, moreover, became a link, if at times a fragile one, between the Nova Scotians, Maroon settlers and the recaptives. Further, it enabled some of the recaptives to rise economically, acquire status and the marks of 'civilisation' and thus merge with the settler population.

In addition to the important part it played in education and the spread of western ideas and attitudes the Church also provided opportunities for the acquisition of administrative skills. Members of church committees learnt the basics of committee work while others, as class leaders, learnt the principles of organisation. The management of property was another skill which resulted from membership of church trusts formed to manage church property.

Many recaptives embraced Christianity with enthusiasm, and were particularly attracted to the Baptist and Methodist Churches. There remained, nevertheless, a strong attachment to traditional religious beliefs and practices despite the missionary attempts to stamp them out. For example, with the withdrawal of the CMS from their administrative activities in the villages of the colony peninsula, traditional religion strongly reasserted itself and this, according to one scholar, formed the real beginnings of Creole society.[12] Belief in and the use of magic and charms became a much more prominent feature of Christian, and for that matter, Muslim life. Specifically African practices were incorporated into the Christian rites of passage such as baptism, marriage and funeral services. For instance 'awujo', the western Nigerian, Yoruba traditional practice of celebrating wakes and mourning for the dead, was incorporated into the Christian funeral service.

While some recaptives never became Christians in the first place, some converts abandoned Christianity for the traditional religion. Both of these groups – and doubtless some Christians – joined in the Shango processions which were held in Freetown every week. In addition, secret societies such as the 'Agugu' and the Bundo and Poro societies survived and even flourished in such places as Freetown, Fourah Bay and Hastings. Traditional religion thus formed an important part of the religious beliefs of the settlers and recaptives.

Missionary activity in the interior of Sierra Leone

So far the discussion has been concerned with the settlers and the recaptives – the Creoles – while nothing has been said about the indigenous people of Sierra Leone. Missionaries and Creoles began moving inland in the nineteenth century. By the second half of the nineteenth century the staff of some of the Protestant missions in towns such as Rotifunk, Tarma and Shenge were for the most part Creoles, and their missionary and 'civilising' work among the Temne and Mende peoples was largely unsuccessful. The missionaries were seen by some of the Mende as government agents and were mistrusted. The Mende also poured scorn on the European dress and attitudes of the Creoles, while the latter referred to the indigenous people as 'heathens' and 'aborigines'. The impression conveyed is that the missionaries were on the whole simply tolerated and occasionally found to be useful rather than appreciated for their teaching about Christianity and 'civilization'.

By 1840 there were about 1,500 full members of the CMS. The Society was in charge of some fifty schools which catered for about 6,000 pupils. The Methodists had about 2,000 full members and about 1,500 pupils in their schools.[13] These apparently meagre results need to be seen in a wider context. The missionaries' political links with the European authorities, the strength of the traditional religion, the spread of Islam and the high death rate among missionaries – 109 died in Sierra Leone in twenty-five years – the indifferent attitude of some Europeans to the teachings and practices of Christianity, and the fact that the settlers themselves were westernised and did not easily make contact with the indigenous population all account for the slow progress made in the hinterland.

Liberia: the resettlement of ex-slaves from North America

The history of Christianity in Liberia in the first half of the nineteenth century followed a similar course to that of Christianity in Sierra Leone. In the United States in the early years of the nineteenth century there were over 250,000 ex-slaves, in addition to about 1,770,000 black people still enslaved.[14] As in Britain, the question of the future of these former slaves was one which had begun to exercise the mind of, among others, Quaker philanthropists and missionary organisations. Some consideration had in fact been given to this question in the eighteenth century before the American War of Independence. It was not, however, until the early years of the nineteenth century, when the freed slave issue came to be seen as an acute social problem by white North American society that any moves were made to solve the problem by returning the former slaves to Africa. The majority of North Americans were, as was the case in Britain, unwilling to welcome the liberated slaves into the wider community as equals.

Some of the ex-slaves, it is true, had gained limited acceptance into predominantly white North American society as small traders and salesmen. But the majority had little or no access to the wider society and were seen as a threat to its peace and stability. Some of the freed slaves encouraged those still in bondage to revolt and also attacked wealthy white homesteads. This led to the suggestion by the Virginia State Legislature that the most troublesome of the freed slaves be sent to Africa and the rest to a destination of their own choice. This suggestion was put forward in 1816, the same year as the foundation of the American Society for the Colonization of Free People of Colour of the United States (ASC).

Some members of the ASC were philanthropists with strong

missionary interests and saw in the freed slaves repatriated to Africa a band of Christian missionaries who could spread Christianity right across the continent. The organisation, however, was backed by politicians and many others who saw in it a means of ridding society of people they did not want.

The first attempt by the ASC in 1817 to establish a freed slave settlement on the Sherbo island off the coast of Sierra Leone failed. Other attempts followed. For example, in 1820 eighty-two freed slaves left the United States, again for Sherbo island. The freed slaves were Christians and were ministered to by a Methodist, David Coker. Twenty-two died soon after arriving and the rest headed for Sierra Leone. Then in 1821 two further shipments were made, the first one taking twenty-eight freed slaves to Sherbo. They also ended up in Sierra Leone, as did the small group of emigrants who followed in November of the same year. But land was soon purchased from the indigenous people at the mouth of the Mesurado River, several hundred miles to the south-east of Sierra Leone, and in April 1822 all those freed slaves still remaining in Sierra Leone were transferred to this settlement. The settlers came under attack from the local population almost immediately. Led by a clergyman, Jehudi Ashmun, the freed slaves put up strong resistance and had consolidated their position by 1830.

By 1830 relatively few freed slaves had been resettled in Liberia and this provoked dissatisfaction among some whites in North America with the performance of the ASC organisation. The outcome was the formation of the Maryland Colonisation Society (MSC) in 1831. Uprisings in Virginia and attacks on white property alleged to be the work of former slaves pushed a number of legislatures in the southern states of North America into taking speedy action to repatriate freed slaves. The Maryland State Legislature financed repatriation through the MCS to Cape Palmas, south of Monrovia, in 1831 and 1832, and the states of New York and Pennsylvania followed with the establishment of a settlement at Bassa Cove. Mississippi established its settlement at Greenville on the Sinoe River, and other settlements were founded by Louisiana and Georgia.

In 1837 the various settlements became the Commonwealth of Liberia, governed by Thomas Buchanan, and under the control of the Board of Directors of the State Societies for repatriation. Repatriation, however, was not a success. Men like W.L. Garrison had from the outset opposed the foundation of the ASC and argued that the answer to the freed slave question lay in integration not repatriation. Moreover, the former slaves themselves, never consulted about the repatriation scheme, did not on the whole wish to be arbitrarily despatched to Africa. Further the United States government showed very little interest in Liberia. This made it easier for the leadership of the settlement to declare Liberia an independent republic in 1847, albeit with a constitution modelled on that of the United States.

Virtually all of the settlers were Christians and according to a report of 1834 religion (meaning Christianity) 'is respected and in general appreciated by the settlers of Liberia. . . . The Sunday is regularly observed and the public service is frequented by almost everyone.'[15] The settlers belonged to a variety of different Christian denominations, and consequently in each of the settlements different Christian Churches were established. This diversity was increased with the arrival of the various Christian missionary denominations, the first of which was the Evangelical Missionary Society of Basel (Switzerland) which began work in Monrovia (formerly Cape Mensuado) in 1827.

The first Basel mission achieved virtually nothing by way of converts to Christianity. Interdenominational rivalry, lack of interest and concern among the settler Christians in the conversion of the local inhabitants, the hostility between these two groups and the lack of support from the authorities all contributed to the failure of the Basel mission from its beginning in 1827 to its decision to leave Liberia in 1831.

The American Methodist Episcopal Church (AME), also sent several missionaries to Liberia during this period. One, Melville Cox, arrived in Monrovia in March 1833 and died there two years later. Two other clergymen of the same Church, and the first Christian woman missionary to West Africa, Miss Farrington, arrived in Monrovia in 1834. One of the clergymen soon died while the other left for home. At this point Miss Farrington was joined by a clergyman of West Indian origin, John Seys, who directed the mission for the next ten years.

Seys was undoubtedly among the most successful of the early missionaries to Liberia. When he arrived at Monrovia in 1834 the mission had 13 preachers, 6 teachers for 200 students, and 204 Church members.[16] Seys brought in another missionary from the United States and a doctor to promote missionary activity among the indigenous people of Condo. He also established a college for training clergymen, an industrial school and a printing press which produced the mission journal 'Africa's Luminar'.[17] By 1840 Seys and his fellow workers had converted a number of indigenous chiefs, including the chiefs of Haddington and Robertsville and a number of their people. When Seys was forced to return to North America in 1841, allegedly because of his interference in local politics, his Church had an estimated 1,000 members, 150 of whom were local people while the rest were settlers. And there were 600 students in the school.

The American Baptist mission, although several of its clergymen had been in Liberia from the beginning of the settlement, began sending missionaries there from 1835. One of the most active of these early Baptist missionaries was Crocker, who struggled to learn the language of the Bassa-speaking people in order to convert them to Christianity. He enjoyed a relatively high degree of success converting some forty of the Bassa from Eldina (Bassa Cove) between 1835 and 1840.[18]

Other North American missionary bodies that became involved in missionary activity in Liberia in the 1830s included the American Presbyterian Mission, the American Board of Commissioners for Foreign Missions and the Protestant Episcopal Church, a branch of the Anglican Church. The American Presbyterian Mission, known from 1837 as the Board of Foreign Missions of the Presbyterian Church of the United States, attempted to use its small number of adherents from among the settler population at Cape Palmas and elsewhere as a base for spreading Christianity into the interior of the country. The American Board adopted a different strategy, going directly to the indigenous people, the reason being that it had no established local church which could be used as a launching-pad into the interior. But neither missionary body made very much impact on the indigenous population prior to 1840 and not a great deal during the rest of the nineteenth century. The American Board was to leave Liberia in 1843, and by the 1890s the Presbyterian Church of the United States had an estimated 332 full members, only fifty of whom were from among the indigenous population.

The American Board had established itself in seven different areas of the country, had opened a number of schools and had translated parts of the Gospel into Grebo before being hit by a severe financial crisis and a number of untimely deaths. When the Board left Liberia in 1843 the Protestant Episcopal Mission took over a number of its missions and went on to make a relatively large contribution to the christianising of the indigenous people of Liberia.

By 1840, however, the missionary societies as a whole had not made any noticeable impact, as far as the growth of Christianity was concerned, on the indigenous people. Liberia had many churches and chapels, indeed it has been suggested that there were too many.[19] In 1840 the sixteen existing churches and chapels mainly served the 5,000 settlers and as was the case in Sierra Leone, the settlers were for the most part indifferent and even at times hostile to the idea of incorporating the indigenous population into their Christian communities. This can be explained in part by the fact that the settlers had come to see their Christianity as a symbol of their higher status and a mark of their identity. They were unprepared to lower or 'dilute', as it were, their own status and blur the distinction between themselves and the indigenous population by extending what they regarded as the prestige, benefits and status conferred by Christianity. As one scholar has pointed out, for the Americo-Liberian settlers in Liberia the Christian religion was, and to some extent still remains, an essential distinguishing mark of their 'civilization', along with the English language and European dress.[20]

While this goes some of the way towards explaining why there were only an estimated 300 Christians in Liberia by 1840, another part of the explanation lies in the reaction of the indigenous people themselves. They likewise were anxious to protect their identity, beliefs, customs and way of life and did not, therefore, welcome conversion to Christianity which many of them regarded as the religion of foreign invaders.

For the Liberian settlers their Churches had functioned in the United States as political, social and religious institutions, and this continued to be the case in Liberia. In Liberia and in Sierra Leone, as we have seen, the Churches also provided members of the settler communities with opportunities for leadership and advancement.

Most of Liberia's leaders in this period and many of Sierra Leone's were from the Churches. This remained so for a long time to come. It is worth noting one important difference between the Liberian situation and that prevailing at the time in Sierra Leone. While the settlers in Sierra Leone were soon outnumbered by the recaptives, those in Liberia continued to outnumber the recaptives by about four to one during the whole of the period under discussion. This made the Americo-Liberian or settler community in Liberia a much more closed, separate society, and a society that strove to perpetuate itself by, among other things, restricting Christianity to those schooled in the western education system.[21]

Some Churches in fact were to make literacy in English a prerequisite for baptism.[22] In the eyes of one Protestant missionary who worked among the Grebo at Cape Palmas in the nineteenth century a good Christian was someone who had some western education and 'who observed Sunday, pulled down greegrees, . . . refused to participate in traditional sacrifices . . . wore western clothes, built a western house, married only one wife and cultivated gardens of flowers.'[23] Converts, moreover, would also be expected to support the settler community in any disputes – and there were many – with the indigenous population,[23] and to isolate themselves geographically as well as in other ways from the wider non-Christian society. Shut away in mission schools they would learn to disown their past.[24]

Ghana (formerly the Gold Coast)

The modern Christian missionary movement got under way in Ghana in the 1820s. The Basel mission (see p. 31 and p. 39), began work there in 1828. At first the mission concentrated its efforts on the villages of Ossu and Mingo which were situated close to the Danish fort of Christiansborg. In 1832 the missionaries moved into the mountainous regions of Akwapin where the climate was more amenable. However, despite the better climatic conditions, the Basel mission in Ghana had accomplished very little by 1840. The death rate among missionaries was high. Furthermore, the policy of the Danish administration at Christiansborg and the rivalry between Denmark and England on the West African coast made the task of the mission exceedingly difficult. The Basel Mission Committee had sent out missionaries to the Gold Coast (Ghana) 'to open schools and in general live in brotherly love with the Africans'.[25] The Danish administration, on the other hand, demanded that the missionaries devote themselves exclusively to work among the Danish congregation at Christiansborg. One missionary, Heinze, a doctor, was appointed to the post of medical doctor at the fort and was 'forced' to act for a time as chaplain to the local Danish congregation. Another, Riis, partly in order to escape from the control of the Danish authorities, moved the headquarters of the Basel mission to Akropong in the Akwapin Hills.

This move, even though it had a number of advantages particularly as far as the health of the missionaries was concerned, also had the disadvantage of involving the mission in political infighting. The Akwapin region, while it came within the Danish sphere of influence, was coveted by the British who were anxious to establish and maintain close commercial and trading links with the indigenous population. The

Basel missionary Riis, for his part, though without any personal political ambitions, appears to have favoured the British presence to that of the Danes. Riis believed that the Akwapin people had more confidence in the authority of the British governor, Maclean, than in the Danish authorities. This positive attitude of Riis towards the British aroused the suspicion and hostility of the Danish authorities. In 1837 King Ado of Akropong staged a rebellion against the Danish authorities and Riis was arrested on suspicion of having engineered the rebellion. Later released, Riis returned to Akropong, but he and his missionary colleagues were unable to engage in any in-depth missionary work among the local people for fear of being suspected by the Danish authorities of involvement in subversive activity. According to Riis the local people were not opposed to Christianity, but none of them became Christians in his time.

The Wesleyan Methodist Missionary Society (WMS) which started its operations in Ghana in 1835 experienced few of the problems – the high mortality rate apart – encountered by the Basel mission. The WMS, based at Cape Coast, also had a firmer foundation upon which to build. The 'government' school at Cape Coast trained a number of students in reading, writing and Bible Knowledge, and it was one of the school's former students, William de Graft, who played an important part in arranging for the WMS to establish itself at Cape Coast. Then in 1838 the well-known Wesleyan missionary Thomas Birch Freeman began his long missionary career in Ghana. Assisted by the 'graduates' of Cape Coast school, the recaptives who had returned home, and supported by the British authorities, Freeman and the other Wesleyan missionaries were able to establish mission stations in many towns and villages and overcome some of the opposition from local rulers such as the King of the Asante. Freeman visited the Asante capital Kumasi in 1839 and reported that the King's opposition to missionary activity 'was removed by a promise of all necessary assistance on the part of his excellency President Maclean'.[26]

The impact of the WMS on the Gold Coast in the period under discussion was understandably slight. Seven years, as one missionary expressed it in 1842, was too short a time to expect 'any of those great changes which would be desirable'.[27] The 'Great Object' was to implant Christianity and 'civilisation'. The approach was to get people to renounce their 'sins' and 'evil' ways, and convert to Christianity. Sermons given in English through an interpreter attacked idol worship, insisted on the necessity of repentance and spoke about redemption through the love of Christ.

Very few rulers converted to Christianity in this period, though many were apparently neither unsympathetic nor hostile to it. Initially there was some scepticism about the establishment of Christian schools, but this for the most part was overcome when chiefs began to discover that these schools could serve to bring about improvements in agriculture, trade and other areas. Though they were few in number the schools nevertheless made a considerable impact on the social and cultural life of the people. New tools for furniture-making and farming were introduced in this way, and the use of European languages and style of dress became more widespread. For some local converts, Christianity became the symbol of higher social status.

The Senegambia (Senegal and The Gambia)

From the outbreak of the French Revolution in 1789 until about 1817 Senegal's several thousand Christians were without any resident missionary. Occasionally they were visited by Catholic priests from the Cape Verde islands, but for much of the period (1789–1817) the island of Gorée, part of Senegal, and St Louis, Rufisque and Joal, the other main centres of Catholicism in Senegal, and normally served by priests from France, were under British control and therefore had little contact with Catholic clergy. The British handed back the territory to France in 1815, having first destroyed the main buildings including the churches. Something of a new beginning was made by Catholicism in Senegal with the arrival of the French missionary sisters of the Order of St Joseph of Cluny (see p. 31). The sisters took charge of the hospital and opened a school for girls in Gorée in the 1820s. They were responsible for sending three Senegalese – Moussa, Fridoil and Boilat – to France to train for and later be ordained to the priesthood. The first, Moussa, returned as a priest to St Louis in 1840, and Fridoil and Boilat followed in 1843.

Fr. Boilat's account of the state of Catholicism in the Senegambia as he found it on his return from France is worth considering here. According to Boilat, there were many Catholics at St Louis who had been baptised in 1820 by a priest who never even left his ship. Children of at least five years of age and many adults were taken to the ship where they were baptised. These people, Boilat observed, remained attached to Catholicism in the absence of priests, passing on to their children all they knew, which was only a few prayers.[28] The Catholics in Joal were said by Boilat to be 'superstitious like the Muslims and Traditionalists'. Moreover, in Joal in the 1840s two old Catholic lay teachers, Papaille and Michel, had been in charge of the Catholic community for so long that they came to look upon themselves as priests.[29] And when Fr Gallais arrived to take charge of the Joal mission in 1848 he found that many Catholics had several wives and that some were quite happy to distinguish themselves from Muslims solely by the criterion of 'excessive beer drinking'.[30]

Although many of the Christians of Joal knew little more than the sign of the cross in Portuguese and the names of Jesus and Mary they tended to regard themselves as superior to their non-Christian neighbours. They saw themselves as educated, better protected from the ravages of the slave trade than others, in control of the flow, direction and quantity of European merchandise, not liable to tax, and 'partners' of the Europeans. They wanted in fact to be treated as Europeans and even demanded to be addressed as the 'whites of Joal' on account of their 'Portuguese' descent and baptism. As Boilat put it: 'In a word, to be a Christian is to be white, for to be white is to be free, it is to have the right and the means to drink.'[31]

There were also a number of Roman Catholics in The Gambia, south of

Senegal, in this period. The Wesleyan rather than the Catholic
missionaries were the most active there until the arrival of the French
Catholic missionaries of the Holy Ghost Congregation in the late 1840s.
Between 1821 and 1849 the Wesleyans established missions in Combo,
Barra, Georgetown, MacCarthy Island, Wuli and Bathurst (Banjul).[32]

By the 1840s there was a relatively strong Muslim presence in the
Senegambia and this was to have a profound impact on Christian
missionary thinking and strategy. The Christian encounter with Islam is a
topic that will be discussed in some detail later (see Chapter 8,
pp. 214–19). Here it is worth pointing out that as early as the 1820s the
Wesleyan missionaries saw Islam as the greatest obstacle to the expansion
of Christianity in The Gambia regarding it as an 'impenetrable barrier'.

In Banjul (formerly Bathurst) missionaries were in a fortunate position.
This city was founded as a settlement for English and African traders
forced to leave Gorée when the British returned the island to France in
1815, and as a home for recaptives. In the first fifty years or so of its
existence Banjul had a majority of Christians over Muslims. However,
once the era of settling the recaptives had come to an end in the 1860s, the
Christian community in Banjul grew only very slowly and was soon
outnumbered by Muslims who moved there from the hinterland. As was
the case in Liberia and Sierra Leone, and for much the same reasons, the
Christians made little real effort to extend Christianity to the hinterland.[34]

Conclusions

During the period discussed in this chapter (1790–1840) the Christian
missions made little headway in converting the indigenous people of
West Africa to Christianity. The vast majority of the 10,000 or so
Christians in West Africa in 1840 were either settlers or recaptives. In
addition, there were a similar number of children attending mission
schools. A few hundred at most of the indigenous population had been
converted to Christianity by the end of this period.

Although one cannot judge success and failure purely in numerical
terms, one can ask why the Christian missions had such a slight impact on
the local indigenous population. This question has in large measure
already been answered. The death rate among missionaries was high,
and this aggravated what was already an acute problem, namely the
shortage of trained missionary personnel. This factor alone, however,
does not explain adequately the very slow growth of Christianity among
the indigenous population. Many of the indigenous rulers needed to be
persuaded of the advantages – moral, intellectual, cultural, political and
economic – to be gained from conversion. These as we have seen were by
no means obvious or self-evident.

Further, the fact that many of the settlers and recaptives saw in
Christianity a symbol or mark of their more 'civilized', more 'advanced'
way of life, and a means of distinguishing themselves from the
indigenous people did little to advance the cause of Christianity among
the latter. The climate, the lack of knowledge and information on the part

of the missionaries about the people they were attempting to convert, their harsh and strident condemnation of the latter's way of life, their inability to communicate in the local language, and their lack of resources when viewed against the immensity of the task undertaken all contributed to defeat their aims. Some missionaries, further supported by government administrators and spurred on by the desire to put an end to the slave trade by replacing it with what was termed 'legitimate' commerce, did not always make a clear enough distinction between the political, economic and cultural interests of Europe and the task of spreading Christianity. To say all this is not to criticise individual missionaries for the sake of it. Nor is it to ride roughshod over the undoubted courage and dedication of many of them, but simply to attempt to explain why the results they achieved by the 1840s were so much less spectacular than what they had hoped for when they set out in the 1790s.

Notes

1   R. Gray, The Origins and Organization of the nineteenth-century Missionary Movement. In O.U. Kalu (ed.), *The History of Christianity in West Africa*, Harlow: Longman, 1980: 14 ff.
2   A.F. Walls, Missionary Vocation and Ministry: the first generation. In O.U. Kalu (ed.), op. cit., pp. 22 ff.
3   O.U. Kalu (ed.), op. cit., p. 12.
4   G.E. Simpson, *Black Religions in the New World*. Columbia University Press, 1978, 216–28.
5   Quotations from E. Kendall's, *The End of An Era. Africa and the Missionary*. London: SPCK, 1978: 28.
6   J.F.C. Harrison, *The Second Coming: Popular Millenarianism 1780–1850*. London: Routledge and Kegan Paul, 1979.
7   E.M. Hogan, *Catholic Missions and Liberia*, Cork: Cork University Press, 1981: 13.
8   J. Peterson, *Province of Freedom*. London, Faber, 1969.
9   C. Fyfe, *A Short History of Sierra Leone* (New Ed.) London: Longman, 1979: 28.
10   A.F. Walls, *The Nova Scotian Settlers and Their Religion*, Sierra Leone Bulletin of Religion, June 1959.
11   A.T. Porter, *Creoledom*. Oxford: Oxford University Press, 1963: 88.
12   J. Peterson, *Province of Freedom*, pp. 187–92.
13   J. Faure, *Histoire des Missions et Églises Protestantes en Afrique Occidentale des Origines à 1884*. Yaoundé, 1978: 54.
14   J.D. Hargreaves, *African Colonization in the Nineteenth Century*. In J. Butler (ed.), Boston University Papers in African History, Boston 1966, Vol. ii, p. 59.
15   Faure, *Histoire des Missions et Eglises Protestantes en Afrique Occidentale des Origines à 1884*, op. cit., p. 54.
16   ibid., p. 63.
17   ibid.
18   ibid., p. 66.
19   ibid., p. 70.
20   M. Fraenkel, *Tribe and Class in Monrovia*. London: International African Institute, 1964: 7.

21   J.C. Wold, *'God's Impatience in Liberia'*, Michigan University Press, Michigan: 1968: 57,

22   J.J. Martin, *The Dual Legacy: Government Authority and Mission Influence Among the Grebo of Eastern Liberia*, 1834–1910. Ph.D. Boston, 1968 (University Microfilm, Ann Arbor, Michigan): 206.

23   ibid.

24   M.A.G. Brown, Education and National Development in Liberia, Ph.D. Thesis, Cornell, 1967 (University Microfilm, Ann Arbor, Michigan, 1967).

25   This quotation is to be found in S.K. Odamtten, *The Missionary Factor in Ghana's Development (1820–1880)*. Accra, 1978: p. 32.

26   Thomas Birch Freeman, *Various Visits to Ashanti* (3rd Ed. with Introduction by H.M. Wright) London: Frank Cass, 1968: 12.

27   Quotation in Odamtten, op. cit., p. 36.

28   L'Abbé Boilat, *Esquisses Sénégalaises*, Paris, 1853: 214.

29   ibid.

30   Holy Ghost Fathers' Archives, Paris, *Sénégambie*, Boîte No. 152, Doss B. Lettres et Divers, 1840–1850.

31   L'Abbé Boilat, op. cit., p. 109.

32   F. Renner, Muslim-Christian Relations in The Gambia in the 19th and 20th Centuries. M.A. Dissertation. Area Studies, London, Sept. 1979: 16 ff.

33   ibid., p. 19.

34   F. Mahoney, *Government and Opinion in The Gambia*. Ph.D. Thesis, University of London (School of Oriental and African Studies), 1963.

3

Towards the establishment of 'self-governing, self-supporting, self-propagating' African Churches 1840–1890.

By the 1840s it had become clear to many missionary societies that if Christianity was to take root and expand in Africa it would be necessary to raise a class of highly trained Africans to govern and administer the local African Churches. European missionaries wanted to create Christian nations in Africa, but given the problems of climate, shortage of manpower and inadequate financial and material assistance, they began to see themselves more and more simply as guides and advisors who would eventually be replaced by Africans. In the meantime the Africans would act as their agents.[1] From this approach the policy of 'native agency' emerged and it was implemented by a number of missionary societies for much of the period under discussion.

While the CMS was among those missionary bodies that laid great emphasis on the establishment of 'self-governing, self-supporting, self-propagating' Churches in Africa, the Roman Catholic emphasis was placed almost exclusively on the training of an indigenous clergy. Colleges were established very early on in this period by the Catholic missionary order, the Holy Ghost Fathers, in Senegal, but the results as we shall see, were meagre.

To christianise Africa it was not only thought necessary to raise a trained African clergy and a people knowledgeable in the Bible, but also to instil 'new' attitudes towards work and leisure, to replace the slave trade by 'legitimate' trade, to introduce new agricultural and other skills, and to isolate the Christian community from what were seen as the 'corrupting influences' of the wider society, allegedly fostered by traditional religion and Islam. Islam, as its influence increased in the nineteenth century, came to be regarded as the foremost obstacle to the spread of Christianity, and as 'responsible for all the evils of Africa'.[2]

Though they condemned the trend towards secularism and materialism in Europe, many missionaries were convinced that Europe had arrived at an advanced stage of social, cultural, political and economic development, because at base it was Christian. Africans, by coming to know the truths of Christianity and by hard work – in other words by means of the 'Bible and the Plough' as it is sometimes put – could emulate Europe. It was maintained that Islam, which made progress by accommodating itself to the current norms, values and attitudes of African societies would decline since it would cease to appeal to the mission-trained, 'enlightened', 'civilised' African.[3]

These, then, in broad outline were the hopes and aspirations, the policies and methods of most of the Christian missionary societies in West Africa from the 1840s until the age of the Scramble for Africa which began in the mid 1880s. Those missionary societies committed to the establishment of self-governing, self-supporting African Churches did not have to look very far for trained and educated African co-workers, whose contribution towards the implementation of these policies was crucial.

In the late 1830s former slaves and recaptives from Brazil, Cuba and Sierra Leone began to make preparations to return to their homelands in Nigeria, Togo, the Republic of Benin (formerly Dahomey), Ghana and elsewhere. This homeward movement of freed slaves and recaptives gained momentum in the 1840s. Several hundred more freed slaves from North America were to be resettled in Liberia in this period. On their own initiative and independently of missionary societies many of the Christians among these returnees – not all were Christians; some were Muslims – planned to bring Christianity and legitimate commerce to their homelands.[4] However, before considering the role of these African agents in the spread of Christianity in Nigeria and elsewhere we will first of all continue with the history of Christianity in Sierra Leone and then Liberia.

Sierra Leone

By the 1840s the vast majority of Christians in Sierra Leone were from among the settlers or recaptives rather than the indigenous Africans. Moreover, as we have seen, (see Chapter 2, p. 44) for many of these Christians their allegiance to a Christian Church was not only a matter of religious faith but also a mark of their identity and a symbol of their prestige and status. For example, membership of the Anglican Church of St George in Freetown, which became a cathedral in 1852, was widely recognised as conferring considerable social prestige and status. As people rose up the social ladder they tended to transfer their allegiance from the less prestigious denominations and chapels to St George's, and even some of those who did not go this far still arranged to have weddings, funerals and other public services there.

Elements of African religious thought and practice either remained or re-emerged as part of the belief system of the Creoles, paralleling to some extent the development of the language they spoke – Krio – which was a fusion of English and African elements. By the 1840s the term *Creole* was a label that was applied in the main to the Nova Scotian, Maroon and liberated African members of the population, thus blurring the distinctions between these three groups.[5]

In the period 1840–1890 the Creoles were a relatively prosperous and successful community and one upon whom the British administration relied very heavily. Moreover, missionary societies such as the CMS felt the Creoles ought to be allowed greater scope and freedom in the administration and organisation of the church. Thus in 1861 the Native Pastorate Church (later called the Sierra Leone Church) was set up to be governed by committees composed of clerics and lay people, both African and European. Africans were appointed as principals of schools such as the Freetown Grammar School. James Johnson, however, born of Yoruba parents in Sierra Leone, and at the time a clergyman and later to become a bishop in Nigeria, while welcoming the establishment of the Native Pastorate felt the CMS and the British administration should be prepared to grant full autonomy over their own affairs to the people of Sierra Leone. He expressed this view in a letter to the governor in December 1872 in which he wrote:

> We see nothing around us that we can call our own in the true sense of the term; nothing that shows an independent native capability – excepting this infant Native Pastorate institution; for this reason and for the conviction we have that it is capable of being made a mighty instrument to develop the principles which create and strengthen a nation we cleave to it . . . . Whilst we value our connection with England and use the service of a valuable English bishop, I say that the use of the services of a native prelate and our own Liturgy and Canons, is a mere question of time.[6]

The Native Pastorate idea, thus, was a step in the right direction, but did not go far enough in such matters as the appointment of African bishops, the formulation of the liturgy and ecclesiastical law.

Though missionary societies tended to concentrate their efforts in and around Freetown, they did not entirely neglect the people of the interior such as the Temne and Mende. The CMS, in addition to its educational and other activities in Freetown, established mission stations at Port Loko and elsewhere in what became known as the Protectorate, and the Methodists became involved in the evangelisation of the peoples of the Mabanta and Limba areas, also in the Protectorate.[7] The American missionaries of the United Brethren Church (UBC; later the Evangelical United Brethren and today the United Methodist Church of Sierra Leone) set up mission stations in the interior among the people of Mano Bagru, Imperi and the surrounding area. They provided facilities in their schools for acquiring technical, entrepreneurial and other skills, and those interested in trading were given goods on credit and encouraged to preach the gospel while trading.

When Governor Cardew visited one of the UBC mission stations at Rotifunk he reported:

> it was pleasing to observe the advance that had been made in the school and the industrial training of 'native' youths through the efforts of the American mission of the United Brethren . . . . This work is principally carried out by ladies from the United States under the superintendence of a minister. . . . The system of education seems thorough and complete and is principally imparted by object lessons; amongst other apparatus in use is a human skeleton for instruction in anatomy and physiology . . . . The Industrial Training is very practical and consists of brick-making, building and carpentry. . . . The

establishment of mission stations on such lines as the above cannot but be productive of much good in the interior and the civilising influences of the one at Rotifunk were very apparent on the 'natives' of the place.[8]

Many of the people outside the colony tended to remain suspicious of the missionaries, whether European or African, regarding them as government agents. Gradually, and despite the occasional outbreak of hostility against the Creoles who were labelled 'the white men's children', increasing numbers of Temne, Mende and others began to send their children as wards to be educated by the Creole families in Freetown. As a consequence some of these wards became Christians, but even this did not necesssarily lead to full integration into Creole society.

The arrival of the Catholic missionaries

Religious life in Sierra Leone became even more diverse and varied with the arrival there of the Catholic Missionaries of the Society of African Missions (SMA) in 1859. The mission got off to a bad start with the death of all its missionaries in Freetown during an outbreak of yellow fever there in 1859. But the Catholics began again with another attempt by the Holy Ghost Fathers in 1864. Later, in 1866, the priests were joined by the sisters of the Order of St Joseph of Cluny. The latter opened schools in Howe Street and concentrated their efforts on the socially and economically deprived sectors of the population of Freetown. The membership of the Catholic mission remained small for some time, consisting of a few Jolof from Senegal, some Portuguese-speaking Africans, a number of French traders, some Irish NCOs and a few soldiers from the West Indian Regiment.[9]

The situation in 1890

By the beginning of the 1890s Christianity in Sierra Leone was still in large measure confined to Creole society. In 1891 there were an estimated 15,350 Creoles in Freetown out of a total population of 30,033.[10] Very few of the remainder of the population – Temne (2,897), Mende (1,015), Kru (1,234), Susu (1,434), Mandinka (1,256), Limba (693), Fula (244), Loko (114), and several thousand others – were also Christians.

Missionaries concentrated on the 'school approach' to conversion with the intention of building up an élite of educated Christians who would go forth to 'civilise' and evangelise the rest of the country. But by 1890 there were very few schools up country, while the indigenous peoples were reluctanct on the whole to abandon their way of life and culture in exchange for what they regarded as an alien way of life. The Christian Creoles, the principal agents of evangelisation, while retaining many African ideas and rituals in their practice of Christianity, failed or were unwilling on the whole to adapt their faith to the needs and outlook of the indigenous peoples. Furthermore, missionary societies, often engaged in rivalry and competition with each other, now had to face even greater competition from Islam both in the colony and the protectorate.[11]

While many Muslims in Sierra Leone were craftsmen or small-time traders, others like Sattan Lahai Yansanneh and his descendants controlled large tracts of land in northern Sierra Leone. Furthermore some Muslims became advisers to local rulers, and others, chiefs or almamies (rulers in this case) of indigenous or stranger communities. In some cases these influential Muslims built mosques and centres of Islamic learning like Medina in Bullom and Gbileh on the Kolente River. Blyden, who visited Gbileh in 1872, spoke of it as the 'Oxford University of the region where are collected over five hundred men studying Arabic and Koranic literature.'[12] And Burton observed that the Muslim Mandinka were as advanced educationally as any other group in Freetown.

Muslims, many of whom were literate and skilled and successful in business, came increasingly to stand out as people to be admired, becoming in the words of one writer, 'a positive reference point' for many Sierra Leoneans.[14] And as the influence and appeal of Islam grew, the Christian Creole community experienced some serious setbacks. From the 1890s the colonial administration adopted a more antagonistic, intolerant and prejudiced approach towards the Creole community, thereby increasing the already existing tension between itself and that community, and indirectly between the European-led mission Churches and the Creoles who, as we have seen, were the principal agents of evangelisation. The idea of self-governing, self-supporting African Churches, while it lost much of its appeal in European missionary circles, became more than ever the goal of the Christian Creoles in the colony.

Liberia

For most of the period from 1840 to 1890 missionary societies such as the Presbyterians and Baptists confined themselves almost entirely to work among the settlers leaving the indigenous people to themselves. On the other hand, the American-based Methodist Episcopal Mission (AME), the Lutherans and the Roman Catholics devoted a considerable amount of their time to the indigenous population.

From 1856 the Methodist Episcopal Mission came to rely almost exclusively on African clergy. In 1856, the mission was allowed its own bishop, Francis Burns, which meant that from then on clergy could be ordained in Liberia without, as was formerly the case, having to go to the United States for this purpose. Bishop Burns and his successor Bishop Roberts who took over in 1866 sent a number of missionaries trained in Monrovia to work among the Grebo, Vai, Gula and Kwaia speaking peoples of Liberia. By the 1880s this mission had established twenty-seven mission stations in Liberia and had a membership of about 2,500.[15]

The Lutheran Church, which became involved in missionary activity in Liberia in 1860, decided from the beginning to work among the indigenous people. However, for this Church as for the others, christianising meant 'educating and civilising the natives', using the school as the main vehicle for this.[16] It was not until 1927 that the first non-mission employee or school boy or girl was baptised. The baptising of the non-western educated in the 1920s was something of a new departure.[17]

Most of the missionary societies realised the absolute necessity of training local clergy. The black American, Alexander Crummell, a member of the North American-based Protestant Episcopal Church, who worked in Liberia from 1853 to 1873 was a strong advocate of black missionaries from North America and of an indigenous clergy.[18] Crummell also stressed the necessity for women missionaries if real progress was to be made. Crummell's insistence on the need for black evangelists did not mean, however, that he looked forward to the emergence of a truly independent African Church. He never questioned the assumption held by many white missionaries that Africa needed to be civilised along western, Christian lines. Indeed, he worked extremely hard to this end, believing that God had entrusted this work to black American Christians.[19]

Edward Wilmot Blyden, of West Indian origin, and well known for his writings such as Christianity, Islam and the Negro Race, was at times an even more ardent advocate of the use of black missionaries in the evangelisation of Africa than Crummell.[20] Africans, Blyden maintained, were better equipped than whites or mulattoes to withstand the difficult African climate. Blyden, however, was not always consistent, at times stressing the need for white missionaries whose commitment and abilities, he argued, were indispensable in the short term to Africa's advancement.[21]

North American black Churches and Liberia

It was not until the last quarter of the nineteenth century that black-led Churches in the United States directed their attention to missionary work in Africa in an organised and systematic way. This was in some measure due to the fact that the mission movement in the United States which had previously concentrated most of its attention on American Indians only began to develop a sense of worldwide mission in the 1880s. By the late 1880s Christian organisations in the United States such as the Student Volunteer Movement began to speak of 'the evangelisation of the world in this generation'.[22]

With the Civil War over, slavery abolished, and the frontier Indians nominally Christian, Americans began to look to the wider world for 'good causes' and found one in the international missionary movement. Between 1880 and 1900 the total number of American missionaries rose from 2,465 to 4,728, an increase of almost 100 per cent.[23]

At first, the American missionary societies were led by whites who came to the conclusion quite early on that if Africa was to be christianised this would have to be done by Africans. In its report of 1874 the Southern Baptists Convention of the United States concluded:

Nearly every white missionary has fallen a victim on the field or has been compelled to return to America (because of disease). If Africa is evangelised,

coloured men must be the agents of that great work . . . . Young coloured
brethren could be encouraged to prepare for the work of preaching the Gospel
to people of the same color in Africa. At present they are our only hope of
success.[24]

White missionary societies in the United States made great efforts to
interest black Americans in the evangelisation of Africa. Members of
these societies gave lectures on black university campuses such as Atlanta
University, quoting the biblical psalm 'Ethiopia shall soon stretch out
her hands to God', and claiming that God had ordained slavery as the
means of creating a new christianised, educated and 'civilised' African
élite in the United States that would go forth and 'bring Africa to Christ'.[25]
It was the duty of the black American Christian, the white missionaries
stressed, to 'cover Africa with homes and schools and churches and
Christian states, and 'to overcome the ignorance and barbarism of African
tribes'. This was the 'Theory of Providential Design', adapted by
missionaries for their own purposes.

A number of black American missionaries working in Liberia like the
already mentioned Alexander Crummell and Edward Blyden were in full
agreement with many of these views. Crummell believed that black
Americans were a chosen people that had been exposed to Christian
civilisation, tried and tested by slavery, and freed for the purpose of
civilising Africa. This was Crummell's version of the 'Theory of
Providential Design'.[27]

Black American evangelists had been active in West Africa long before
the last quarter of the nineteenth century, for example in Liberia and
Sierra Leone. Daniel Coker, a founder member of the American Episcopal
Church, was one of the party of colonists who went to Sierra Leone in
1820 and worked there for several years. Then there was Crummell
himself who worked in Liberia from 1853 to 1873. But it was not until the
1870s that North American black-led Churches began to get seriously
involved in missionary work in West Africa. Until then, and even later,
some black Americans believed that it was more important for them to
establish their rights and privileges as American citizens than to take
upon themselves a leading role in 'civilising' and christianising Africa. To
commit themselves to Africa would, some believed, obscure and weaken
their objectives as American citizens. While some shared many of the
goals and values of the wider American society, others believed that
white missionaries were just as suitable as blacks, as far as the 'civilising'
and christianising of Africa were concerned. Then there were those, a
minority, who saw missionary work as a form of imperialism and
Christianity as a corrupting influence. There was also the problem of
finance. African-led Churches in the United States, less financially secure
than white-led Churches, would have to find the money to support a full-
scale missionary movement in Africa.

Despite the financial and other limitations black-led Churches in North
America, in particular the Baptist and Methodist Churches, with such
members as the African Methodist Episcopal Church (AME) and the

African Methodist Episcopal Zion Church (AMEZ) began sponsoring their own missionaries from the 1870s. Between 1875 and 1900 black-led Churches in North America sponsored sixty-five black American missionaries, the majority of whom served in Liberia, while a few others went to Sierra Leone and South Africa.

These missionaries opened mission stations among the Vai people of Western Liberia and in other parts of the country. However, missionaries from these black-led Churches experienced the same financial and health problems as the missionaries in the other Churches. The AMEZ mission in Brewerville, Liberia, was short of funds and consequently was unable to expand, and by the 1890s much of its work had to be curtailed.

Most of these missionaries were part of an emerging black élite in North America that regarded Africa as a 'heathen' and 'uncivilised' land. Pressure was put on them to think of Africa in this way. As one writer expressed it, 'The myth of African barbarism was continually held over their heads . . . (and) this definition was imposed by a white population which was determined not to let blacks fully assimilate into American society.'[28]

Nevertheless, many of the black American missionaries took pride in being members of the black race and saw it as part of their duty to that race to 'civilise' and christianise it. This, they believed, was their destiny and why God had allowed them to be enslaved.

They also saw their missionary work in Africa as a way of obtaining respect from white Americans. By building a 'civilised', Christian society in Africa some of these missionaries believed they would prove to whites their capacity for leadership and thereby gain the respect that was their due. And this also explains to some extent the determined efforts made by some of them to turn Africa into an American-type society and why the indigenous people of Liberia and Sierra Leone responded to them in the same way as they did to other missionaries. In Liberia, Crummell made every effort to preserve the country's American character and even for a time wanted it turned into an American protectorate. Blyden, likewise, wanted Britain to extend her influence in and control over West Africa for a limited period of time.[29]

He thought, wrongly as it happened, that Britain would simply agree to come in and take control for a short time to assist Africans in the process of 'modernising', industrialising and 'civilising' their country and then depart.

Blyden was fully committed to the eventual establishment of black, independent African states and strongly opposed any notion of permanent or even long-term foreign control over Africa. Others, like Bishop Harold Turner of the AME shared Blyden's views on the European presence in Africa. There were also those who gave their support to colonial regimes and opposed attempts by the indigenous people to put a halt to colonial intrusion.[30]

The indigenous people of Liberia tended on the whole to judge and respond to a missionary on the basis of the latter's attitudes, opinions and actions rather than on the basis of race or colour. The same was true in

Sierra Leone and Nigeria. Thus if a missionary, whether white or black, attempted to impose exclusively western notions of culture and a totally western form of Christianity he or she was regarded as a 'foreign' missionary. Those missionaries, both black and white, who believed Africa to be the 'Dark Continent', condemned its culture and made little effort to identify with it, naturally met the same indifferent response from the local people. However, with the passage of time, some of the black missionaries from North America changed their outlook and came to play an important role in the establishment of the African independent Churches (see Chapter 6, pp. 156 ff.).

The arrival of Catholic missionaries in Liberia

Until the 1840s all the missionary societies working in Liberia were Protestant and from the United States. Then, in the early years of the 1840s, as a result of the interest of Bishop England the American Bishop of Charlestone in North Carolina, Catholic missionaries travelled to Liberia. Bishop England was not concerned so much, if at all, with converting the indigenous African peoples to Christianity but rather with the spiritual care of a small number of his former congregation who had been resettled in Liberia. For this reason he called for volunteers from among his clergy to go to Liberia and the Irish-born American Fr Barron responded, and led a party consisting of himself and two others to Liberia in 1842.[31]

The territory consigned to Barron's care by the Catholic Church was vast. It was known as the Vicariate of the Two Guineas and stretched from north of the River Senegal, to the Orange River in South Africa. The northern sector to Gabon was referred to as Upper Guinea, and Gabon to the Orange River was known as Lower Guinea. While in Europe in June 1842 in search of more priests, Barron met Francois Libermann, founder of the French Catholic missionary congregation of the Immaculate Heart of Mary. This congregation was to join with the much older French Congregation of the Holy Ghost in 1848 and, as we have seen, take the name of the Congregation of the Holy Ghost and the Immaculate Heart of Mary, usually referred to simply as the Holy Ghost Fathers.

In 1843 Libermann agreed to send ten of his missionaries to assist Barron in his vast territory of the Two Guineas. Five of the missionaries were to be based at Gorée, Senegal, and to work in the Senegambia while the remaining five were to be stationed at Cape Palmas in Liberia. Due to a misunderstanding all ten missionaries arrived at Cape Palmas in October 1843. By January 1844 several of the missionaries had died or were in very poor health and Barron decided to withdraw from Liberia to the Ivory Coast and Gabon. This was the end of Catholic missionary activity in Liberia until 1884.

In that year missionaries of the Congregation of the Holy Ghost based in Freetown, Sierra Leone, responded to a request from the Liberian Minister of the Interior to assist with government schemes designed to improve the standard of education in Liberia. So far very little had been achieved by way of 'civilising' the indigenous people by means of the schools. Of course, as the previous chapter discussed, many settlers did not want to extend either education or Christianity to the local people.

Two Catholic missionaries arrived in Monrovia in February 1884 and by October of the same year had opened a 'model school' which catered for between thirty to forty Americo-Liberian children. In addition they began teaching Christianity to the indigenous people of Monrovia in that part of the city known as Krutown. One of the missionaries learned the Kru language and translated hymns and the principal teachings and practices of the Catholic Church into Kru. But although the Catholics were welcomed by the Kru, a number of Protestant missionaries objected to their presence. The latter reacted by publicly attacking Protestant teaching and practice. This interdenominational conflict, a variety of other pressures and threats, and the failure to make Catholic converts either of the Americo-Liberians or the indigenous peoples led to the withdrawal of the Catholic missionaries from Liberia in 1888. The next Catholic mission to Liberia was not to open there until 1902.

The situation in 1890

At one time or another all the Protestant missionary societies involved in Liberia became convinced of the need to train more indigenous clergy without whom the work of evangelisation could not succeed. The indigenous clergy were to begin as auxiliaries and eventually to take over full control of the Churches. However, by about 1890 almost all of these missionary societies had begun to have strong reservations about this policy. Foreign controlled missionary bodies were not only critical of the indigenous clergy but also of the settler clergy. The principal reason given for this reversal of policy was that the African clergy were very poorly trained for the task in hand. Even Blyden demanded qualifications from Liberian clergymen that were unusually high. They had to be, in his opinion, intellectually the equal of – if not the superior – to the most enlightened of their congregation; they had to be scholars 'who would not be content to take at second hand the view of the meaning of (scriptural) passages; . . . but should repair to the fountainhead.'[33] Few missionaries white or black, apart from a handful like Blyden himself, were trained to such a high degree in scriptural exegesis or anything else.

By the 1880s there was a growing antipathy towards educated Africans in the political, administrative and clerical spheres and this may account, as much as anything else, for the abandonment in Liberia, Sierra Leone and elsewhere, of the policy of developing self-governing, self-supporting African Churches. Because of the competition clerical positions that conferred status and prestige were becoming increasingly difficult to obtain in parts of Europe such as Britain. As one LMS missionary in England stated, such posts were as 'rare as a snowstorm in July'.[34] This sent a number of clergy 'scrambling' for posts abroad. For while there was a comparative lack of scope for clergymen at home, there was still room for expansion overseas. Missionary work carried high prestige in some European countries and provided an outlet for the evangelical zeal and millenarian beliefs of young, often well-educated and privileged members of British society. This was highlighted by the development of the Niger mission and the opposition to the Nigerian bishop, Samuel Ajayi Crowther (see below, pp. 65 ff.).

These developments do not fully explain why the policy of establishing self-governing, self-supporting Churches was abandoned. As far as the Churches were concerned, the policy was defeated by difficulties concerning the financial viability of self-governing African Churches and the methods used in missionary work. The building of schools and churches and the training and maintenance of clergy were very costly and beyond the means of the local Churches. For financial reasons if for no other, therefore, the local Churches were obliged to retain their links with the parent body as long as Church life continued to be organised and administered along North American or European lines.

The method of evangelisation employed by the missionary societies also militated against the implementation and success of the plan for the establishment of self-governing and self-supporting African Churches. The approach to conversion was never likely to result in more than a handful of converts and, therefore, of potential clerics. The educational and cultural restrictions on conversions have already been mentioned (see pp. 51–2). It might well be asked how the Lutheran mission, as one example, established at Mutilerberg in Liberia in 1860 and adopting the approach that it did, should hope to make any noticeable impact on the wider society. The mission gathered together children between the ages of six and twelve, and these children, now cut off from the local environment, were taught through the medium of English, Christianity and the three Rs until they were twenty-one years of age. Then, if they had shown 'good will', they were given a plot of land to cultivate for their own needs. This boarding school idea with its restrictions on numbers was clearly an *exclusive* rather than *inclusive* institution, and did nothing for anyone except its pupils.

Of course, in analysing the way missionaries went about the task of evangelisation it is worth bearing in mind that they used those methods which they believed would lay a firm foundation for the future. Moreover, it was not easy simply to go wherever one wanted to preach the Gospel. The interior of Liberia was difficult to penetrate due to a lack of roads and at times was disturbed by conflicts between the indigenous inhabitants.

Ghana, The Republic of Benin (Dahomey) and Togo

Much of the mission history of Ghana (formerly the Gold Coast), Benin (Dahomey) and Togo in the period 1840 to 1890 centred around the activities of the Wesleyan Methodist, Basel and Bremen missions and to a lesser extent the Roman Catholic mission of the SMA.

Ghana

Thomas Birch Freeman, of West Indian descent, is the best known of the

Wesleyan missionaries of this period and his strategy as superintendent of the mission in the 1840s and 1850s consisted of establishing central mission stations along the coast of Accra, Cape Coast, Anamabu and in the large cities in the interior such as Kumasi. From these centres missionaries, relying on auxiliaries, the majority of whom at the time were Fante, would branch out and establish out-stations in the surrounding villages.

The Wesleyans also placed a great deal of emphasis on 'civilising' the people by means of the school. Prior to the 1840s the education provided by the missionaries was rather narrow in scope consisting of learning the Scriptures and reading and writing. From the 1840s attempts were made to broaden the curriculum to include such subjects as agriculture, commerce and joinery. In this way people would be taught the habit of sustained application to work and this in turn would lead to a more 'civilised' and economically prosperous society.

However, the attempts made by the Wesleyan Methodist missionaries to introduce agriculture and commerce into the school curriculum were not successful.[36] Lack of funds and the vast amount of time devoted to teaching Christianity proved to be the principal reasons for this lack of success. The Basel missionaries were better in this area than their Wesleyan Methodist counterparts. But the latter never abandoned the attempt to provide agricultural, technical and industrial training for boys and such subjects as needlework for girls. As time wore on the Wesleyan Methodists began to introduce teaching in the vernacular. They published translations of the Gospels and Fante grammars, but here again they do not seem to have enjoyed as much success as the Basel missionaries.

The Wesleyan Methodists did not convert large numbers of indigenous people of the Gold Coast in this period. By about 1885 the mission there had an estimated 5,300 active members and 77 schools with 2,356 students.[37] The mission at Kumasi established in 1843 was closed down for virtually the whole period under discussion. In 1876, when the Wesleyans decided to reopen the mission just after the Asante war had ended, the Asantehene (king of the Asante) pointed out that he would only allow the mission to operate if the missionaries would help to keep the peace and ensure that trade flourished. He also told the missionaries that they should not attempt to educate the children since the latter had more important work to do 'than to sit down all day long idly to learn "hoy, hoy, hoy" (a corruption of Holy, Holy, Holy and here meaning the Holy Scriptures).[38]

The Wesleyans decided to delay their return to Kumasi until 1884 when they made an impact on a number of outlying areas such as Bekwai. It was not, however, until after Asantehene Prempeh I had been exiled in 1896 that Wesleyan missionary and educational activities in Asante began to have a significant impact on the society.

Of course, given Freeman's connections with the British administration one could not expect the rulers of Asante to greet the Wesleyan missionaries with open arms. Freeman seems to have favoured an extension of British control in West Africa, and in 1853 and 1872 he accompanied, and appears to have approved of, British expeditions against the Asante.

The Basel missionaries made a second attempt to establish themselves in Ghana in 1843, and from that moment set about training an African clergy who would become their partners in spreading Christianity and eventually take over complete control of evangelisation from the European missionaries. They also laid great stress on preaching Christianity in the local languages.

One of their outstanding African linguists in this period was Johann Gottlieb Christaller who worked in Ghana from 1853 to 1868. Among his many translations into Twi were the four Gospels (1959), the New Testament (1864), the Psalms and Proverbs (1866) and the whole Bible (1871). He wrote a Twi dictionary which has received very high praise indeed from scholars.[39] In addition to their emphasis on the use of the vernacular languages the Basel missionaries also stressed the importance of agricultural and industrial training. Trading schools were opened in Akropong, Eburi and many other towns and villages. They also developed a 'home school' system where girls were taught the domestic sciences by the wives of the missionaries. By 1890 the Basel mission had 441 girls in its schools, a higher number than the Wesleyan, Catholic and government schools combined.[40]

The Basel mission gave most of its attention to the people of the interior but the end result was not always what they had intended. While they gave a significant boost to agricultural and industrial training they were to find that many of those whom they had trained for agriculture were to abandon this work for clerical jobs. The financial rewards and the status attached to such agricultural work were low, and these two factors in large measure explain why young people then, as they do today, leave the land and the rural areas for more prestigious jobs in the towns.

Although their contribution to the development of education in Ghana was significant the Basel mission, like other missionary bodies, tended to develop Christian communities that were cut off from the rest of society. They prohibited their students – and they had over 1,500 of them by 1890 – from taking part in local political and economic affairs and even from participating in traditional music, dancing and other social and cultural activities. Moreover, Christians living with non-Christians were encouraged not to eat with the latter.[41] The same prohibitions were imposed on Christians by other missionary societies elsewhere in Africa, for example in Nigeria, as Ajayi has noted.[42] While the aim was to create a Christian élite whom others would admire, listen to and emulate, the result was often social cleavage. However, there were some missionary societies like the Bremen mission which adopted a less isolationist policy.

The Bremen mission from north Germany, like the Basel and Wesleyan missions, also considered educational work to be an integral part of evangelisation. It also believed very strongly in the creation of an indigenous Church, and in 1864 established a college for the training of indigenous pastors. Great importance was attached to preaching

Christianity in the vernacular and by 1877 the New Testament as well as hymn books and catechisms had been translated into Ewe. One of the driving forces behind this translation work was Dr Zahn whose ideas on missionary methods were widely followed, especially in Togoland.

The Bremen mission appears to have adopted on the whole a much more positive approach to African society and culture than some other missionary societies. It did not concern itself so much with condemning and eradicating African customs, traditions and rituals, nor did it seek to withdraw Christians from their local surroundings. The mission did emphasise the importance of establishing Christian homes, but this did not entail a complete rejection of polygamy. Some Bremen missionaries in fact admitted polygamists to baptism and holy communion, maintaining that Christ did not make polygamy a barrier to entry into the Christian Church.[43]

On the question of a self-governing Church, to return to this important question, the Bremen missionaries were frequently reminded by their home base to train local converts from among the elders for leadership positions as quickly as possible. From these elders a consistory was to be set up which would take care of the day-to-day running of the Church. But very little progress was made in this direction by the outbreak of the First World War when German missionaries were obliged to leave West Africa.

The arrival of Catholic missionaries in Ghana

Catholic missionaries established themselves in Ghana for a second time (see Chapter 1, pp. 17 ff.) during this period. The main work of these missionaries of the SMA was in the field of education. By 1890 they had several hundred pupils in their schools after only a few years of missionary activity. One reason why they had such an impact in such a short space of time was that they confined themselves to a relatively small area, about one-quarter of the size of the Wesleyan sphere of influence, and employed twice as many missionaries in this smaller area as the Wesleyans did in their much more extended territory. Later on, the Catholic mission was to benefit much more from government financial aid than the Wesleyans. In fact, from 1881 many Wesleyan and Basel schools began to close down. In the 1890s when there was a remarkable increase in educational activity, the Catholic and Basel mission schools fared well, but Wesleyan schools never regained the position they had once occupied prior to 1881.[44]

The Republic of Benin and Togo

The Wesleyan Methodist Missionary Society in Benin (Dahomey) and Togo formed part of the Society's Ghana mission until 1878. Benin proved to be a difficult terrain for the Wesleyans. Freeman approached King Ghezo of Dahomey about the possibility of establishing a mission in 1843, but King Ghezo was suspicious of the latter's links with the British. Ghezo did, nevertheless, consign some children to the care of Freeman.

It was not until 1857 that the Wesleyans began their attempt to evangelise Whydah, the capital of the Dahomeyan Kingdom, in the person of the African pastor James Dawson. Then Thomas Marshall, son of a traditional religionist from Badagry, began work in Porto Novo, only to be expelled in 1867 apparently because people persuaded the ruler that it was impossible to keep a minister of religion who served the gods of the white man.[45] Marshall was allowed to return in 1876, but in the meantime the Wesleyan mission had been almost completely closed down, due in the main to persecution by Mikpon, ruler of Porto Novo, who suspected the Christians of spying for the British Governor of Lagos.

The Catholic mission in Benin was revived in the 1830s and 1840s by freed slaves, many of them from Brazil. A woman back from Brazil, Venossa de Jesus, had a church built at Agoué in 1835. The church, dedicated to Senhor Bon Jesus da Redempçao in memory of a church in Bahia, north-east Brazil, was destroyed by fire and later reconstructed by a group of freed slaves from Brazil led by Joaquim d'Almeida.[46]

Not all of the freed slaves who became Catholics in Brazil showed such devotion to their faith on returning home. Some of those who were converted to Christianity from Islam when they arrived in Brazil, reverted to Islam when they returned to Benin. As one put it, 'I was a slave when I arrived (in Brazil) and I was baptised; I was in the power of my master then.'[47] Those who reverted to Islam retained their Brazilian names – Paraiso, Marcos, Lopez, Da Silva, etc – and also retained the strong ties of friendship forged in exile with those ex-slaves who remained Catholics on returning home.[48]

In 1860 the SMA priests assumed overall responsibility for Catholic missionary activity in Benin, and when the first priests of this missionary order, an Italian, Fr Boghero and a Spaniard, Fr Fernandez, arrived in Whydah in 1861 they found a number of willing assistants among the former slaves. The ruler (Yevogan) of Abomey adopted a positive attitude towards the Catholic missionaries. The missionaries lived at first in the Portuguese fort at Whydah and from there opened mission stations in 1862 and 1863 at Porto Novo, Adjara, Adjassi and Atsioupa. By 1864 the Catholic missionaries had baptised 31 adults and 288 children, but this rapid progress was soon to be halted.

In 1865 the priests were expelled from the Portuguese fort at Whydah after traditionalists had accused them of being responsible for the death of a child. The Catholic missionaries then made Porto Novo their headquarters and Whydah was served by priests from São Tomé. Additional Catholic missions were opened by the SMA missionaries at Agoué and Grand Popo, both in Benin (Dahomey) and Anecho, and Port Seguro, Atakpamé and Keta, all in present-day Togo, between the mid 1870s and 1890. The mission in Atakpamé was abandoned in 1887, mainly because of the hostility of the traditional religionists. The Bremen, Basel and Methodist missions also had mission stations in Togo and these were mainly among the Mina in the Anecho region.

The situation in 1890

While the Roman Catholic Church, the last of the missionary bodies to arrive on the scene, gave little serious attention to the establishment of a self-governing African Church, the other missionary societies operating in Ghana, Benin and Togo laid great emphasis on this. The Basel and Bremen missions in particular worked consistently towards this end. The Wesleyan Methodist Mission, a strong supporter of devolution at the outset had begun, by the 1880s, to slow down the process. This was in part due to the arrival of a 'new' breed of European missionary in the 1880s.

In the 1860s and 1870s Wesleyan Methodist missionaries, in order to carry through their policy of devolution, sent a number of Ghanaians to England for training. However, when these Ghanaians returned home they found that a shift had taken place in the Methodist outlook and policy. Newer and younger missionaries committed to retaining control had replaced the older ones who had sent them abroad for training for leadership. The Ghanaians, regarded by the new breed of European missionary as 'indolent' and 'untruthful' were sent to distant corners to superintend circuits. Far from the corridors of power and influence some of them, like the Revd S. Attoh Ahima joined with other Ghanaians – teachers, lawyers and doctors, among them John Mensah Sarbah and Casely Hayford – in the struggle to preserve African identity, values and culture from being eroded by a legalistic, culture-bound type of Christianity. A similar situation emerged in Nigeria.

Nigeria

By about 1850 some 3,000 recaptives and ex-slaves, the majority of whom were of Yoruba descent, had returned home to Nigeria from Sierra Leone, the West Indies and South America. It was from among these returnees that the missionary societies chose their 'agents' or 'auxiliaries' who were to assist and eventually take full responsibility for the spread and development of Christianity and 'civilisation' in Nigeria. As Buxton expressed it, these returnees could be used 'to create cells of civilisation from which the light would radiate to the regions around.'[49] The leading CMS strategist Venn was more than ever persuaded, given the vastness of Nigeria, that the only way his society could make any significant impact there was by establishing a Church that was led, administered and maintained by Africans, that is a 'self-governing, self-supporting, self-propagating' Church. It was also Venn's ambition to encourage the growth of an African middle class that would undermine the subsistence economy on which he believed slavery was based and thereby destroy slavery.[50] However, before the end of the period under review, both Venn's missionary policy and his policy of development were to be rejected by some of his missionary colleagues and discredited by some of the African middle class (see below, pp. 66 ff.).

The missionary advance into western Nigeria

As Ajayi points out, the arrival at Badagry, south-western Nigeria in September 1842 of Thomas Birch Freeman, the Wesleyan Methodist minister from Cape Coast (see p. 42) marked the effective beginning of the 'modern' missionary enterprise in Nigeria.[51] With his Ghanaian 'assistant missionaries', William de Graft and his wife, Freeman conducted services for the returnees from Sierra Leone who had settled there. The majority of the latter, however, soon moved on to Abeokuta, and leaving the de Grafts behind in Badagry Freeman followed them there in December 1842. Abeokuta, founded in 1829 by the Egba chief, Sodoke, had a population of around 40,000 at the time.

The CMS missionary Townsend had also begun to explore the possibilities for missionary work in Badagry and Abeokuta. But it was not until January 1845 that the first CMS mission station was opened in Nigeria at Badagry, and among the Society's first missionaries was Samuel Ajayi Crowther, the Nigerian recaptive, who from 1822 had been trained and educated by the CMS in Sierra Leone and then Britain. Crowther was later to become Bishop of the Niger Delta before being humiliated and 'forced' to resign (see below, p. 67).

In 1846 Crowther and Townsend established a CMS mission at Abeokuta, the great hope of CMS missionaries, indeed the symbol of Christian missionary hope in Africa, 'the sunrise within the tropics' as it was once called. By fostering 'civilisation' and Christianity in Abeokuta missionaries and philanthropists believed they would light a torch which would shine throughout Africa. Mission houses, schools and churches were built, but converts were slow in coming. It was not in fact until February 1848 that the first converts to Christianity, three in number, were baptised. All three were women and one of them was Crowther's own mother.

The success of a mission depended as we have seen on many factors, including the reaction of the local ruler and the traditional priests. While Chief Sodoke had welcomed the missionaries and had facilitated the establishment of the mission, difficulties emerged after his death in 1845. Traditional priests reacted strongly against the growing influence of Christianity and to make matters worse the missionaries and the British consul of what were then known as the Bights of Benin and Biafra, became involved in the hostilities between the Dahomey and Abeokuta in 1851. Moreover, around the same time the missionaries played a part in involving the British government in a dispute in Lagos between Chiefs Akintoye and Kosoko.[52]

Nevertheless, by 1854, four CMS mission stations had been opened in and around Abeokuta. Then in 1856 an Industrial Institution was established at which brick-making, carpentry, dyeing and other trades were to be taught. In 1859 a school for catechists was started and a church magazine published in Yoruba. The mission also started a cotton plantation in the town.

The steady, if slow, progress made by the CMS in Abeokuta and

Ibadan, Oyo and Ife where missions were opened in 1852, 1857 and 1858 respectively, was halted by British political and military involvement, particularly in Lagos which was proclaimed a colony in 1861. There were also internal wars, for example the war between Ibadan and Ijaye in 1862 which brought about the destruction of both the CMS and Baptist missions at Ijaye. Missionary association and involvement with British political and military exploits led to the temporary expulsion of Europeans from Abeokuta in 1868.[53] From this moment Lagos became the headquarters of CMS missionary activity in Nigeria. Crowther had effectively been detached from the Yoruba mission and based at Lagos from the 1850s when he was placed in charge of the Niger mission.

Another prominent African Church spokesman and later bishop, James Johnson (see p. 100) was to be assigned to Lagos to become pastor of St Paul's Breadfruit Church in 1874. He held this post until 1876 and again from 1880 to 1900. Though he regarded orthodox European Christianity as the true and universal religion, Johnson encouraged the growth of self-governing, self-supporting, self-propagating African Churches on the lines laid down by the CMS. Moreover, he was one of the pioneers of the cultural nationalist movement that began to gain momentum in West Africa in the 1870s.[54]

Johnson was appointed superintendent of the Yoruba missions in 1876, and moved from Lagos to Abeokuta to lead a Christian community of some 2,500 people which had lacked any effective leadership since 1868. On CMS instructions Johnson attempted to eradicate domestic slavery and worked towards the establishment of a self-supporting, self-propagating Church in the interior of Yorubaland. His self-support programme met with resistance from Egba and Ibadan Christians, and supported by European missionaries they openly opposed Johnson's aggressive, tough approach and methods.

In 1880 Johnson was removed from his post as superintendent of the Yoruba mission in the interior and reassigned to St Paul's Breadfruit Church in Lagos. Educated Africans in Lagos saw Johnson's removal as a clear indication that the CMS was in the process of abandoning its commitment to the policy of creating a self-governing, self-supporting and self-propagating Church in West Africa. They also regarded it as a clear sign that European missionaries refused to accept that Africans were capable of leadership. As we shall see, bishop Samuel Ajayi Crowther was to experience similar disappointment and humiliation some ten years later when he was in effect forced to resign as superintendent of the Niger missions.

The Southern American Baptist mission which arrived in western Nigeria in 1850 appears to have done even less than the CMS to encourage the growth of a self-governing Church in the region. Controversy and dissension within this Church over questions of the training of clergy and racial discrimination led to secession from the mission Church and the establishment of the Native Baptist Church in the late 1880s (see Chapter 6, pp. 159 ff.).

The Niger mission under bishop Samuel Ajayi Crowther (1857–1890)

The vast Niger mission, effectively under bishop Samuel Ajayi Crowther's control from 1857, covered all the peoples of the Niger River from its delta northwards up to and including the northern states of present-day Nigeria. Starting in 1841, Crowther had made several journeys up the Niger. On the 1857 journey he was accompanied by, among others, the Ibo-speaking clergyman, James Taylor, and twenty-five evangelists and school teachers, all of whom had returned from Sierra Leone. On this occasion Crowther opened a mission at Onitsha and another at Igbebe at the confluence of the Niger and Benue Rivers, opposite Lokoja.

Crowther's zeal and good sense were rewarded when he was consecrated a bishop of the Anglican Church in 1864, an event which Venn regarded as a clear sign that the day of a 'self-governing, self-supporting, self-propagating' Church in Africa was near. However, even though he was now a Bishop, Crowther did not have jurisdiction over mission centres such as Lagos, where there were European missionaries who would not and did not accept African leadership.[55]

Crowther opened many other mission stations in addition to those mentioned above. He established a flourishing mission at Bonny in 1865, another at Brass in 1868 and the Kalabari mission in 1874. In the opinion of one scholar Crowther and his colleagues had turned the Niger Delta by the closing decade of the nineteenth century 'into the scene of a most flourishing Christian civilisation'.[56]

Like other bishops, Crowther was short of clergy despite his numerous attempts to recruit more missionaries. In the words of Taylor, a colleague of his who was born in Sierra Leone of Ibo parents, his clergy, though African, were 'for the most part colony born from Sierra Leone . . . (and) perfect strangers to the country at large.' And Taylor added 'It is true that Africa is Africa . . . (but) no one should hold it out as a criterion that the climate is ours. We have to undergo the system of acclimatising on the Niger.'[57]

Many of the African missionaries attached to the Niger mission did not speak the language of the people among whom they worked, nor did they know or always respect the customs of these same people. They preached and upheld the doctrinal and moral teachings and practices of the Anglican tradition of Christianity, and condemned the 'idolatry' and 'evil' ways of the traditional religionists, and when they encountered Muslims which was not very often – their ways too. Even the tolerant, mild-mannered Crowther could liken the growth of Islam to the 'growth of pernicious weeds'.[58] Christian pronouncements on Islam were consistently negative and hostile in the 1840s and 1850s, becoming less so as time went on.[59] The whole question of the Christian view of and approach to Islam is taken up in Chapter 8.

Although African, the missionaries on the Niger did not always find that rulers and people alike were willing to accept them and their message. Crowther and his assistants were to meet with opposition from rulers, traditional priests and others who saw them as a threat to their political, economic, cultural and religious way of life. Jaja of Opobo, head of the Annie Pepple House from 1863, was convinced that belief in the traditional religion made for political stability and was good for trade, while Christianity presented numerous political and economic problems. It involved, for instance, a new, untried way of establishing trading agreements and ensuring that these agreements were adhered to, and a new way of settling disputes. These were matters which, in Jaja's opinion, were sufficiently well catered for in the traditional system of oath-taking and in the divinity cults respectively. An important element, therefore, in Jaja's opposition to Christianity was the belief that he was defending tried and tested traditions against attack from something that was new and untried – namely, Christianity.

Crowther and his colleagues nevertheless continued with their efforts and reached the Upper Niger. They attempted to convert Muslim rulers such as Masabu of Bida and to obtain permission to open mission stations in Muslim-ruled areas. On a visit to Masabu in September 1870 Crowther gave him a gift on behalf of the CMS mission, and attempted to persuade him of the benefits of Christian-Muslim co-operation pointing out that Britain, a Christian country, was co-operating with Turkey and Egypt, both Muslim countries, over the Suez Canal.[59] Again on a subsequent visit to Bida in 1873 Crowther tried the same approach, informing Umaru, Masabu's successor, that the Shah of Iran had visited Britain to request the British to build railways in Iran 'to facilitate communications and commerce'. Then Crowther put the question to Umaru: do not Muslim rulers in Africa also desire a foreign power, albeit Christian, to improve their country?[60] Umaru, like Masabu, was open-minded and interested, and agreed to continue to protect the Christian missions.

Though a Christian presence had been established on the Upper Niger there were few converts in contrast to the situation further south. By the mid 1880s there were just under 4,000 Christians in the Delta, some 800 of whom were communicants, and therefore full members of the Church.[61] This constituted a fairly large, settled Christian community, albeit with a number of problems which were to be exacerbated by the growing criticism of the leadership of Crowther by certain members of the CMS.

The undermining of Crowther's authority and leadership, and the establishment of the 'Native Pastorate'

There was a marked revival in missionary enthusiasm in parts of Europe in the 1870s–1890s. In Britain, for example, the CMS sent out as many missionaries between 1882 and 1900 as they had sent out in the previous eighty-two years.[63] There was also a noticeable change in the social background of the 'new' missionaries of the 1870–1900 period. By this time the CMS was recruiting far more university graduates and fewer artisans and manual workers than was previously the case. Until 1880 the total number of graduates sent to the missions by the CMS had been 156, while from 1880 to 1900 the number rose to 284, or 43 per cent of the total.[64] Many of these missionaries were full of 'trail-blazing zeal', inspired by evangelical motives and millenarian ideas. They regarded the missionary role as one that carried high social status, considerable prestige and great responsibility. It was from missionaries such as these that Crowther's mission, leadership and authority came under increasing criticism from the late 1870s.

Ajayi describes some of these missionaries as 'able, young, zealous, impetuous, uncharitable and opinionated'.[65] The oldest of this group discussed by Ajayi was the Revd J.A. Robinson who was appointed secretary of the Niger mission at the age of twenty-nine. This type of missionary, in a hurry to convert the whole world to Christianity, and with his own rather narrow view of missionary work, began to probe and question Crowther's capacity for leadership and the moral integrity and suitability of some of his assistants. The latter were accused of immorality, illegitimate trading, slave dealing and other irregularities. There was also one alleged case of manslaughter.[66] The CMS investigation into the situation in the Niger mission began in earnest in 1881.

Crowther's reaction was not to deny that there was evidence to support some of these charges, but he did emphasise that most of it was based on hearsay. After reporting this to a CMS committee Crowther was then asked to investigate further and this he did with the assistance of Archdeacon Dandeson Crowther (his own son) and Henry Johnson. Crowther, after examining the cases, acquitted all the accused except one, who was transferred to another mission.

Although some scholars maintain that Crowther was perhaps a little too lenient in his judgement, almost all would agree that he himself was unjustly treated by some members of the CMS who eventually forced his resignation. The attack on Crowther's leadership was seen by some Christians at the time and by historians subsequently as having been motivated by racialism as much as anything else.[67] The criticism and 'trial' of Crowther came at a time when the policy pursued by Venn, Buxton and others of the CMS of establishing self-governing, self-supporting, self-propagating African Churches was losing its appeal among certain elements in the CMS who approached questions of leadership and discipline in a one-track minded, almost military-like fashion. Moreover, it came at a time, as we have seen, when positions of responsibility and leadership in the Church in Britain were becoming increasingly difficult to obtain and when ordinary, routine pastoral work did not carry the same prestige and status as missionary work abroad.

Crowther, who gradually acquired in CMS circles – in the words of Ajayi – 'the reputation of an over-indulgent father shielding the wrong of his children',[68] strongly opposed wholesale condemnation of his assistants by Europeans. Although he himself was never accused of wrongdoing, he came to regard himself as being on trial with those accused and as a defender of the African's capacity for leadership against those who maintained that 'the Negro race shows almost no sign of "ruling" powers'.[69]

By 1890 Crowther, no longer able to tolerate the abuse criticism and interference to which he was being subjected, decided to resign from the CMS Niger Finance Committee and in effect from his post as superintendent of the Niger mission. With the death of Crowther in December 1891 'the transmutation', as Ajayi has written, 'of Europeans from guides to rulers was complete in the Church.'[70]

Some of Crowther's assistants still clung to their interpretation of Venn's policy, and made the Niger Delta Churches which were named the 'Native Pastorate' into a separate entity from the CMS Niger Delta Mission. Many other African Independent Churches were to begin to emerge in Nigeria now, and these are considered in Chapter 6.

Missionary activity in south-eastern Nigeria (Calabar)

The main mission Church in Calabar in this period (1840–1890) was the Presbyterian Church, introduced to Calabar by the Jamaican-born missionary Hope Waddel in 1846.

The Presbyterians spread out from Calabar to Creek Town, Duke Town and Old Town among other places, using the school and instruction in the compound as the principal means of evangelisation. But it was not until 1853 that the first convert was baptised, and the missionaries had very little success with their attempts to convert the local rulers. Like many other missionaries both then and since Hope Waddel and his missionary colleagues attributed their slow progress to the people's strong attachment to polygamy.

Although they accepted the principle of self-governing, self-supporting and self-propagating Churches in Africa the Presbyterians at Calabar advanced towards this goal with great caution. After the departure of Hope Waddel in 1857 it was only with reluctance that Africans were placed in charge of their local Churches. One Presbyterian minister writing in 1880 spoke about the 'inability' of an African 'to initiate a scheme', and added, 'I think we should not settle down to the belief that our native agents will relieve us of the pioneering.'[71]

There was no full agreement between the European missionaries themselves in Calabar as to how they should carry out the work of christianising and 'civilising' the indigenous people. Part of the problem arose from the fact that the older missionaries preferred to concentrate all their energy and efforts on a very limited number of areas and build secure, solid foundations in this way, while the newcomers like Mary Slessor wanted to expand outwards as quickly as possible, believing that the whole region could be turned into a Christian stronghold overnight.

The newcomers also wanted an aggressive onslaught on local religious traditions, practices and local culture which they regarded as 'barbarous'. The authorities endorsed the approach of the newcomers, thereby helping to split the Presbyterian Church in Calabar. Local politics also fuelled the flames of dissension in the Calabar mission, the 'old' missionaries supporting the Archibong House in a dispute with the Eyamba House which received the backing of the 'new' missionaries.

One of the latter, Ross, with Eyamba support, withdrew from the main mission in Calabar taking with him a number of teachers and quite a large part of the congregation, thus creating a split at the institutional as well as the ideological level in the Presbyterian Church in Calabar.

During this time the Qua Ibo mission from Belfast, Northern Ireland and the Primitive Methodist mission from England arrived in the south-eastern region of Nigeria in 1887 and 1893 respectively.

The arrival of the Catholic missionaries

The Roman Catholic mission began to take steps towards re-establishing itself on a permanent basis in Nigeria in the 1860s. A Catholic missionary based in Porto Novo in present-day Benin visited Lagos in 1863 and found there a Catholic community consisting of a catechist, Pa Antonio, and several thousand Portuguese-speaking returnees (saros), former slaves who had returned home to Nigeria from South America. Pa Antonio was born in São Tomé and spent his youth and early manhood as a slave in Bahia in north-eastern Brazil. After emancipation he travelled to Lagos via Whydah, São Tomé, Fernando Po and Porto Novo, and there took on the role of spiritual adviser to the repatriates from Brazil.[72]

Pa Antonio's community was served by a Catholic priest from Porto Novo until 1868, when it was decided to establish a permanent base in Lagos. A mission house was opened in Broad Street and a decision was taken to spread the Catholic faith by means of the school system. By 1890 the Catholic mission in Lagos had eight schools attended by over 600 students. The size and influence of the Catholic community there was increased by the emancipation of the slaves in Brazil in 1888. They also played a very important role in the development of music, song, dance and cultural life in general in Lagos.[73]

By 1890 Catholic missionaries were also working in eastern Nigeria. And while the French SMA Fathers in Lagos favoured the school system the French Holy Ghost Fathers who arrived at Nkissi near Onitsha Wharf in September 1885 began by favouring the system of the 'Christian village'.[74] This system consisted essentially in redeeming slaves; that is, buying them from the slave dealers, and settling them in villages where they would be taught the Christian faith, employed by the mission and trained as evangelists. The entries in the mission journal of Holy Trinity Mission near Onitsha, opened by the Holy Ghost Fathers in January 1886, document the buying of slaves for this purpose. The entries in the journal are repetitive in the following manner: '12th June (1886). Buying of a slave . . . 90 francs', '6th August (1886). Buying of a three-year-old boy for 12 sacks of salt'. And a letter written in March 1887 by the superior of the mission, Fr Lutz, to his headquarters in Paris states that there were fifty people at Holy Trinity Mission, twenty of whom had been bought out of slavery.[76]

This method of evangelisation used to a greater or lesser extent by the Holy Ghost Fathers and other Catholic and Protestant, missionary societies in Africa was soon to be abandoned. The Holy Ghost Fathers in eastern Nigeria had come to realise that it was expensive, slow and unproductive in terms of gaining converts and replaced it with the school system of evangelisation.

The situation in 1890

The Christian Church in Nigeria, despite the policies pursued by Venn and like-minded individuals, was still governed from outside, from England and North America, and operated through missionary intermediaries both European and African, the latter occupying the position of middlemen and/or assistants.

Christianity had made some progress in the south-west, east and south-east of the country, where at times conditions were far from ideal. For instance, much of Yorubaland was affected by intermittent warfare for over a decade, beginning in the late 1870s. This was also a time of increasing European rivalry and political and economic interference in the region.

Within many of the Churches there were disagreements over the method and approach to evangelism between the 'old' and the 'new' missionary. Members from both these camps strongly criticised the failure of certain missions to expand more rapidly. Further, they had little or no confidence in the ability of Africans to manage and lead a Christian Church. The real problem, however, was not one of leadership but concerned the relevance of Christianity, as preached and practised, to the totality of the African experience of life. This was a problem very similar, as we have seen, to the one in Ghana.

The Senegambia

Senegal

When the French missionary congregation of the Holy Ghost Fathers arrived in Senegal in the 1840s, there were a small number of Christians in St Louis, Gorée, Rufisque, Joal and Portudal (see Chapter 1, pp. 14 ff.). Although only nominally Christian by the late eighteenth century, many of them, descendents of sixteenth-century *lancados* (Portuguese settlers) who had gradually identified with their Serer neighbours in language and culture, clung tenaciously to aspects of Christianity such as the rite of baptism. In the minds of many, there was still the belief – and this particularly the case among the Christians at Joal – that high social status and the profession of Christianity went together.

While the Christians of Joal, strongly influenced by traditional religion, would have nothing to do with Islam others, in St Louis for example, combined in their ritual and worship elements of the Christian, Muslim and traditional religions. Regarding the Islamic influence on Christians in St Louis in the second half of the eighteenth century a contemporary wrote that 'Many of the Christian habitants . . . bear all the outward marks of Muhammadanism. There are those who having been to mass then make salaam and pray with equal fervour to Jesus Christ and Muhammad'.[77]

With the arrival of the Sisters of St Joseph of Cluny in the 1820s, followed by the French Holy Ghost Fathers, in the 1840s, the modern Christian missionary movement in Senegal began to take shape. The French Protestant missionaries of the Society of the Evangelical Missions of Paris did not arrive in Senegal until 1863 (see below, pp. 78–9).

The Catholic missionaries believed that if Catholicism was going to triumph it would be necessary above all else to train an indigenous clergy and to curb the growth of Islam. On both counts they had little success during the period under discussion.

At the outset the missionaries were extremely confident that they could halt the progress of Islam. In his notes on the Senegambian Catholic missions compiled in 1844–5 the head of the mission, Truffet, reported that 'since the Muslims know little more than the name of Muhammad and practise circumcision and a few other superstitions there will be no problem converting them to Catholicism'.[78]

It would appear that the missionaries underestimated the strength and depth of the commitment of the Senegambians to Islam. They overlooked the historical, socio-economic and political dimensions of religious adherence. Catholic missionaries were not alone in pointing out that Senegambian Islam was 'syncretist' but they were virtually alone in concluding that the adherence of the Senegambians to Islam was 'superficial' and could easily be broken. Coelho, who travelled in the Senegambia in the second half of the seventeenth century, wrote 'The Wolof are all Muslim and for that reason are difficult to convert'.[79]

The strategy of the Catholic missionaries was to convert the marabouts (the Muslim teachers). It was, they believed, the latter and not the local rulers who had more influence over the people. The more educated marabouts, the missionaries imagined, would be easier to convert because they would be less attached to their 'gris-gris'. Education would be the principal means of converting them, whereas the semi-literate marabouts could be converted by giving them gifts. Further, the children of the marabouts could be taken away and educated in the mission school. Missionaries learned Arabic and studied the Qur'an 'in order to be able to persuade by instruction the Muslims that Christianity was superior to Islam.' A Fr Arragon found the marabouts very friendly and interested 'even though I say very strong things against Mahomet'. Several marabouts were converted to Christianity and Arragon wrote to another missionary, 'You will only need to remain here for about two more years and there will be no more Islam, . . . only Catholicism'.[80]

At the personal level relations between Muslims and Christians were friendly in the nineteenth century. The missionaries, moreover, were encouraged by the fact that the Muslims were tolerant. A number of Muslims on the Municipal Council of St Louis assisted at High Mass on the Feast of St Louis. In Joal in the 1840s marabouts visited the mission and debated with the Catholic missionary Abbé Gallais. On one occasion the Bour of Sine and the leading marabout came to Joal with 1,000 warriors and questioned Abbé Gallais about the Christian faith. A dialogue ensued between the marabout and the missionary concerning the Old Testament, and ended by the marabout and Bour asking permission to attend the missionary's 'salam' (prayer). Gallais was informed by the marabout that Issa (Jesus) was the second most important prophet after Muhammad, and the Bour said that he was prepared to accept both Jesus and Muhammad and incorporate them into his Serer belief system. Gallais himself became known as the Bour's white marabout.

The interest shown by marabouts and influential Muslims in Roman Catholicism convinced the missionaries that the move from Islam to Catholicism was inevitable. The Catholic missionaries were to discover, however, that on one key doctrinal issue Muslims were immovable: the doctrine of the incarnation. It is the same to this day. When Father Arragon visited the King of Dakar in 1844 to seek permission to build a school he was refused this permission on the grounds that the school might destroy the people's religion – Islam. The king asked the missionary to change his religion and Father Arragon replied that he would if he found the king's religion (Islam) better. The king, on the other hand, Father Arragon stated, would have to become a Christian if he found that religion better. The proposition was accepted by the king and the missionary then entered into a debate with him. The king stretched for his Qur'an bound in cow's skin and showed it to the missionary. He then displayed a drawing of Muhammad's tomb and sketches of Mecca and Medina. The missionary in turn showed the king a number of pictures, one of which was the adoration of Jesus by the three kings. At this juncture Father Arragon stated that one of the kings who came to adore Jesus Son of God was black. Arragon continued, 'At the words "Son of God", the king left, dismissing the pictures as superstition.'[81]

Other marabouts such as Al-Hajj Umar were even less disposed to dialogue with Christians. Al-Hajj Umar associated Christianity with European imperialism and was only prepared to tolerate Christians if they paid the *jizya* or tribute payable by non-Muslims under Muslim rule. He warned the children of N'Dar (Senegal) that they had a duty to make war on those 'who neither believe in God nor in the Last Judgement', and on those 'who although they have received a revelation do not follow the true religion until they are forced to pay the *jizya* and are humbled – the Christians'.[82] The Senegalese were not to live with the Christians and 'he who shall join them is an infidel like them; you shall not live promiscuously with Jews or Christians; he who shall do so is himself a Jew or Christian.'[83] This exclusivist, hard-line attitude was continued by a number of influential and important marabouts. Al-Hajj Amadou Dem (b. 1892) from Kaolack in Senegal preached that the Qur'an spoke of the Christians as 'lost'.[84]

Others took a different line, for example, Cheikh Kamara (1864–1943). He wrote a treatise, *The Possibilities of an Understanding Between Christianity and Islam*.[85] The circumstances which led Cheikh Moussa Kamara to seek a rapprochement between Islam and Christianity are interesting. He met three young French girls, one of whom, aged about 20, was praying. Cheikh Moussa asked her what prayer she was saying and the reply he received was, 'In the name of the Father, the Son and the Holy Spirit, God all-powerful, Creator of heaven and earth, I believe in You.' The Cheikh translated this prayer into Tokolor, then Arabic, discovering in the process that Christians were monotheists, as he had read in the works of the Lebanese Maronite poet Boutrous. This motivated him to compose his book on Christian-Muslim dialogue in which he singled out the areas of agreement between Islam, Christianity and Judaism. Once again the doctrine preventing complete unity was that of the incarnation. Nevertheless, Cheikh Moussa Kamara stressed that Muslims and Christians ought to emphasise what they held in common.

By the 1870s, after a quarter of a century of effort, the Catholic missionary view of and approach to Islam had begun to change. The optimism of the 1840s and 1850s was to give way to resignation and even despair by the 1870s. Many missionaries were indeed at a loss as to what to do, believing that in order to christianise Africa they had first to destroy Islam. Yet they had become aware of the strength of Islam, of the hold it exercised over the people of the Senegambia. It was no longer considered to be a religion that people loosely adhered to for want of something better but 'a religion of fanaticism . . . responsible for the evils of Africa'.[86]

A missionary, Fr Speisser, wrote a report of his tour of the Catholic missions in the Senegambia in 1877. In the addendum to this report Speisser gives some general reflections on thirty years of missionary work in the Senegambia and attempts to answer why the progress made by the missions had been so slow and difficult. The main reason, he believed, was that 'all our missions are situated in Muslim country, that is, in territory where Muslims form either the majority of the population or an important minority'. He then comments: 'To work to convert Muslims is almost a waste of time'.[87]

By the 1870s the Catholic missionaries in Senegal had virtually abandoned all direct attempts to convert Muslims and instead were increasingly turning their attention to the non-Muslim peoples, such as the Diola of the Casamance region and the Serer. Once converted these would, it was hoped, not only constitute a barrier against the spread of Islam but could also be used as evangelists in the surrounding Muslim areas.

The mission stations of Sedhiou and Carabane were established in the 1870s precisely for these reasons. Sedhiou, then a small village on the right bank of the River Casamance was, when the Catholic mission was opened in February 1876, an important French *comptoir* (warehouse) and military base. It had a permanent population of about 600 people: Sosé, Mandinka, Balentes and Diola. Moreover, during the trading season it attracted many others from St Louis, Dakar, Gorée, Cacheo, Bissau, Ziquinchor and Banjul. Sedhiou was considered to be a very good choice for a mission station; its population was largely non-Muslim. It was also in an area where trading in slaves was common practice and this enabled the missionaries to 'redeem' slaves, settle them in 'Christian villages', and in this way lay the foundations of a Christian community, a policy already mentioned (see pp. 69 ff.).

However, by 1890 the mission at Sedhiou had been abandoned as a central mission and was served from Carabane and Ziquinchor. Few converts had been made, while the surrounding villages remained Muslim, as they were at the outset. The decline of Sedhiou set in around 1886 when the French, after taking over the Portuguese enclave of Ziquinchor, moved their business there from Sedhiou. The small-business people, workers and others followed, leaving Sedhiou with a few Muslims and a larger, but still relatively small, number of non-Muslims.

Carabane, a small peninsula about two kilometres from the mouth of the Casamance River, was raised to the status of a central mission in the 1880s and was also regarded as being very favourably placed. As one missionary wrote:

> That small locality (Carabane) owes all its importance to its favourable position . . . . It commands the River (Casamance) and is a centre of communication with Sedhiou and other places on the River, and also with Gorée and Dakar, and even with St Mary of the Gambia and the Portuguese colony of Cacheo. This is without any doubt the reason why the French Government constructed and retains a military base there.[88]

There were on average about 600 people settled in the village on a permanent basis, but this number rose to 1,000 during the slave trading season. The majority of the inhabitants were Diola, and in addition to their own language also spoke Wolof. There were also a number of Roman Catholics among the inhabitants from Rufisque, Dakar, Gorée and St Louis. The missionaries were very optimistic about Carabane, an optimism based not only on the fact that Carabane was so well situated but also on the fact that the attitudes and dispositions of the Diola appeared to them to be extremely favourable. 'We can legitimately hope', a missionary commented, 'for the success of a mission at Carabane.'[89] There were at least a dozen villages that could be reached from Carabane within a few hours, and Carabane itself also offered a good opportunity for 'redeeming' slaves and establishing 'a small, solid, active Christian community'.[90] Thus from Carabane the missionaries could carry the good news to all the surrounding areas and preserve them from, among other things, contact with Islam.

The early history of the Carabane mission resembled very much that of Sedhiou outlined above. The mission was closed for a time in the late 1880s and re-opened in 1890. By 1905, after twenty-five years of missionary activity, there were an estimated 1,050 Christians in what by then had become the Carabane-Elinkine mission.[91] And when the Roman Catholic bishop Jalabert visited Carabane in 1910 although 'the clocks sounded, and the guns were fired in salute', there were only a few Christian families remaining in what had become a predominantly Muslim village, and most of its business and commerce had moved to Ziquinchor. By 1916 in the Carabane-Elinkine mission stations there were only 800 Christians.[92]

The Catholic missionaries also expected great advances to be made from the establishment on a permanent basis of a mission at Ziquinchor to the south of Carabane in 1888. Previously manned by Portuguese missionaries, Ziquinchor became an 'outstation' in 1877 and was looked after on an *ad hoc* basis by the Holy Ghost Fathers, until it became a permanent base in 1888. In 1877 a Senegalese priest, Fr Sene, visited Ziquinchor and it was reported then that the people of the town were 'full of faith and entertained an implacable hatred for Islam'. It was stated that by order of the Portuguese Governor of Cacheo Muslims were forbidden to remain for more than a short period in the locality. The report adds that in four days Fr Sene baptised fifty children 'and instructed a great many adults who demanded the same grace (baptism)'.[93]

The people in and around Ziquinchor were non-Muslims and the majority were Diolas. In the first years of the twentieth century the mission was staffed by four priests, an unusually large number. But the progress made was slow and difficult. By 1905 there were about 1,300 Catholics in and around Ziquinchor, and by 1910 the Catholic missionaries had begun to despair of the mission. A report on the mission looked at the problems of evangelisation and pointed to the fact that in this area Christianity had become associated in some people's minds with slavery because, for one reason, the missionaries before the abolition of slavery had baptised some of the chiefs' sons and his slaves.[94] Moreover the mulattoes, of Portuguese descent and Christian, were said to despise the Diolas and to look upon them as mere slaves and units of labour. The report also pointed to the fact that very little work had been done by the missionaries in Diola villages, partly because travel was very difficult. It referred also to the language problem and the inability of the missionary to communicate with the Diola in their own language, and to the influence of Muslim 'propaganda'. With reference to the Muslims who 'favoured commerce and who were seriously influencing the minds of the simple people' in the area, the report stated: 'Soon it will be too late to cast our nets; a few good souls would still come and willingly allow themselves to be caught, but the prestige of the Crescent will eclipse forever that of the Cross . . . . The mission is lost in a corner of the village.'[95] This forecast was a little too pessimistic for, as we shall see, it was from Ziquinchor that 'successful' missions such as Bignona in the region of Fogny were established.

In addition to the Casamance region the Catholic missions also attempted to prevent the further spread of Islam in the Serer states of Sine and Saloum. For most of the nineteenth century there were only two Catholic missions in this region, one at Joal and the other at Ngasobil, both within the boundary of the state of Sine. Joal, a trading community dependent on Sine, was once a Portuguese settlement, and when it was officially reopened as a mission station in 1848, there still remained traces of Catholicism (see pp. 70–1). However, from the 1850s, largely because of the military campaigns in the regions by the French Governor Faidherbe and his successors, and the impact of the *jihads* (holy wars) led by Ma Ba Diakhou Ba and others in the Senegambia, Joal ceased, to all intents and purposes, to be a centre of missionary activity for almost fifty years.

The mission at Ngasobil, north of Joal, was opened in 1850 and then closed by the Bour (King) of Sine in 1851, who maintained that he could not guarantee the safety of the mission against attack from the *tyedo* (the warrior party). Opened again in 1863 the mission set to work on the development of a cotton plantation to provide 'legitimate', useful employment and commerce and the founding of an orphanage for those left homeless by military campaigns and *jihads*. By 1868 the cotton plantation scheme ran into difficulties and had to be abandoned.

In the 1870s further attempts were made to evangelise Sine and Saloum. In 1879 a mission station was opened at Fadiouth. This is a mainly Serer island village near Joal, and by 1905 there were an estimated 1,084 Catholics in this mission which was at the time an 'out station' of Ngasobil. But while a considerable number of Serer from Sine were turning to Christianity by the end of the nineteenth and the beginning of the twentieth century, many more from both Sine and Saloum had converted to Islam.

Another people that the Catholic missions placed their hopes in were the Bambara. In 1884 plans were drawn up for the establishment of a mission among the non-Muslim Bambara who inhabited the region in and around Beledugu. There is no point, the superior of the Catholic mission commented, 'in beginning a mission among the Muslims of the region (Haut-Sénégal) since they belong to the Tokolor (the most fanatical of the Muslims)'.[96] From the point of view of the Catholic missionaries the establishment of a mission among the non-Muslim Bambara had numerous advantages. Not only were they non-Muslim, but they were also considered to be more 'civilised' and industrious than other peoples of the region. The Bambara language was also 'extremely easy to learn' and in 1887 the Catholic mission produced a Bambara grammar.[97]

The missionaries, however, were not completely free to establish mission stations wherever they liked. The French government at the time was in the process of extending its control over this and other areas of Senegal. Although it did not oppose the establishment of a mission among the Bambara of Beledugu it pointed out that Samory's resistance to French penetration meant that the project would have to be delayed. The missionaries then decided to prepare for the evangelisation of the Bambara of Beledugu by training those Bambara living in St Louis for the work of evangelising their own people in the not-too-distant future. In 1866 the Catholic mission at St Louis established within the mission compound a Bambara 'Christian village'. Then in 1888 after agreeing to certain conditions laid down by the French administration the first 'Bambara' mission in the interior was established close to Kita in present-day Mali.

However, by 1891 the mission at Kita was, in the words of one missionary, 'threatened with ruin', because, 'all the infidels [traditional religionists] of the locality who used to come to us for instruction and who gave us hope for the future have left us to become Muslims'.[98] They had in fact become part of the resistance movement that opposed the French military occupation of the Soudan (Mali). In 1899 there were only 150 Christians in the mission at Kita, and according to the mission report for that year the Bambara and Khassonke in whom the missionaries had placed so much hope were now either Muslims or inclining towards Islam.

By the 1890s the Catholic missionaries in Senegal and the Soudan (Mali) were in a very pessimistic mood. The confidence of the 1840–70 period had been shattered. Islam had proved to be an irremovable obstacle and had extended its influence considerably. As the head of the Senegambian Catholic mission wrote in 1892, 'Cayor which was mainly "pagan" some fifty years ago is now almost completely Muslim'.[99] The missionaries were not even confident of their future prospects in the non-Muslim areas and accused the government of placing obstacles in their path by appointing Muslim chiefs in these areas. Missionaries in fact felt beleaguered on all sides and were convinced that the growing anti-clericalism voiced in the semi-official newspaper *Reveil du Sénégal* in the 1880s was a threat to the very existence of Catholic missionary activity in the Senegambia. And this was all the more serious given that very few Senegalese had been trained for the priesthood.

In 1892 there were thirty-four European and only five Senegalese priests working in the Senegambia. In addition to the priests there were eighty missionary sisters of St Joseph of Cluny and fifty-five lay brothers. The Catholic mission had committed itself at the outset to the formation of an indigenous clergy who would take control of the Senegambian mission. But after almost fifty years only 100 Senegalese had commenced training for the priesthood and of these only seven completed the training. Of the seven, one died while very young, another a few years after his ordination while yet another became seriously ill almost immediately after completing his training.

The training provided for future Senegalese priests was 'assimilationist', in that the students were obliged to 'follow exactly the same course as in a French seminary'.[100] The principal aim of this training was to 'form the minds, hearts and character of the students with a view to making them assistants of the European missionaries'.[101] In addition it was designed to inspire the students with:

a taste for and love of work, and to transmit to them a knowledge of agriculture . . . which would lead to the provision of some of those resources necessary for the maintenance of the mission community and thereby reduce the amount of money needed from the Propagation of the Faith (one of the institutions that financed the Catholic missions).[102]

The curriculum at the seminary training centre for future clergy included Scripture, Church History, Latin, French and Wolof. Apart from the teaching of Wolof the curriculum, life style, tone and ideals of the seminary in Senegal differed little if at all from those prevailing in a seminary in France. However, it had failed by the 1890s to produce the number of Senegalese priests required to enable the Catholic mission to make any real impact on the non-Muslims, not to speak of the Muslim areas of Senegal. This failure convinced the Catholic missionaries of the necessity of devoting more time to the training of catechists (see Chapter 4) and to the use of the school as a means of evangelisation.

Evangelisation through the schools was a complex issue in Senegal and in other West African territories under French domination. The Sisters of St Joseph of Cluny had opened a school for girls at St Louis in 1819 and another at Gorée in 1822. Then the Brothers of Ploërmel, a religious order of Catholic laymen from France, established schools for boys at St Louis (1841), Gorée (1843), Dakar (1864), Rufisque (1888) and Ziquinchor (1901).[103] The French colonial administration was to take direct control of all public schools run by missionaries in Senegal and elsewhere in French West Africa. This same administration, while it promoted the extension of French civilisation through the school system, was at times strongly opposed to any attempt to use the schools as a means of Christian evangelisation. Thus societies like the Brothers of Ploërmel were in a sense obliged to be more actively involved in carrying through the French policy of assimilation than in spreading Christianity.[104]

The Holy Ghost Fathers did, of course, have 'private schools', in contrast to the public schools run by the Brothers of Ploërmel, and these 'private schools' (such as the seminary at Ngasobil mentioned above), orphanages and mission schools all had as their goal the advancement of Christianity. The Holy Ghost missionaries, however, were not always willing to use their schools for the purpose of extending French culture, believing that this might impede the development of Christianity. They were afraid that if their pupils were taught French and mathematics they might be tempted to leave the mission in search of more attractive and financially rewarding work elsewhere. Nevertheless the French administration turned a blind eye to the existence of those 'private' mission schools, and even at times encouraged their development, especially where it proved difficult to establish 'public-schools' and staff them with lay teachers.

In the first fifty years then of renewed Catholic missionary activity in Senegal, little had been accomplished by way of halting the progress of Islam or the creation of an indigenous clergy. When the Catholic mission began to give much more serious thought and consideration to the training of catechists only then did it begin to take root in Senegal (see Chapter 4).

The arrival of the Protestant missions in Senegal

Protestant missionaries from the Paris Evangelical Mission Society arrived in Senegal in 1863 and established a mission at Sedhiou in the Casamance region in 1864. This mission had to be abandoned in 1867 owing to a shortage of missionary personnel. Then in 1870 another mission was opened at St Louis in the north of the country, and here again the beginnings were difficult. The Franco-Prussian War (1870–1) made it difficult for the missionaries to obtain supplies, funds and personnel.

In fact, whatever success the mission enjoyed in the 1870s and 1880s was attributable in large measure to Mr Taylor, born in Sierra Leone of Nigerian parents from Abeokuta, and at one time a trader in The Gambia. Pastor Taylor, who provided the mission with its first converts from among the Wolof, was to find himself in charge of the mission at St Louis from 1878.

Taylor, like the Catholic missionaries, concentrated on the Bambara at St Louis, and by 1880 he had established a 'Christian village' composed in the main of Bambara freed slaves. And while the headquarters in Paris stressed the need to train pastors with a view to establishing an indigenous Church Taylor, who had only two assistants, was almost totally pre-occupied with the 'Christian village'. It can be seen with hindsight that this was probably a mistake since by concentrating on Bambara freed slaves who were strangers to St Louis the mission failed to root itself in the local soil of that city.

The Gambia

Catholics and Quakers entered The Gambia in 1821. While the Catholics soon left to return again in the 1840s the Quakers, under a Mrs Hannah Kilham, established an industrial mission at Bakau some seven miles outside Banjul (formerly Bathurst). The Wesleyans, however, were the most active Christian mission society in The Gambia in the first half of the nineteenth century, opening missions at Combo, Barra, Georgetown, McCarthy Island, Wuli and Banjul.

In the 1840s Sisters of the Society of St Joseph of Cluny and the Holy Ghost Fathers recommenced Catholic missionary work in Banjul, a city inhabited at the time by people from many parts of West Africa including among others Akus (people of Yoruba descent from Sierra Leone) and Manjaks from Guinea Bissau. The Akus were almost all Protestants, while many of the Manjaks were nominally Christian. In addition to these two groups there were numerous Wolof, Serer, Diola and Mandinka speaking people. Wolof and Krio were the two most widely spoken languages.

By 1850 Banjul had become, according to one Catholic report, 'the most beautiful and flourishing mission on the coast of Africa'.[105] In the same year the Catholic mission began work on the Cathedral of St Mary's which was not completed until 1881. In addition to building churches the Catholic mission opened schools, convinced as it was that 'the future of the mission depended on the education of the young'. The latter, 'living in continual contact with "pagans", Muslims and Protestants', would have their faith strengthened through the school which 'provides them with sound instruction in Catholicism'.[106] While Catholics had little time or respect for 'pagans', Muslims and Protestants, the latter likewise were hostile towards and critical of not only 'pagans' and Muslims but also of Catholics.

Catholic missionaries, while concentrating most of their energies on the young, regretted the fact that the Aku population of Banjul was mainly Protestant, and staunchly so, and this deprived the mission of 'valuable, effective, African agents, of the strong part of the population, of those who dominated and gave the tone to the place, of those whom others imitated'.[107] Many of the Akus were rich business people, and people of influence, but try as they might to win them over to Catholicism, the Catholic missionaries had little success.

Outside Banjul the Catholic missions made little headway. One of the reasons for this was the fact that they had few missionaries and another was that most of the people, apart from the Diola, were Muslims. None the less, the mission did establish an agricultural and/or farming school at Combo, and an orphanage for freed slaves. By the 1890s the Catholic mission in The Gambia had an estimated 1,500 members.[108] And while the Protestant missions, with a larger membership by this time, were still determined to convert the Muslms of Banjul, the Catholic mission, realising that Islam had long since gained the upper hand there, was to redouble its efforts in the interior of the country among the non-Muslim peoples.

The situation in the Senegambia in 1890

By about 1890 Christian missionaries in the Senegambia, apart from a few exceptions in The Gambia, had given up all hope of converting Muslims to Christianity, and had begun to concentrate on the non-Muslim areas. The intention was not only to convert these areas to Christianity but also to stem the tide of Islam. They were not very successful (see Chapters 4 and 5).

Christian missionaries felt beleaguered on all sides. Islam was advancing rapidly with, they believed, the 'connivance' and support of the French administration which, they were persuaded, was attempting to undermine Christian missionary activity. In support of this view they pointed to the criticism and abuse of the clergy in the *Reveil du Sénégal*, and to the reduction in government subsidies to the missions.

Furthermore, in respect of European personnel, finances and the training of local clergy the Catholic missions in the Senegambia were encountering severe difficulties. Between 1889 and 1892 five missionaries under the age of forty-five died, leaving only thirty-four European and five African clergy. In addition there were over eighty missionary nuns and over fifty missionary brothers, but very few catechists. The involvement of increasing numbers of catechists was to make a very great difference to the progress of Christianity in the Senegambia in the twentieth century.

Cape Verde, Guinea Bissau, São Tomé e Principe

These former Portuguese colonies were largely ignored by the Catholic Church for most of the eighteenth and the last half of the nineteenth century. Missionaries whose assignments had ended or who had died were often not replaced by the authorities in Europe, and of those that remained the vast majority were concentrated in the more heavily populated areas.

In the 1850s the Portuguese Bishop Moniz opened a school at Ribeira Grande (Cidade Velha) on the island of Santiago. Students came from other islands in the archipelago and from Guinea Bissau on the West African mainland to attend this school. A few of the promising Cape Verdean students, among them the future portrait painter Joao Rodriques de Brito, would be sent from this school to study at Church-sponsored institutions such as Casa Pia at Lisbon in Portugal. Then in 1876 a seminary for the education of laymen as well as for the training of priests was established in Vila De Ribeira Brava (São Nicolau), and for over fifty years this institution was the centre of Cape Verdean literary and educational life.

Even by the second half of the nineteenth century some 400 years after the arrival of Catholicism many Cape Verdeans on the lesser populated islands such as São Vicente and in the remote villages rarely saw a missionary. The Catholic Church was still, in many senses of the term, a 'mission church', being controlled, administered, directed and led from outside. Furthermore, most of the Christians, and especially those in the rural areas, continued to believe in, practise and value aspects of the traditional religion. Adaptations and parallel forms of the Catholic liturgy also emerged in Cape Verde, Guinea Bissau, São Tomé e Principe, as in Senegal and elsewhere. 'Lay priests', for example, were designated by the local community to say or sing Mass on certain feast days. Then there were funeral and other ceremonies which in the opinion of one scholar had little in common with official Catholic practice.[109] A number of politico-religious prophets came to the fore in Cape Verde, as elsewhere, in the second half the nineteenth century. One of the best known was Domasio Lopes (1850–1930) who took the name Nhô-Nacho. In addition to prophets there were also innumerable mystics, mysticism being a central concern of Cape Verdean Christians, as were rituals and customs connected with the belief in the continued presence and intervention in everyday affairs of the souls of departed relations.

The Catholic mission in Cape Verde was also responsible for missionary activity in Guinea Bissau throughout the period under discussion and until 1940. However there was very little mission activity in Guinea Bissau in the nineteenth century, and as late as 1929 there was only one Catholic priest in the country.

Nor was there much Christian missionary activity in São Tomé e Principe during the second half of the nineteenth century. In fact, by 1900 the overwhelming majority of the small population of these islands still continued to adhere to the traditional religion. But the period 1900 to 1960 saw a considerable increase in the percentage of Catholics in the country as a whole.

Conclusions

Apart from one or two exceptions the Christian Churches established in

West Africa in the period from 1840 to 1890 remained 'foreign' institutions. They were not only under foreign control but were also dependent on clergy and financial support from abroad for their survival. Little attempt was made to adapt the liturgy, ritual, symbolism and teachings of these Churches to the African setting. The Christian missionary of the nineteenth century was not on the whole prepared for alternative ways of thinking about and practising the faith if these appeared to conflict with the form and content of the Christian tradition of which he or she was the bearer.

With the arrival of the 'new', more aggressive, often arrogant, breed of missionary in the last quarter of the nineteenth century any hope that existed of establishing 'self-governing, self-supporting, self-propagating' African Churches was for the most part extinguished. Like other Europeans at this time the 'new' missionary – with some notable exceptions – was on the whole more determined to 'rule' over Africans than to participate in the creation of autonomous African Churches. The Catholic Church for its part, although it subscribed to the theory of an African Church in the sense of a Church manned by an indigenous clergy, had no intention of establishing an autonomous Church in Africa, but looked ahead rather to the creation of African provinces of the Church.

Furthermore, the attempt to win over Muslims to Christianity had completely failed. The next step was to attempt to limit Islam's expansion by winning over the so-called 'pagan' areas to Christianity and thereby erecting a barrier against further Muslim penetration.

Notes

1   J.F.A. Ajayi, Nineteenth Century Origins of Nigerian Nationalism. *JHSN* **2** (1), 1961: 2.
2   P.B. Clarke, The Methods and Ideology of the Holy Ghost Fathers in Eastern Nigeria 1885–1905. In Kalu (ed.) op. cit., pp. 43 ff.
3   P.B. Clarke, *The Christian Encounter with Islam in Africa c. 1840–c. 1982*. Forthcoming.
4   C. Fyfe, *A History of Sierra Leone*. Oxford: Oxford University Press, 1962: 212.
5   C. Fyfe, *A Short History of Sierra Leone*. London: Longman, 1979: 76.
6   C. Fyfe, *Sierra Leone Inheritance*. Oxford: Oxford University Press, 1964: 211.
7   The British divided Sierra Leone into two areas in 1896 – the colony and the protectorate. This division lasted until independence was regained. See Fyfe, *A Short History of Sierra Leone*, pp. 112 ff.
8   C. Fyfe, *Sierra Leone Inheritance*, pp. 260–1.
9   C. Fyfe, *A History of Sierra Leone*, p. 326.
10 M. Banton, *West African City*. Oxford: Oxford University Press, 1957: 24.
11 P.B. Clarke, *West Africa and Islam*. London: Edward Arnold, 1982: 179 ff.
12 ibid., p. 180.
13 ibid.
14 D.E. Skinner, 'The Role of the Mandinka and Susu in the Islamization of Sierra Leone'. Conference on Manding Studies, School of Oriental and African Studies, University of London, 1972, p. 11.
15 J. Faure, *Histoire des Missions et Eglises Protestantes en Afrique Occidentale des Origines à 1884*. Yaoundé, 1978: 234.

16 J.C. Wold, God's Impatience in Liberia. Michigan: Michigan University Press, 1968: 99.
17 ibid., p. 103.
18 L.E. Ejofodomi, *The Missionary Career of Alexander Crummell in Liberia 1853–1873*. Ph.D. Boston University 1974 (University Microfilm, Ann Arbor, Michigan 1974).
19 W.L. Williams, *Black Americans and the Evangelization of Africa 1877–1900*. Wisconsin, 1982: 11.
20 ibid., pp. 12–13 and *passim*. See also H.R. Lynch, *Edward Wilmot Blyden. Pan-Negro Patriot 1832–1912*. Oxford: Oxford University Press, 1967: Chapters 3 and 6, and *passim*.
21 H.R. Lynch, *Edward Wilmot Blyden. Pan-Negro Patriot, 1832–1912*, p. 142.
22 W.L. Williams, Black Americans and the Evangelization of Africa, 1887–1900. Wisconsin: University of Wisconsin Press, 1982: 4.
23 ibid., p. 7.
24 ibid., p. 6.
25 ibid.
26 ibid., pp. 6 ff.
27 ibid., p. 11.
28 ibid., p. 97.
29 H.R. Lynch, op. cit., p. 173.
30 W.L. Williams, op. cit., p. 135.
31 E.M. Hogan, *Catholic Missions and Liberia*. op.cit., 12.
32 ibid., p. 28.
33 H.R. Lynch, p. 46.
34 S. Potter, The Making of Missionaries in the Nineteenth Century. In M. Hill (ed.) *A Sociological Yearbook of Religion in Britain* 8, London: SCM Press, 1975: 120.
35 M.A.G. Brown, Education and National Development in Liberia. Ph.D. Thesis, Cornell, 1967: 141.
36 C.K. Graham, *A History of Education in Ghana*. London: Frank Cass, 1971: p. 68.
37 J. Faure, *Histoire des Missions et Eglises Protestantes en Afrique Occidentale des Origines à 1884*. Yaoundé, 1978: 248.
38 Quotation from C.K. Graham, op. cit., p. 101.
39 ibid., p. 125.
40 ibid., p. 131.
41 S.K. Odamtten, *The Missionary Factor in Ghana's Development, 1820–1880*. Accra, 1978: 156.
42 J.F.A. Ajayi, *Christian Missions in Nigeria 1841–1891*. London: Longman, 1965.
43 E. Grau, *Missionary Policies As Seen in the Work of Missions with the Evangelical Presbyterian Church, Ghana, in Christianity in Tropical Africa*. Edited with an Introduction by C.G. Baeta, Oxford: Oxford University Press, 1968: p. 68.
44 C.K. Graham, op. cit., p. 118.
45 R. Cornevin, *La République Populaire du Benin* (2nd ed.). Paris: Editions G-P Maisoneuve et Larose, 1981: 297.
46 ibid., p. 298.
47 P. Marty, *Etudes sur l'Islam au Dahomey*. Paris: Ernest Leroux 1926: 18.
48 ibid., p. 34.
49 Quotation from O.U. Kalu, (ed.) *The History of Christianity in West Africa*, Vol. 1, p. 2.
50 J.F. Ajayi, *Henry Venn and the Policy of Development* in O.U. Kalu, op. cit., pp.

63–75.
51   J.F.A. Ajayi, *Christian Missions in Nigeria 1841–1891*, p. 31.
52   ibid., pp. 66 ff.
53   ibid., pp. 201 ff.
54   E.A. Ayandele, *Holy Johnson*. London: Frank Cass, 1970.
55   G.O.M. Tasie, *Christian Missionary Enterprise in the Niger Delta*, Leiden, 1978: 49–50.
56   ibid.
57   G.O.M. Tasie, John Christopher Taylor, Missionary Strategist and Pioneer Ibo 'Nationalist': A Bibliographical Note (copy in author's possession) p. 8.
58   P.R. McKenzie, *Inter-Religious Encounters in West Africa*. Leicester: Leicester University Press, 1976: 24.
59   ibid.
60   *C.M.S. Intelligences* (Feb. 1871) Vol. VII. New Series.
61   ibid., Sept. 1873.
62   G.O.M. Tasie, *Christian Missionary Enterprise in the Niger Delta*, op. cit., pp. 141 ff.
63   S. Potter, The Making of Missionaries in the Nineteenth Century. In M. Hill (ed.) *A Sociological Yearbook of Religion in Britain* 8, 1975: 117.
64   ibid., p. 118.
65   J.F.A. Ajayi, *Christian Missions in Nigeria*, p. 250.
66   G.O.M. Tasie, *The Story of Samuel Ajayi Crowther and the C.M.S. Niger Mission Crisis of the 1880s: A Re-Assessment*, pp. 53–4 (copy in the author's possession).
67   J.F.A. Ajayi, *Christian Missions in Nigeria*, pp. 250–5. Also E.A. Ayandele, *The Missionary Impact on Modern Nigeria 1842–1914*. London: Longman, 1966: 210.
68   J.F.A. Ajayi, *Christian Missions in Nigeria*, op.cit., p. 249.
69   ibid., p. 250.
70   ibid., p. 269.
71   ibid., pp. 179–80.
72   E. Isichei, 'An Obscure Man: Pa Antonio in Lagos (c.1800–c. 1890)'. In E. Isichei (ed.) *Varieties of Christian Experience in Nigeria*. London and Basingstoke: Macmillan, 1982: 28 ff.
73   M.J.C. Echeruo, *Victorian Lagos*. London and Basingstoke: Macmillan, 1977: 73 ff.
74   P.B. Clarke, *The Methods and Ideology of the Holy Ghost Fathers in Eastern Nigeria 1885–1905* in O.U. Kalu, op. cit., pp. 36–62.
75   ibid., p. 38.
76   ibid.
77   D.H. Lamirel, *L'Afrique et le Peuple Africain*. Paris, 1789, p. 43.
78   H.G.F. Archives, Paris, Boîte 147, Sénégal-Travaux Divers.
79   N.I. de Moraes, *La Petite Côte d'Après Francisco de Lemos Coelho (XVIIIe siècle)*. BIFAN T.XXXV, sér. B, No. 2, 1973, p. 251.
80   H.G.F. Archives, Paris, Boîte No. 152, Doss. B. Lettres etc. Sénégambie.
81   ibid.
82   Quotation in J.D. Hargreaves (ed.) *France and West Africa*, London: Macmillan, 1969: 132.
83   ibid.
84   H.G.F. Archives, Paris, Boîte 157. Doss. B. Lettres-Divers.
85   Cheikh Moussa Kamara. *L'Islam et le Christianisme, traduction et notes par Amar Samb*, BIFAN T.XXXV, sér. B, No. 2, 1973.
86   H.G.F. Archives, Paris. *Report on the Senegambian mission by Revd Fr Speisser –* 6/8/1877.

87   ibid.
88   ibid.
89   ibid.
90   ibid.
91   H.G.F. Archives, Paris, Boîte 164, Sénégal, Lettres-Divers.
92   ibid.
93   Speisser report, op. cit.
94   ibid.
95   ibid.
96   H.G.F. Archives, Paris, Boîte 159, Sénégambie, Lettres-Divers.
97   ibid.
98   ibid.
99   ibid.
100 ibid., Boîte 147.
101 ibid.
102 ibid.
103 D. Bouche. La Participation des Missions au Développement de l'Enseignement dans les Colonies Françaises d'Afrique Occidentale de 1817 à 1940. *Etudes d'Histoire Africaine*, **VIII** (1976), pp. 173–97.
104 ibid., p. 177. And D. Jones, The Catholic Mission and Some Aspects of Assimilation in Senegal, 1817–1852. Journal of African History (JAH) **21** (3), 1980: 323–40.
105 H.G.F. Archives, Paris, Boîte No. 152, Doss. B. Lettres-Divers.
106 ibid.
107 F. Mahoney, Government and Opinion in The Gambia 1816–1901. Ph.D. Thesis, School of Oriental and African Studies, University of London, 1963.
108 F. Renner, Muslim-Christian Relations in The Gambia in the Nineteenth and Twentieth Centuries. M.A. dissertation. Area Studies, London: September, 1979.
109 N.E. Cabral, Les Iles de Cap Vert. Cinq Siècles de Contacts Culturels, Mutation et Mélange Ethnique. Doctoral Thesis, Sorbonne, Paris, 1979.

4

The Christian missionary movement during the colonial era 1890–1960 in former British West Africa and Liberia.

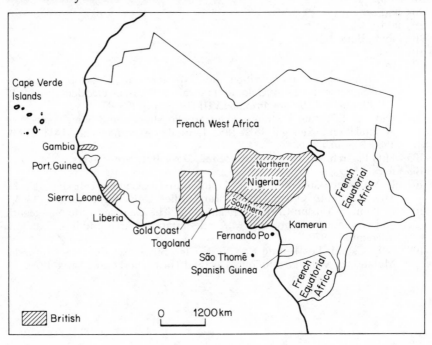

II   British influence in West Africa, 1914

This chapter considers three particular aspects of Christian missionary activity in West Africa during the colonial era. In the main it concentrates on Sierra Leone, Liberia, Ghana and Nigeria; that is, all of what is sometimes referred to as Anglophone West Africa, excluding The Gambia. The Gambia, a former British colony, is discussed alongside Senegal, the rest of former French West and Equatorial Africa, and former Portuguese West Africa in Chapter 5.

Although African resistance to European conquest and occupation was never completely quashed, the colonial powers were effectively in control of most of the main centres in West Africa – with the exception of Liberia which was never formally colonised – by the outbreak of the First World War in 1914. The new colonial administrators, like many of the 'new' missionaries mentioned in the last chapter – the Bremen missionaries being among the exceptions – were determined that they would give the orders and that Africans would obey. Moreover, as was the case in some of the mission Churches, the number of Africans promoted to senior posts in the administration was to decline between the 1890s and the outbreak of the First World War. For example, in Sierra Leone in 1892, just under half (eighteen) senior posts were filled by Africans whereas in 1912 the latter occupied only fifteen out of ninety-two senior posts.[1]

The First World War, though its impact was uneven,[2] went some way to altering this situation. The war made it necessary for a number of missionaries to leave West Africa for chaplaincy and other work in the armed forces. Those German missionaries still remaining in Nigeria, Togo and Cameroon were deported by the British and French governments. This reduction in the number of European missionaries led to a greater reliance on African partnership and leadership, but only in one or two instances did it mean a full-scale return to the policy of Venn. For this, one has to wait until the post-Second World War era when the twin processes of nationalism and decolonisation were well advanced.

Another characteristic of mission Christianity during this period (at least until the outbreak of the Second World War) was the emphasis placed on the necessity of halting the advance of Islam, principally by getting to the 'pagans' first and converting them to Christianity before Islam came on the scene. This, of course, did not happen everywhere and in some instances where it did occur, for example in Senegal, it was simply a continuation of a previous policy rather than something completely new.

In the period 1890 to 1960 far greater use was made of the school as a means of evangelisation; so much so that in the minds of many West Africans a Christian was someone who had been to or was attending a western-type school. But there were some differences here between the British and French colonies in West Africa. It was during this period that the mission Churches came to a greater realisation of the crucial role of the catechist in the work of spreading Christianity.

The above themes – European control of the Churches, the race against Islam, evangelisation through the schools and the role of the catechist – are discussed below, within the framework of a general outline of missionary expansion in the colonial era, in first anglophone and then francophone West and Equatorial Africa, and former Portuguese West Africa. Such issues as Christianity and the independence struggle, and the relationship between Church and State in the colonial era form part of Chapter 9.

Sierra Leone

From 1896, as we have seen, Sierra Leone was divided by the British into the two administrative units of the colony and the protectorate (see Chapter 3, pp. 48 ff.). In the colonial era, as was previously the case, the main strength of the mission Churches in Sierra Leone was in the colony.

By the end of the First World War there were over 100 churches in the colony with some 20,000 members, while the protectorate had only a handful. Mission schools in the protectorate were few and far between, and this was partly because the administration felt that western schools might prove to be a breeding ground for rebels. The colonial regime had already faced one serious uprising in the form of the Hut Tax Rebellion in 1898. In this rebellion several missions were destroyed and a number of missionaries and some 300 Creoles were killed. This may well have caused missionaries, some of whom had preached on the duty of paying taxes to 'Caesar' to feel that their presence in the protectorate would not be tolerated, despite the assurances to the contrary given by Bai Bureh and the Mende who were among those involved in the rebellion.

Many other factors contributed to the slow growth of Christianity in Sierra Leone, among them the individual as opposed to the collective approach to conversion. By extracting and alienating individuals and their families from the local culture and attempting to convert them in isolation from their surroundings, the missions to some extent limited the influence and impact of the Christian way of life. A further drawback was the official policy of most denominations with regard to polygamy which severely limited the number of those who could become full members of the Christian churches. The reluctance of the Creoles to spread Christianity among the indigenous peoples and the unwillingness of many of the latter to accept Christianity from 'outsiders' also explain Christianity's slow growth in Sierra Leone. And the development of Islam inevitably offset possible progress attainable by Christianity.

From the 1950s there was a large increase in the number of Muslims in Sierra Leone, though it is difficult to say with any accuracy what percentage of the population is now Muslim. According to some accounts Muslims make up 25 per cent[4] of the population, while others put the figure much higher, at around 50 per cent.[5] On the other hand, after over 150 years of missionary activity only just over 3 per cent of the population is Protestant and just under 2 per cent Roman Catholic.[6]

While Blyden attempted to present a positive and objective – if somewhat paternalistic – view of Islam as a religion and way of life,[7] many of his contemporaries and those who followed him spent a good deal of their time denouncing it and working to counteract its influence and expansion.[8] None the less, among ordinary people in such places as Freetown there was, in general, a high level of tolerance between Muslims and Christians, particularly among the Akus – the liberated slaves of Yoruba descent – of whom a substantial minority were Muslims. But just as there were Christians who were strongly anti-Muslim, there were Muslims, particularly among the Ahmadiyya, who were militantly anti-Christian. Using a vigorous missionary approach modelled to some extent on the 'school approach' of the Christian missionaries, the Ahmadiyya movement, which entered Sierra Leone from India in 1921,[9] set out both to purify Islam and limit the spread and influence of Christianity. The Ahmadiyya, regarded as unorthodox by Sunni (orthodox) Muslims in Sierra Leone, made little headway until the 1950s.

But by 1959 there were six Ahmadiyya primary schools in the country, and by the late 1960s the movement had substantially increased the number of its schools and started to open secondary schools, to the number of five by 1973.[10] Other Muslim communities in Freetown became deeply involved in western education and this likewise was to some extent in response to the pattern of evangelisation set by the Christian missions.[11]

With the passage of time, increasing numbers of people from the protectorate, especially on entering Freetown, turned to Islam in preference to Christianity. By 1950, of the approximately 65,000 inhabitants of Freetown about 72 per cent came originally from the protectorate while the remaining 28 per cent were Creoles.[12] And apart from the Kru and Bassa very few of the Mende, Temne, Kono, Kissi and Limba from the protectorate were either Christians on arrival in Freetown or became Christians later.[13] Not all of them became Muslims either, but what did give rise to a greater harmony of outlook and belief among Muslims and between Muslims and traditional religionists in both the colony and protectorate from the late 1940s was the determination not to allow the Christian Creoles to take over from the Europeans at independence and run the country. Some Mende chiefs, for example, were afraid that the situation in Sierra Leone might parallel Liberia where 'two or three hundred Creole families run the place for their own benefit'.[14]

Some Creole Christians, although they still regarded Christianity as an integral part of their identity as a group, had begun by the 1950s to forge closer links with the indigenous culture and people by, for example, adopting African names. E.N. Jones, for instance, changed his name to Laminah Sankoh. In fact, the decline in support among Creoles in the 1951 and 1957 elections for Dr Bankole Bright's National Council, which stood for the old Creole attitudes of aloofness and superiority indicates very clearly the changes then taking place in Creole perspectives and attitudes.[15] But the extent of this change in attitude on the part of the Creoles should not be exaggerated. Moreover, a wide gap at the political, cultural, economic and religious levels between the colony and protectorate still existed in the 1950s.

Somewhat earlier, in the 1920s and 1930s, some of the Christian missions, among them the Roman Catholic mission, began to have a much greater impact in the protectorate and this was due in some measure to the improvements made in the catechist system and the greater emphasis placed on the school as a means of evangelisation. According to one writer, the Catholic mission in the 1930s began to develop 'an increasingly satisfactory catechist system in several missions'.[16] One of the Mende has left an outline of the catechists and their work prior to the 1930s. They were, he says,

great itinerants . . . . These gentlemen went about from place to place touching and baptising the old, the sick and the dying. Their sphere of work was unlimited and each of them travelled through many chiefdoms only returning to the mission at the end of the month . . . . The first great harvest of the Serabu Mission then, was the hundreds of Holy Souls sent to Heaven through these baptisms.[17]

Few and far between, these catechists could do little more than give the last rites to the dying.

In the 1930s more and more outstations established schools and more catechists were enlisted from among the school teachers to provide instruction in these schools. But just as the Catholic mission was about to reap the benefits from this new approach to evangelisation, the Second World War broke out and many of the better qualified teachers and catechists left the mission for the armed forces or for other more lucrative posts in the administration. Then after the war when the government started paying teachers' salaries, salaries that were higher than those paid by the mission to its catechists, the status of the latter, when compared with that of the teacher, declined considerably. The end result was that some missions found it increasingly difficult to recruit suitably qualified catechists.

The changes in the catechist system had, nevertheless, made a remarkable difference to the Catholic mission. While in the mid 1920s almost 90 per cent of those baptised by the Catholic mission in Sierra Leone were either young children or people on their death bed, over half of those baptised in the second half of the 1930s were adults. The problem of the better salaries paid to teachers by the government was only partly overcome by the greater involvement of the Catholic mission in education both in the colony and the protectorate. This increased involvement, as far as the protectorate was concerned, was made possible by the fact that more people had come to realise that there were certain advantages to be derived from western education. Improved communications, urbanisation, the growth in the modern sector of the economy and the consequent increase in the number of opportunities there, the growing number of salaried posts for clerical workers – all this attracted people towards the school. It was this kind of socio-economic change that made western education more attractive to the Mende and others.

For their part the missionaries believed that by concentrating more on schools in the protectorate they would be able to provide a Christian education for the youth who, even if they left for the towns, would eventually return to the rural areas and act as leaders of the Christian community. This missionary hope was in general never realised. As one missionary wrote in 1944: 'The catechist question is really important. The schools are necessary and good as far as they go . . . but the Mende are an agricultural people who will not stay on the land.'[19] Like the more qualified, better trained catechists many of those who had completed their mission school education moved away from the district and were, therefore, of little direct help to mission expansion.

Nevertheless, the Catholic and other missions continued to use the school as a principal means of evangelisation. Some elders objected, arguing that western-educated children not only lost respect for their seniors and for local traditions and customs, but also their appetite for 'real' work such as farming. The more the missionaries concentrated on evangelising the young through the schools the wider became the gulf between the youth and the elders of the community. The Western schools were creating a new type of adult who was unacceptable in many respects to the elders of the community. They had not for instance, undergone the traditional initiation rites into adulthood conducted by such Secret Societies as the Poro. Western schools were introducing a new way and a new set of criteria for deciding questions of status, influence, ability, authority, and power in the community.

A critical issue for the missionaries themselves as well as for the rest of society turned on the question of the education of girls. One of the principal aims of the Christian missions was the formation of Christian families, but to do this successfully there was a need for sufficient numbers of well-educated Christian girls who would provide suitable marriage partners for the young men educated in the mission schools. Until 1945 however, there were only two Catholic schools for girls in Sierra Leone, both of them run by nuns, and throughout the period under discussion there were always far fewer girls than boys attending school. Even though the Catholic mission opened a house 'for training prospective wives' for their Christian, educated young men they were unable to establish to their satisfaction a system of ensuring viable Catholic marriages.

By the end of the Second World War the Catholic Church in Sierra Leone, still a 'foreign' church with no indigenous priests, felt somewhat beleaguered. It had little money, its missionaries were few in number and stretched to the limit, its 'new' catechist system had suffered a severe setback, and its policy of evangelising through the schools did not appear to be making much headway. The mission recognised that some of its problems were of its own making but it also had its scapegoats in Islam, the secret societies and the Protestant Churches in particular. In its view Islam was gaining ground because it was pragmatic, and prepared to accommodate itself to local aspirations and needs in a way that Catholicism, true to its beliefs and principles, was not. As for such secret societies as Poro these, it was often alleged, were immoral and retained their hold over people by fear and various unacceptable means of social control. And the Protestant missions, like the Muslims, were accused of enticing away potential converts to Catholicism. Similar allegations were made against Catholics by various Protestant and Muslim groups.

Despite its problems the Catholic mission, which had set out with great determination in the 1920s to overtake its Protestant rivals in the protectorate had come close to achieving that goal at least in the sphere of education by the 1950s. It was responsible for two teacher training colleges, and 33 secondary schools out of a total of 105 in the country, and more primary schools in the protectorate than any other Mission with the exception of the Evangelical United Brethren. Of course, more schools meant that there were less missionaries available for 'ordinary' missionary work, and therefore less contact with the non-school going population, a situation that was not helped by the fact that it was becoming incresingly difficult to recruit suitably qualified catechists. Even improvements in transport – the introduction of at first motorcycles and then cars – did not necessarily always bring the missionary closer to the people. For while they made it possible for the missionary to cover more ground they also made it more difficult for him to sink his roots in the villages among the people.

While, therefore, the Christian missions had made virtually no impact at all in the interior of Sierra Leone by 1890 the situation had altered somewhat by 1960. By this time between 2 and 3 per cent of the people of the protectorate were Christians. From the 1920s virtually all the missions gave a high priority to the school approach to evangelisation, assuming that the young would be more open, willing and ready to accept and spread Christianity. Though this approach was successful among the Creoles, over 65 per cent of whom are now Christians, it encountered numerous obstacles when it was introduced into the protectorate. The difficulties involved in maintaining the catechist system, the spread of Islam, the attraction and hold over the people of the secret societies which the missionaries condemned and the failure to establish an indigenous clergy are some of the other principal reasons for the slow growth of Christiantity in the protectorate and in Sierra Leone as a whole. After 150 years of Christian missionary activity the population of Sierra Leone was less than 5 per cent Christian.

Liberia

Here, as in Sierra Leone, most of the Christian missionary activity was concentrated in the nineteenth century along the coast among the settler population (see Chapter 3). For the Americo-Liberian settlers, as for the Christian Creoles in Sierra Leone, the Christian religion was and remained throughout the period under discussion one of the essential distinguishing marks of their identity as a group and a basic ingredient of their 'civilisation'. They did not regard Christianity as something that could simply be passed on to all and sundry alike or even to potentially sincere and devout believers from the interior who were prepared to accept its teachings and religious practices. Something more, such as a knowledge of the English language, was required. Several denominations made literacy in English a prerequisite for baptism (see Chapter 3, pp. 51 ff.). Until the 1920s, and even later in some areas, Christianity was restricted to those schooled in the English language. Some of the people of the interior did not object to these restrictions and, as was the practice in Sierra Leone, sent their children as 'wards' to Americo-Liberian families where they would be given a western education. A number of schools were established in the interior of the country. The Lutheran Church, which entered Liberia in the 1860s, concentrated its work among the peoples of the interior. This Church was in part responsible for breaking the Americo-Liberian monopoly of higher education when the Episcopal and Methodists Churches established

Cuttington College after the Second World War. This college, situated 100 miles inland from Monrovia, provided the people of the interior with access to higher education for the first time and enabled them thereby to challenge the all-powerful Americo-Liberian educated élite. The latter had made Liberia College (established in 1862) and from 1951 the University of Liberia their own preserve, and attendance at it a condition for high political office. However, Cuttington College was in time to acquire a certain status and respectability and to open up the educational system at the tertiary level to a wider public.[20]

In addition to the above-mentioned Churches the Roman Catholic Church also became involved in various educational schemes for the purpose of christianising and 'civilising' the interior of Liberia. Re-opened in 1903, closed down in 1905 and re-opened again in 1906 the Roman Catholic mission, staffed by priests of the Society of African Missions (SMA) was to act, in the understanding of the Liberian government of the day and of its own administrators in Europe, as a 'civilising influence' on the peoples of the interior by establishing schools. Some of the missionaries on the spot, however, felt that the mission's headquarters should be in Monrovia and that out-stations could then be set up within easy reach of the capital. To penetrate deeply into the interior, these missionaries maintained, given the poor conditions of the roads and of communications in general, would be to cut the mission off from supplies.

It even proved difficult for the Catholics to establish a mission in Monrovia, and in 1911 they moved 150 miles west of Monrovia to the Kru coast. From there the intention was to establish a network of high-quality Catholic schools, and create by this means an educated Catholic élite that would go on to play an important role in the government of the country. Central missions stations were established in the heart of Kru country at Old Sasstown, New Sasstown, Betu and Grand Cess. But as was the case in Sierra Leone, attempts to attract people to Catholicism through the schools often proved to be ineffective. Kru elders regarded western education as a waste of time, energy and money, and others saw no reason to go to school when Americo-Liberians monopolised opportunities in government and trading companies. For the Krus the only openings into the modern sector of the economy were work in the dockyards, on ships, or on foreign plantations.

By the end of the First World War only some 700 people had been baptised Catholics and the majority of these were young children or old people who were baptised on the point of death.[21] The war itself made things even more difficult for the missionaries than would have otherwise been the case. It contributed to a shortage of food supplies, building materials and financial aid, and to a decrease in missionary personnel when some of the French priests working in Liberia were enlisted to serve in the French army as chaplains.

It should be noted that a number of positive developments took place in the Catholic mission in Liberia during the First World War as was the case elsewhere in West Africa, and in parts of East Africa.[22] The missionaries not only performed numerous humanitarian acts such as obtaining and distributing food and generally alleviating distress – particularly during the influenza epidemic of 1919 – but also attempted to protect the Krus from the excesses of the Liberian Frontier Force (LFF) which sought to establish government control over the coastal regions from Monrovia to Cape Palmas. But even more important was the greater involvement of the Krus themselves in the activities of the Catholic Church. They organised such things as fund-raising schemes and in this way anchored the mission in the Liberian soil.

Another development that assisted the Catholic and other missions in Liberia in this period was the appearance of the prophet William Wade Harris, whose activities and impact are discussed at greater length in Chapter 6. Harris, a Liberian, who began his work of Christian evangelisation in the Ivory Coast and Ghana in 1913, visited the Kru Coast in 1916, 1917 and 1918. He preached that all the churches were 'good' and singled out the Catholic Church for special mention describing it with approval as the 'old Church'. According to one Catholic missionary writing in 1920, Harris was a 'boon' to the Catholic mission. The same missionary continued,

> Our missions are going ahead by leaps and bounds . . . . This is due not least to the former teaching of the famous prophet Harris. When the extraordinary man passed this way he ordered all idols to be burned. His success was simply marvellous. Now the 'pagans' deprived of their old gods stream to our churches and ask for religious instruction.[23]

The progress made among the Krus, however, was not maintained during the 1920s and 1930s and this was due in large measure to the decision taken in 1920 to move the headquarters of the Catholic mission to Monrovia. The mission's stations at New Sasstown and Betu fell into decline, along with other outstations at Wappi, Wessa, Topo, Dayepo, Suronki and Niffu. Almost all the resources at the disposal of the Catholic Church were poured into the Monrovia mission and this made the establishment of schools among the indigenous impossible. By 1948 in fact there were only 16 Catholic-run elementary schools in operation in Liberia, though for some time in the 1930s that number had been much higher.[24] These schools were run for the most part by teacher-catechists who in concentrating on teaching had little time for evangelisation, and this to a very large extent explains the slow growth of the Catholic Church in Liberia between 1920 and 1950.

The Kru opposition to control by the central government, resulting in the Kru wars of the 1930s, and the Second World War which adversely affected the mission's financial position – it was heavily dependent on supplies of foreign aid which either did not arrive or were delayed – also hindered the progress of the Catholic Church in Liberia in these years. One possible way out of the financial difficulties and the difficulties arising from shortage of personnel was to make the mission in Liberia more self-reliant.

The Catholic mission did not move in this direction. Instead, it grasped at what it believed was a golden opportunity to solve its financial problems. It agreed after the Second World War to participate in a North American-sponsored scheme designed to develop Liberia's medical, educational and economic institutions, involving itself in the medical and educational parts of the scheme. The scheme, however, never got off the ground, and by 1950 the mission had returned to the approach it had adopted at the outset but had then very soon abandoned; that is, the 'school approach' to evangelisation. This approach, welcomed by the Liberian government, was to prove highly successful from the 1950s.

Other Churches in Liberia, some of which were strongly opposed to Catholicism, had been opening up their own schools in the interior, partly in response to the late President Tubman's policy of 'civilising' the interior by means of the school. Some of these schools, like the Lutheran one at its Kpolo Kpele mission station, were no more than small-scale churches used during the day as a classroom. One former pupil at Kpolo Kpele has described it as it was in her time in the late 1940s:

> The school, was like most other schools around, a one-room rectangular building where church services were held. Different classes sat in different sections of the room. All our teachers were Liberians and discipline was strict . . . . Our chief motivation for being on time or doing our homework was fear of punishment. At the school the daily routine for boarders . . . was prayer in the dormitory at five in the morning, a cold bath in the creek, school, siesta, evening chores, evening bath, evening prayers and then to bed.[25]

In the case of this pupil the way Liberian church workers and pastors were treated by missionaries from overseas produced in her 'a deep distrust of missionaries and a cynicism towards Christianity generally'.[26]

The Lutheran mission ceased to exist as a separate mission having been absorbed into the Evangelical Lutheran Church in Liberia established in 1947. By the 1960s this Church was responsible for a number of primary and secondary schools, a nursing school, several literary centres, an agricultural extension programme, two hospitals, eight dispensaries and three community centres. The Protestant Episcopal Church from North America developed an even more extensive educational programme than the Lutheran Church, being responsible for over forty primary schools, ten secondary schools and, along with the Lutherans and Methodists, for Cuttington College and Divinity School. In addition, this Church has also concentrated its efforts on the evangelisation of the peoples of western and north-western Liberia.

Pentecostal missionaries also from the United States and who entered Liberia in 1908, directed their attention to the peoples of eastern Liberia where they established several Bible schools and a leper colony. The Seventh Day Adventists, who began missionary work in Liberia in 1927, also opened up schools, hospitals and literacy centres in the interior.

The response of the peoples of the interior to the educational and other services provided by the missionaries as part of the 'civilising' process has on the whole been positive. The process, however, has by no means been a complete success. Many of those from the interior on becoming

Christians decided to retain their African names and in some cases their membership of the traditional secret societies, despite missionary objections. The Liberian press and the government for their part began, after the Second World War, to lend their support to those educated Liberians from the interior who, on becoming Christian, decided in the face of missionary opposition, to retain their African names and their membership of African societies. For example in 1958 *The Liberian Age* condemned a group of Liberian Christians who, encouraged by missionaries, destroyed some Poro masks and ritual objects, and commented that such secret societies 'do not in any way conflict with the Christian belief', and 'in the true sense support the cause of Christian fellowship'.[27] The government fined and imprisoned the missionaries for their part in this activity against the Poro, a secret society into which President Tubman and several leading politicians were symbolically initiated in order to demonstrate the existence of bonds of solidarity between the Americo-Liberians and the indigenous peoples of Liberia.

These concessions to indigenous opinion and practices did little to close the gap, in the political and religious spheres, between the Americo-Liberians and the people of the interior. The former continued to dominate the upper echelons of the government, civil service and the Church, and higher status continued to be attached to membership of the 'older' churches than, for example, to the Pentecostal Churches which in some respects were more indigenous in character than the former. Of course, in Liberia and elsewhere in West Africa the African independent Churches have contributed most to the indigenisation of Christianity (see Chapter 6).

Ghana

In Ghana, as was the case in other West African states, many missionary societies either turned to or consolidated their educational activity in this period. By the end of the First World War the Basel Mission, for example, was responsible for 180 schools which catered for an estimated 10,000 pupils.[28] It is worth noting that the number of girls attending these schools was relatively high – one girl to three boys – when compared with Wesleyan and government schools where the ratio was one girl to six and seven boys respectively.

Most of the Basel Mission schools were boarding schools and had as their main objectives the establishment of Christian communities and the formation of the future leaders of the Church. At the apex of the Basel educational system was a seminary in Christiansborg where students pursued advanced courses in biblical studies, pastoral care and church history, and were also trained as teachers. Considerable emphasis was also placed on vocational education so that Christianity and 'civilisation' might be promoted through legitimate trade. The mission established a trading factory with an affiliated commercial company and numerous workshops for shoemaking, bookbinding, pottery, joinery, blacksmithing, masonry and other crafts and skills.

With the conquest of Kumasi by the British in 1896 the Basel Mission was able to establish itself in Asante territory, but its progress there, due in part to the competition from colonial government-sponsored schools was slow. By 1910 the Basel Mission school in Kumasi had only 95 students compared with 300 in the colonial government school.[29] But even colonial government progress in the sphere of western education was slow. In addition to Asante suspicion and hostility towards Europeans generated by the Anglo-Asante wars of the nineteenth century which dragged on until 1901, the social structure of Asante society by way of contrast with the situation among the Fante[27] appears to have militated against the rapid and widespread acceptance of western education whether sponsored by the colonial government or the missions. The Asante, like the Mende, realised that western education could destroy among other things the prevailing system of promotion to positions of authority and change the outlook, perspective and role of the local ruler. Traditionally, the principal criteria for recruitment to office were descent and ascription, not wealth and achievement, and the role of the local ruler was to conserve and not to change the status quo. Western education, it was feared, would lead to the abandonment of such criteria and to entry to office on the basis of achievement, thereby undermining traditional values and norms.

Consequently, at the outset and for some time to come it was mainly those of lower social status who welcomed western education. Over time, with the further development of the modern sector of the economy the criteria for advancement to traditional office began to change, but this did not necessarily favour the Christian missions. Whatever the criteria for election to traditional office the chief would still be expected to officiate at or perform traditional ceremonies and rituals, many of which were condemned as 'pagan' by the missionaries. The chief was therefore barred from full participation in the Christian Church. The rise of African independent Churches went some way towards resolving this dilemma (see Chapter 6).

During the First World War the Basel and the Bremen Missions lost many of their European personnel who, being German subjects, were obliged by the British to leave Ghana. The mission societies however had attempted with some success to train Africans for leadership and consequently, when the Germans had to leave these Churches, they were able to operate as self-governing institutions, with some assistance from the United Free Church of Scotland. The Basel Mission, known from 1926 as the Prebyterian Church of the Gold Coast, was fully independent by 1950. And though more reluctant when compared with the Methodist, Anglicans and Roman Catholics to launch out into secondary education, the Presbyterian Church in 1958 was responsible for the education of an estimated 15 per cent of Ghanaian school children in primary and middle schools.[30]

Education, as we saw in the last chapter, had been from the second half of the nineteenth century an important concern of the Wesleyan Methodist Mission in Ghana (see Chapter 3, pp. 58 ff.). This mission was also intent on establishing a self-governing African Church, a policy considered premature – if not opposed outright – by the 'new' missionaries who arrived in Ghana in the last decade of the nineteenth century. Bishop Small of the North American-based African Methodist Episcopal Zion Church (AMEZ), when he visited Ghana in 1898 strongly criticised the Wesleyans reluctance to promote more Africans to positions of leadership, and even Thomas Birch Freeman's son compared what he saw as discrimination in the Wesleyan Church with the practice in the AMEZ, a Church which, he said, 'was composed by Africans' and was 'entirely governed and worked by Africans'.[31]

The Wesleyans were not the only missionaries 'who were not', to use the words of Freeman's son, 'above the colour question'.[32] But by the 1920s they had begun again to devolve authority for Church affairs on Ghanaians, and the pace of this devolution was rapidly increased after the Second World War, the Methodist Church of Ghana becoming fully autonomous in 1961. Furthermore, through its schools such as Mfantsipim the Wesleyans made a very important contribution to the development of secondary education in Ghana. Mfantsipim secondary school, opened in 1876 was, it is worth mentioning, on the point of being closed down by the 'new' breed of missionaries mentioned above, but was kept open by the efforts of the Ghanaian John Mensah Sarbah who had been a student at the school before going to London to study law. Sarbah became a stout defender of Ghanaian laws and customs and organised the Fante Society for the purpose of preserving these laws and customs.

The Anglican and Roman Catholic Churches also entered or perhaps more correctly re-entered the field of education during this period. In 1910 the Anglicans opened Adisadel grammar school in Accra for the training of clergy, catechists and teachers for its missions. While the Anglicans concentrated their efforts in and around Accra, the Catholic mission extended itself over a much wider area. In addition to the Cape Coast where the SMA priests recommenced Catholic missionary activity in the 1880s, the Catholics moved into Kumasi and then to Navrongo further north. The mission at Navrongo among the Nakana and Kassena was opened by a French missionary order, the White Fathers, in 1905 and a school for the training of catechists followed in 1910. Other mission stations opened in this region included one at Bolgatanga (1924), and others at Wiagha (1927), Jirapa (1929), Kaleo (1932) and Nandom (1933).[33]

The growth of the mission at Jirapa and among the Dagari in general in the early years was very rapid. By 1931 the mission at Jirapa had an estimated 7,000 preparing for baptism. This interest in the Catholic Church continued and it was reported that in two days in July 1932, 1,000 people came to the Jirapa mission to inquire about the possibility of membership of the Church.[34] The Dagari had been experiencing considerable suffering and hardship caused by a prolonged drought and it was quite widely believed that the prayers of the missionaries had brought rain to the area. This might in part explain the tidal wave of recruits to the Catholic mission, which led to the opening of mission stations at Kaleo, near Wa, and south of Jirapa in 1932, and at Nandom, north of Jirapa in 1933.

During the period under review the development of the Catholic Church in Ghana was quite remarkable, rising from a few thousand members in 1906 to well over 50,000 by 1924 and to over half a million by 1950. And after 1950 this kind of expansion continued, bringing the membership up to over one million by 1970.[36] The widespread use of catechists and the 'school approach' to evangelisation provide an important part of the explanation for this rapid rise of Catholicism in Ghana.

While both the Catholic and the Protestant Churches saw the school as the 'nursery' of the Church, Catholics seem to have made greater efforts to ensure the success of this method of evangelisation. Though Wesleyans had been working among the Fante long before the Catholics returned in the 1880s the latter, as we have seen (Chapter 3, pp. 60 ff.) were soon attracting far more students to their schools than the former. This no doubt had a great deal to do with the fact that Catholic schools were completely free of charge, there being no charge even for books. Moreover, the Catholic tendency to adopt the method of group rather than individual conversion, as was the case among the Dagari in the 1920s and 1930s, may also form part of the reason for the relatively rapid expansion of this Church.

Nigeria

The Niger Delta

The years of misunderstanding, criticism and confict of opinion over the approach to missionary activity generated by the Crowther crisis (see Chapter 3, pp. 66 ff.) impeded the development of the Niger Delta mission for some time. After the death of Crowther in 1891 the Anglican churches on the Lower Niger, while giving some recognition to the new bishop, Tugwell, pressed forward towards self-government and financial independence. In 1891 the Delta mission had 902 full members, but by 1893 the number had dropped to 397, and by 1898 there were only 263 members.[37] But by 1930 the Niger Delta Pastorate under Archdeacon Crowther and without the assistance of missionaries from Europe or America 'had grown from the first mud and thatch building at Bonny to eleven districts with an average of nearly sixty churches in each, and all self-supporting'.[38] The number of full members had risen from 263 in 1898 to 13,852 by 1930.[39] This was clear proof, if any such proof were ever needed, of the competence and capability of the local clergy to lead, administer and organise the local Church. By 1930, full co-operation and harmony had been restored between the Niger Delta Pastorate and the Church Missionary Society. Of course, the links between the Niger Delta Pastorate and the CMS had never been completely severed, and the CMS continued to open missions in parts of the Niger Delta after the death of Bishop Crowther in 1891.

The Nigerian bishop, James Johnson, a member of the CMS, played an important role in building up the Christian Church in the Benin area, regarded as part of the Delta, in the early years of this century. With almost no encouragement or support from the CMS Johnson undertook to open missions in, among other places, Benin, Warri and Sapele in what is today Bendel State. He employed African personnel, mainly Yoruba-speaking, to run these missions. The Sapele mission in particular expanded at a very rapid pace and was serving fifteen congregations by 1914. Christianity also spread very rapidly in the first two decades of this century in Isokoland to the south of Benin and Warri. A woman evangelist called Bribrinae from Patani played an important role in the expansion of Christianity in parts of Isokoland, for example in Igbide and surrounding areas.[40] Not only here but elsewhere in Nigeria, for instance in Plateau State,[41] the role of Nigerian women in the spread of Christianity was crucial. Another example of female evangelism was provided by Madam Emadu, who was responsible for bringing Christianity to Illue-Ologbo. These women evangelists and other Nigerian pastors, though few in number at the time, were by and large responsible, as the historian Ikime has pointed out, for laying the foundations of Christianity in Isokoland.[42]

The principal method of evangelisation employed by these early evangelists was preaching in public. It was not until the 1930s that the CMS began seriously to consider using the school approach to evangelisation in this region of the Niger Delta Pastorate. The Roman Catholic mission for its part, though it arrived in the area later than the CMS, laid great emphasis on the 'school approach', and by 1935 had 'planted schools in myriads of Urhobo villages and towns in most of which the CMS maintained only worshipping congregations'.[43] The organisation of the building of many of those mission schools, it is worth noting, was the work of clan heads who used clan labour. This was how Isoko Central School at Oleh, and many others in Isokoland, were built in the 1920s and 1930s.

Further east among the Ibo-speaking people much more emphasis was to be placed on the 'school approach' to evangelisation by all the missionary societies, and in particular by the Catholics from the time of the arrival at Onitsha in 1902 of Bishop Shanahan. It was not in fact Shanahan, as some writers have suggested, who introduced the policy of evangelisation through the schools but Fr Lejeune, his predecessor as superior of the Holy Ghost Fathers in Nigeria. Lejeune wrote to his superiors in Paris in 1901, 'It is perilous to hesitate, the Christian village must go and all our concentration must be on the schools otherwise our enemy the Protestants will snatch the young'.[44] By 1902 there were thirteen Roman Catholic primary schools with an estimated 800 pupils in eastern Nigeria, which led Lejeune to comment 'Education is our principal work and our hopes for the future are based on it'.[45] Shanahan developed the 'school approach' believing, as he said in 1905, that 'those who hold the schools hold the country, hold its religion, hold its future'.[46] While Shanahan and his colleagues attached a great deal of importance to the role of the catechist, and to visiting people in their local communities, he saw the school as the most effective means of conversion pointing out in 1909 that 'If we go from town to town talking only about God, we know from experience that much of our effort brings no result. But no one is opposed to schools'.[47]

By the outbreak of the First World War the success of the schools policy was obvious to all. Archdeacon Dennis of the CMS testified to this when in 1913 he wrote that the policy 'has . . . been vigorously sustained up to the present and with a large measure of success.'[48] Schools were established in remote villages as well as towns and the Catholics were prepared to teach whatever 'secular' subjects the government proposed. The CMS for its part was at first relunctant to include in the school curriculum such 'secular' subjects as book-keeping, accountancy and carpentry, but the rapid progress made in such a short space of time by the Catholics did much to change this narrow view of the curriculum and the society's somewhat haphazard, tentative approach to the policy of evangelisation through the schools.[49]

By 1921 the Catholic mission was responsible for 533 schools in the eastern and south-eastern regions of Nigeria, while the CMS was not so far behind with responsibility for 380 schools, the vast majority of which were in Owerri and Onitsha.[50] In 1924, Shanahan established a college for the training of priests at Igbariam and another for the training of teachers in 1928. The CMS and other Anglican and Protestant missionary societies had already opened centres for the training of indigenous clergy, and both they and the Catholics made relatively rapid progress in this field in eastern Nigeria.

In 1930 in Onitsha alone the CMS had three churches, one of which had 1,000 members, a boys' grammar school and a girls' grammar school, several elementary schools, a bookshop, and a ninety-bed hospital.[52] And the Catholic mission, assisted from 1924 by the Sisters of the Holy Rosary was expanding in every direction, to the north, east, south and west of Onitsha.

From the 1940s, and to a limited extent even before then, the policy of evangelisation through the schools was to become a little more problematic. Nationalists in the National Council of Nigeria and Cameroons Party (NCNC) were determined to gain control of the schools in order to use them as instruments of nationalist and national policy. The Churches resisted until eventually the state took over the schools after the civil war which ended in 1970.[53]

South-eastern Nigeria

In the early years of this century the CMS moved into south-eastern Nigeria to join the Scottish Presbyterian, Primitive Methodist, Qua Ibo, and United Free Church of Scotland and other missions already working in the area (see Chapter 3, pp. 68 ff.). The Catholic mission was to enter the region later. The Qua Ibo Mission was in some respects unique among these missionary societies for it was free from denominational sectarianism. This mission was not concerned with making people Catholics, Anglicans, Baptists or anything but Christians. It was a Church that sought in a very literal and real way to be indigenous, self-governing and self-financing.

In terms of expansion the Qua Ibo Mission began slowly with only 250 full members in 1910, some twenty years after beginning work in Nigeria. Then between 1910 and 1939 the growth rate increased considerably, bringing the membership up to 42,000 in 1939.[54] During and for some time after the Second World War there was a fall-off in membership, and this decline may have something to do with the arrival in the area in 1947 of the North American-based Church of Christ. Within a matter of fifteen years this Church, which based everything on the Bible, had an estimated 475 congregations and 30,000 members in the Calabar region.[55]

The Scottish Presbyterian mission which became the Presbyterian Church of Eastern Nigeria in 1954 likewise experienced a decline in membership just prior to and for some time after the Second World War. The Catholic Church on the other hand, mainly through its schools such as St Patrick's College and St Thomas' Training College established in 1935 and 1937 respectively experienced a fairly consistent growth rate in and around Calabar, Ikot Ekpene, Ogoja and other areas of the southeast.

Western Nigeria

Though the rate of expansion was uneven, all the missionary societies made headway in western Nigeria from 1890 to 1960. The Independent Baptist Church, which broke away from the Baptist mission in 1888 only to be reunited with it again in 1914, gained many aherents in Ijebu, Ekiti and Ibadan; the Baptist mission, which became heavily involved in education, attracted considerable numbers in Abeokuta, Oyo, Ogbomoso Shaki and Iressi. The Wesleyan Methodists also began to concentrate their energies on education and went so far as to make literacy in Yoruba a condition for conversion to Christianity. This mission, supported by Prince Ademuyiwa Haastrup, a relative of the Oloja (ruler) of Shagamu, made rapid progress in Ijebu-Remo, the more southerly section of Ijebuland from the 1890s until the outbreak of the First World War. Haastrup also used his influence with the ruler of Ilesha on behalf of the Wesleyans, and as a result the latter were allowed to open a mission there in 1895.

There may be the impression that mission development in education brought greater success in terms of the number of converts gained than any other form of evangelisation. This was not always so, as the Wesleyan experience makes clear. Prior to the 1920s when the Wesleyans were less involved in education their progress was much more rapid. Indeed, it is possible that the Wesleyans placed too much emphasis on their policy of providing a 'thorough' training and education for the Christians within their churches. They became too involved in 'civilising', and neglected as a consequence the work of conversion. They had hoped to educate Christians who would constitute an élite that would ·attract others to

Christianity. By the 1950s the Wesleyan Methodists still had no centre in western Nigeria for the training of indigenous clergy, and what is more they had relatively few catechists.[56]

By way of contrast the CMS in western Nigeria by this time had 'succeeded to a remarkable extent in forming an indigenous ministry, with over 140 clergy, mostly Africans'.[57] Some of these clergymen, however, decided to enter the teaching profession while others gravitated towards administration, thus creating a shortage of clergymen for the work of preaching, visiting and general pastoral activity. In fact, given the length of time it had been active in western Nigeria, the Anglican Church had not made the impact one might have expected by the 1950s. By 1957 only an estimated 33,000 people in western Nigeria were full members of the Anglican Church. The rise and expansion of the African Independent Churches, especially after the First World War, had much to do with this (see Chapter 6).

Meanwhile, the Catholic Church had begun to expand in western Nigeria as a whole. By 1890 the Catholic mission in Lagos was responsible for eight schools attended by over 600 pupils (see Chapter 3, pp. 66 ff.). In 1894 the Catholics opened a mission at Oke-Are, Ibadan, and in 1900 a school was started in the same city.[58] Progress in Ibadan was slow due to the shortage of personnel and the fact that access to Oke-Are was at that time very difficult. The headquarters of the mission at Ibadan was therefore moved to Ogunpa in the heart of the city in 1907. The area around this mission became known as Oke-Padre, (pronounced Oke-Paadi). Converts to Catholicism were still slow in coming and by 1909 only seven adults had joined the Catholic Church. In 1912 sisters of the Congregation of Our Lady of Apostles opened a convent school for girls at Idikan. By the outbreak of the First World War the Catholic community in Ibadan consisted of a small number of local converts, a few Nigerians who had returned from Brazil and a handful of Lebanese traders.

After the First World War, with the ever-increasing pace of urbanisation in Nigeria which had an enormous influence on the development of Ibadan, Catholics from other parts of Nigeria arrived in the city making the Catholic Church much more of an organised, going concern. This development led to the opening of another mission centre at Oke-Ofa in 1931 which had for its primary objective the conversion to Catholicism of the indigenous people of Ibadan. However, by 1950, there had been little success in this area, partly because there were on average only three priests directly engaged in the work of conversion in the whole of Ibadan during the 1930s and 1940s, and this despite the fact that a college for the training of an indigenous clergy had been opened at Oke-Are in 1908.

There were a number of problems involved in staffing the Ibadan Catholic Mission with local clergy. First, there was a large drop-out rate among those who entered the college at Oke-Are, and moreover those who finished their studies there were obliged to go elsewhere for further training, until the establishment of the senior training college or seminary of St Peter and St Paul at Bodija, Ibadan, in 1956. Students who entered

Oke-Are and later completed their training were not necessarily appointed to churches in Ibadan, but could be sent to parishes in, for example, Lagos, Ijebu, Ife and other parts of western Nigeria. Still by the early 1970s the college at Oke-Are had helped to train about 120 indigenous priests, the first being ordained in 1929.[59] However, it was the catechist as much as, if not in some respects even more so than the clergy, whether European or African, who was responsible for the early development of the Christian Church in its Catholic, and other forms, in Ibadan, in Nigeria as a whole, and throughout West Africa. The Catechist Training Centre opened at Oke-Are, Ibadan in 1921, and staffed by individuals like Mr Jolasun, the chief catechist, provided the Catholic mission with a number of highly effective evangelists, particularly in the rural areas. Unfortunately as far as the mission was concerned, the expansion of western education went some way towards undermining the status and role of the catechist who came to be regarded as a rather low salaried, semi-literate assistant of the clergy. The clergy themselves did little, until recently, to counteract this trend; it should have been possible to elevate the catechists to a rank below that of priest (e.g. that of a deacon) and thereby confer on them and their role greater status, prestige and recognition.

It was with the help of catechists from Ibadan, Lagos, Abeokuta, Ijebu and others from Ekiti, that the Catholic mission established itself in 1917 in what is today Ondo State in western Nigeria. From the central mission at Ado catechists and helpers went out into the surrounding areas to teach and preach, and within a few months of their arrival the missionaries had opened St George's School on the mission compound at Ado, to train more catechists or 'young Apostles' as they were sometimes called. Carrying catechisms and prayer books to the outstations the catechist, in addition to preparing them for baptism taught the people how to read and conduct a simple service in the absence of a priest or one of themselves.

By the later 1920s there were Catholic mission stations in Ado, Akure, and virtually every town and village of any size in what is today Ondo State. In 1928 there were 100 Catholic churches, sixteen schools, fifty catechists and four priests in the area. Some of the first converts were former members of the CMS who broke away to join the Catholic Church, thus increasing the rivalry and tension that already existed between Catholics and Anglicans in western Nigeria and elsewhere in the country. But it was mainly through the schools that the Catholic Church increased its membership in Ondo, the policy being to open a school wherever there was a mission station. It became increasingly difficult after the Second World War to implement this policy, since the government had decided that there was to be only one school in each village, which in practice meant that if one denomination had already established a school in a particular village all other denominations were excluded.

By the 1940s the problem of the role and status of the catechist had become acute. The old type of catechist whose main task was to teach religion and serve the church disappeared to be replaced by teachers with higher educational qualifications for whom the teaching of religion however important it might be was simply one of their many duties.[60] Part of the answer to the problem lay in the total restructuring of the system of training catechists and in improving their status and position in the Church (see Chapter 7, pp. 207–8).

While the Roman Catholic, Anglican, Methodists and several other missionary societies spread out over western Nigeria in the period under discussion, eager and willing to establish schools wherever they went, the Sudan Interior Mission (SIM), adopted a different approach. The SIM concentrated its activity on Yagbaland in north-eastern Yorubaland where it attempted to shield the people from the corrupting influences of western civilisation.[61] Though it began work among the Yagba in 1908 the SIM only opened its first, organised mission school in 1930.

The policy of the SIM, an evangelical, fundamentalist society, was to provide people with a basic, Christian theology, whereby believers depended totally on the Holy Spirit for guidance. Rigorous examinations were given to potential converts before baptism to ensure that each baptism was a 'believer's baptism'. As a consequence there was no baptism of children. To protect the faith of their members the society kept them away in so far as this was possible and feasible from western education and other dangerous influences. The building of dispensaries, hospitals, and other similar institutions was encouraged, and took place, but schools were frowned upon.

This protectionist policy proved impossible to implement. Many of the younger converts travelled south to Ibadan and elsewhere in search of education, or left the SIM to join other Churches. Eventually, by the 1930s the SIM was obliged to change and began to open schools and training colleges which produced the majority of the first generation of the Yagba western-educated élite. It is worth noting, though I do not posit a direct cause-effect relationship for this, that SIM membership increased steadily as schools were established from a few hundred in the 1920s to over 6,000 in the 1950s.[62]

The Benue

The two principal Christian missions working among the Tiv, Jukun and Idoma of the Benue region during the colonial era were the Dutch Reformed Church of South Africa (DRCM), which operated for a short time under the aegis of the Sudan United Mission (SUM), and the Roman Catholic Mission, staffed in the main by the Holy Ghost Congregation.

The DRCM which became in 1957 part of the Church of Christ in Tivland – *Nongo u Kristu Ken Sudan hen Tiv* – established a mission at Sai (Salah in Hausa) in 1911. The DRCM, like the SUM, laid great emphasis on the creation of an indigenous clergy, and regarded the use of the Tiv language in church and mission school and the translation of the Bible into Tiv as essential to the success of this policy. Further, illiteracy was made a barrier to full church membership. It was 1917 before the first Tiv were admitted to full membership of the Church.

New mission stations were opened over the years, for example at Zaki-Biam (1913), Sevav (1919), Mkar (1923), Adikpo (1923), Turan (1926) and Kunav (1927), and many others followed later. But by the time Kunav had been opened in 1927 very few Tiv, in fact less than half a dozen, had become full-time members of the Church. The fact that Tiv society was highly decentralised with the people living in small groupings some distance from each other may have made the area somewhat more difficult to evangelise than, for example, western Nigeria which was much more urbanised and where the people were more accessible. The slow growth was possibly also due to the fact that the mission school system proved to be, prior to the later 1920s, an ineffective means of evangelisation in this region. An education in the Tiv language and Biblical knowledge qualified one for very little in an area where most people were agriculturalists. The administration also preferred to recruit local staff from among those who could speak Hausa and English and where these languages would have been considered useful by those intending to enter the expanding trading and commercial networks. As the well-known early Tiv Christian convert Akiga expressed it, the education provided by the mission was 'simply a waste of time'.[64] It was also generally regarded among the Tiv at this time, according to Akiga, as the European's concern, as 'his own natural heritage'.[65]

When the colonial administration began to organise and finance education from local funds on a small scale there was a more positive response from the people. In the primary schools sponsored by the colonial administration such subjects as English, Agriculture and Mathematics were taught, and successful students could gain admission to Katsina Ala, opened in 1922 and raised to a Middle School in 1930. But like the SIM in Yagbaland the DRCM was reluctant to introduce English as the medium of instruction and to teach too many 'secular' and 'morally corrupting' subjects. The mission was also worried that if its students became too highly qualified they might look for employment beyond the confines of the Church.

While this protectionist policy did ensure that the mission possessed a ready supply of trained catechists, it did not prevent former students of the mission schools from establishing numerous non mission-controlled Bible schools during what became known as the 'Awakening' in the central and eastern areas of Tivland in the 1930s. The Bible schools' Movement won over many people to Christianity and at the same time obliged the mission to give greater recognition to the Bible school teachers, by allowing them to participate to a limited extent in the decision-making process in the Church and by the creation of the order or office of Bible School Leader. Nevertheless, access to the higher offices in the Church remained a difficulty, and no serious attempt was made to indigenise the higher ranks of the clergy till the 1940s.

The Roman Catholic mission in the Benue began when the railway was extended from Enugu to Makurdi in 1924. The catechist, Christopher Ilobi, looked after the primary school and other Catholic interests in the area until German priests of the Holy Ghost Congregation established a permanent mission station at Makurdi in 1930. Like the one at Makurdi, many of the early Catholic mission stations in the Benue were established close to the railway line that ran northwards from Enugu. This was the case with the missions at Utonkon opened in 1930, at Oturkpo (1934) and Taraku (1935). The construction of the railway line northwards from Enugu to link the tin mines of the Jos Plateau with the coalfields of Udi went ahead in stages of ten miles, and at each stage a base camp was erected to provide accommodation for the workers. The camps attracted people from the surrounding areas and others, in particular Ibos, who travelled there to trade. The Catholic priest accompanied by the catechist would go from camp to camp to minister to a predominantly Ibo Catholic community, until these camps became the large villages and towns of Otobi, Utonkon, Uturkpo, Taraku and Makurdi in which mission stations were opened.[66]

It was not long before the Catholic mission became involved in education. In March 1931 the colonial administration gave permission for a school to be opened at Utonkon 'provided that no English is taught and no instruction is given in English'.[67] And in 1933 permission was granted to open a school at Oturkpo. A primary school had already been opened at Makurdi and by 1932 it was being attended by seventy pupils. In the same year the German Catholic missionaries started a brick-making factory in Makurdi, and in 1935 they set up a printing press at Taraku which by 1938 had produced a prayer book and reader in both Idoma and Tiv.

By 1940 when the German missionaries were interned by the British government in Jamaica the Catholic mission had extended itself far beyond the railway line to other parts of the Benue region. A mission was opened at Korinya in 1934, and between 1933 and 1938 a central mission and a school were established at Gboko, and another at Wukari in 1940.

The Catholic mission in the Benue area, handed over to the English priests of the Holy Ghost Society in 1946, began to witness a steady increase in membership from the late 1940s. This growth coincided on the one hand with the expansion in primary and secondary education in which the mission played an important role, and on the other hand with the increase in the number of catechists trained and employed by the mission. In 1950 the Catholic mission in the Benue was responsible for an estimated 392 schools attended by almost 12,000 students. In 1940 the mission had less than 50 schools attended by 1,400 pupils. Moreover by 1950 the mission was employing 514 catechists compared with less than 50 in 1940.[68]

This numerical growth was not as spectacular as that achieved by the Irish priests of the Holy Ghost Society working in the Onitsha-Owerri region to the south. Between 1939 and 1946 the number of Catholics increased in this region from 163,564 to 250,000, and from 1946 to 1948, from 250,000 to 321,511.[69] This growth rate can also be related to some extent to the mission's expansion of its primary school system in particular. By 1948 it was either running or supervising some 850 such schools.[70] The situation in the Benue was, of course, different in many respects from that which obtained in and around Onitsha and Owerri. In the Benue the people were more dispersed and scattered and this meant that the missionary had to cover much more terrain where roads and communications were poor. There was also the question of personnel, the Benue having far fewer missionaries than the Onitsha-Owerri area. By 1939 there were four Nigerian priests working in Onitsha and Owerri regions and eleven by 1946,[71] while the Catholic mission in the Benue did not have any of its own Nigerian priests until the early 1970s.

The Protestant mission in the Benue on the other hand ordained five indigenous clergy in 1956, one of whom took over responsibility for the DRCM mission which, as we have seen, became the Church of Christ in Tivland in 1957. It is worth mentioning here that the Church of Christ in Tivland was one of a number of Protestant Churches that grouped themselves into the Fellowship of the Churches of Christ in the Sudan – in Hausa, *Tarayyar Ekklesiyoyyin Kristi a Sudan* (TEKAS), in 1960. In 1957 it began to receive assistance from the American branch of the SUM known as the Christian Reformed Church, SUM. From 1957 there occurred a spectacular increase in the number of those attending its Sunday services: from 24,000 in that year to 73,140 in 1962. On the other hand the number of full and/or communicant members was still only 6,152 in 1962.[72]

The Catholic mission with approximately two and a half times as many full members in 1962 did not have as many people attending its Sunday services. Writing in the 1960s the then superior of the Catholic mission stated 'the slow development of the indigenous clergy is the main worry . . . . Most missions are too large to be run by one or two priests and not enough attention can be given either to consolidating our Christian communities or to extending our apostolate'.[73] This, it would appear, was a fairly accurate assessment of the situation. Nevertheless, though less than 10 per cent of the peoples of the Benue region taken as a whole regarded themselves as Christians by 1960, the Christian missions had acquired considerable influence throughout the region.

The northern states

Prior to 1890 several attempts had been made to establish Christianity in the northern parts of Nigeria (see Chapter 3, pp. 65 ff.). A group of CMS missionaries known as the 'Sudan Party' made the conversion of the Muslim areas of northern Nigeria their principal objective. The missionary view was that no one became a Muslim for sound intellectual and religious reasons. Muslims, however, in particular the Hausa-speaking Muslims, were not regarded as unintelligent or incapable of 'sound' reasoning. The missionary believed that once the foundations of the Muslim political economy had been destroyed the Hausa, with their sophisticated culture and capacity for understanding 'the high metaphysical truths of Christianity', would be attracted by the fact that Christianity was intellectually superior to Islam and become 'providential instruments for the Christianisation of even the less healthy and less enlightened part of the African continent'.[74]

This view of the Hausa was also shared by the CMS and other missionary societies. The colonial administration, for its part, tended to emphasise the military skills and aptitudes of the Hausa and their 'innate' capacity for leadership and administration. On the very day the Northern Region of Nigeria became self-governing the outgoing colonial governor of the north spoke, in his address to mark the occasion, of the 'administrative genius of the Hausas with their Islamic culture' which, along with other factors such as the 'British gift for empiricism and improvisation', enabled this region 'with its varied tribes, creeds and traditions' to enter 'its new status with a united purpose'.[75]

The Roman Catholic missionaries began work in northern Nigeria with the opening of a mission at Lokoja in 1886 and went on in the first decades of this century to open stations at Dekina (1904) and Shendam, off the southern escarpment of the Jos-Bauchi plateau, in 1906. The CMS established itself even further north in Zaria in 1905. Prior to this, in 1901 the Sudan Interior Mission (SIM) began work in Pategi, a small Muslim emirate in Nupeland. The Sudan Pioneer Mission, founded in England in 1902 on the initiative of the German, Karl Kumm, and which later became the Sudan United Mission, opened a mission at Wase in present-day Benue State in the same year. Wase was at the time the headquarters of a small Muslim emirate south of the Jos-Bauchi plateau. The work at Wase was abandoned in 1909 as a result of objections made by the emir to the presence of Christian missionaries.

The Hausa mission in Zaria apart, the colonial government, though not anti-Christian missionary *per se*, was for a number of reasons extremely reluctant to allow Christian missionaries to work in the main Islamic centres of northern Nigeria such as Kano, Sokoto, Katsina, Bauchi and Maiduguri. However, the development of the *sabon gari* system, whereby 'strangers' lived and worked in separate areas on the periphery of the old Muslim centres in the north led eventually to Christian missionaries being allowed to work not actually in – unless invited to do so by the emir, as was the case for a time at Zaria and Bida – but on the borders of northern Muslim towns.

When it became clear that they would not be permitted to evangelise in the Muslim areas the missionary societies sought to 'stem the tide of Islam'. In its Annual Report of 1908 the SUM referred to the 'crisis in the West Central Sudan, where unless the Gospel of Christ be brought within the next few years to Northern Nigeria, the million numbered pagan people of that new British Protectorate will go over to Islam'.[76] Indeed, it was the fear that these people would go over to Islam that led to the Protestant Churches joining together to form the Sudan United Mission. 'Stemming the tide of Islam' was in line with the strategy proposed at the Edinburgh and Lucknow World Missionary Conferences, held in the early years of this century, where it was stressed that the 'whole strategy of Christian missions in Africa should be viewed in relation to Islam'.[77] The Lucknow conference proposed the establishment of 'a strong chain of mission stations across Africa, the strongest links of which will be at those points where Muslim advance is most active'.[78]

Once again in the Nigerian context, as was the case in the Senegambia, the evolutionary theory of religious development seems to have been fairly widely accepted in missionary circles. The SUM missionary Kumm regarded Islamic civilisation as a 'higher' form of civilisation than African civilisation, while Christian civilisation was 'higher' than both.[79] However, a consideration of Kumm's comments and writings on Islam make it difficult to see in what ways he regarded Islam as a civilisation as being 'superior' to African civilisation. In the words of one scholar Kumm depicted Islam as 'excelling in works of evil'.[80] He seemed on the one hand to be able to excuse 'Christian civilisation' for its role in such barbarities as the trans-Atlantic slave trade, while on the other hand being completely incapable of in any way toning down his harsh, virulent abuse of Muslims for participating in slavery.[81] Kumm contrasted the benefits of western civilisation with the 'evils' of Islamic and African civilisation. For Kumm, thus, western colonialisation was divinely ordained; it was God's instrument for bringing, in the name of Christ, liberty and justice to Africa.[82]

Kumm was not alone in his presenting this almost totally negative view of Islam. Some Roman Catholic missionaries in eastern Nigeria and American Protestant missionaries, among others, expressed similar sentiments to Kumm concerning Islam. Moreover, like their Protestant counterparts, those Catholic missionaries working in northern Nigeria in particular had as one of their principal objectives the stemming of the tide of Islam. As the head of the SMA congregation who made an extensive tour of northern Nigeria in the early 1920s explained, his missionaries were engaged in a struggle in northern Nigeria to 'defend them (the traditional religionists) against Islam', and if they were successful they would not only improve their 'barbarous' customs but also 'hand them over to the true God'.[83]

The views of Islam expressed by one of the most prominent CMS missionary figures in the Hausa mission in Zaria, Walter Miller, differed little from those outlined above. Miller, like Kumm and some of the Roman Catholic missionaries, maintained that there was a direct causal link between Islamic beliefs and practices and destitution, poverty and low morality. As one scholar explains, 'evil' was, in the mind of Miller and others, the direct consequence of religion in so far as Islam was concerned.[84] These Christian missionaries were not completely blind or oblivious to the many 'evils' perpetrated in so-called Christian countries. But these 'evils' were not, it was argued, directly attributable to Christianity; they existed rather 'in spite of Christianity'.[85]

This strong opposition to Islam was not only the result of ingrained cultural and historical prejudices, but was also the result of fundamental doctrinal disagreements: principally the fact that Islam formally rejected Christian teaching on the divinity of Christ and on the role of Christ as saviour. While the traditional religionist was simply ignorant of Christ, and therefore to some extent could be excused for his 'low morality', the Muslim knew of Christ but repudiated him, and in doing so attacked the very foundations of Christian missionary endeavour. The dominant perspective on salvation and 'evil' of many of these Christian missionaries was what might be termed 'conversionist'. Salvation and the conquest of 'evil' were to be achieved by the individual undergoing a profound inner conversion and/or transformation of self, a conversion which could only be initiated and brought to completion by Christ. This was the means to salvation offered by the missionaries in Nigeria and elsewhere in Africa, but it was a means that Islam categorically rejected, and for doing so was considered by many missionaries to be in essence 'the spirit of the anti-Christ'.[86]

In a very real sense, Christian missionary encounters with Islam produced a clash at the cultural level. The missionary believed God had worked wonders for European civilisation centuries ago when by means of Christianity he transformed the English, the French and other Europeans from 'savages' and 'barbarians' into cultured and civilised people. Now – but for Islam which rejected colonial rule and Christianity – the same process could speedily be got underway in Africa. European civilisation was, of course, considered to be the highest form of civilisation, and in refusing to accept it Muslims were perpetuating the 'evils' generated by Islam's inferior form of civilisation.

Apart from the few missions established inside Muslim towns such as the CMS missions at Bida and Zaria, the SIM mission at Patigi and the SUM mission at Wase, abandoned in 1909, the missionary societies henceforth concentrated their energies on the so-called 'pagan' areas of northern Nigeria, such as the Jos Plateau. Though the Christian missions spread themselves far and wide over the whole of northern Nigeria their impact, in terms of the numbers converted to Christianity, was negligible prior to the outbreak of the Second World War. The history of the SUM mission among the Birom at Forum on the central area of the Jos Plateau, today part of Plateau State, will serve to illustrate this point. The aim of the first Sudan United missionaries on the Plateau was to lead *individuals* to *full* repentance and conversion, to wean them away completely from all 'idolatrous' practices and social activities such as beer drinking.[87] The result in the Birom village of Forum was that there were only three such converts between 1910 and 1921.

The field station reports for 1921 made by the missionaries serving at Forum and Du throw considerable light on the situation in that year. Referring to the mission work at Du, an outstation, the report for July 1921 states 'The work at Du is not easy. One woman is very interested'. And another for the same mission for November 1921 reads 'People are on their farms mostly. When at home they gather for usual harvest beer drinking rather than hear the Gospel'. And the report for the Forum mission also for November 1921 records that 'The school is very poorly attended because of the harvest season. No catechumenate class because no one attended'.[88]

One of the numerous problems encountered by the missionaries was the multiplicity of languages on the Plateau and this even made the task of the local catechist extremely difficult. Some catechists, however, like the Birom woman evangelist Vo Gyang who, with her blind husband

Bot Dung, brought Christianity to the neighbouring Ganawuri not only learnt the language of these people but also many of their customs in order to communicate effectively with them.[89]

When the missionaries decided to change strategy and devised the policy of 'group movements', that is, the establishment and development of Christianity within homogenous units by means of indigenous pastors and evangelists, the conversion rate to Christianity was much higher.[90]

The missionaries nevertheless still faced the problem of the lack of an indigenous leadership. SUM congregations, partly because of its laws against polygamy and beer drinking, were composed mainly of boys and girls. One author has spoken in the same vein of the Catholic mission which he described as a 'Church of children' in the early years of its existence on the Plateau.[91]

Not only were the Birom men excluded from Christianity on the grounds of polygamy, but also to an extent by the fact that they themselves had to consider the political, social, religious and economic consequences of conversion. Becoming a Christian might involve the renunciation of a position of authority in the community or dissociation from the ritual practices of the society which ensured one's social and economic well-being. A trader might well have to suffer by being excluded from the trading network. Plateau trade was dependent to a great extent on such networks. A person's success depended, not only on the cheapness of wares and the number of customers one had, but on the number of trading friends one enjoyed. Thus to isolate oneself from the community could mean economic disaster.

In the minds of the Birom, moreover, missionaries were identified with and on occasion regarded as agents of the colonial administration. Thus there was strong and consistent opposition to them from many Birom societies. Pastor Ghey left Gyel in 1910 because 'the people couldn't really understand what he wanted in their country'. In the period 1900–30 the missionaries concentrated on converting the chiefs, but their only success was that of Gwom Chai Mang of the Ganawuri, a conversion achieved in abnormal circumstances. The missionaries were far more dependent on the village communities than the latter of them. One reason being that villages did not accept money or trade goods and as one missionary put it, 'The one connecting link between the natives and ourselves is salt'.[92] Further problems arose in Kuru, Rafan, Tahoss, Forum, Fulle and among the Ganawuri when Christians were driven out and excluded from marriage. Thus the problem of getting wives for converts arose. In addition, there were the problems of language, and in some areas there were restrictions on preaching and Sunday observance.

By the 1930s missionary bodies were better organised than in the early years of the twentieth century. Attempts were being made to unite the various missionary denominations, hospitals (Vom 1924) and schools (Gindiri 1934) had been established, and parts of the Bible had been translated into Hausa and some of the local languages. Associations such as the 'Boys Brigade' had been founded 'to keep the converts from their old ways', and 1938 saw the ordination of Pastors Bot, Lot and Bali. The

Second World War forced the missionaries to realise even more the necessity to train African evangelists. It also led to a great demand for schools which the missionaries attempted to meet. By the end of the Second World War the problems of local leadership had been partly solved. Many of the first Christians had been through school, or had worked in the tin mines, or as clerks or scribes in government service and had acquired relative wealth and achieved some status in the 'new' society. They, along with the newly-trained pastors and evangelists, provided the Plateau Christian community with leadership.

By the 1930s the traditional political, economic, social and religious institutions of the Birom – and this was the case in many other parts of Nigeria and throughout West Africa – had been to a considerable extent undetermined by the cultural, political and economic changes that had taken place in the previous thirty years, either as a direct consequence of or under the aegis of colonialism. As a particular result of the political, economic and social changes traditional religion had become increasingly irrelevant in all of these spheres. One of its primary functions had been to enable its adherents to cope with all aspects of life. Moreover, it provided the community with an element of stability and cohesion. But with the development of the modern sector of the economy on the Plateau, mainly through the opening up of the tin-mining industry, with the construction of roads and the emergence of towns such as Jos, and the break up of the traditional politico-religious system by the introduction of indirect rule by the British, traditional institutions and the old religion lost much of their relevance. This in turn facilitated the spread of Christianity and Islam in the region. These religions were, many thought, more appropriate and relevant to a changed and changing society. Not everyone, of course, saw things quite in this way.

By the 1950s there were countless mission societies and mission stations scattered across the length and breadth of northern Nigeria from Sokoto in the north-west to Maiduguri in the north-east. These missions for the most part sprung up around a school or dispensary and in most cases the first local Christians took it upon themselves to work as evangelists.

In the 1950s, as we have seen, many of the Protestant Churches joined the fellowship of Churches known as TEKAS. The SIM, with the largest number of missions of any missionary society in northern Nigeria, in an attempt to completely indigenise itself, formed from the churches for which it was responsible the association called ECWA (The Evangelical Churches of West Africa). In the 1950s both the TEKAS Churches and ECWA began to concentrate far more than was the case in the past on education, and by 1960 had developed an extensive education network to add to their hospitals and leprosariums. By 1960 the main strength of both the TEKAS and the ECWA Churches in northern Nigeria in numbers of converts was in the Jos Plateau region, a substantial increase in membership beginning to take place in the 1940s. Nevertheless, even with this acceleration the membership, relative to the size of the population of northern Nigeria, was still very small by 1960.

It was in the 1930s that the Catholic mission began to establish itself on a firm foundation in the northern areas of Nigeria. The mission station at Shendam had been opened by the SMA Fathers as early as 1906, and the same missionary society had visited Kano and other parts of the north in the 1920s. A mission was estabished in the *sabon gari* area of Kano in 1922. In Yola in present-day Gongola State a small Catholic community composed in the main of migrant workers from the south was established around 1930, while in 1938 Irish priests of the Order of St Augustine (OSA) took charge of Roman Catholic activities in an area stretching from Jos across Bauchi and Adamawa to the Northern Cameroon.

In the 1940s missions were opened at, among other places, Sugu, Jimeta, Bare and Kaya. Maiduguri, close to both Chad and Cameroon was visited by Catholic priests in the late 1930s. As was the case in Yola, the Catholic community in Maiduguri at this time was composed almost entirely of people from southern Nigeria, the majority of whom, like the Catholics at Potiskum, were artisans who had travelled north to work in the construction industry. At first the Catholics, mainly Ibos, worshipped in the Anglican and/or CMS church opened in 1935 by Mr King from Sierra Leone and a Yoruba, Mr Vaughan. The 'church' was in fact a rented room and was situated in the town. However, when the local Muslim population disapproved of the holding of Christian services in the town a site was provided outside the town gates and a small church was erected there in 1936. In order not to antagonise the Muslim population the church was named the 'Foreigner's Club' and classes in English as well as Sunday services were held there. The interdenominational worship came to an end in 1941 when the Catholics of Maiduguri, among them Mr Rapu from the west, a Mr Obuna from the mid-west (Benin) and a Mr Anyanwu from the east of Nigeria, opened their own church.[93]

In addition to Maiduguri many of the other Catholic missions established in the Borno region and indeed elsewhere in northern Nigeria were composed in the main of people from the southern parts of the country. This was the situation at Nguru in Borno State where the 'leader' of the Catholic community was from Benin and most of the members were also from either eastern or western Nigeria. The mission established in 1952 at Gashua, also in Borno State, was also composed of Catholics from eastern Nigeria. The Catholic Church developed in the same way in Bauchi, Jos, Kaduna, Kontagora, Katsina, Kano, Yelwa and Sokoto. Prior to the 1960s western education, like that provided by the CMS, did little to change the composition of the Catholic community, since it attracted in the main the inhabitants of the *sabon gari* who showed much greater enthusiasm for it than the local people.[94]

While many of the Protestant Christian communities in various parts of northern Nigeria were, like the Catholic Church, composed in the main of 'internal migrants' (of people from areas other than the north), there was one Christian community in the north where the membership was made up almost entirely of 'local' people. This was the CMS community in Zaria founded by the Revd Dr Miller in 1905. By 1913 there were some 120 Christians, many of them descendants of the followers of the unorthodox, nineteenth century Muslim preacher Malam Ibrahim who were known collectively as *Isawa* (The Jesus People), because they appear to have placed Jesus on a higher plane than the Prophet Muhammad.[95] Assisted by a West Indian clergyman, the Revd Thompson, Miller opened a CMS school in Zaria and in this way gave the mission a firm foundation. Many of the leading Christian families from northern Nigeria are products of this school.[96]

In 1928 the mission in Zaria, which was the only Christian mission in the north situated within a Muslim town, moved outside the city to nearby Wusasa. As a result of this move the mission became more of a base to teach Maguzawa than a centre for attracting Muslims to Christianity. Although the mission's secondary school, St Paul's and the hospital were to attract many Hausa, very few of the latter became Christians during the period under discussion. Nevertheless, Wusasa remained the only Hausa Christian community in northern Nigeria.

Conclusions

Although the main priorities of the missionaries underwent some change with the passage of time, it is possible to single out what they were during the colonial era and the means the missionaries adopted to attain their objectives. Most of the missionary societies concentrated on establishing Christian families and where possible Christian communities, and one of the principal means used to achieve this was the school. And while this method of evangelisation proved highly successful in some areas such as eastern Nigeria it had numerous drawbacks, and to a lesser extent the same applies to the system of catechists. The training of a sufficient number of indigenous clergy to serve the people was also an area where there was little advance among Roman Catholics in particular. Missionaries too often saw themselves solely as leaders, and felt that there was little or nothing to be gained from an open, equal partnership with African Christians. They only very rarely blamed their slow progress on their own methods and approach, and almost always on extrinsic factors such as Islam, the policy of the colonial administration, the secret societies or the lack of self-sacrificing altruism on the part of Africans.

The race with Islam preoccupied a great deal of missionary thinking in certain areas, and this question will be treated again at some length in Chapter 5. Lack of success here led to the development of a variety of explanations, for the most part extremely negative and disparaging, for the advance of Islam (see pp. 110 ff. and Chapter 5). Another drawback for the missionary societies was that they brought their theological and other differences with them from Europe to Africa, pursuing their accusations and counter accusations, their recriminations and feuding, which did little good to the image of Christianity. With some exceptions like the Qua Ibo Mission (see pp. 101 ff.) each mission society tended to believe that it alone was in possession of the full 'truth' of Christianity and this made for a narrow, authoritarian, exclusivist presentation of the Christian message. A more co-operative, tolerant, ecumenical approach

II Church made of mud, Wusasa, Zaria, Nigeria

III The altar in the church at Wusasa. The Hausa inscription means 'Holy, Holy, Holy'.

began to emerge in the colonial era and is now widespread throughout West Africa and Africa as a whole.

Nevertheless it is clear that by the 1950s, as most West African states moved quickly towards their political independence, the mission-established Churches had achieved a considerable amount. Indeed, in some missionary circles, for example in eastern Nigeria, there was a certain euphoria over the number, size and quality of the schools, hospitals and churches under their control. But in their excitement over schools and training colleges some missionary societies were paying insufficient attention to the development of a national education system. They were placing their faith in the teachers under their charge, regarding them as the pillars of the Church while tending to overlook the important – in fact indispensable – role of the catechist in the local church, especially in the rural areas. Little was being done to improve the status, position and training of the catechist and yet once the schools were taken over by the government (and it was clear in many cases that they would be), the mission-established Churches would have very little option but to have recourse once again to the catechist system.

While the mission-established Churches in most of former British-occupied West Africa and Liberia were experiencing a boom in terms of the number of converts in the 1950s, a boom generated in large measure by their increasing involvement over the years in education, a number of important and pressing issues, shelved for so long, remained to be solved. Undoubtedly, although the number of 'foreign' missionaries was on the increase, the most pressing need of all was the need for ever-increasing numbers of African clergy, assisted by well trained, well qualified catechists. Without the latter, the rural areas in particular could not be served, and without the former there was no prospect of a transfer of ecclesiastical authority, and responsibility from European to African, at the higher and intermediate levels and therefore no prospect of creating some of the necessary conditions for the emergence of a truly indigenous Christian Church.

Notes
1 C. Fyfe, *A Short History of Sierra Leone*. Oxford: Oxford University Press, 1979: 133.
2 P.B. Clarke, *West Africans at War, 1914–1918 and 1939–1945*. London, Ethnographia Publishers Ltd, forthcoming: Chapter 1.
3 W.L. Avery, Christianity in Sierra Leone. In O.U. Kalu, (ed.) *The History of Christianity in West Africa*. London and New York, 1980.
4 ibid., p. 113.
5 J.M. Cuoq, *Les Musulmans en Afrique*. Paris, 1957: p. 168.
6 ibid., p. 168.
7 E.D.A. Hulmes, 'Christian Attitudes to Islam: A Comparative Study of the Work of S.A. Crowther, E.W. Blyden and W.R.S. Miller in West Africa'. D.Phil, Oxford, 1980.
8 P.B. Clarke, *The Christian Encounter with Islam in Africa*. Forthcoming, Chapter 2.

118   West Africa and Christianity

9   H.J. Fisher, *Ahmadiyyah: A Study in Contemporary Islam on the West African Coast*. Oxford: Oxford University Press, 1963.
10   H.J. Fisher, The Modernization of Islamic Education in Sierra Leone, Gambia and Liberia: Religion and Language. In G.N. Brown and M. Hiskett (eds) Conflict and Harmony in *Education in Tropical Africa*. London: George Allen and Unwin, 1975: 187–99.
11   L. Sanneh, Modern Education among Freetown Muslims and the Christian Stimulus. In E. Fashole-Luke *et al* (eds) *Christianity in Independent Africa*. London: Rex Collings, 1978: 316–34.
12   M. Banton, *West African City*. Oxford: Oxford University Press, 1957: 24.
13   ibid., p. 140.
14   D.J. Scott, The Sierra Leone Election, May 1957. In W.J.M. Mackenzie and K.E. Robinson (eds) *Five Elections in Africa*. Oxford: Clarendon Press, 1960: p. 226.
15   ibid.
16   A.J. Gittins, Mende and Missionary: Belief, Perception and Enterprise. Ph.D. University of Edinburgh, 1977 (2 volumes). Vol. 2, p. 452.
17   Citation in A.J. Gittins, op. cit., p. 453.
18   ibid., pp. 462 ff.
19   ibid., p. 473.
20   T. Awori, The Revolt Against the 'Civilizing Missions': Christian Education in Liberia. In E.H. Berman (ed.) *African Reactions to Missionary Education*. New York and London: Teachers' College Press, 1975: 116–33.
21   E.M. Hogan, *Catholic Missions and Liberia*. op.cit.: 80.
22   M.L. Pirouet, East African Christians and World War I, Journal of African History (J.A.H.), **XIX** (1), 1978: 117–30.
23   Citation in E.M. Hogan, op. cit., p. 103.
24   ibid., p. 127.
25   T. Awori, op. cit., pp. 121–122.
26   ibid., p. 122.
27   M. Fraenkel, *Tribe and Class in Monrovia* op.cit., 172–3.
28   C.K. Graham, *The History of Education in Ghana* op.cit., 150.
29   F. Yao Boateng, The Catechism and the Rod: Presbyterian Education in Ghana. In E.H. Berman (ed.) *African Reactions to Missionary Education*, op. cit.,: 75–92.
30   C.K. Graham, op. cit., p. 183.
31   F.Y. Boateng, op. cit., p. 70.
32   F.L. Bartels, *The Roots of Ghana Methodism*. Cambridge: Cambridge University Press, 1965: 118.
33   A. Proust, *Les Missions des Pères Blancs en Afrique Occidentale avant 1939*. Paris (n.d), p. 146.
34   ibid., p. 150.
35   ibid., pp. 151–2.
36   D. Barrett (ed.), *World Christian Encyclopaedia. A Comparative Survey of Church and Religions in the Modern World A.D. 1900–2000*. Oxford: Oxford University Press, 1982: 324.
37   J.B. Grimley and G.E. Robinson, *Church Growth in Central and Southern Nigeria*. Michigan: Eerdmans, 1966: 289.
38   ibid.
39   ibid., p. 290.
40   S. Erivwo, *A History of Christianity in Nigeria. The Urhobo, The Isoko and The Itsekiri*. Ibadan: Ibadan University Press, 1979.
41   P.B. Clarke, Birom Woman Evangelist: Vo Gyang of Forum., In E. Isichei

(ed.) *Varieties of Christian Experience in Nigeria*. London and Basingstoke: Macmillan, 1982: 163–77.
42 O. Ikime, *The Isoko People*. Ibadan: Ibadan University Press, 1972: 62.
43 S. Erivwo, op. cit., p. 61.
44 See P.B. Clarke, Methods and Ideology of the Holy Ghost Fathers in Eastern Nigeria, 1885–1905. In O.U. Kalu, op. cit., p. 51.
45 ibid., p. 52.
46 ibid., p. 53.
47 ibid., p. 54.
48 ibid.
49 F.K. Eketchi, *Missionary Enterprise and Rivalry in Igboland 1857–1914*. London: Frank Cass, 1972.
50 Fr J.C. Okoye, *Bishop Joseph Shanahan*. Onitsha: R.C.M. 1971: 20.
51 J.B. Grimley and G.E. Robinson, *Church Growth in Central and Southern Nigeria*, op.cit., p. 331.
52 A.E. Afigbo, The Missions, the State and Education in South-Eastern Nigeria 1956–1971, and C.M. Cooke, Church, State and Education: The Eastern Nigerian Experience, 1950–1967. In E. Fashole-Luke *et al.* (eds) *Christianity in Independent Africa*, op.cit., pp. 176–93 and 93–207 resp.
53 ibid.
54 J.B. Grimley and G.E. Robinson, op. cit., p. 344.
55 ibid.
56 G. Parrinder, *Religion in an African City*. Oxford: Oxford University Press, 1953: 93.
57 ibid., pp. 86–7.
58 For a brief history of the Catholic Church in Ibadan, see P. O'Neil, *The Catholic Faith in Ibadan Diocese 1884–1974*. Ibadan: Ibadan University Press, 1981.
59 ibid., p. 21.
60 Fr Oguntuyi, *A History of the Catholic Church in Ondo Diocese*. Ibadan: Ibadan University Press, 1970: pp. 105–6.
61 A. Ijagbemi, Christian Missionary Work and Change in North-East Yorubaland. Staff and Postgraduate Seminar Paper, Dept. of History, University of Ibadan, Dec. 1977, p. 19.
62 ibid., p. 13.
63 *The Coming of the Gospel into Tivland*. Christian Reformed Church Publication, n.d., p. 4.
64 Akiga, *History of the Tiv*. MSS, University of Ibadan Africana Collection, p. 325.
65 ibid.
66 Holy Ghost Fathers' Archives, London, Bulletin General, Vol. 45, pp. 209 ff.
67 ibid., Utonkon Diary – Entry for March 11th 1931.
68 ibid. Bulletin General, op. cit.
69 ibid. Bulletin General, Vol. 43.
70 ibid.
71 ibid.
72 J.B. Grimley and G.E. Robinson, op. cit., p. 226.
73 Holy Ghost Archives, London, Bulletin General, Vol. 51, p. 393.
74 P.B. Clarke, Methods and Ideology of the Holy Ghost Fathers in Eastern Nigeria, 1885–1905. In O.U. Kalu (ed.), op. cit., p. 42.
75 E.P.T. Crampton, *Christianity in Northern Nigeria*. Zaria, 1975: pp. 79–80.
76 J.B. Grimley and G.E. Robinson, op. cit., pp. 43–4.
77 ibid., p. 44.

78 ibid.
79 J.H. Boar, *Missionary Messengers of Liberation in a Colonial Context. A Case Study of the Sudan United Mission*, Vol. I. Amsterdam: Editions Rodopi N.V., 1979: p. 128.
80 ibid.
81 ibid., p. 128.
82 ibid., p. 129.
83 R.P. Chabert, L'Islam Chez les Sauvages et Les Cannibales de la Nigéria du Nord. Conférence, Institut Catholique, Paris, op. cit., p. 188.
84 J.H. Boer, op. cit., p. 170.
85 ibid.
86 ibid.
87 J.L. Maxwell, *Half a Century of Grace*. London: S.U.M., 1954.
88 SUM Archives Jos Field Station Reports Du and Forum 1920/21.
89 P.B. Clarke, Birom Woman Evangelist. Vo Gyang of Forum. In E. Isichei (ed.), *Varieties of Christian Experience in Nigeria*. London and Basingstoke: Macmillan, 1982: 163–77.
90 J.L. Maxwell, op.cit.
91 B. O'Brien, Marriage Among the Birom. Ph.D., Rome, 1973.
92 'The Lightbearer'. *Journal of the SUM IV* (4), June 1907, p. 203.
93 R. Hickey, OSA, *Heralds of Christ to Borno*. Jos, 1978, pp. 29 ff.
94 ibid., and P.B. Clarke, The Religious Factor in the Development Process. In Nigeria: A Socio-historical Analysis. *Genève-Afrique*, **XVIII** (1979): 45 ff.
95 I. Linden, The Children of the Israelites in Northern Nigeria: Islam and Change in Nigeria, 1850–1918. *Seminar Proceedings*, Centre of African Studies, University of Edinburgh, 1979, pp. 75–94.
96 E.P.T. Crampton, *Christianity in Northern Nigeria*. Zaria: Gaskya Press, 1975: 115.

5

The Christian missionary movement during the colonial era in former French West and Equatorial Africa and former Portuguese West Africa

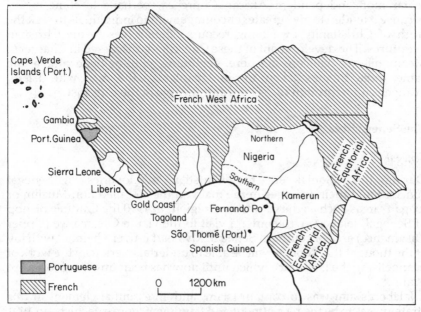

III   French and Portuguese influence in West Africa, 1914

While there were similarities there were also differences in the way Christianity developed and in the type of Christianity that emerged in the different colonial spheres of influence in West and Equatorial Africa during the colonial era. In the ex-French territories, as in some of the former British colonies, great emphasis was placed on the race with Islam in a bid to win over the traditional religionists. There was also in both cases a development in Christian missionary thinking on the role and importance, indeed indispensability, of the catechist. What was somewhat different, however, was the role played by the schools in the work of spreading Christianity. In the former French territories colonial government legislation made the school approach to evangelisation more problematic and therefore less widely used than in the former British colonies. The situation, of course, differed from one territory to another and from one period to another depending on the decrees enacted and the attitudes, needs and concerns of the governor general and the governors of each territory.

In the previous chapter, it was noted that there were differences in the way Christianity was spread and also in the type of Christianity that emerged in the different territories. A more uniform, dogmatic and less evangelical and scriptural form of Christianity characterised the former French and Portuguese territories where Catholic missionaries were for the most part the only Christian missionaries. In the British colonies where innumerable Protestant Churches and the Roman Catholic Church emphasised different aspects of Christian belief and practices, Christianity was a much more diversified phenomenon. It also gave rise to far more independent African Churches, perhaps to some extent because it tended to give greater encouragement to individuals to seek the truth of Christianity by having recourse themselves to the Christian Scriptures. The development of these Churches is discussed in Chapter 6. Meanwhile we will consider here, beginning with the Senegambia, the same three themes taken up in Chapter 4: the race with Islam, evangelisation through the school and the role of the catechist.

The Senegambia

Senegal

During the colonial era the Christian missionaries in Senegal concentrated their activities in the main on the so-called non-Muslim or 'pagan' areas such as the Casamance region. In 1910 the Catholic Bishop of Senegal, Jalabert, wrote after a visit to the Haute Casamance (Upper Casamance) area of southern Senegal 'My heart is overwhelmed with joy at the thought that soon *we* will be able to undertake seriously the work of evangelising the Diola race which until now has been unwilling to accept Islam'.[1]

Jalabert's aim was to contain Islam, and an essential element in this strategy was to be the recruitment and training of more catechists. In 1901 there were only thirty-three Catholic missionaries working in Senegal, and the likelihood of there being sufficient numbers of indigenous clergy in the foreseeable future appeared very remote. There was, moreover, a certain disillusionment and disenchantment among European missionaries with indigenous clergy. The latter were said to be incapable of administration and of positive action except when under orders, of being over pre-occupied with material and temporal concerns 'since their religious duties do not give them enough money for the upkeep of their dependents' and, moreover, they were far from being 'prophets in their own country'.[2] This explains more about the methods of training (see Chapter 3, pp. 77 ff.) indigenous clergy, than it does about the indigenous clergy themselves, and smacks very much of the same attitudes and prejudices found among other missionaries at this time, for example among some of the CMS missionaires in the Niger Delta (see Chapter 3, pp. 66 ff.). The shortage of both European and indigenous clergy and government measures that aimed at imposing a secular education system in Senegal and throughout French and Equatorial West Africa all posed serious problems for the Christian missions and indigenous clergy, and made the role of the catechist even more crucial.

After 1903, missionaries in Senegal and some other areas of French West Africa had little choice but to place less emphasis on the school approach to evangelisation. A decision to secularise or laicise all education in French West Africa was taken in Paris in 1903. This decision was implemented in a modified form in Senegal in 1904. In theory it meant that in Senegal, and elsewhere in French-occupied West Africa, only lay people would be allowed to teach in public, government-supported schools, and that while certain missionary societies would be allowed to retain their 'private schools', such as schools for the teaching of the catechism and the training of the clergy, these schools would not receive any financial support from the state.[3]

Different missionary societies responded in different ways to this decision by the French government. While the teaching Order, the Brothers of Ploërmel, reacted by handing over their schools to lay people and leaving Senegal, the Sisters of St Joseph of Cluny and other societies simply closed their schools, retained possession of the premises, and within a short space of time were once again admitting students, albeit without permission from the Administration. Other 'clandestine' and 'private schools' run by missionaries continued to function in Senegal, Benin (Dahomey), the Ivory Coast and elsewhere. In fact, by the outbreak of the Second World War about 15 per cent of the school population of French West Africa was attending schools run by the mission societies. However, government interference and the lack of personnel and resources created a certain reluctance on the part of these mission societies to become involved in education in the period between the First and Second World Wars.

Although the role played by the mission-run schools in the work of evangelisation in former French West Africa should not be underestimated it is nevertheless the case that they were of much less significance in this respect in the inter-war years than, for example, in Nigeria and other former British West African colonies. After the Second World War the Catholic missions in Senegal and elsewhere in former French West Africa stepped up their involvement in education.

Although strongly convinced of the necessity to train and employ more catechists, the Catholic missionaries were rather slow to do anything about this. Despite Jalabert's recommendation in 1910 that the number of catechists should be greatly increased, the catechist training centre at Ngasobil was not opened until 1916. Once this centre began to turn out catechists in ever-increasing numbers between 1920 and 1945 the number of catechists rose from a mere handful to 500. The difference they made was significant. In fact, between 1920 and 1945 the number of Catholics in Senegal increased by about 100 per cent. Ironically, some of the missionaries had been reluctant at first even to consider the deployment of more catechists. After assessing the situation in Senegal in 1921, one

Catholic missionary wrote to his superiors in Paris, 'The employment of catechists is not only desirable; it is necessary. No mission can make progress without them. And those missionaries who do not want them are as unpardonable as those who do not learn the language of the people to whom they are sent.'[5]

While in 1921 some missionaries still entertained serious doubts about the value of the catechists – it was said for example that they were not as effective as a European missionary, that they were expensive, that they did not persevere and that where they had been tried they had failed – by 1938 the superior of the Catholic missions in Senegal could write 'The catechists are our most valuable asset'.[6] Mission stations such as Oussouye in the Casamance in 1938 had two main churches and seventy-nine outstations, and only two priests. The twenty-six catechists employed by the central mission did most of the teaching of the basics of Catholicism while at the same time attending to the spiritual needs of the people in the outstations.[7] The situation was the same at Bignona, another flourishing mission in the Casamance, and elsewhere in Senegal.

During the post-war, pre-independence period 1945–60, the Catholic missions in Senegal turned their attention more to education, social action programmes to cater for the growing urban proletariat, and the indigenisation of the clergy. By 1960 the Catholic missions in Senegal were responsible for eighty-one primary schools, eight secondary schools, and several social and cultural centres.[8] A community of clerics was established in Dakar for the purpose of carrying out sociological research into industrial, urban, economic and social issues. Some progress towards the indigenisation of the clergy had also been made permitting a Senegalese, Mgr Thiandoum, to become Archbishop of Dakar in 1962. The vast majority of the clergy, however, were still expatriates, although in the women's religious orders a large proportion of the members were Senegalese.

Finally, perhaps one of the most important developments which began in the 1950s and has continued since independence was the change in the thinking and attitude of Christians, both Catholic and Protestant, towards Islam.[9] Competition and rivalry began to give way to a search for ways in which Christians and Muslims might co-operate and this search provided the impetus for Christians and Muslims to join together in the establishment and administration of the Service Oecumenique d'Entraide (Ecumenical Centre for Mutual Aid) at Bopp, Dakar, in the 1950s. The Centre seeks to provide people, whatever their religious faith or lack of it, with assistance in the fields of education, health and culture. This change in the Christian attitude and approach to Islam will be explored further in Chapter 8.

The main Christian denomination in Senegal, and throughout French West Africa is the Roman Catholic Church, as in France. In Senegal and most of French-speaking West Africa in ordinary conversation the words Catholic and Christian are interchangeable. There are, however, as we have seen (see Chapter 3, pp. 78–9), other Christian denominations in Senegal. In addition to the Protestant Evangelical Missionary Society from Paris, which today comprises the Protestant Churches of France which have come together in the French Evangelical Association for Apostolic Action (DEFAP), there is also the Worldwide Evangelical Crusade which arrived in Senegal from Britain in 1935. After the Second World War Pentecostalist Churches from the United States, such as the Assemblies of God, began operations in the country using radio broadcasts as their main instrument of evangelisation. But most of these Churches arrived after the country had been almost entirely islamicised and consequently their combined membership of around 1,000 is small when compared with the estimated 120,000 members of the Roman Catholic Church, which of course has had a much longer history in Senegal.

The Gambia

The history of Christianity in The Gambia, as far as numerical growth is concerned, resembles very much that of Senegal in this period. In the 1890s Catholic missionaries abandoned their attempts to convert Muslims, but the Methodists continued with their efforts in this direction. Their task was made even more difficult when the government decided to establish a Muslim school in Banjul (Bathurst) in 1903, thus indirectly depriving the missionaries of one important means of converting Muslim children to Christianity.

In the protectorate most Muslims simply refused to allow their children to attend mission-run schools. It was not in fact until the late 1920s when the government opened Armitage School at Georgetown and left religious education in the hands of the local Muslim teachers that Muslim parents in the protectorate felt confident about sending their children to school. With the creation of such schools as Armitage, which provided among other things a pool of recruits for junior posts in the administration, mission schools were, at one time, in danger of having to close down.

By the 1930s the Methodist missionaries had decided to abandon their aggressive approach to Muslims, and a policy of appeasement was adopted instead. A great deal of effort was made from then on to create an atmosphere of mutual tolerance and respect between the two, for example by exchanging gifts at feast days. Incidentally and somewhat ironically one of the effects of this policy of appeasement was to attract an increasing number of Muslim children to mission schools.

The Catholic mission for its part strengthened its appeal in the 1930s, and especially in 1934 during the cholera epidemic, by providing medical care for people irrespective of their religious affiliation. And from this moment on the Catholic Mission became the largest Christian church in The Gambia with a membership of about 8,000 at independence in 1970. By this time there were still no indigenous Catholic priests, the mission being run entirely by expatriate clergy, Gambian and expatriate sisters, and a large number of catechists. Moreover most of the Catholics, and the Christians as a whole, were descendents of the Akus, the freed slaves (see

Chapter 3, pp. 79–80). Since the Catholic Church continued to cling to the old liturgical traditions and to Latin as the language of worship, the image of a foreign Church was allowed to persist at a time of increasing nationalist sentiment.

A hundred and fifty years of missionary activity in The Gambia produced a Christian community of about 10,000, while in the same period Islam, admittedly starting from a wider base, had forged ahead to become the religion of the vast majority of the country's inhabitants.

Mauritania

The population of Mauritania which lies to the north of Senegal is virtually 100 per cent Muslim.[10] Under the 1961 constitution it is stated that Islam is the religion of the Mauritanian people. Since the beginning of the twentieth century Catholic missionaries, based at St Louis in Senegal until the 1960s, have been serving the mainly expatriate, both French and African, Christian communities living and working in Nouakchott, Nouadhibou, Atar, Zouerate, Kaedi and elsewhere. There has been little or no attempt to convert the local Muslim population. In addition to carrying out their pastoral and religious functions among the Christian communities and the provision of such educational services as adult literacy classes the missionaries see their task primarily as one of silent witness to the Christian faith, regarding their own presence and that of the Christian community in Mauritania as a sign of the Kingdom of God.[11]

Guinea (Conakry)

Christian missions had been established in what is today the Republic of Guinea prior to the formal colonization of that country by France in the 1890s. A Catholic mission was opened by the Holy Ghost Society at Boffa in Lower Guinea, to the north of the capital Conakry in 1877, in response to a demand made by the brother of the ruler of Rio Pongo.[12] From the outset, the Catholic missionaries concentrated their activities on Lower Guinea and in particular on the Soussou (also written Sosso or Susu) people of that part of the country. By 1890 a catechism and a part of the Gospels had been translated into Soussou and other works such as a Soussou-French dictionary were to follow.

In the first decade of the twentieth century as the colonial regime stamped its authority, often by military might, across Lower Guinea and the forest zone the Catholic mission extended its influence in these areas, opening mission stations among the Kissi at Brouadou and Mongo. One missionary described the French occupation of Guinea as 'a providential invitation' to missionaries to preach the Gospel there.[13] Not only in Guinea, but elsewhere in West Africa, missionaries, both Catholic and Protestant, appeared at one stage to justify the colonial occupation of the region, even by force of arms, on the grounds that it made their task – the preaching of the Gospel and the spread of 'civilisation' – easier to accomplish.

On occasion, moreover, the missionary himself was part of the so-called 'pacification' process. For example, at the outbreak of the First World War when the Kissi, Toma and other peoples of Guinea were about to stage another revolt against French rule, the mission at Mongo intervened and played an important, albeit indirect part, in the containing and suppression of the uprising.[14] Some of those displaced and dispossessed in this and other uprisings occasioned by the French conquest and the local resistance that it invited were settled in mission-run Christian villages such as the one at Pakédou near Mongo. The intention was to turn them into Christian evangelists but this approach was soon abandoned (Chapter 3, pp. 69–70). These villages, however, often proved to be a considerable asset to the missions by providing a readily available work force for the development of the coffee, cocoa and mango plantations in and around Mango, which proved to be an important source of income for the local Christian community.

During this period the Catholic Church opened a number of mission stations in Upper Guinea, for example at Siguiri, Kouroussa and Kankan in an attempt to evangelise the Malinke.[15] But it was in the south especially, among the Toma, Guerze and Manon in the Nzérékore district in the forest zone that the Catholic mission made most progress, though even here the progress was slow. By 1960 the majority of the 25,000 Catholics in Guinea were in this area.[16]

Part of the explanation for this slow progress lies in the fact that the missionaries do not appear to have made the best use of the catechist system until the 1930s. Although statistics do not provide conclusive proof they nevertheless lend some support to this view. In the Brouadu mission in 1903 the number of catechumens – that is, people preparing for baptism – increased threefold between 1925 and 1945, an increase roughly proportionate to the increase in the number of catechists in the mission over the same period.[17] And with the employment of more catechists the same or similar increases occurred in the number of catechumens in the districts of Kankan and Nzérékore over the same number of years.[18] Bishop LeRouge, responsible for the Catholic missions in the Ivory Coast, had come to realise by the 1930s that catechists were, to use his own word, 'indispensable'.

LeRouge also concerned himself with the training and formation of an African clergy, but with little success. The first indigenous Catholic priest was not ordained until 1940, and by 1960 there were only six Guinean priests in all.[19] A notion shared by LeRouge and other Catholic missionaries on the formation of an African clergy was that future African priests required a long and arduous training during which they would be introduced to and would gradually internalise values, attitudes, and ways of thinking and behaviour that were considered appropriate, regardless of whether these were relevant to the task in hand.

As LeRouge noted, the system of training indigenous priests in Guinea was exactly the same as that in France except for the fact that it took longer – from fifteen to seventeen years – in order to make sure that those being formed had the 'right' attitudes. It was a test of perseverance and stamina, applied to people who were considered to be unpredictable, and who needed in LeRouge's view to wage a constant battle lasting for many years against their 'disorderly' and 'wayward' tendencies. LeRouge wrote 'it is serious proof of a vocation if a student stays the course'.[20] Moreover, LeRouge's main concern was not so much that African priests should be equipped to work among ordinary people in the rural areas but rather that they be given a complete intellectual formation: 'they will have to mix with the lay élite – doctors and so on – and will have to be able to hold their own'.[21]

LeRouge believed, like so many others, that he had time on his side. He did not go all out for growth. In fact he was perhaps a little suspicious of rapid results. Catholicism he believed was not an easy option even at the best of times and in the case of people 'steeped in paganism', as he put it, stronger proof was needed of sincerity and commitment, lest people should slip back into 'paganism', or turn to Islam.

According to LeRouge Islam was the main obstacle to the christianisation of Guinea. He was so convinced of this that he even went so far as to admit that his great adversaries the Protestant missionaries, such as the Seventh Day Adventists who arrived in Guinea in the early 1920s from the United States, might indirectly be able to do some good for Catholicism by holding back the forward march of Islam. LeRouge wrote: 'The Protestants may help to prevent some tribes from becoming Muslims and then it will be easier for us to recover these converts to Protestantism than to convert Muslims'.[22] Of course, all of this, like so much else, would depend on whether or not there were sufficient funds to increase the number of catechists and pay them a decent salary. The salaries paid to catechists were, in LeRouge's view, 'derisory' when compared with those received by others with similar qualifications who worked for the administration. And this made the situation of the catechist in the society at large intolerable.[23]

In the 1940s Catholic missionaries in Guinea were still pointing to Islam as the principal obstacle in their way and explaining that this was the reason why they concentrated their activity in the regions inhabited by the Toma and the other largely non-Muslim inhabitants in parts of the south. By this time any hope of progress in Kankan and other Muslim strongholds had been virtually abandoned.

What the Catholic Church had built up in Guinea by the 1940s and 1950s was a number of relatively isolated Christian communities, the Christian villages being among the best examples of this. Of course, factors such as language, culture and geography on occasion made integration difficult even among Christians. There were cases where, for example, parents of Toma Christian children refused to allow the latter to marry Christians from other ethnic groups, and the missionaries agreed not to insist on this.[24]

There were instances, however, when the Catholic Church intervened decisively in an attempt to determine the way matters developed, for example in post-Second World War social and political affairs of the country. LeRouge was never very keen on having too many Catholic intellectuals for the simple reason that they might prove to be 'dangerously' critical of both the civil and ecclesiastical authorities.[25] He also opposed at first the proposal for a Christian-based trade union movement, and then only gave his approval for it in 1946 when he realised that it might provide a counterweight to the socialist-orientated CGT (General Confederation of Workers) introduced into the country from France in 1945.

LeRouge appears to have been opposed to anything that might be construed as socialism and in 1943 even went as far as closing down a study circle organised by one of his priests for the purpose of examining the social teaching of the Catholic Church. Sekou Touré, the late President of Guinea, was a member of the circle and after its closure decided, along with others, to frequent the discussion groups which considered in-depth Marxist analyses and interpretations of social, political and economic change.[26] LeRouge's move against the study circle proved counter productive.

In the 1950s, believing the PDG (Guinea Democratic Party) to be Communist-inspired, some of the missionaries became directly involved in politics advising Christians to vote for certain candidates rather than others, while at the same time refusing to speak out openly in favour of independence. But they lost out, even in areas where Catholics were relatively numerous and where the candidate was a Catholic. For example, in the 1954 legislative elections in Macenta Sekou Touré managed to defeat the Catholic candidate Samoe Gnankoï. The opposition between the Catholic Church and the PDG was to continue into the independence era. In 1967 all European missionaries were expelled from the country, and this left the Catholic Church with only eight indigenous priests. The situation, however, immediately improved when a group of thirteen African clergy from Benin (Dahomey), Upper Volta, Togo and Senegal were allowed to enter the country in the service of the Catholic Church.

The Catholic Church's relations with the colonial government in Guinea were not always harmonious either. The nature of Church-State relations in the colonial era in Guinea depended to a great extent on the attitudes and ideas of particular Church leaders and governors. According to some scholars Guinea was a veritable hotbed of freemasonry, particularly during the governorship of Poiret (1916–29), and this did not meet with the approval of the Catholic Church.[28] But in the 1930s LeRouge wrote of 'the excellent relations between Church and state' in Guinea.[29]

In Guinea by 1960 there were an estimated 25,000 Catholics out of a population of over three million. Islam was by far and away the dominant religion. The influence of Catholicism cannot be gauged, however, from a consideration of its numerical strength. As one Guinean observer has pointed out the Catholic Church, though it had failed to show much respect and tolerance for the customs of the country, had nevertheless contributed in a positive way to its educational, social and economic development and for this reason many Guineans, whether Catholics or not and whatever their political views, recognise and appreciate its performance in these areas.[30] In Chapter 7 we will consider how the Catholic Church coped in Guinea after the expulsion of the European missionaries in 1967.

Mali

In contact with Islam since the eleventh century,[31] Mali formed a large part of the Segu-Tokolor empire founded by Al-hajj Umar Tall and destroyed by the French in the 1890s.[32] During the colonial era the French named this large, predominantly Muslim though sparsely populated area, the Soudan.

Catholic missionaires of the Holy Ghost Society began working among the Bambara of Mali in the late 1880s (see Chapter 3, pp. 76–7) and by 1895 the White Fathers had reached Bamako (at that time a small village), which by the 1920s had become the centre of the colonial administration in the former French Soudan. In the early years of this century the White Fathers took over the missions opened by the Holy Ghost Society, and established others at Segou, San, Mopti, Gao, Timbucktu and elsewhere, and like their predecessors they were confident that they would be able to win over the non-Muslim peoples, in particular the Bambara.

Initially, the school was regarded as an important means of evangelisation and schools were opened at Timbucktu (1895) and close to and in Segou in 1896.[33] These schools, however, made little headway. The school at Timbucktu started with only five students and by 1907 when the White Fathers closed down their mission at Timbucktu there had never been more than fifty students on the register during any one school year.[34] The colonial administration was convinced that the problem of recruitment arose from the fact that the school was situated in a strongly Muslim area and was regarded by the people as an instrument of Christian evangelisation. The missionaries for their part, though they intended to use the school system for purposes of conversion, believed that the local people turned against the school at Timbucktu because they saw no good reason why their children should learn French and, further, because they were persuaded that the teaching of French was a device used by the colonialists in order to alienate their children from their own society. It would appear that this, if not a more important reason, was at least as important as the religious reason given above for the failure of the school at Timbucktu.[35]

The Segou schools suffered a similar fate to the one at Timbucktu. Very few pupils had been enrolled during the years from 1896 to 1904, and with the implementation of the laicisation policy in 1904 the schools were reduced to little more than centres for the teaching of Christian doctrine and some basic agricultural theory and method. These developments were not unwelcome as far as the missionaries were concerned. Obliged both to teach French and to teach *in* French prior to 1904, after that date, since their schools were no longer public schools but private, unassisted institutions, they were able to teach in the local language and to concentrate on religion and agriculture, leaving aside subjects such as French which they believed had a corrupting, demoralising influence on the students.

The White Fathers in Mali in the early years of this century, like the CMS missionaries in Nigeria and some colonial officials, wanted to isolate the local people from what they saw as the demoralising influence of western secular subjects such as French and English. There was always the fear on the part of some missionaries that people who were too highly educated would desert the work of the mission for better pay and conditions in the administration, or become rebellious and critical of their authority. On the other hand, some colonial officials, both French and British, were worried that the mission schools could create problems by, for example, spreading 'subversive' ideas such as the notion that all men were equal, thereby blurring the distinction they wished to preserve between Europeans and Africans. Lugard in Nigeria – and he was not the only colonial official to express this kind of concern – warned the missionaries not to preach the equality of Europeans and Africans, for it was an idea which 'however true from a doctrinal point of view is apt to be misapplied by people in a low state of development and interpreted as an abolition of class distinction'.[36]

Anything that tended to obliterate or even blur the distinction between Europeans and Africans or that tended to undermine white superiority was seen, especially in the early days of colonial rule, as an attack on the very foundations of colonialism. For example, the recruitment and deployment of black troops both with and against white troops in Europe during the First World War was opposed by many colonialists from France, Britain, Belgium and Germany on the grounds that this would, by exposing Africans at first hand to the disunity, division, and weaknesses of the Europeans, undermine their 'respect' for the latter's authority and as a result weaken the European grip over the colonies.[37] Necessity, however, won the day and hundreds of thousands of West Africans, the majority from former French West Africa, fought on the European front during the First World War.[38]

It was among the Bambara of Segou and elsewhere, as we have already noted, that the Catholic missionaries hoped to make their biggest impact. Segou itself was, in the early years of this century, a small town with about 10,000 inhabitants, almost all of whom were Muslims. The missionaries therefore moved about in the surrounding rural areas visiting numerous agricultural settlements or villages consisting of between 150 and 200 people and inhabited by the so-called 'pagan' Bambara. Full of optimism, the head of the Catholic mission wrote in 1902 of the situation in Segou and beyond:

> Now the momentum is everywhere; from the Niger to the Bani Rivers the indigenous people are asking for instruction; they call the missionaries to their villages and show an extraordinary eagerness to attend catechism classes. Forty-two villages regularly receive visits from missionaries, priests and sisters, and catechists . . . . The village chiefs themselves, although polygamous, are

involved . . . . In the last three or four months the number of those who listen to us has increased from 1,000 to 4 or 5,000.[39]

This optimism was shared by many missionaries, including those at the mission at Patyana in the Banankourou area by the Bani River. Catechists were installed in the Bambara villages and missionaries made regular tours of the area. Apparently hostile to Islam, the Bambara, it was hoped, would soon convert to Catholicism *en masse*. However, as was so often the case, this optimism had almost disappeared by 1910. By then the Catholic Church had ceased to expand and had decided to cut down on its commitments. Bambara interest and enthusiasm for Catholicism had waned, and this was in part due to the misguided policy adopted by the missions towards Bambara customs such as circumcision. The missionaries demanded that the Bambara abandon the rite of circumcision on the grounds that this was a Muslim practice and therefore signified their adherence to Islam. Circumcision had little if any religious significance for the Bambara, who refused to comply with the demands of the missionaries. The end result was that the Catholic Church became a Church of young children: 'Only the young children came to the mission and the majority left at the moment of puberty, the demarcation line between these two "classes" being clearly marked by the rite of circumcision'.[40] And according to the same source, 'Throughout the land of the Bambara it began to be said that Christianity was a religion for children'.[41] A similar situation developed, albeit for somewhat different reasons, on the Jos Plateau in Nigeria (see Chapter 4, pp. 111–12).

Some of the other factors that contributed to the stagnation and even decline of the Catholic missions among the Bambara were the lack of financial resources, the shortage of personnel made worse by the famine of 1903 during which a number of priests died, the long distances to be travelled to reach a mere handful of people in this sparsely populated region, and the introduction by the colonial administration of what was in practice a system of indirect rule. Recognising that while very little French was spoken compared with Arabic the administration used both Arabic and French as official languages. It also decided, given the shortage of qualified European personnel, to make use of Muslim officials such as *qadis* (judges) even in non-Muslim areas, thereby extending indirectly the influence of Islam. Furthermore Muslim institutions established during the era of the Segu-Tokolor empire were left in place until such time as they could be replaced, and this included Qur'anic schools.

The Catholic mission also experienced problems with its catechists on whom it relied so heavily. Very poorly paid, some of the catechists who had learnt to read, write and speak French left the service of the mission for that of the administration. Without catechists very little could be done; it was they who did virtually all the work of preparation and instruction for baptism in the outstations, in addition to organising and leading the worship on Sundays and feast days.

During the First World War many of the European missionaries were obliged to serve in the armed forces, and at a time when there was considerable resistance to Europeans and to European colonialism, the catechists did much to keep the Catholic mission functioning. During the inter-war years (1918–39), the situation began to improve. The number of missionaries – both priests, nuns, and catechists – increased considerably, and communications and means of transort improved dramatically. In the early 1920s the rail link between Dakar and Bamako was completed, and in 1932 another stretch of railway cutting across from Abidjan in the west reached Bobo-Dioulasso in the east. These developments and the introduction of the motorcycle made a vast difference to the scope of missionary work, and to the pace and efficiency, especially with regard to the deployment of personnel, with which it could be carried out.

Between 1918 and 1939 the Catholic Church in Mali opened several new mission centres, and began to take seriously the question of training an indigenous clergy. The medical work of the mission, especially among lepers, was also extended. By the outbreak of the Second World War there were an estimated 6,000 Catholics in Mali compared with less than 2,000 in 1919. But in 1940 there were still only two indigenous priests and those priests after some fifteen years of training had acquired, in the words of one missionary 'the capacity to think in French', an aptitude which made working in their own language something of a difficulty.[42]

Between 1945 and 1960 the number of indigenous clergy rose from two to eight, and the number of Catholics from just under 7,000 to about 18,500. The growth rate since independence has been even more remarkable, rising from 18,500 in 1960 to around 55,000 in 1980.[43] Some of the reasons for this growth in recent times will be discussed in Chapter 7.

Although their efforts were at first and for some time devoted to converting the Bambara, the Catholic and Protestant missions also had better results among the less islamicised Bobo, Wala and Dogon peoples of Mali in the regions of San and Mopti. Churches, both Catholic and Protestant, became active throughout the country. For example, the Protestant Gospel Missionary Union (GMA) and the Evangelical Church of Mali, two of seven Protestant Churches in Mali, though they concentrated their efforts on the south-eastern region when they first arrived in the early 1920s, now have Bible schools for training church leaders in many parts of the country. But Mali remains a predominantly Muslim country with Christians forming less than 2 per cent of the population. In Burkina Faso Christianity is numerically and in other ways much larger and more influential.

Burkina Faso (Upper Volta)

In many respects the development of Christianity in Burkina Faso resembled that of Mali and other areas of the Western Soudan formerly occupied by the French. Much of the territory was sparsely populated and communications until the 1920s were poor. There were, however, a number of differences, one of them being the fact that Islam was much more thinly spread in Burkina Faso than in these other areas. Further, many of the Muslims in Burkina Faso were Hausa, or Diola or Fulani, 'strangers' that is, from outside the territory.[44]

Since they were under the direct control and authority of the Catholic mission in Mali the Catholic missionaries in Burkina Faso adopted much the same approach to Islam and the same methods of evangelisation. In Mali, as we have seen, the missionaries sought out the non-Muslim peoples, in particular those Bambara who still adhered to the traditional religion, hoping that by converting them they would halt the progress of Islam which they considered to be the major obstacle to evangelisation. It was a question, as far as the mission authorities were concerned, of going into those areas where Muslims were few in number. One of the reasons why the mission in Timbucktu was closed down in 1907 was the fact that it was in an area heavily populated by Muslims.[45]

Burkina Faso in the view of the Catholic missionaries was just such a place. They were convinced that the Mossi in the Wagadugu (Ouagadougou) region were so hostile to Islam, for historical reasons, and more importantly because they themselves drank alcohol, that they would never become Muslims.[46] As for Christianity, the missionaries were persuaded that the Mossi would regard it as a religion of liberation, since it had entered their territory just behind the French troops. As one missionary wrote 'The Christian religion has had the immense advantage of appearing as the religion of the liberators'.[47] The manner in which the Catholic missionaries entered Wagadugu in 1900 indicates quite clearly that they not only approved of the colonisation and 'pacification' of the region by France but regarded their association with these twin processes as being of benefit to the cause of Christianity. This is borne out by a description written by a missionary of the entry of the first Catholic missionary to Wagadugu. It reads:

> Bishop Hacquard (the superior of the Catholic missions in the Western Soudan) arrived at Wagadugu via Sabtenga, and made his solemn entry. Seven or eight kilometres from the town horsemen joined his caravan . . . and then the Captain Commandant, with his officers, arrived to meet him 'to show to the Africans' the Captain said, 'how we as well as them know how to honour our religious leaders' . . . . At Wagadugu there was a solemn high mass for Lieutenant Grivard [a French officer killed in the resistance to French 'pacification'][48]

Bishop Hacquard was very impressed by all of this and commenting afterwards on the prospects for the Catholic mission at Wagadugu wrote: 'I am fully satisfied that here we will probably have the best mission field in the whole of the Vicariate (which covered virtually the whole of the Western Soudan).'[49] Of course, Mossi resistance to Islam did not imply, any more than did that of the non-Muslim Bambara in Mali, that they were prepared to accept foreign rule or automatically to abandon their religion and way of life for Christianity.

The first Catholic mission to be established in Burkina Faso among the Mossi was opened at Koupéla, some 150 kilometres south-east of Wagadugu, in 1900. The mission at Wagadugu followed in 1901. Schools were started in both missions and these schools, though run by the White Fathers, were official schools in the sense that they were under the control and direction of the colonial administration. In practice, this meant that the schools were to be used as a vehicle for French penetration and as a consequence were expected to give considerable attention to the teaching of the French language. Three hours of each school day were given over to the teaching of French, and all conversation even during times of recreation had to be in French.[50]

Both schools enjoyed remarkable success in terms of recruiting students in the first two or three years after opening but then came the problems with the colonial administration over laicisation, and this led to their closure in 1906 as official or public schools. From this moment the schools were regarded as private establishments in which religion and the local language only were to be taught. As a consequence they became less attractive and the number of students attending declined appreciably. The missionaries were not unduly perturbed by the restrictions placed on their educational activity by the colonial administration after 1904, largely because they had never really wanted to provide a general education. To them the school was first and foremost a means of evangelisation, and the situation in which they found themselves after 1904 gave them the opportunity to use it for this purpose, providing, of course, they had the finances to do so which was not always the case.

The Catholic mission, nevertheless, felt that it was being victimised by a pro-Muslim colonial administration. For while the administration was busy closing down its schools, taking away its students and refusing it financial assistance for its educational work, it was at the same time raising Arabic to the status of an 'administrative language' second only to French and appointing Muslims as chiefs and judges even in non-Muslim areas. However in 1911 Governor-General William Ponty, who regarded every Muslim official and teacher as a potential threat to French rule, went some way to reversing what the missions saw as the pro-Muslim policy of the French administration. In that year Ponty ordered that local chiefs be appointed in their own area, and put an end to the use of Arabic as the second language of the administration.

Before the outbreak of the First World War the Catholic mission was attempting to expand its activities to include, in addition to the Mossi, the Voltaic peoples inhabiting the region between the Black and Red Volta Rivers. But the war created further problems for the mission, depriving it of a number of missionaries which entailed the closure of several mission stations. The missionaries who were left became involved in the drive to recruit African soldiers for the war effort and this left them little time for evangelisation. It also led to reprisals against the mission itself from those who resisted the attempts being made to forcibly and brutally recruit them into the army. At least two mission stations in Burkina Faso were destroyed during uprisings sparked off by recruitment campaigns. To make matters worse, many people not only began to stay away from the missions out of mistrust, but also to avoid all contact with the missionaries. For example, in 1915 at the mission at Reo among the Lele,

Nouna and other Voltaic groups, known collectively to the Mossi as Gourounsi, it was reported that the number of people attending the central mission, and the outstations in the villages, had fallen considerably and that this was due to recruitment.[51]

After the war the situation improved. The school opened at Pabre in 1915 provided the missions with some recruits for the ministry and a continuous if small number of catechists. Most of the catechists were to come from the training centre at Guilongou, situated to the north-east of Wagadugu. The catechist course at Guilongou lasted for four years and the language of the Mossi, Môre, was the medium of instruction. By 1939 there were over 250 catechists in Burkina Faso, the majority of whom worked in the rural areas instructing people in the Catholic faith and preparing them for baptism.

The fact that many of the catechists were young posed a number of problems in a society where respect and authority were given in the main to the older members. The poor pay of the catechists further increased the problem of authority. But there were some benefits, such as exemption from the indigénat, the system whereby certain offences were created and summarily punished by the administration. The indigénat was not abolished until after the Second World War.

Missionary activity continued to be confined for the most part to the Mossi and the peoples south of Wagadugu. The more northern and eastern parts of the country were left virtually untouched. Both the shortage of personnel, and some of the methods of evangelisation employed made it impossible to expand into these areas. Missionaries and catechists, both of whom were relatively thin on the ground, spent a great deal of their time fighting polygamy and other traditional customs and practices, in the hope of making what they termed 'solid conversions'. Christians who became polygamists were regarded as public sinners and in addition to being confined to a corner at the back of the church were not allowed to act as godparents, or contribute in any way to the mission, and were even refused burial. Missionaries tended to concentrate, as was the case in Nigeria and elsewhere, on the formation of a Christian élite which it was hoped would become for others, including Muslims, a reference point and a clear, visible sign and proof of the benefits to be obtained from becoming a member of the Catholic Church. Some missionaries tended to evaluate success in terms of the numbers of Christians they had helped to acquire positions of status and responsibility.[52]

In Burkina Faso, as in other parts of West Africa, the period 1945–60 was one of relatively rapid expansion for the Christian missions, both among the Mossi and Dagari and others in the above-mentioned Voltaic regions to the south of Wagadugu. In contrast to the Mossi, the Voltaic peoples were not, for the most part, grouped together in centralised states or large chiefdoms. The area between the Black and Red Volta Rivers where many of these people lived was thinly populated and consisted for the most part of small villages. This, along with the fact that there were numerous dialects and different languages, made missionary work more complex and difficult than was the case among the Mossi. To the missionary the absence of states with a strong central authority and the social, cultural and political situation in general in the Volta region smacked of chaos and anarchy. As one wrote: 'There is no social or political authority, no large ethnic groups, (only) small pockets of (different) people all with their own language . . . . There are twenty-three in Bobo-Dioulasso . . . a great problem for the missions.'[53] Nevertheless, through the work of catechists in particular, significant numbers of the Dagari and other peoples of the region converted to Christianity.

By 1960 the Catholic Church in Burkina Faso was in a much stronger position, at least in so far as size of membership is concerned, than in Mali, and a number of other former French West African colonies such as Guinea (Conakry), Niger and Senegal. This to some extent can be attributed to the early development of a well-planned programme for the training and employment of catechists and, to a lesser extent, of indigenous clergy and to the fact that throughout much of the country, Islam had very little influence.

Islam began to expand much more widely and rapidly during the colonial era than previously, a development which the Catholic missionaries attributed to the pro-Muslim policy of the administration. After a visit to former French West Africa in 1939 the Catholic bishop in charge of the White Fathers at the time commented, 'I must confess that I am worried by the progress being made by Islam in French West Africa under the benevolent eye of France.'[54] Until the 1950s 'official' Christianity in Burkina Faso not only lamented the progress of Islam but was also reluctant to consider any form of dialogue. However, a quite dramatic change in attitude did begin to take place around this time.[55]

Among the Protestant Churches working in Mali in this period (1890–1960) were the Assemblies of God and the Sudan Interior Mission (SIM). The former entered the country in 1919 and since then has established a wide network of Sunday Schools, numerous training courses for church leaders and many publishing programmes. The SIM, beginning in 1930, concentrated on the Gurma region south-east of Wagadugu, and in a relatively short period of time made a considerable impact.

Niger

Occupied by France after stubborn and prolonged resistance Niger was governed for a time as a military territory. Among the first Christian missionaries to work in this region in the modern period were the Protestant SIM missionaries. Starting in 1923 this mission has been active ever since in the Maradi and Dogondoutchi areas in the south of the country. For the most part the SIM has concentrated on educational, medical and social schemes which include numerous dispensaries, a leprosarium at Maradi and a large hospital at Galmi. A number of other Protestant missionary societies, among them the Methodists, several Evangelical Churches and the Jehovah's Witnesses also became involved in missionary activity in this predominantly Muslim country in the colonial era.

The Catholic mission, although it took an interest in Niger from the very outset of colonial rule, only in the early 1930s began to establish a permanent base at Niamey, which replaced Zinder as the capital of the territory in 1926. By 1960 there were only a very few Christians (10,000) and the majority of these came originally from the Republic of Benin and Togo. The majority of the indigenous Christians were Zerma-Songhai from Dolbel and Hausa from Dogondoutchi. By 1980 the Christian population had risen to around 15,000, but less than 2,000 of these were local inhabitants of Niger. It is a country in which for many years now, co-operation and dialogue have characterised relations between the minority Christian population and the Muslim majority. The emphasis has been placed on what both religions have in common rather than on differences.

The Republic of Benin (Dahomey)

The early history of Christianity in the Republic of Benin, which after stout resistance was conquered by the French in the 1890s, was outlined in Chapter 3 (pp. 60–1). Missionary activity continued to be confined for the most part to the southern part of the country until the outbreak of the First World War in 1914. Apart from missions in the north at Fada N'Gourma and Kouandé opened in 1901, the rest of the Catholic missions established or restarted before 1914 – among them Atakpamé, Keta, Athiemé and Zagnanado, Abomey, Cotonou, Bohicon and Cové – were in the south-central area of the territory.[56]

Partly because the colonial administration had neither the resources nor the personnel and partly because of the positive if highly pragmatic attitude of the then governor, Liokard, the Catholic mission in Benin was at first encouraged to pursue an active role in education. By 1903 the Catholic missionaries of the Society of African Missions (SMA), assisted by a grant from the administration, was responsible for fifteen schools, attended by almost 1,700 students.[57] And even after the decision was taken in 1904 to implement the laicisation decree of the previous year the SMA struggled successfully to keep open their existing schools as private institutions, and in fact by 1912 had established five additional schools at Bohicon, Cové, Dohoua, Ekpé and Djefa.[58] Other schools were to be added later and in 1922, when a decree was issued forbidding the establishment of private schools in French West Africa, the authorisation of the governor of a colony, the Catholic mission in Benin was responsible for twenty-one schools of this sort. One of the largest and finest Catholic schools in the whole of former French West Africa was the school at Porto Novo where the attendance rose in the 1920s to over 1,000 students in any one year.

By this time the Catholic mission had begun to concentrate more of its efforts on the interior, establishing missions at Sokponta, Allada, Savé, Tchaourou, Azaourisse and elsewhere. The 1930s, 1940s and 1950s saw further expansion, this time into the more northerly districts of Fada

N'Gourma, Kandi, Natitingou, Parakou, Djougou, and even as far north as Banikouara. At independence in 1960 there were some fourteen Catholic mission stations and forty-five schools in northern Benin, and some 12,500 Catholics who were served by fourteen European priests and ninety-nine catechists.[59]

Although all the missionaries in the northern region were Europeans there was a relatively large number of indigenous priests in the south. The Catholic Church began training an indigenous clergy in 1913 and by 1961 there was almost an equal number of indigenous (fifty) and expatriate clergy (fifty-seven) in the country.[60] In addition there were some eighty-four indigenous nuns or sisters, some of whom were involved in running a leper colony, others in teaching in the secondary school for girls while others acted as counsellors to the women's section of the Organisation of Catholic Youth which aimed at bringing Catholicism to the masses. Catechists were also quite numerous, totalling 376 in 1961. Between 1890 and 1960 the Catholic population in Benin increased from 5,000 to 250,000, a faster growth than in any other former French West African colony.

Most of the Catholic population resided in the south of the country where there was less competition from Islam, and this might to some extent explain this relatively high rate of expansion. The many primary and five secondary schools run by the missions was also another important factor. In the southern and central areas of the country in particular the short distances between one town or village and another undoubtedly made evangelisation that much easier, as did the early formation of an indigenous clergy and the training and employment of numerous catechists.

Among the Protestant missionary societies the Methodists from Britain, the first Christian missionaries to enter the country in the nineteenth century (see Chapter 3, pp. 57 ff.), emerged as the largest during the period under discussion. They likewise concentrated their activity for the most part on the southern part of the country, and on the area from Anecho eastwards in particular.

Numerous Methodist churches were opened in the coastal towns of Porto Novo and Cotonou during the inter-war years (1918–39), and even further inland at Dossa-Zoume and Savé-Kilibo. During the Second World War in 1942 a mission was opened at Djougou in the north. The Methodists, like the Catholics although to a lesser extent, devoted a considerable amount of their energies to education, opening numerous primary schools and one secondary school. And from the 1920s they began to give serious attention to the formation of an indigenous clergy.

The Assemblies of God, another Protestant mission, entered Benin in 1946 and confined their activity almost entirely to the north-western part of the country, opening missions at Natitingou, Tanguieta, Boukoumbé and Kouandé areas. Growth was slow, the total number of conversions by 1960 amounting to less than 2,000. This was perhaps inevitable, since in an area where traditional religion was strong and Islam had some influence the Assemblies of God, a rather evangelical, fundamentalist type of Christian denomination, retained its policy of baptising adults only and relied solely on preaching as a means of evangelisation.

The Sudan Interior Mission (SIM), today part of the Evangelical Churches of West Africa (ECWA), entered Benin shortly after the Assemblies of God in 1947 and established itself mainly in the central and north-central areas of the country at Niki, Kandi, Djougou, Parakou, Sinendé and elsewhere. This mission devoted considerable time to medical work, education and the translation of the Bible into the various local languages. After producing a number of these translations the SIM reached the conclusion that, given the multiplicity of local languages, French was the most suitable and effective language of evangelisation.

In 1960 Christians, the vast majority of them Catholics, accounted for about 18 per cent of the population which then stood at just over two million; nearly 70 per cent were adherents of the traditional religion. The remaining 12 per cent were Muslims, who were to be found mainly among the Nago Yoruba in the south and the Fulani, Dendi and Bariba in the North. The fact that Muslims were relatively few in number meant that in Benin Christian missionaries devoted less of their time and energy to holding back Islam. Instead they focused their attention on Benin's traditional religions.

Togo

The course taken by Christianity in Togo during the period 1890–1960 was similar in many respects to the one in the Republic of Benin. Togo was a German colony from 1884 until the First World War when it was taken over by Britain and France. During the period of German rule Christian missionary activity was confined almost entirely to the south of the country. Prior to the German occupation of the country French Catholic missionaries had opened a mission at Agoué, but because of the possibility of conflict between themselves and the German administration, they left in 1892 and were replaced by German missionaries of the Society of the Divine Word. Although their activity was confined to the south of the country until 1912 these German missionaries with the assistance of returnees from Brazil provided the Catholic mission with a firm foundation before they were forced to leave the country in 1914. At the time of their departure there were over 20,000 Catholics in Togo.[61]

The first Protestant missions to be established in Togo in modern times were opened by Africans trained in mission schools in the Gold Coast, now Ghana. The Anecho Methodist mission was opened in 1870 in this way and was run by a catechist from Lagos from 1876 until the arrival at Anecho of the first European Methodist missionary in 1880. The German-based Bremen mission established itself in Lomé, the present-day capital of Togo, in 1893, and concentrated its efforts on the areas inhabited by the Ewe (now part of Ghana) while the Basel mission worked mainly among the Twi. The Bremen mission from very early on made a determined effort to train an indigenous clergy and this was to pay dividends when its

German missionaries were expelled from Togo during the First World War.

Before its departure from Togo the German administration, through the Christian missions, had developed an extensive educational system. Restricting their activities to a particular area assigned to them by the government the Bremen, Catholic and Methodist missionaries established a combined total of 307 elementary schools, six high schools, two of which were for the training of an indigenous clergy. The government itself was responsible for only two elementyary schools and three high schools, including an Agricultural College. Thus in 1914 there were 324 western-type schools in Togo staffed by 49 Europeans and 408 African teachers, and attended by 13,347 students.[62] The German system of education in Togo, like the French system in operation elsewhere in West Africa, was essentially assimilationist in that its primary aim was to turn Togolese into Germans. The missions, however, did not always lend their support to this policy, insisting in some cases on teaching through the medium of Ewe in the primary schools, on retaining the Christian character to which the government was at best indifferent, and on introducing English into the secondary school curriculum.

Education was for the most part confined to the south of the country, the north – and in particular those areas regarded by the administration as Muslim areas – being closed off to missionaries and other Europeans until 1912.

The expulsion of the German missionaries at the outbreak of the First World War had a profound impact on the development of Christianity in Togoland and in particular on the Bremen mission. This mission intended from the outset to establish a self-governing, self-supporting and self-propagating African Church (see Chapter 3, pp. 59–60). But as one writer points out, 'slow progress was made in the actual implementation of the intention until the First World War caused the removal of the missionaries'.[63]

After the First World War the United Free Church of Scotland took over responsibility for the Bremen mission in both British-controlled Togo and Ghana and pressed ahead with measures to strengthen the independence and autonomy various Bremen congregations had acquired during the war period. Although they retained control over the educational activity of the Church, the Scottish missionaries stressed from the early 1920s onwards that European missionaries would have to act, more so than was the case in the past, simply as advisers and accept the decrees of the Church Synod which was presided over by Africans. While some missionaries felt that this emphasis on African leadership was premature and were unable to accept it, an indigenous, Ewe-led Church emerged out of the Bremen mission, adopting the name of the Ewe Presbyterian Church in 1927.

By the early 1950s the Ewe Church, known from 1954 as the Evangelical Church of Togo, had taken over responsibility for educational and social as well as pastoral concerns. It was now fully responsible for, among other things, numerous primary schools, several secondary schools, hostels, clinics, social and literacy centres and an agricultural institution. In that part of Togo under French mandate Protestant missionaries of the Society of Missions in Paris provided the Bremen mission with assistance from the 1920s.

Relying heavily on its catechists, schools and youth workers, the Evangelical Church of Togo spread rapidly among the Ewe, especially in the Palimé district and more slowly among the rest of the population, although considerable headway was made among the Kabre who, from the 1930s, provided the bulk of the Church's catechists in the Lama-Kara area in the north. The Assemblies of God, however, have been the most active of the Protestant missions in the north since the 1950s. On their arrival from the Togo the Assemblies of God installed themselves at Dapango in the far north of the country and then at Mango (1950) and Bassari (1951). Assisted by catechists trained at Natitingou in the Republic of Benin, and relying on preaching as the principal method of evangelisation this Church which baptises adults only had attracted 1,500 adherents, about two-thirds of whom were baptised by the time of independence in 1960. The Evangelical Church of Togo with close on 37,000 members was by far the largest Protestant denomination in Togo, at this time, and this is still the case today.

The Catholic mission in Togo had established itself throughout the country by the time of independence in 1960. Its main strength, however, was in the south, and in and around Lomé in particular where there were an estimated 150,000 members of this church at independence. After making steady progress during the inter-war years, this mission saw a dramatic increase in membership after the Second World War from 91,878 baptised Catholics in 1945 to 214,114 in 1960. This clearly made it the largest Church in the country.

The progress made by the Catholic Church in Togo, though somewhat more even throughout the country, was very similar in other respects to that made in the Republic of Benin and for much the same reasons (see above, pp. 138–9). While the Protestant Churches tended to become less involved in education as time went on, the Catholic Church stepped up its activity in this sphere. In 1912 there were 163 Protestant compared to 181 Catholic schools in the country. But by the early 1970s the former were responsible for only 72 primary schools and one secondary school, whilst the number of schools run by the Catholic Church had by this time risen to 265, of which 236 were primary schools and 29 were secondary schools.

It would seem to be the case that in the Togolese context, as in others already referred to, the greater use made by the Catholic Church of the school approach to evangelisation goes a long way to explaining its more rapid growth rate. In the words of one historian, 'The Catholic advance has almost followed the school, an inducement for the young and symbol of prestige for parents'.[64]

The colonial regime in Togo was somewhat exceptional in the way it assisted financially and morally the growth of mission education. Between 1945 and 1960 Catholic secondary schools and institutions were established right across the country from Lomé in the south as far north as

Dapango. Moreover, from very early on, efforts were made to train an indigenous clergy and a sufficient number of catechists. The role of the 'traditional' catechist in the development of Catholicism in Togo was not as crucial as was the case elsewhere, the emphasis being more on schools and organisations such as the Young Christian Workers (JOC) movement and the Social Secretariat, both of which did remarkable work, especially among the displaced, uprooted inhabitants of the urban areas.

In Togo as in Benin the Christian missions had little competition from Islam which was confined in the main to Sokodé, Mango and Dapango in the north. Allegiance to the traditional religion, however, remained strong. Today there are still priests who offer regular sacrifice to the Ewe Supreme Being Mawu, regarded as mother, creator, judge and lawgiver, while Sakpata, the god of smallpox, and So, the god of thunder, also have their devotees. In 1960s the majority of Togolese were in fact adherents of the traditional religion, a phenomenon found elsewhere in West Africa, including the Republic of Benin and the Ivory Coast.

The Ivory Coast

After establishing a protectorate over Grand Bassam in 1842 the French set about extending their influence and control over the whole of the Ivory Coast following the Treaty of Berlin (Nov. 1884–Feb. 1885). In 1893 the Ivory Coast was declared a French Colony, but it was not until 1915 that the resistance movement was finally broken and the country declared 'pacified'.

Despite its largely unsuccessful attempts to establish itself in the Ivory Coast on previous occasions the Catholic Church returned there with a new sense of mission in the 1890s. And once again, as in Togo and Benin, it was mainly the French priests of the Society of African Missions (SMA) assisted by the Sisters of Our Lady of Apostles, who were responsible for Catholic missionary activity in the Ivory Coast in the earlier and indeed for the greater part of the colonial era. The Protestant missions did not make any serious attempt to evangelise the Ivory Coast until the early 1920s. The best known and most successful Christian evangelist in the Ivory Coast, whose activities benefited both Catholic and Protestant missions was the Liberian Prophet William Wade Harris (see Chapter 6, pp. 178 ff.).

Although it installed itself in Korhogo in the north of the country as early as 1905, the Catholic mission made most progress in the south, and in particular in the urban centres such as the capital Abidjan. During the 1890s and until after the First World War Catholic missionaries in the Ivory Coast were few in number, and of those who worked there during this period many died young, the yellow fever epidemics of 1899, 1902 and 1903 making thirty-two the average age of death. The average life span of the missionary greatly increased during the First World War the average age at death in this period rising from thirty-two to forty-nine years.[65]

The paucity of missionaries, the delay in training indigenous priests and the fact that missionaries were seen as agents of the administration, explain in large measure the slow growth of the Catholic Church in the Ivory Coast between 1895 and 1914. Called in by Governor Binger in 1895 the Catholic mission was entrusted by the administration with the task of education. It was to be one of the government's principal agents of 'civilisation', and for some time the mission willingly accepted this role. But after the decision to laicise the schools, a decision that began to affect the French West African colonies from 1904–5, the missionaries, while continuing to uphold many of the interests of France, began to take a more independent line of the government as far as the activities and organisation of the Catholic Church were concerned. As we shall see, it concentrated on opening mission stations in non-Muslim areas rather than running schools.

The view was quite widespread among Catholic missionaries that after a little hard work, tact and gentle persuasion the adherents of the traditional religions would flock into their missions. Some saw no need to confront the traditional religious systems head on and were somewhat more cautious and less direct in their efforts to undermine these systems than their Protestant counterparts. In fact, the Protestants attributed the greater success of the Catholics to the latter's easy-going, tolerant approach to traditional religion.[66] The Catholic Church, of course, was as determined as the Protestant Churches to make clear the distinction and the differences between Christianity and the traditional religions of the country, but it avoided for the most part the policy adopted by the Protestants and by the Prophet Harris of direct confrontation with the priests and devotees of these religions.

Nevertheless prior to 1914 there were very few conversions to Catholicism. But from around 1915 the situation began to change dramatically, and this was due to a considerable extent to the preaching of the Prophet Harris. The latter, as we have seen, entered the Ivory Coast in the latter part of 1913 and in the villages and towns along the coast he preached to the people telling them to abandon the traditional god and gods and to accept and worship none other than the god of the Christians. He burned the masks, amulets, religious objects and altars used by the traditional priests and convinced the people to accept baptism which, he maintained, would protect them from harm. Rather than simply undermining the traditional religion, leaving people with nothing or only a limited participation in a different, 'foreign' religion, Harris offered them a form of Christianity designed to cater for their worldly, everyday needs and expectations as much as anything else.

Harris's success was phenomenal and news of him reverberated along the coast of West Africa and into the interior.[67] His fame was so widespread and his following so large that the French colonial government came to see him as a possible threat to their authority and so expelled him from the country in 1914. Among those who benefited most from this expulsion were first the Catholic and later the Protestant missions. From 1915 Harris's converts began to enter what was until then a rather poorly attended and little sought-after Catholic mission. Only a few hundred strong in 1915, the number of those wanting to join the Catholic mission had increased to 8,000 by 1917, and to over 20,000 by 1922.[68] One Catholic missionary commented with reference to the impact of the Prophet Harris: 'What he did none of us would have been able to do, indeed because the methods were forbidden to us. That hallucinating man, who was also a charlatan, did, in barely three months, what we, ministers of Our Lord Jesus Christ were not even able to begin doing in twenty years.'[69]

Another Catholic missionary made the same point, saying that Harris's work 'helped the cause of Catholicism; "pagans" burned their idols and joined the catechumenate'.[70] He also described Harris's appearance on his arrival at Lahou in the Ivory Coast:

A very tall and ageing black, with his beard neatly trimmed. He was clothed completely in white and on his head he wore a white skull cap. He was accompanied by his two wives and one of his daughters, also dressed in white. He declared that he was sent by God and inspired by the angel Gabriel. In his right hand was a long cane topped by a cross like one sees in the popular representations of St John the Baptist. In his left hand there was a bible, resting on it a calabash used as a container for the baptismal water. And dangling from the same hand was another calabash containing seeds and covered with a net made of glass pearls and cowries. Beside him stood his two wives holding similar gourds. On entering a village he would summon the men and women and tell them to bring the sorcerers. Once the latter had arrived he would put his cane between their hands. Then he would look around at everyone, before adding: 'Now witness the power I have from God. You (the sorcerers) can no longer speak.' Immediately their tongues were tied.[71]

To the Catholic missionary this 'power' exercised by Harris over the 'sorcerers' was nothing more or less than hypnotism. Moreover, in their view he preached 'a neo-Christianity tinged with spiritualism'.[72] The content of his preaching according to the missionaries consisted for the most part in admonishing people not to drink alcohol, not to take their neighbours' belongings, not to worship idols, and to respect the Sabbath. He also explained to the people that they were allowed, like the Patriarchs, to have more than one wife. He would then ask his listeners if they accepted his message, and if the response was 'yes', he baptised them. Then after baptism Harris told his disciples 'to follow any Christian missionary they chose because there was no difference between them'.[73]

While, as we have seen, many Harris converts joined the Catholic mission even more were to join the Protestant missions. It was in the first half of the 1920s that the missionary Platt, who was in charge of the Methodist mission in Benin (Dahomey) and Togo, began his efforts to bring into the Methodist Church the large number of Harris converts in the Ivory Coast. The Catholic mission saw this as a sinister plot to win over converts who would otherwise – and this was also the hope of the administration – become Catholic. Platt also had to counter opposition from French Protestants of the Paris Evangelical Missionary Society who seem to have resented the fact that an Englishman was attempting to take charge of missionary activity in a French colony. Platt nevertheless managed to counter these various forms of opposition and in 1924 a small party of Methodist missionaries and catechists arrived in the Ivory Coast from Benin (Dahomey) and Togo.

In less than two years Protestant missionaries had taken over responsibility for some 160 congregations. One Methodist missionary wrote in 1926:

> More than 32,000 people had their names on our church registers – illiterate people suddenly precipitating themselves into our arms, all needing to be taught, and eager to learn the first principles of the Gospel. A mass movement? It is rather an avalanche! We have known nothing like it in our century and a half of missionary work.[74]

By 1926 it would appear from a message most probably dictated by Harris himself to the Protestant missionary Benoit that the prophet was no longer prepared to allow his disciples the liberty to choose between the Catholic and Protestant Churches, but had instructed them instead that their only option was the Protestant Church if they were to be true to him. Part of his message to his disciples reads 'All men, women and children baptised by me must enter the Methodist Church. No one must join the Roman Catholic Church if he wants to remain faithful to me'.[75] The Catholics regarded the message as fraudulent and part of a Protestant conspiracy. However, as one scholar points out, the Catholics unlike the Protestants had made no real attempt 'at establishing themselves as the prophet's successors',[76] and this may explain Harris's decision in favour of the Protestant Church.

Catholic churches were not likely to continue attracting large numbers of Harris converts as long as they placed the emphasis on the correct pronunciation of Latin in the liturgy, the importance of the Mass rather than the Bible, and as long as they opposed polygamy, dancing to calabash rhythms and the feasting which had become part of the Christian life of many of Harris's disciples.[77] Furthermore, unlike their colleagues in Togo and Benin the Catholic missionaries in the Ivory Coast were not only reluctant but were also unable to make much use of the schools as a means of evangelisation. This remained the situation between 1908 and 1922.

In the Ivory Coast, as in the Soudan (Mali), where there were serious difficulties with the administration over schools the Catholic missions decided in 1908 to abandon almost entirely their involvement in education. In 1914 the mission was responsible for only one school and saw its limited role in education as an advantage rather than a setback. The mission, however, did derive some benefit from the expansion of the system of state-controlled, lay-administered schools. Commenting on the situation in the Ivory Coast at the outbreak of the First World War the superior of the Catholic mission made the point that his missionaries, because they were not tied down with school work, were free for 'the work of evangelising the unlettered masses, while the official schools provide us with their best students'.[78] At Bingerville, for example, the students from the state school were obliged to spend all of their free time at the Catholic mission.

From 1922 the Catholic mission in the Ivory Coast, in response to a demand from the government as much as anything else, became involved once again in the establishment and administration of private schools. But largely because of financial difficulties very little progress was made until the 1930s. At the outbreak of the Second World War there were twenty-six mission-run primary schools and sixty catechists in the Divo area alone. This type of concentrated evangelisation, for the most part in the south of the country, along with the natural increase of the Catholic population which stood at over 60,000 in 1939, made for rapid growth. By 1960 there were 150,000 baptised Catholics in the country and another 50,000 preparing for baptism.[79] It was not all progress however either here or elsewhere in West Africa, for by this time a process of de-christianisation had set in, especially in the urban areas.

The Protestant missions benefited even more than the Catholics from the teaching of the Prophet Harris. The 32,000 people, most of them Harris converts, registered with the Methodist Church in 1926 had grown to over 42,000 by the mid 1930s.[80] Others had joined the Protestant missions opened by the Paris Evangelical Mission Society and those of the Christian Missionary Alliance from the United States. It should be noted that quite a number of Harris converts refused to join either a Protestant or Catholic mission, deciding instead to become involved in what one writer describes as 'strange, new cults', such as 'The Church of William Wade Harris and his Twelve Apostles', founded by Grace Thannie, at one time a traditional priestess and who, although a follower of Harris, apparently refused or was unable to abandon many of her 'old' beliefs and practices.[81] In a number of villages in the Lahou district and elsewhere Harris converts, in particular the older ones, wished to remain independent of the mission churches, sometimes from political and financial as much as cultural and religious considerations. Then there were those Harris converts who having joined one or other of the mission churches came to disagree with certain aspects of Church teaching and discipline and decided therefore to break away again. These Harris converts and those others already mentioned, anxious to safeguard their independence, ensured the survival and indeed growth and expansion of the Harris Christian tradition in the Ivory Coast. The majority of the first Harris converts and their descendants organised themselves as an independent church (see Chapter 6, pp. 178 ff.).

Despite the efforts of Harris, of other founders of African Churches and of the Christian missions African traditional religions retained the allegiance of considerable numbers of people in the Ivory Coast throughout the colonial era. A majority of the Kulango, Lobi, Gagu, Anyi, Dan, Baule, Brong and Senufo, among others were – and in some cases contine to be – adherents of traditional religion, worshipping the Supreme Being and Creator known by various names such as Nyam, Nyangka, and Zra.

While at the outset of colonial rule Muslims were confined for the most part to certain areas in the north-west of the country, making it possible for the administration to describe the Ivory Coast as non-Muslim territory, Islam very soon began to spread throughout the country. The impact was such that by the Second World War, as one historian has pointed out with a certain amount of exaggeration, 'an Islamic Ivory Coast was a reality'.[82] At independence in 1960 Islam was not far behind Christianity in terms of numerical growth, accounting for some 22 per cent of the total population, and in southern towns such as the capital Abidjan around 45 per cent of the inhabitants were Muslim.[83]

Former French Equatorial Africa: Cameroon

Cameroon was a German protectorate from 1884 until 1916 when it was overrun by British and French colonial armies and divided into British and French zones. The Treaty of Versailles of 1919 upheld this division and in 1922 Britain and France received a mandate from the League of Nations to administer their respective zones. From 1946 until independence in 1960 Cameroon was a United Nations Trusteeship under British and French Administration. The eastern region, occupied and adminstered by France, was much larger than the western sector under British control. And today, although there are Catholics and Protestants in both regions, the former constitute a majority of the Christians in the east, while a majority of Christians in the west are Protestants.

Christianity, as was the case in many of the other former French and British colonies, began and developed mostly in the southern region of the country. The first missionary to enter the territory was Joseph Merrick from Jamaica who opened a mission at Douala in 1843. Then came Alfred Saker, the Baptist missionary from Britain, who established a school and a mission also at Douala in 1845.[84] Later, just after the German occupation, efforts were made by the different Protestant missionary societies to hand over responsibility for their establishments in Cameroon to the Basel mission which had begun working there in 1886. When it proved impossible to integrate the various Protestant missions the Basel mission decided to go it alone and consolidate and extend its activities throughout the Douala region and beyond to cities such as Foumban further north and Edea to the east. In 1906 a large church was built in Foumban in the Bamoun region where the Muslim ruler Njoya, who was later to develop his own religion before finally returning to Islam, believed the Christian missions would be of great benefit to himself and his people.[85] When Njoya declared himself a Muslim the Christian church was destroyed, and the Christian schools were closed. But his ultimate aim was to establish his own religion with a view to bolstering his authority among his people and to prevent it from being undermined by Christianity, Islam and the administration. Part of one of the prayers which he ordered his people to recite reads: 'May God glorify the Sultan so that he may be above all through the ages, that thousands upon thousands may bless and acclaim the Sultan, through the grace of Muhammad. Amen.'[86] By 1919 Njoya had returned to Islam, and prior to that date, in 1917, the

Christian missions had been allowed to re-enter his kingdom.

The fastest growing Christian Church in Cameroon between 1890 and the end of the Second World War was the Roman Catholic Church. From the date of their arrival in 1891 until their forced departure in 1916, German Catholic missionaries had established twelve centres stretching from Doula eastwards to Yaoundé and northwards to Foumban. During the First World War a number of missions were destroyed while others were left without priests, and in this situation it was the catechists who according to one account kept the Catholic Church alive.[87] And even with the arrival of small contingents of mainly French priests during and after the war the catechists proved to be indispensable. According to one source, numerous flourishing, orthodox centres of Catholicism were established in the rural areas on the sole initiative of the catechists.[88]

By 1930 the number of Catholics in Cameroon had reached 200,000, and already a seminary had been established for training indigenous priests. Each year from 1935 a small number of Cameroonians were ordained. But for some time the total number of clergy, African and European, was quite small, never much more than 100. But this shortage was compensated for in large measure by the existence of some 2,500 catechists working for the Catholic Church in the Douala and Yaoundé regions in 1946. Of course, even these numbers of catechists were inadequate to cope with the estimated 410,000 people who were then to some degree members of the Catholic Church.

In East Cameroon, administered by the French and where the Catholic Church has been most active, it is clear that from the 1930s the school approach to evangelisation proved to be just as effective as the catechist system. Here the French administration was perhaps more willing than it was elsewhere to rely on private education. Thus between 1938 and re-unification in 1961 some two-thirds of the school-going population attended private mission-run rather than public government-controlled schools.[89] And while most of the Christian missionary societies established extensive educational programmes the Catholic mission was the most active in this field in the French-administered zone.

The situation was somewhat different in the west where the British were the administrators. Here the English-speaking Presbyterian Church, which originated with the Basel mission in 1884 was the largest Church in the territory by 1957, when it became autonomous. Most of the Protestant missions were stronger in the west than in the east, while neither themselves or the Catholic Mission made much progress in the more Islamicised northern region. In the east also where there was a considerable Muslim presence the French administration restricted the expansion of the Christian missions, but this hardly lessened the impact they were able to make through the schools.

At independence in 1960 the Christian-established mission Churches in Cameroon including the Catholic Church had one of the highest percentages of indigenous clergy in the whole of West and Equatorial Africa combined. Moreover, many of the Protestant Churches were by this time fully autonomous.

Chad

Situated to the north of Cameroon, Chad was under French military occupation from 1900 to 1910. It then became a colony in French Equatorial Africa until independence in 1960. Chad's contacts with both Islam and Christianity reach far back into the past. Islam first began to penetrate northern Chad in the eleventh century and today most of the people of northern and eastern Chad are Muslims. Christianity's first contacts with Chad were made in the second half of the seventeenth century, but it was not until the late 1920s that the first permanent Christian missions were established in the country.

In 1929 Catholic missionaries based in Bangui in the Central African Republic opened a mission in the south of the country and again it was in the south that the Christian Churches made most progress. While at independence in 1960 Christians formed less than one per cent of the population of the northern region, they accounted for over 20 per cent of the more densely-populated southern region. And the Christian mission schools and colleges produced the administrative and political elite at independence.

In addition to the Roman Catholic mission a number of protestant societies also began working in Chad during the inter-war years. These included the Sudan United Mission (SUM), which joined with the Mennonites and the Worldwide Evangelisation Crusade to form the Evangelical Churches of Chad, the largest Protestant Church in the country. Involved, like the Catholic mission, in education, medical care, rural development programmes and other related activities, the Protestant Churches built up a somewhat larger body of followers than the better organised Catholic mission, a very unusual development in a former French colony. These Churches were to experience a great deal of opposition and even persecution during the presidency of Ngarta Tombalbaye, especially during the authenticity campaign of 1973.

Portuguese West Africa: Cape Verde, Guinea Bissau, São Tomé e Principe

These three countries had to endure a longer period of colonisation than other West African states, only regaining their independence from Portugal after several hundred years of foreign rule in the first half of the 1970s. Guinea Bissau was the first to become independent in 1973, while Cape Verde and São Tomé e Principe both had to wait until 1975 before becoming independent republics.

In all three countries there was officially only one Church until this century and that was the Catholic Church. To be a citizen was to be counted by the civil authorities as a member of the Catholic Church. In practice for many of the people the Church was not as important in many respects as their own culture. While it gave authority and an air of dignity to solemn ceremonies, promoted to a limited degree western education, and kept the only official birth, death and marriage records it did not and could not replace the popular festas and parallel forms of liturgy and ritual that emerged (see Chapter 3, pp. 81 ff.).

Throughout the twentieth century the Catholic Church in these three countries remained a 'mission Church', in the sense that the direction and leadership came from outside. Among the thirteen Catholic priests in Cape Verde in 1946 none were Cape Verdeans. The fact that the Portuguese authorities closed the seminary at Santiago in 1910, allowing it to be re-opened in 1917, does not in itself explain why at independence in 1975 only ten out of the fifty priests in the country were Cape Verdeans, nor why it was not until a few weeks before independence in 1975 that the first Cape Verdean was appointed Bishop of the islands.

Administered from Cape Verde until 1940, when the concordat between Portugal and the Vatican was signed giving the Catholic Church a special status in all Portuguese territories, Guinea Bissau then became an independent mission territory. In the same year Lisbon handed over the responsibility for Catholic activities in São Tomé e Principe to the Bishop of Luanda in Angola.

The Catholic monopoly in these countries as far as the preaching of Christianity was concerned was broken in the twentieth century. In the late nineteenth century Protestant evangelists made their first conversions among the Cape Verdean community in North America and one of these, Joao Dias, returned to Brava in Cape Verde in 1901 as a missionary of the Church of the Nazarene.[91] Opposed and even imprisoned by the authorities for preaching a religion other than Roman Catholicism, Dias persevered and established a small but active and committed community of Protestants before retiring to the United States in 1936. Though the Protestant Churches – Nazarene, Baptist and Seventh Day Adventists – remain numerically small, accounting for less than one per cent of the population, they have added vigour and dynamism to Christianity in Cape Verde, and even stimulated a revival among Catholics in the country.

While Cape Verde and São Tomé e Principe are largely Roman Catholic, Guinea Bissau has a far higher proportion of Muslims and traditional religionists than Catholic and other Christians combined. While Islam is strongest in the north-east of the country among the Soninke, in the south-east among the Fula and Susu, and in the west among the Diola, the vast majority of the Banyun, Bijago, Manjaco-Papel, Balante and Biafada peoples who are mainly to be found in the west are traditional religionists. The Catholic Church, whose activities in the interior were curtailed by the PAIGC-led nationalist war for independence also has most of its estimated 61,000 adherents – 12 per cent of the population – in the west.

The Worldwide Evangelical Crusade from North America arrived in Guinea in 1939 to become the only Protestant Church of any size in the country. In addition to its three missions on the Bijagós islands, this mission, now known as the Evangelical Church of Guinea, has a number of other missions in western Guinea. By 1950 it still had less than 250 members. As a Protestant Church in a country where there was a special relationship between the colonial power, Portugal, and the Catholic Church, the Worldwide Evangelical Crusade was only barely tolerated. It had no schools and confined itself to preaching and medical, social and agricultural programmes. These were its only means of spreading its Christian message. In addition to the Evangelical Church of Guinea there is a small Anglican Mission in Guinea attached to The Gambia.

São Tomé e Principe, with a total population of less than 100,000, is over 90 per cent Roman Catholic. The Protestant presence in the country dates back to the 1930s when an Angolan Christian in exile on São Tomé started the Evangelical Church. Then came the Seventh Day Adventists from Portugal, followed in the 1950s by an African Methodist missionary from Angola who began work in São Tomé. By independence in 1975 Protestants accounted for 4 per cent of the population.

In all of these countries the main Church is still the Catholic Church, but its adherents are – in the words of one writer – more influenced by the rituals and liturgy of Christianity as they understand it than by Catholicism as a body of doctrines and precepts.[92]

Conclusions

The Catholic and other missionary societies that were involved in the expansion of Christianity in the former French and Portuguese territories considered above adopted very similar methods and shared much the same attitudes and opinions as their counterparts in former British West Africa and Liberia (see Chapter 4, pp. 86–119). They set out to contain Islam by being the first to evangelise the so-called 'pagan' areas, concentrating their activities for the most part in the southern and central regions of Benin, Togo, the Ivory Coast, Cameroon and elsewhere. In some instances, such as Benin, Togo, the Ivory Coast and Cameroon the results were quite spectacular, as they were in, for example, eastern Nigeria. And in all of these instances great emphasis was placed on the school approach to evangelisation.

In general, less use was made of this approach in the former French and Portuguese territories than in the British territories, partly because of the different policies adopted by the French and British authorities towards mission schools and missionary involvement in education. The Catholic missionary societies (the Holy Ghost Fathers and the White Fathers) were present in both former French and British West Africa and in both cases their educational programmes were much more developed and much more effective in British-ruled territories.[93]

Involvement in education, while it not only helped to build up a following, also gave the Christian missions and the Christian community an influence far above that merited by its numerical strength. Often, in what were largely non-Christian societies, Christians held most of the senior positions then open to Africans in education, the administration and the armed forces. One of the consequences, perhaps unintended for the most part, of the mission school was the formation of a western educated African élite that was to play a vital role in the nationalist, independence struggle. Whether the role it played or was allowed to play was always in the best interests of Africa is another matter altogether. Some would argue that apart from one or two notable exceptions this élite, so culturally assimilated, simply perpetuated the colonial system and its interests and values when it came to power (see Chapter 9, pp. 227–42).

Given some of the difficulties with the school approach to evangelisation and the slow progress made in training an indigenous clergy, missionaries in the former French colonies, though somewhat reluctant at first to recognise their importance, came to rely heavily on the catechists, especially from the First World War onwards. The catechist system, like the school system, had certain weaknesses from the point of view of the Christian missions. In general, catechists were poorly paid and some, after reaching a certain educational standard (usually not very advanced) sought to improve their lot by accepting such posts as junior clerks in the administration. On the other hand, as the number of those with a western education increased the catechist, who had received only a very basic education, sometimes found his position intolerable. Poorly educated, with no official rank and very little status in the Christian community his voice went unheeded. Often young men, they were obliged to represent the Christian community in societies where it was believed that wisdom came with age. Nevertheless, they were in a very real sense the founders and pillars of village Christianity in the former French and Portuguese colonies as well as in the British colonies. Catechists were to some degree the counterparts in the mission-established Churches of the prophets and apostles of the independent Churches who emerged in great numbers in the Protestant areas of former British West Africa, and to a far lesser extent, with the exception of the Ivory Coast, in the French and Portuguese territories considered in this chapter. It is to the independent Churches that we now turn.

Notes

1 HGF Archives, Paris, Boîte no. 164. Sénégal, 1900–1910. Report by Mgr Jalabert on his tour of inspection of the Senegambian Catholic mission.
2 ibid. Report by Mgr Kuneman, Dakar, to the Sacred Congregation of Propaganda, Rome, on the Vicariate of Sénégal, 1903.
3 D. Bouche, La Participation des Missions au Développement de L'Enseignement dans les Colonies Françaises d'Afrique Occidentale de 1817 à 1940. In *Etudes d'Histoire Africaine* **VIII**, 1976: 183.
4 ibid., p. 188.
5 HGF Archives, Paris, Boîte 261. Doss. A. Les Catéchistes dans les Missions. LeRoy, Senegal, June–July 1921.
6 ibid., Boîte 264. Doss. A. Dakar 1936–1950. Bishop Grimault to Superior General Paris, Dakar 35/11/1938.
7 ibid., Boîte 264. État Statistique Annuel July 1937–July 1938, Mission D'Oussouye et Mission de Bignona.
8 J. Delcourt, Histoire Religieuse du Sénégal. Dakar: Editions Clair Afrique 1976.
9 P.B. Clarke, Christian Approaches to Islam in Francophone West Africa in

the Post-Independence Era (c1960–c1983): From Confrontation to Dialogue. *Bulletin on Islam and Christian-Muslim Relations in Africa*, **1** (2), April 1983: 1–20.

10   On the development of Islam in Mauritania, see P.B. Clarke, *West Africa and Islam*, op. cit. chaps. 1, 2 and *passim*.

11   Interviews with Catholic missionaries serving in Mauritania, Paris, 1981.

12   HGF Archives, Paris, Boîte 265. Doss. A. Guinée (Conakry) Jean Jacques Katty to Mgr Duret, 17/2/1875.

13   ibid. Histoire de la Mission Saint-Michel de Mongo, by Mgr LeRouge.

14   ibid.

15   D. Diane, Le Catholicisme en Haute-Guinée de 1903 aux Années Cinquante, Memoire (DEA), University of Paris, I, June 1981.

16   ibid., p. 33.

17   ibid., p. 37.

18   ibid.

19   ibid., p. 33.

20   HGF Archives, Paris, Boîte 265. Doss. A. Guinée. Quinquennial Report of 1935 by LeRouge. Conakry 1/9/1935.

21   ibid.

22   ibid. LeRouge, Conakry 1/11/33 to the National Director, Oeuvre de la Propagation de la Foi, Paris.

23   ibid.

24   ibid. Quinquennial Report, op. cit.

25   C. Rivière, *Mutations Sociales en Guinée*, Paris: Editions Marcel Rivière et Cie, 1971, p. 351.

26   ibid., p. 352.

27   ibid., p. 354.

28   ibid., pp. 348–9.

29   HGF Archives, Paris, Boîte 265. Doss. A. Guinée, Quinquennial Report, op. cit.

30   D. Diane, op. cit. The same point was made by Diane in an interview with the author.

31   P.B. Clarke, *West Africa and Islam*, pp. 40 ff.

32   B.O. Oloruntimehin, *The Segu-Tokolor Empire*. London: Longman, 1972.

33   L. Harding, Les Écoles des Pères Blancs au Soudan Français, *Cahiers d'Etudes Africaines* (CEA) **3** (8), 1972: 101–28.

34   ibid., pp. 107–8.

35   ibid., p. 110.

36   P.B. Clarke, 'Methods and Ideology of the Holy Ghost Fathers in Eastern Nigeria 1885–1905', op. cit., p. 45.

37   P.B. Clarke, *West Africans at War, 1914–1918 and 1939–1945*, London: Ethnographica Publishers Ltd. forthcoming, Chap. 1.

38   ibid., p. 45.

39   A. Proust, *Les Missions des Pères Blancs en Afrique Occidentale Avant 1939*. Paris (n.d.), p. 68.

40   ibid., p. 70.

41   ibid., p. 101.

42   ibid., p. 133.

43   Annuaire Catholique, République du Mali 1980: 114.

44   P.B. Clarke, *West Africa and Islam*, pp. 212 ff.

45   J. Audouin and R. Deniel, *L'Islam en Haute Volta*. Abidjan and Paris, 1978: 75.

46   ibid., p. 77.

47   ibid., pp. 75–6.

48   A. Proust, op. cit., p. 50.
49   ibid.
50   L. Harding, op. cit., p. 119.
51   A. Proust, *Les Missions des Pères Blancs en Afrique Occidentale Avant 1939* op.cit., p. 106.
52   ibid., p. 143.
53   ibid., p. 146.
54   J. Audouin and R. Deniel, op. cit., p. 87.
55   ibid., pp. 88 ff.
56   R. Cornevin, *La République Populaire du Benin* (2nd Ed.), op.cit., pp. 436 ff.
57   D. Bouche, op. cit., p. 181.
58   ibid., p. 185 n. 58.
59   R. Cornevin, *Histoire du Togo* Paris: Berger-Lavrault, 1969: 441.
60   ibid., p. 448.
61   ibid., p. 199.
62   M. Crowder, *West Africa Under Colonial Rule*. London: Hutchinson 1968, p. 246.
63   E. Grau, Missionary Policies as seen in the Work of Missions with the Evangelical Presbyterian Church, Ghana. In C.G. Baeta (ed.) *Christianity in Tropical Africa*, op. cit., p. 73.
64   R. Cornevin, *Histoire du Togo*, op. cit., p. 312.
65   M. Bée, La Christianization de La Basse Côte d'Ivoire. *Revue Française d'Histoire d'Outre Mer*, No. 62, 1975: 625.
66   ibid., pp. 630–1.
67   G. MacKay Haliburton, *The Prophet Harris*. Harlow: Longman, 1971. And S.S. Walker, *The Religious Revolution in the Ivory Coast. The Prophet Harris and the Harrist Church*. North Carolina: University of North Carolina Press, 1983.
68   S.S. Walker, op. cit., p. 57.
69   ibid.
70   HGF Archives, Paris. Boîte 13, Notes de Mgr LeRouge.
71   ibid.
72   ibid.
73   ibid.
74   Citation from S.S. Walker, op. cit., p. 62.
75   ibid., p. 66.
76   ibid., p. 68.
77   G. MacKay Haliburton, op. cit., p. 170.
78   D. Bouche, op. cit., pp. 187–8.
79   This is an estimate based on figures in M.J. Bane's *Catholic Pioneers in West Africa*. Dublin: Clonmore and Reynold's Ltd, 1956: 188.
80   E. de Billy, En Côte d'Ivoire. Mission Protestante d'AOF Paris (n.d.).
81   G. MacKay Haliburton, op. cit., p. 148.
82   Citation in P.B. Clarke, *West Africa and Islam*, op. cit., p. 215.
83   ibid.
84   Anonymous. 'Alfred Saker Premier Missionaire au Caméroun'. Paris, 1945: 13.
85   P. Dubie, Christianisme, Islam et Animisme chez les Bamoun. *Bulletin de l'Institut Français d'Afrique Noire*, Sér. B. Tom. XIX, nos 3–4, Dakar (IFAN), 1957. 337–82.
86   ibid., p. 349.
87   M. Briault, *Le Vénérable Père F.M.P. Libermann*. Paris, 1946: 523–4.
88   ibid., p. 524.

89　W.R. Johnson, *The Cameroon Federation*. New Jersey 1970, p. 84.
90　C. Bouquet, *Tchad. Genèse d'un conflit*. Paris 1982, p. 175.
91　D.E. Reed, J.E. Wood, J. van Beek, *Upon This Rock. Nazarene Missions in the Middle East, Cape Verde and Europe*. Kansas: Nazarene Press, 1972.
92　N.E. Cabral, op. cit., p. 99.
93　D. Bouche, op. cit., p. 193.

6
The rise, expansion and impact of independent Churches, 1890–1960.

The mission Churches were not the only vehicles for the spread of Christianity during the colonial era. Many West Africans, for a variety of reasons, broke away or seceded from these Churches and established flourishing Churches of their own, referred to collectively as independent Churches.

The independent Churches are not all the same as far as doctrines, forms of worship, organisation and the response they give to the problem of 'evil' in all its manifestations are concerned. Those that retained much of the 'orthodox' forms of doctrine, worship and organisation introduced by the mission Churches, but have as their main distinguishing mark independence from mission support and control are often termed African or 'Ethiopian' Churches.[1] Chapter 4 discussed the tendency to domineer over and even downgrade Africans which developed in a number of mission Churches in West Africa in the last quarter of the nineteenth century, and this was one of the factors – there were many others – that contributed to the emergence of the African or 'Ethiopian' Churches.

Although it does not correspond in every detail to an Ethiopian or African Church as described above, the African Church – also called the National Church of Africa – founded by the Nigerian Adedeji Ishola (1885–1950) was clearly 'Ethiopian' in the sense that it was very much a response in the religious sphere to what was regarded as an attempt by Europeans to control and dominate Africans. Ishola claimed to be the recipient of a divine calling to free Africans from religious bondage and to search for 'a religion which was not tainted with dogmatism nor adorned with colonialism'.[2] This point was made again in article 18 of the 'Objects and Doctrines of this Church' part of which reads 'it is not in harmony with the will of God that any nation or race should be subject to the religious dictates of any foreign nation or race and it is the unchanging and everlasting purpose of God that every nation or race must have its own messiahs'.[3]

The concept of a British, French, German or any other national form of Christianity (e.g. Anglican or Lutheran) was not in itself opposed; on the contrary, it was endorsed by some 'Ethiopian' Christians in Nigeria. What they opposed was what they saw as the imposition of another nation's version of Christianity or any other religion on Nigerians. A religion was universal only in so far as it reflected and respected the character, perspectives, thinking and traditions of each and every society in which it was found.[4] As one Nigerian expressed it: 'Every nation should introduce the rule of God into its own customs . . . . Nations are differently talented and every nation must trade with its own talents otherwise it will be condemned on the day of judgement (Matt. 25, vv. 14–33)'.[5] The Christianity that was introduced into Nigeria was, it was pointed out, 'British Christianity which gave England the privilege to become a powerful nation', and 'teaches the superiority of the white man to the black', while 'God teaches equality and the right of every nation to become a holy nation'.[6] 'No nation', it was stressed, had any right to say to another 'Worship God after my own fashion, sing to God in my own tune, say my own prayers, speak to God in my own language, marry after my own fashion . . . Roman Christianity is the Christianity of Rome, English Christianity is the property of England . . . it isn't African'.[7]

African independent Churches were compared with early Christian Churches and it was pointed out that:

> To say it is premature for us in West Africa, and for that matter in any part of Africa that has accepted Christ, to organise and establish independent Churches, is to say it was premature for Rome, Corinth, Galatia, etc. to have had independent Churches . . . . Philip was not allowed by the Holy Spirit to influence the organisation of the Abyssinian Church, hence the Abyssinian Church, being indigenous, lives to the present day.[8]

In the writings and the preaching of those committed to establishing African independent Churches there is constant reference to the fact that Scripture, not the missionaries, is the basic source of authority and guidance, and to the view that to follow the missionary interpretation of Scripture was to agree to remain in spiritual slavery.[9] What we see in the rise of independent Churches is the sharp edge of a profound spiritual and cultural clash, of a clash of indentities, of a clash concerning the meaning and purpose of religion. While missionaries saw it as part of the function of Christianity to bring about a fundamental change in the thinking, attitudes, customs and traditions of Africans, some of the latter responded by claiming that in doing this the missionaries were using religion to preserve and extend their own foreign culture and traditions at the expense of those of Africa. The Christianity of the early part of this century must have appeared very foreign indeed when it was able to provoke such statements as: 'To worship a foreign God in a foreign Church planted in Africa, to follow foreign customs and ideas, to adopt foreign names and habits . . . this is nothing more than race suicide . . . . We are thus justified in calling into existence an African Church independent of foreign aid and control'.[10]

These aspirations and sentiments were expressed by an increasing number of preachers and writers in Nigeria and elsewhere in West Africa from the late nineteenth century onwards. And though they are to be found for the most part in the context of and as a response to mission Christianity, they are not entirely absent in Islam, in the sense of opposition to Islam as 'foreign', as the case of the Mahdi of Ijebu-Ode, Nigeria, illustrates.[11]

In addition to these 'Ethiopian' or African Churches, numerous others emerged and are often labelled 'Zionist', 'Prayer', 'Spiritual' or 'Prophet' Churches, referred to collectively in Nigeria as *Aladura* (praying) Churches. At the outset and for some time afterwards these Churches or movements which emphasised revelation from the Holy Spirit, prayer and faith healing, tended to attract a considerable number of converts who, though they had experienced both directly and indirectly many of the frustrations and deprivations that resulted from the impact of colonialism, had not been to any great extent detached or cut off from their own culture and surroundings by, for example, an extensive and in-depth education in a mission-run school. They did not conform on the whole to the pattern of the 'good Christian' as described by the Protestant Episcopal missionaries working in Liberia in the nineteenth century: the well-educated mission-school student who 'observed Sunday, pulled down greegrees, refused to participate in traditional sacrifices . . . wore western clothes, built a western-style house, married only one wife and cultivated gardens of flowers'.[12]

Many who joined the prophet movements were among those who regarded the new colonial order as having no legitimacy whatsoever and demonstrated this by their opposition to new forms of taxation.[13] They were realists and pragmatists, people who had not been persuaded or who had seen no evidence to convince them that western medicine, western education and the other 'benefits' associated with colonial rule would either in the here and now or in the long term lead to an overall improvement in their condition.

They had, on the contrary, evidence all around them pointing to the shortcomings, and the limitations of both the traditional and western 'scientific' approach to sickness, disease, infertility and related matters. They were fully aware that many people taken into European hospitals such as the one in Ibadan during the influenza epidemic of 1918 died none the less. They soon realised, furthermore, that western education, while it was of benefit to a very small minority, brought frustration, upheaval and unemployment to the majority. As a contributor to the *Yoruba News* wrote in 1929,

> Education in Nigeria from the last 20 years has come to naught. It has been an increasing source of prolific afflictions among the younger generation. Many formerly employed are now unemployed . . . . A man who was eating from the table before is now eating from a leaf . . . . In olden times we see that there were employments suiting everyone and all abilities and desires in the world. But what happens now we do not know.[14]

For many of the converts to these 'Zion', 'Prophet', 'Spiritual' or 'Praying' Churches colonialism and the 'modernisation' that went with it not only had little or no economic value but was also lacking in meaning at the moral, religious and cultural levels. Of course, discontent with colonialism and the stimulation it gave to the development of a modern enclave economy were not the only reasons for the emergence and expansion of independent Churches and prophet movement.

It is worth noting that the vast majority of independent Churches that emerged in West Africa during the colonial era were established in the more Protestant areas of former British West Africa and Liberia. Although a number of these Churches subsequently emerged in or entered the former French colonies such as the Republics of Benin, Togo and Niger from Nigeria, Ghana and elsewhere, these colonies with the exception of the Ivory Coast produced very few independent Churches. And even in the Ivory Coast the largest indigenous Church, the Harris Church, arose as we have seen through the preaching of the Liberian Grebo prophet William Harris. The more hierarchical, authoritarian, ritualistic, community orientated, less individualistic and less scriptural approach of Roman Catholicism, the predominant Christian tradition in former French West Africa might to some extent account for this, as indeed might the strict controls over religious organisations and activities that were imposed by the French colonial administration.

The origins of the independent Church movement in West Africa can be traced back to the first half of the nineteenth century when Lott Carey and Colin Teaque, Black American missionaries, founded in Monrovia in 1822 the Protestant Baptist Church, followed by the establishment of the West African Methodist Church by Nova Scotian settlers in Sierra Leone in 1844. However, it was only with the onset of overt colonialism in the 1880s that independency really got underway, starting in Nigeria.[15]

Nigeria: the rise of African Churches

In 1888 a temporary split occurred in the American Baptist Missionary Society in Lagos resulting in the formation of the African Baptist Church. The Nigerian Mojola Agbebi was one of the most prominent members of this Church. The secession occurred at a time of some confusion among the Nigerian élite in Lagos over what names to adopt, what style of dress to wear and how many wives to marry. Many of them were returnees and during their time in Sierra Leone, Brazil and the Caribbean missionaries had considered it necessary to eliminate all traces of their so-called 'pagan' African past. On returning home and finding themselves in a new, less artificial situation, many like Mojola Agbebi, baptised David Vincent, began to discover the meaning and depth of African culture and expressed their pride in it by adopting African names and customs. Agbebi and others also wanted to change the 'foreign', élitist image of Christianity and adapt it to the social laws, the religious and political aspirations and the style of Africans. In his view 'hymn books, harmonium, dedications, pew constructions, surpliced choir, the white man's names, the white man's dress, are so many non-essentials, so many props and crutches affecting the religious manhood of the Christian Africans'.[16] He was insistent that Christianity in Africa should make itself relevant and indigenous, using wherever possible 'African style and fashion' in worship.

This was one of the principal reasons why the United Native African Church was formed by ex-members of the CMS in Lagos in 1891. A majority of foreign missionaries and some African clergy and lay Christians were not in agreement with this approach, an approach adopted to some extent to counter the success of Islam, which many people like Agbebi believed was largely because it had adapted itself better than Christianity to the African context (see Chapter 8, pp. 215 ff.). Those who opposed the indigenisation of Christianity and the emergence of independent Churches saw all of this basically as a lowering of the moral standards of Christianity, and dismissed these Churches as refuges for the weak and immoral.

These independent Churches arose not only as a response to the past in Sierra Leone, the Caribbean and Brazil or out of a desire to adapt Christianity to African society, enabling it to better compete with Islam and serve society's needs, but also as a reaction to the increasingly negative assessment of African capabilities for leadership by nearly all European and North American missionary societies operating in Nigeria and West Africa at the time. The split in the Baptist Church in Lagos in 1888 was as much about who should control the Church – Africans or Europeans – as anything else. Likewise the United Native African Church mentioned above was dedicated to the evangelisation of African society by means of African evangelists and under African leadership, having no doubt concluded after the Crowther crisis that Europeans had repudiated any idea of a 'self-governing, self-supporting, self-propagating' African Church (see Chapter 3, pp. 66 ff.).

In the case of the Baptist Church it is clear that the dismissal of the first Nigerian Baptist Pastor Moses Ladejo Stone from his pastorate in Lagos in 1887 by the missionary W.J. David, in a way incidentally that was contrary to Baptist Church practice, was the immediate, direct cause of the secession and the establishment of the Native Baptist Church in 1888. What made the dismissal even more difficult to accept was the fact that during the American Civil War, 1861–5, when the American missionaries had been withdrawn from Nigeria, the Baptist Church in Lagos had been under African leadership. And almost from the moment the Americans returned in 1875 a clash between them and the Nigerian Baptists over the question of leadership and other matters seemed inevitable.

Again the resolution of the United Native African Church, established in 1891, makes it clear that the founders of this Church were no longer prepared to accept the view or presumption that it was for foreign missionaries to rule and Africans to obey. Part of the resolution drawn up at a meeting in Lagos in 1891 states 'That this meeting in humble dependence on Almighty God . . . resolved that a purely Native African Church be founded for the evangelisation and amelioration of our race, to be governed by Africans'.[17] The resolution also pointed to a second important reason why these Churches emerged: to change Christianity's alien, foreign image. The United Native African Church, while altering very little of the teachings inherited from the Anglican Church, held its services in Yoruba, allowed polygamy and introduced African music and chant into the liturgy.

The establishment of the African Church (Incorporated) in Lagos in 1901 was also occasioned by what some Anglican Church members saw as the unjustifiable removal of the Nigerian bishop, James Johnson, from his post as pastor of St Paul's Breadfruit Church, Lagos. While Bishop Tugwell and other CMS missionaries saw the secession as an act of disaffection perpetrated by resentful malcontents, 600 or so Nigerian Christians (the majority of whom were parishioners of St Paul's) did not agree. They met at Rose Cottage, Marina, Lagos, in December 1901 to open the Bethel Church, the African Church's first branch. What these Nigerian Christians appear to have been objecting to as much as anything else was the lack of consultation, the paternalism and the autocratic manner of the CMS authorities. The reasons for the break were neither theological nor moral, nor was polygamy an issue at the time of secession. The only changes made by the African Church consisted in the introduction of services in Yoruba, and of a new hymn book which provided greater opportunity for African chant. Later, with regard to the question of polygamy, this church, basing itself on such scriptural passages as 1 Timothy 3:2, 3:12, decided that while the clergy should remain monogamous, Christian laymen were permitted to take more than one wife. Although it kept close to Anglican teaching and liturgy, this African Church felt itself to be very much a part of the struggle for African independence, a point made on the occasion of the inauguration of the Church when it was stated 'This day we lay the foundations of the Church of the Black race'.

The fact that about one-third of the parishioners at St Paul's Breadfruit, including Bishop James Johnson, did not secede from the Anglican Church, must cast some doubt on the above interpretation of the secession. Johnson, like Blyden, was a staunch advocate of an African Church, and a leading advocate of cultural nationalism throughout his life.[18] But neither man was prepared to go to the same extent as Majola Agbebi in putting their ideals into practice. While the latter became convinced that dependence on foreign missions was a 'curse' and meant, as he expressed it, 'doing the baby for aye', both Johnson and Blyden believed that foreign missions and foreign powers such as Britain and France had an important, if only temporary, role to play in the political, economic and cultural development of Africa. Therefore, though they deserve credit for the support they gave to African independence, their actions and life style did not match up to their rhetoric.

James Johnson's decision, to concentrate on him, not to secede from the Anglican Church in 1901 shows clearly that he was not entirely consistent in his approach to the establishment of an African Church. In previous years he had urged Bishop Samuel Ajayi Crowther to declare the Niger Delta Churches independent of the CMS. He also campaigned for an African to succeed Crowther as Bishop of the Niger Delta Pastorate, and supported the Delta Church's decision to go independent of the CMS in 1892. And in that same year he refused an appointment as one of two assistant bishops, under a European archbishop whom the CMS had chosen to replace Crowther. However, by 1900 Johnson was prepared to accept this post and became the 'half bishop' of the Niger Delta Pastorate. In 1901, when removed from St Paul's Breadfruit Church, Lagos, Johnson had the opportunity to join an independent African Church with himself as Bishop, but did not do so, thereby disappointing many and undermining his position in and influence on the nationalist movement which he had championed.

It was not that Johnson believed that more could be done to further the cause he supported by remaining inside rather than seceding from the Anglican Church. Where he differed from other opponents of foreign missionaries – and from those who like himself wanted to see African Churches established – was in his understanding of the nature of Christianity and his attitude to certain African traditions. While Agbebi and others were not only convinced that Christianity could be adapted and made more relevant to African society than was the case, Johnson appears to have viewed Christianity more as a necessary alternative to existing African religious systems, ideas and practices. Ardently conservative and well meaning, he sought to establish in Africa the Anglican model of Christianity, a task for which Europeans were for many reasons unsuited.

A further secession occurred in Lagos in 1917, this time from the Methodist Church with the formation of the United African Methodist Church (UMAC) also known as the UAM *Eledja* (fish) Church, from the fact that it began in a location close to the fish market. This was a wealthy Church and one that emphasised that polygamy, since it was a basic social and economic institution in Africa, should be permitted. All the Nigerian independent Churches mentioned so far began in Lagos, and without going into too much detail it would be appropriate to develop the 'reasons' or 'causes' of independency.

It was perhaps inevitable that the Christian Church, based in England or North America, so close in style and attitude to the colonial government and riddled with division should contribute to separatism and independency. These independent Churches were part of the struggle against colonialism, forerunners of the independence movements. But they were not simply a response to colonisation, or to the attack by the 'new missionaries' on the competence of Africans to manage their own affairs. They were also about making Christianity relevant to the totality of the African experience of life.

White mission Christianity at this time and for some time to come was unable to understand or even contemplate that in the form it was presenting itself it was of only limited relevance to African life. Africans saw matters in a somewhat different light and demanded that certain of their views at least be respected, and the contribution they were capable of making at all levels to the building of a Christian society in Africa be acknowledged. These Churches, and some of the others discussed below, formed part of that debate which still continues to this day, concerning the extent to which Christianity should and is able to adapt to the African situation which has its own character and individuality, and yet remain a universal religion.

Missionaries did not, of course, appreciate the extent to which the Christianity they preached had been adapted and moulded by European history and culture. They believed they were transmitting to Africa Christianity in its pure, universal, unalterable form. And as they strove to preserve their version from being contaminated by what they saw as the essentially 'superstituous' nature of African religion, many Africans were struck by the alien form of the Christianity preached to them.

The missionary gave little or no consideration to the relationship between religion and society in the African context of the time. Whereas the Christianity brought from Europe had been influenced and even transformed by industrialisation, capitalism and the process of secularisation, all of which not only lessened its control over and impact on the wider society but also made for a clearer distinction between the religious sphere and the political, economic and other spheres, by way of contrast much of West Africa was still largely unaffected by these processes. Religion and society were much more integrated, and this made for less tension between religious values and common values.

As a consequence people and missionary tended to see the purpose and functions of religion in a different light. For example, West Africans saw religion as representing the values of their societies, and religious beliefs and rites as expressing the sharing of a common heritage and destiny. Religion was an integrative force, a force that emphasised common values, one that trained people to abide by the norms of society. Christianity on the other hand often bore the appearance in Africa of a religon that had for its primary object the loosening, if not the complete undermining of social norms. It was presented as a religion in conflict with African society and its values while upholding many of the values of European society. Its European character was made even more explicit by the fact that on occasion it allowed itself to be used by the colonial power, and even went as far as actively seeking the support of that power for the purpose of extending European civilisation, which was regarded as a necessary foundation for the spread of Christianity.

Of course Christianity was in many respects far more than a mere appendage of the colonial administration, far more than a 'European' religion, and when its autonomous, universalist character did manifest itself there was often tension and even hostility between Church and State (see Chapters 4, 5 and 8), a tension and hostility also evident in the relations between prophet movements and praying churches and the government, as the history of the Braide Movement shows.

Prophet Garrick Sokari Braide

Garrick Sokari Braide was an important figure in the independent church movement in Nigeria.[19] From Bakana in what is today the Rivers State in Nigeria Braide came into contact with the Anglican Church through CMS missionaries in the 1890s and was made a full member of that Church by Bishop James Johnson in 1912. In this same year Braide claimed that he

IV   Garrick Sokari Braide

had been called by God to be his messenger.

By 1915 Braide, a fisherman and warden of St Andrew's Church, Bakana, had gained a reputation as a wonder worker and healer throughout the Delta region and as far north as the Benue. Like the Prophet Harris, Braide launched a strong attack on indigenous religion, publicly destroying objects of veneration, charms and shrines, while at the same time attempting to adapt Christianity to the local situation. In addition to placing considerable emphasis on prayer and fasting, he introduced into Church services the singing of hymns in the vernacular, dancing and hand clapping. As one Nigerian bishop expressed it, 'he (Braide) taught the African how to worship God in his own way'.[20]

By 1914 a rift had begun to develop between Braide and the Anglican Church, and by 1916 his followers, who now referred to him as Prophet Elijah II, saw him as their divinely inspired leader and requested the Church authorities to recognise him as an authentic prophet of God. The Church, or more precisely, Bishop James Johnson who at the time was responsible for the Anglican Church in the area, refused to grant such recognition, whereupon Braide and many of his followers left the Church and formed the movement known as the Christ Army Church.

By 1916 Braide was in conflict not only with the Anglican Church but also with the colonial authorities. Braide's movement, referred to by a leading British newspaper, *The Times*, as a 'dangerous pseudo-Christian movement'[21] that threatened government authority and Christian influence, had developed, by this time, into a nationalist movement. The prophet had begun to preach independence and to predict that power would soon pass from Europeans to Africans once the British, French and Germans had destroyed one another in the war.[22] Before his arrest by the colonial authorities in 1916 Braide's preaching had created anxiety not only in government circles, but also among those involved in the liquor traffic. As one writer points out 'he did more within a short time to stop the liquor traffic in his area than all the international conventions and anti-gin lobby had been able to do in decades; his only sin was the challenge he posed to constitutional authority.'[23]

Garrick Sokari Braide died in 1918, the year in which the Aladura movement began to emerge in western Nigeria.

The Aladura (praying) Churches and societies: the Precious Stone – Faith Tabernacle Movement

This was the first of many Aladura churches and societies to emerge in Nigeria. It began in Ijebu-Ode, in present-day Ogun State, western Nigeria, in 1918. As with so many of these Churches, dreams and visions played an important part in its beginnings. Joseph Shadare, known popularly as Daddy Ali, a member of St Saviour's Anglican Church, Ijebu-Ode, saw in a dream a church divided into a larger, dark section and a smaller section that was ablaze with light. The darkness was attributed to the neglect of prayer by the majority while the brilliant light was explained by the fact that a minority of people in the church practised constant prayer.

This dream came to Shadare at a time when Nigeria, and much of the world was suffering from the ravages of an influenza epidemic. Shadare, with the young teacher Sophia Adefobe Odunlami who had recovered from an attack of influenza, formed a prayer association for the purpose of combating the epidemic. Describing the encounter between Shadare and Odunlami the former's son explained: 'God showed her in a vision to go and meet someone at No. 2 Idere Lane . . . to go and meet one Shadare there. And God showed my father here that a lady is coming to him to help him establish a Church . . . . She was to help him to deliver a prophecy . . . as a woman she was a special sign from God. It's unusual to have women prophets'.[24] Sophia Odunlami, claiming to be the recipient of a personal revelation from the Holy Spirit insisted, along with Shadare, that people should rely entirely on prayer and should not have recourse to medical treatment for their sicknesses. This emphasis on healing through prayer and the use of consecrated water only, is at the very heart of the Aladura movement.

To Yoruba Christians and to the Yoruba in general there was not necessarily a great deal that was completely new or original in the approach to healing as presented by Shadare and Odunlami. The same is true of the approach of the Prophet Harris. Among the Yoruba there existed a strong belief in the intrinsic power of certain words, prayers and incantations. An Ifa priest, for example, would pronounce certain words over water to infuse medicinal or healing properties into it. Or he might direct a person to pray over water in the following way: 'May this water be charged with medicinal power, charged for stomach ache and for dysentry . . . may this water become medicine'.[25]

In Yoruba society it was the traditional priest, the *babalawo*, who diagnosed the cause of an illness and prescribed the appropriate treatment. Illness was seen as part of the problem of evil in the world (*aiye*), and therefore had a religious or non-material side to it. There would be an incantation for a difficult pregnancy or for various types of illnesses, and if the correct words and especially the correct names were used then, it was believed, the desired effect in the overall scheme of things would come about. The names of God in particular were believed to have considerable intrinsic power and when used in the form of a prayer were regarded, as was prayer in general, as much more than a simple request or petition but rather as 'the invocation of a law which carries with it its own fulfilment'.[26] Also, when a person or group had said the prayer and pronounced the words 'Amen (*ase*) in the name of the Lord', they believed in a very real sense that their prayer had effected some change, whether visible or not. Early Yoruba Christians, known as *Onigbagbo*, claimed that because of their faith in Jesus who had overcome all things they were in possession of 'word power' which was an indispensable part of healing.

Pastor Shadare and Sophia Odunlami, therefore, in emphasising the miraculous, healing power of consecrated water and prayer were not so much breaking new ground as giving greater significance and importance to a long established belief in the power, efficacy and indispensable role of prayer in the healing process. This in part explains the widespread response to the praying bands, associations, societies and churches.

By 1920 the prayer group started by Pastor Shadare and Sophia Odunlami had become the basis of the Precious Stone Society, an organisation that was still at this time within the Anglican Church. Then a member of the society, a businessman named Odubanjo, came into contact with the Faith Tabernacle movement during a visit to the United States. This society also stressed the crucial importance of prayer in the healing process and on his return to Nigeria Odubanjo circulated its literature among members of the Precious Stone Society.[27] Very soon afterwards the Society adopted the name Faith Tabernacle and came to reject the practice of infant baptism in favour of adult baptism. At this point the Anglican Church decided to sever ties with the movement and in 1923 Shadare accepted from Pastor Clark of the United States an appointment as a minister of the Faith Tabernacle.

The movement did not, however, abandon all the teachings, practices, forms of worship and organisational procedures of the Anglican Church, though by way of contrast with that Church the Faith Tabernacle placed much more emphasis on faith healing and prophecy. In the records there are numerous references to healings effected by means of prayer. An entry in the diary of the Precious Stone Church Ijebu-Ode for 27 October 1922 reads: 'Woman cursed by witches for six years – had been to doctors, and came to church, confessed her belief in Christ and was healed with a divine touch'.[28] And another for 12 January 1923 states, 'Mr Joshua Adukoya received a divine touch at the hour of prayer'.[29] It is recorded that on 20 May 1923 a certain Pastor Nathaniel Claudius Vincent came to reside at the Precious Stone Church and 'received teaching in the divine healing and was prayed with on May 25th for eyesight. He received a real divine touch.'[30]

A Faith Tabernacle church was opened in Ibadan in 1925 by Isaac Akinyele and John Ade Aina, and for this church also there are records of numerous miracles, as they were called. The following table lists some of the miracles that allegedly occurred in Ibadan on 2 and 3 October 1930:

No. of people	Illness	Average duration	Prayer time	Result
4	Weakness	10 years	6 days	All healed
10	Stomach trouble	12 years	15 days	All healed
19	Witch disease	40 years	20 days	All healed
3	Rheumatism	10 years	14 days	All healed
3	Cough	20 days	2 days	All healed
2	Headache	3 years	10 days	All healed
1	Liver Complaint	3 years	8 days	Healed
1	Beelzebub	1 year	7 days	Healed
1	Dreams	2 years	25 days	Healed
3	Tobacco (smoking)	—	—	Rejected (not cured)

(Church Records, Precious Stone Church)

One person, moreover, is said to have risen from the dead, while others were 'cured' of leprosy, sores, barrenness, fear, smallpox, eyepain, evil spirits and so on.[31] There is, as we will see, considerable similarity between the Aladura and the traditional Yoruba explanation of the causes of ill health and misfortune.

After severing its links with the North American Faith Tabernacle movement in the mid 1920s and after a few years of declining membership, the Faith Tabernacle movement in Nigeria experienced an extraordinary revival from the late 1920s and reaching a climax with the Great Revival in 1930. Among those who played a key role in this revival were Daniel Orekoya, Joseph Babalola and Isaac Akinyele.

The Christ Apostolic Church (CAC)

The Faith Tabernacle movement affiliated itself to the British Apostolic Church, a pentecostal, faith-healing movement, in the early 1930s. Then in 1940 Akinyele, a long-time friend of Shadare decided with a number of others, including Joseph Babalola, to sever ties with the British Church and went on to establish the Christ Apostolic Church (CAC) as an independent body. This Church also renounced the use of western medicine and relied for healing on prayer and faith. It also forbade smoking and the use of alcohol, and Akinyele himself is said to have abstained from sexual relations even within marriage.

The Christ Apostolic Church under Akinyele's presidency established a number of its own faith healing homes, opened numerous churches and schools, particularly in Ibadan, and organised frequent revivalist campaigns. The aim was in essence to reform society by first reforming the individual, and by the 1950s the CAC had become one of the three largest and most active Churches in western Nigeria.

The contribution made by Joseph Babalola and Daniel Orekoya to the development and expansion of this Church, to the Aladura movement as a whole and to Christianity in general in western Nigeria was enormous. In October 1928, a 22 year-old mechanic and a driver of a steam roller called Babalola believed he had received a call from God to abandon his work in road construction and maintenance in the Ilesha area and to concentrate on preaching. Although he believed that if he failed to obey this call he would die within a year Babalola apparently chose to ignore it on two occasions. Hearing the call for a third time and finding that the engine of his steam roller failed to start, Babalola took this as a final warning and decided to begin preaching.

According to a colonial government report for November 1931 many people, in particular women, went to Ilesha to hear Babalola. A section of the report reads 'Ijebu women flock in great numbers to Ilesha to Babalola to get blessed water. The roads to Ilesha and the market are chock-a-block with lorries which have brought passengers in from a distance'.[32] Various attempts have been made to explain the widespread interest among women in the Aladura movement. According to one writer there are the special health problems of women, centring in the main on pregnancy and childbirth, and 'which send many women to traditional doctors or Aladura healers'.[33] In such Aladura movements as the Cherubim and Seraphim Society these women are given 'continued and unhurried attention; the illness is not considered as physical only but as a manifestation of a total social and spiritual condition'.[34] The same care and attention was simply not possible in a western-style hospital in Nigeria. In 1919 there were eleven principal hospitals in what was then called the Colony and Protectorate of Nigeria. The one in Ibadan admitted 480 patients in 1918–19 and of these, 32 were Europeans, all men, and of the remaining 448, all of whom were Nigerians, only 18 were women.[35] There was only one day nurse and one night nurse caring for these patients, and thirty-two of the Nigerians died. The medical statistics for the period 1918 to 1930 report a large number of deaths in hospital due to influenza, tubercolosis, bronchitis, meningitis, malaria and so on.[36] The care and attention, then, offered by the Aladura Churches was a major attraction. The greater understanding of, familiarity with and confidence in the approach to healing found in these Churches when compared with that offered by the western-run hospital also was important.

People believed that there were certain diseases which European doctors could not cure and sometimes implored those responsible in the colonial medical service to be allowed to treat in the 'traditional' way their own relatives and friends who were suffering from such diseases. One father wrote to the District Officer of Ijebu-Ode asking for the return of his son who had been taken away to an asylum for the mentally ill. He pleaded:

> Will you please for God's sake set the said Taiyo free and give him to me so that I may hand him over to a native doctor who will cure him. I have made investigations and it is understood that such disease cannot be cured by English doctors . . . . My son's brain was not puzzled before, it was caused when my son was dancing and singing at the native games . . . . The native doctor whom I am handing him over to is a licensed native doctor and has cured so many people of such disease.[37]

The boy was handed over, and the colonial medical service certified some time later that he had been completely cured.[38]

In addition to the Aladura approach to healing which they may well have preferred to others, women may also have soon realised that the Aladura movement opened up for them the possibility of participating much more fully in the life of the Christian community. Coming from a tradition in which women performed the role of priestess and mediator, many women may have welcomed the fact that in movements such as the Cherubim and Seraphim Society they could become 'prophets', a role that carried with it considerable political as well as spiritual power. By way of contrast, according to one writer on independency the mission churches, while they assisted the advance of women by providing schools, nevertheless 'appeared to be practising an unjustified form of social control' by not allowing women the same status and respect accorded to them in the Bible, and 'in attacking the foundations of African society, focused in the family, they were attacking the status of African women and failing to offer them the full status accorded them in the Bible'.[39]

Power in one sense or another, and not necessarily in a negative sense, was at the heart of the Aladura movement. Babalola, Orekoya and other Aladura prophets were seen by Christians as clear proof 'of the Gospels' power', a power that must not be simply talked about but 'that must be seen to exist'. Commenting on the preaching of Babalola and his work of healing, an edition of the *Yoruba News* stated that Babalola's life 'proves that the Gospel has lost none of its power, especially the gifts of the Spirit as recorded in 1 Corinthians Ch. 12'.[40] In another edition of the same newspaper, more than 1,000 cases of recovery attributed to the healing work of Daniel Orekoya were hailed as 'A fulfilment of a Biblical Prophecy . . . as far as we Africans are concerned'.[41] The prophecy in question is to be found in the Book of Joel, 2 vv. 28–29, part of which reads as follows: 'I will pour out my spirit on all mankind. Your sons and daughters shall prophesy, your old men shall dream dreams, and your young men see visions.'

The colonial administration was highly suspicious of these prophets whom they regarded as subversives and a threat to their authority. The Senior Resident of Oyo Province wrote to the District Office of Ife requesting him to inform the Oni of Ife and the Owa of Ilesha that they should not allow the Cherubim and Seraphim or any Aladura organisation to establish itself in any part of the Ife and Ilesha districts. And the reason he gave was that these were not recognised religions, but consisted of 'rascals who use their so-called religion for the enjoyment of promiscuous sexual licence contrary to all native custom and good order and are enemies of Oba and parental control.[42]

Some of the prophecies made and some of the guidance given by Babalola, Orekoya, Abigail, Oshitelu and others undoubtedly smacked of defiance and opposition to the colonial administration. There was Aladura opposition to the level of taxation in many parts of Ondo Province in August 1931, and according to one report 'a favourite subject of the preachings of these people (the Aladuras) is tax and they generally urge the people not to pay more than 3 shillings while one fixed the limit at one shilling'.[43] Oshitelu's prophecies, the so-called 'dangerous prophecies', gave rise to considerable apprehension.

Among those singled out as being the most dangerous was the prophecy which predicted that 'Things will be exhorbitant. Things will be dearer this year (1931) up to about seven years time, which will be the worst year'. And the one which foretold of wars and riots 'in this year (1931)'. Also regarded as especially dangerous was the prophecy which foretold that 'A day will come when this government will be taking money annually from the shepherds taking care of sheep and goats. Because of this most of the sheep will be roaming about without people to care for them'. More threatening was the prophecy which declared 'Something is coming down into the black people's land to an extent that all white men who live in the land will perish'. But perhaps just as worrying for the colonial authorities was the warning given to those who agreed to pay tax: 'Those who accept tax, land fees and other things of such a kind, . . . God's judgement', they were told, 'was upon them'.[44] The Aladura movement was more than a new religious movement that gave prominence in its teachings and practice to faith healing and prophecy. It was also part of the struggle for political as well as religious and cultural freedom and independence and its opposition to taxation should be seen in that context.

V   Members of the Cherubim and Seraphim Society

The Cherubim and Seraphim Society

This branch of the Aladura movement owes its origins to Moses Orimolade Tunolase from Ikare in Ondo State, and Christianah Abiodun Akinsowon from Lagos.[45] Again, dreams and visions inspired the beginnings of this movement. Moses Orimolade, who had been an itinerant evangelist from 1916, decided to settle in Lagos in 1924. A firm believer in faith healing, he claimed to have been told in a vision in 1925 to establish a society and give it the name Cherub and Seraph.

In the same year Orimolade, who became known as Baba Aladura, met Christianah Abiodun Akinsowon, a member of the Anglican Church in Lagos, who was also a recipient of dreams and visions. Believing that Moses Orimolade had cured her of an illness Christianah joined him in starting the Cherubim and Seraphim Society prayer group in 1925. A Praying Band was set up within the Society and its main task was to assist the founder in praying for all who needed spiritual help. In addition to the Praying Band there was the Committee of Patriarchs which was concerned in the main with administration, and the 'Army of Salvation', a youth section, which helped with outdoor activities such as processions.

Until 1928 when Christianah Abiodun known as Captain Abiodun, left the Anglican Church those who joined the society remained members of their own Churches. And even after that date many belonged both to the society and to another Church. In some of its teachings and liturgical practices, the society remained very close to the mainstream Christian Churches and in particular the Anglican Church. As one writer states 'Services and rituals which the C & S has adopted from "orthodox" Churches include Sunday worship, forms of the special services of Baptism, Holy Communion, Confirmation, Soleminisation of Matrimony, Burial, Ordination and some of the important anniversaries and Saints' days'.[46] Many prayers and services were taken directly and used with very little modification from the Anglican Book of Common Prayer. Some of the society's doctrines, however, and its many festivals, style of worship, dress, taboos and organisation distinguished it from the Anglican and other older Christian Churches. But there was little or no attempt to emphasise differences.

One informant, an archbishop of the Cherubim and Seraphim Society, explained the differences between his present and his former Church, the Anglican Church. He stated: 'In the Aladura Church we fast, we depend solely on prayer. This did not obtain in the Anglican Church. But there is only one God and therefore no real differences between us. Of course when I took a second wife I was no longer a full member of the Anglican Church, just a friend of the Church'.[47] The archbishop had no doctrinal differences with the Anglican Church, simply differences of approach, emphasis and interpretation due in his view to cultural factors.

In addition to demonstrating their faith in the absolute efficacy of the prayers of 'faithful' and 'upright' individuals and in the intrinsic power of certain sacred words such as Halleluiah, Iye (life), and Hosannah 'shouted' three or seven times depending on the occasion, the Cherubim and Seraphim like other Aladura Churches made great use in their services of drums, singing, clapping, dancing and stamping on the ground. While these practices had the effect of making Christianity more relevant, they were not done simply for this purpose, or for the purpose of 'exciting' people or attracting attention, but were, it was believed, a means of obtaining spiritual blessings and benefits. Stamping on the ground, for example, was thought to bring spiritual power, well being, prosperity and peace. These beliefs and practices are just as strong today.

Although church services had the appearance of being informal, spontaneous, entertaining, vibrant and perhaps in the opinion of some lacking in due respect and awe and therefore inappropriate for a sacred or holy place such as a church, there was great reverence in the Cherubim and Seraphim and the Aladura movement as a whole for the 'house of prayer'. There was also a strong sense of the sacredness of certain places, and in particular of mountain or hill tops such as Olorunkole hill near Ibadan, and seashores or beaches such as Bar Beach, Lagos. Furthermore, people who are considered to be in some way 'unclean' – women who have just delivered a child, menstruating women, a person who has not washed after sexual intercourse – are not allowed to enter a church or a holy place on the grounds that they would defile it.[48]

Many of the Society's prohibitions were also to be found in Islam, such as the above-mentioned prohibition on menstruating women entering a sacred place, the ban on alcoholic drinks, the eating of pork, the use of charms and the wearing of shoes in holy places.[49] Not all of these prohibitions were observed or strictly enforced, and some of them, such as the ban on the wearing of very expensive material such as Aso-ebi cloth would seem to have been introduced to ensure uniformity and to avoid rivalry and dissension. To so many members of the Cherubim and Seraphim the fact that everyone wore the same basic white dress or praying gown was of great importance. As one member explained: 'It makes us all, like me a mechanic and him a rich somebody all the same. We feel all the same'.[50]

The wearing of Aso-ebi by the wealthy few in western Nigeria caused, as a perusal of such newspapers as the *Yoruba News* and the *Daily Service* in the 1930s and 1940s indicates, a great deal of ill-feeling and animosity, and this as much as anything else may account for the ban on the use of this material by the Cherubim and Seraphim Society. In addition to the ban on Aso-ebi there was also a prohibition on the wearing of black dresses for mourning, and this may well have partly reflected traditional religious practice and custom while at the same time emphasising the necessity of total dedication in life and death to the Church.

The Cherubim and Seraphim expanded quite rapidly throughout western Nigeria and from there to Kano, Bauchi and other parts of the north of Nigeria, and into other West African states such as the Republic of Benin and Togo. The society has, however, been prone to splintering from the outset. Moses Orimolade and Christianah Abiodun, different personalities from different backgrounds, separated in 1929, the former naming his following the Eternal Sacred Order of the Cherubim and Seraphim (ESOC & S) and the latter giving hers the name of Cherubim and Seraphim Society. This split was followed by numerous others, starting with the secession in 1930 of the majority of the Praying Band and some 700 members to form the Holy Flock of Christ. Within ten years of its foundation the society had splintered into six independent sections and by the 1960s there were fourteen larger and over 100 smaller, autonomous Cherubim and Seraphim groups in the city of Lagos alone.

Though highly centralised at the outset the society relied almost entirely on enthusiasm and good will to keep itself together and neglected important matters of organisation and administration. Moreover, the fact that there were in practice two leaders of very different character and background both of whom claimed to be guided in dreams and visions by the Holy Spirit no doubt greatly increased the possibility of division and separation. Furthermore Orimolade, surrounded for the most part by western-educated assistants, appears to have felt insecure in their presence and perhaps as a consequence over-reacted when he detected any sign or hint of disloyalty.

Where there is great emphasis, as is the case in the independent Churches, on dreams and visions and continuing revelation as sources of guidance and direction, and where it is believed that these are to be interpreted and carried out as the Holy Spirit directs, then a high level of splintering would appear to be inevitable.

The Church of the Lord

This Church, like the Precious Stone Society was founded by another former Anglican, also from Ijebuland in western Nigeria, Josiah Olunowo Oshitelu. In 1925 when Oshitelu was still an Anglican, he claimed to be the recipient of a vision from God in which he was commanded to renounce all those aspects of the traditional religion which he had not so far abandoned. Then over the next ten years he continued to hear voices, some 10,000 in all, one of which said, 'I will annoint you as my prophet, even as Elijah annointed Elisha with oil in the olden days, so it shall be unto you'. And another said, 'I will build a new Jerusalem in You. You are the one whom Jesus Christ has sent like the last Elijah to repair the Lord's road and make his way straight'.[51]

Dismissed by the Anglican Church in 1926 as an eccentric, Oshitelu found himself in conflict with the colonial administration in the early 1930s, principally over the so-called 'dangerous prophecies' contained in his booklet Awon Oshotele (see pp. 170 ff.). By this time Oshitelu had produced a sacred script bearing some resemblance to Arabic and based on what had allegedly been revealed to him in a vision. In another vision in 1927 his own sacred name, Arrabablahhubab, and his personal seal which became the seal of his Church, were also revealed to him. Then in 1929 he announced his 'gospel of joy' in ten points. The first three points consisted of an attack on Christians, Muslims and traditionalists for their failures, the next three promised judgement through locusts, famine and war, and the last four condemned superstition, promised divine healing and the cure of all ailments through the water of life given to all who have faith in God.[52]

For about a year the Church of the Lord which was inaugurated in 1930 formed part of the Faith Tabernacle Church before becoming independent in 1931. By 1960 the Church had seventy-two branches, most of them in western Nigeria, while there were others in Ghana, Liberia, Sierra Leone, The Gambia and Togo.

People from all walks of life sought advice and guidance from Oshitelu. Some wrote requesting help in their examinations, and were usually advised to read Psalms 19 and 134.[54] Others who had travelled outside Nigeria for study or other purposes wrote for advice regarding whether or not they should marry non-Africans, or whether they would be promoted on returning to Nigeria. Women wrote to know if they had any hope of giving birth to children. Oshitelu always advised them never to abandon hope and 'to struggle hard with fasting and praying daily'. To one woman who wrote to him asking 'Is there any hope for me about issues [children]?', he replied:

The Lord said you should take a seven day fast and use the Holy Water of Life; be reading Psalm 24 into water and be drinking this with strong faith in the Lord, for you shall be blessed said the Lord God of Hosts. Although enemies are worrying you, you shall overcome them all by paying your tithe into the House of God always, and also, your prayers shall be accepted said the Lord.

To another woman who asked 'What can I do that my husband will be free from his sickness?', Oshitelu sent a similar reply. He wrote:

The Lord said that he must not fear at all, for he will be healed said the Lord. Behold he must pray well, for the stomach trouble is poison from food. Therefore by using Holy Water he shall be healed. Let him be reading Psalms 70, 40 and 35 to [over] a bucket of water and pray into it . . . . He must repeat this several times and with faith and trust in Jehovah alone he will be healed said the Lord God of Hosts.[55]

To a trainee teacher who wanted to know whether he would make progress and obtain promotion Oshitelu replied:

The Lord revealed unto me that there will be progress, prosperity and promotion for you . . . but you must always pray to avert all the snares of enemies against your progress. Fast every Wednesday and Friday. Make a covenant with God to be paying your tithe always into the House of the Lord and be praying with Psalm 16 every morning, for the celestial (face) of Almighty God shall surely shine upon you and you shall have just cause to glorify the name of the Lord.[56]

Here and elsewhere Oshitelu makes reference repeatedly to the need for faith in the power of prayer and to the healing, curing properties of holy water, and in this he stands full square in the Aladura tradition. It is also worth noting his frequent reference to the 'snares of enemies' whom he believes work to thwart the health or progress of his clients. In this respect Oshitelu is using traditional Yoruba notions of cause and effect, used also by the *babalowo* or traditional priest-healer.

According to one scholar Yorubas traditionally tend to seek an external rather than an internal cause or explanation for ill health or misfortune: 'the cause of the problem is usually considered to be some outside agency . . . [and] the practice of the traditional healer is in keeping with these ideas'.[57] This same scholar adds, by way of explaining the link between the traditional healer and the leader or prophet of a new religion such as the Church of the Lord:

The healing procedure of the religious sect only requires the person to perceive his relationship to God. He is a sinner so he prays for forgiveness. His faith is enhanced and it is this faith that heals. The power of the Holy Spirit would overcome illness caused by the devil and evil spirits . . . . This procedure is, therefore, in keeping with the traditional concepts of causation.[58]

At the outset, members of the Church of the Lord came in the main from the established Protestant Churches, though some were from the Roman Catholic Church. They also came from all walks of life but mainly from non-traditional occupations, with the exception of most of the women, the majority of whom were housewives. There were teachers, clerks, electricians, booksellers, motor mechanics, plumbers, bricklayers, policemen and some tailors and carpenters. The Church expanded outwards rather slowly from Ogere to other towns and centres in Ijebuland, to Abeokuta, Ibadan, Lagos and to many parts of western and mid-western Nigeria before it established itself in the eastern and northern regions of the country in the 1950s.[59] One of those most responsible for this expansion was E.A. Adejobi, a former school teacher who succeeded Oshitelu as Primate of the Church on the latter's death in 1966. Between 1943 and 1947 Adejobi established seven congregations of the Church of the Lord in Lagos, in addition to branches at Sapele, Warri and Benin City.[60] One of Adejobi's Lagos converts, S.A. Ogunnaike who was also a former school teacher took the Church to Kano, Kaduna and Jos in northern Nigeria in the 1950s.

From the late 1940s the Church of the Lord began to establish itself outside Nigeria. In 1947 a branch was founded in Sierra Leone and was organised and led by Mende, Kono, Creoles and Ghanaians. By 1960 there were many branches of the Church in the protectorate also. In 1947 the Church arrived in Liberia at the request of a Liberian judge who had visited Nigeria the previous year for healing. Then in 1953 Adejobi, accompanied by a woman minister of the Church from Sierra Leone and by a fellow Yoruba set out to establish the Church in Ghana. On his arrival in Kumasi Adejobi explained the character of his Church and the purpose of his mission to Prempeh II, the king of the Asante, and to the Commissioner of Police. He described the Church as 'purely a Christian religion of no political attachment', and then went on to state the aims of his mission. These were: 1) To teach the Fatherhood of God, 2) The Brotherhood of Man, 3) Development of the spiritual and educative mind of its members, 4) To promote Christian love, healthy living, belief in God and Good-will, 5) To pray, heal, cure and prophesy through Pentecostal power, 6) To propagate Divine healing through the agencies of Holy Water, prayer and divine annointment.[61] Adejobi then described the worship of the Church of the Lord, mentioning that 'during our services we enjoy the shouts of Hallelujah, Hossanah, Hurrah, Laughter, jumping, clapping, drumming, singing and dancing!'.[62]

While the police gave Adejobi permission to hold open services almost immediately the Asantehene took some time to make up his mind, and only took his decision to support the Church after his cousin Princess Victoria Prempeh, had approached him on its behalf.[63] The Church of the Lord in Ghana, though it experienced dissension and splintering, developed and expanded at a relatively rapid pace, much faster than in Sierra Leone and other West African countries with the exception of Nigeria.

As was the case with the other Aladura Churches discussed above, the Church of the Lord experienced secessions from very early on in its history. Turner provides a comprehensive list of these secessions, primary and secondary, which began in the Lagos, Abeokuta and Ibadan areas in the 1930s and continued to occur wherever the Church was established up to the end of the period under discussion and throughout the post-independence era.[64]

Summary of Nigerian independency, 1890–1960

A multiplicity of independent Churches began to emerge in Nigeria from the late nineteenth century onwards. African or Ethiopian Churches such as the United Native African Church came into existence as protest movements that sought to present the Nigerian and/or African perspective on matters of religious belief and practice, a perspective ignored for the most part by the mission Churches. They were the outcome of a spiritual or religious, as well as a political and cultural clash, between Nigerians and Europeans that began in the 1880s and continued throughout the period under review and since.

Following close on the establishment of the African Churches, which at the doctrinal and institutional levels did not differ significantly from the mission Churches, came the praying or prophetic Churches, known collectively as the Aladura Churches. These Churches were established by men and women prophets with extraordinary charismatic appeal. But they would not have been nearly so successful as the case of the Church of the Lord makes clear, without the assistance of able, dedicated and committed lieutenants such as Adejobi.

The Aladura Churches appealed to a fairly wide cross-section of society, and in particular to those in what were then regarded as the new occupations.[65] Many of these people were educated, though not to the highest level, in the western education system, and were no doubt aware of some of the limits and deficiencies of that system, which while it tended to alienate them from their own society, did not guarantee access to the new, emerging order of things. The Aladura Churches on the other hand, though they did not sanction and uphold all that was traditional, nevertheless offered what many saw as an attractive, meaningful, easily accessible method of resolving or coping with their spiritual and other problems of a medical, social, cultural and to some extent political nature.

Many people in western Nigeria in this period, and no doubt before and since, wanted a form of Christianity that would enable them to interpret, understand, and come to grips with their own rapidly changing society. Ijebuland, where the Aladura movement took off, was at the time beset by the influenza epidemic, and unprecedented political, economic and social problems. There and elsewhere in Nigeria many people, experiencing the disintegration of the 'old order', and allowed little or no participation in the political process, looked to religion for remedies and answers to everyday and more long-term problems. In these circumstances some pleaded for a more relevant – and in their view authentic – version of Christianity. As one Nigerian expressed it in the early 1940s,

> Christianity – the old conception of it – as dogmatic and unconcerned with mundane affairs – is spurious and anachronistic. Those who believe in a Christ

of the Gospel believe in a real and not an abstract deity. Christianity is a religion of rebirth and regeneration and has an efficacious prescription for social regeneration. It cannot afford to be mute and must concern itself with every phase of life.[66]

The Aladura Churches, clearly concerned with the here and now as much as the hereafter, to some extent met this demand for a relevant, applicable form of Christianity, expressed in such a way as to encourage active participation. They were concerned with overcoming what they saw as the 'evils' of the time, symbolised in the use of medicine, alcohol, tobacco, various traditional religious beliefs and practices, aspects of mission Christianity and foreign rule.

The Ivory Coast

The Harris Movement

About the same time as Garrick Sokari Braide was beginning to have a decisive impact on the Niger Delta region of Nigeria, William Wade Harris from south-eastern Liberia was 'revolutionising' the religious life of a large part of southern Ivory Coast. In the latter part of 1913 and during 1914 Harris converted many thousands of Ivorians to Christianity.

Born sometime between 1850 and 1865 of illiterate, non-Christian parents in the village of Graway near Cape Palmas, Liberia, Harris was a merchant sailor who became a Methodist and later a lay preacher in the Episcopal Church in Liberia. Like many of the Nigerian prophets and founders of the Aladura Churches discussed above, Harris strongly condemned a number of the beliefs and practices of the African traditional religions. Like the leaders of the Nigerian independent Churches, Harris claimed to be the recipient of a vision in which he was told by the Angel Gabriel that God had chosen him as one of His prophets and had assigned to him the mission to preach to all those who had not as yet heard the word of God. The Angel Gabriel is said to have appeared to Harris while the latter was in prison for a treasonable offence, which consisted in displaying his opposition to the Liberian government in February 1909 by lowering the Liberian flag and hoisting the British flag in its stead.

After his release from prison and dressed in his long white robe, black scarf and small white hat (see Chapter 5, p. 145) and having failed to attract much of a following in Liberia, Harris accompanied by two women companions, made for the Ivory Coast in 1913. Claiming to be a prophet who was above all religions and beyond the authority and control of men, Harris was an instant success in the southern region of the Ivory Coast, and in the south-western part of Ghana. According to one political report compiled in 1915 for the French colonial administration, 'The hypnotic action of the "prophet" [Harris] was very effective in the administrative regions of Assinie, Bassam, the Lagoons, Lahou and in parts of the Indénié and N'Zi-Comoë administrative regions, involving the

VI   Prophet Harris

conversion of about 100,000 people.'[67]

Harris, who employed a number of clerks (many of them Methodists) to assist him in his conversion campaign, publicly burnt the ritual objects used in traditional religion for purposes of protection, explaining that if people accepted baptism this would be the best possible way of protecting themselves from their adversaries and from all evil influences. The fact that Harris did not simply dismiss the belief in evil spirits and influences and destroy the material objects designed to protect people from them, but accepted the belief and offered people straight away a new means of protection in baptism goes a long way towards explaining his success. As one writer observes, 'a major element of Harris's technique of conversion, of key importance in his success, was his provision of an immediate replacement for the system of belief and protection that he asked the Ivorians to relinquish'.[68]

This approach contrasted sharply with that of the mission Churches. They demanded that people renounce at once and entirely the traditional religious belief system and required that they serve a long apprenticeship before being admitted to full membership of the Christian community. In many cases people – for example, those who practised polygamy – were never admitted to full membership. This meant that many of those for whom religion was an important means of explaining, interpreting and understanding the world were expected to live without the full support and benefits of either traditional religion or Christianity. On the other hand, Harris offered to baptise anyone who agreed to renounce the traditional religion and lead a 'Christian life'. These people in Harris's view were full members of the Christian community with access to all the benefits and supports, material as well as spiritual, which it had to offer.

Just as the Aladura prophets preached that prayers said in faith and with the right dispositions had, if God so willed, the power to heal both physical as well as spiritual sickness, so likewise did the Prophet Harris preach about the material as well as the spiritual benefits to be derived from living a 'Christian life'. He preached a 'this worldly' religion explaining to people that if they observed and practised the faith that he had brought to them for a set number of years, seven in all, they would prosper materially – they would be able to afford, for example, two-storey houses – and advance educationally. In adopting this approach the Prophet Harris was encouraging people to model their way of life on that of the Europeans. This, however, did not mean that Harris's message was seen as an endorsement of colonialism. Far from it – for some of the people who accepted his message and turned to Christianity steadfastly refused to obey the orders and comply with the demands of the French colonial administration.[69] Harris was not overtly critical of the French administration in the Ivory Coast, and in fact some of the things he accomplished met with the approval of that same administration. The fact that he was instrumental in bringing greater unity and cohesion to the southern region of the Ivory Coast and in generating enthusiasm for certain development projects devised by the colonial regime met with the approval of the authorities. However, the French administration very soon came to fear the growing authority, stature and influence of Harris in the Ivory Coast and in due course expelled him from the colony.

There were many reasons for Harris's success, some of which have already been touched upon. As we have seen, he did not simply demand that people abandon their traditional beliefs and practices. He in fact accepted many of those beliefs, such as the belief in evil spirits, and agreed that people needed to be protected from such spirits. But as far as he was concerned, this protection was to be found in baptism and not in the rituals and symbols and the material objects of the indigenous religion. Therefore, while he challenged the power and authority of the traditional priests and destroyed the external trappings of traditional religion, he did not regard the beliefs themselves as necessarily erroneous. While many indigenous religious beliefs and aspirations, moral and social norms were respected they were nevertheless to be understood from a different perspective, the Christian perspective, and from within a different framework: that of Christianity.

In matters of religious belief, Harris did not demand a clean break with the past, nor did his teaching entail large-scale disruption of the existing social system. Indeed, as one writer points out,

> The Harris movement . . . supported the indigenous social structure at a time when it was being shaken by external pressures. The chiefs, elders and traditional priests acquired renewed power and authority by converting to the religion of the Prophet Harris. Rather than developing as a substitute for social institutions that were breaking down or loosing their hold, the Harris movement fitted into the existing social structure and helped to reinforce and perpetuate it.[70]

Those who accepted Harris's message were not obliged, therefore, to break off all social and cultural links with their own community. For many of them, conversion did not involve anything like total separation at any level, intellectual, emotional, psychological or social, from family and friends since group rather than individual conversion was the norm where Harris was concerned. Harris usually converted a whole community or a large part of it all at once, thus making the transition from the indigenous religion to Christianity less divisive and disruptive of the existing social order.

There was, further, nothing completely new to Ivorians in Harris's manner, style of address, and methods, or in much of what he had to say. Prior to Harris's conversion campaign in the Ivory Coast, traditional priests from Liberia who also wore white garments had brought what they claimed were more powerful spirits for the protection and well-being of the Ivorians. And though Harris differed from these traditional priests or prophets in as much as he claimed to be sent by the only true God, he nevertheless resembled them in this and in many other respects. For example Harris's form and style of worship – which included the playing of the gourd rattles and singing and dancing – resembled the traditional manner of worship. Indeed, Harris is said to have told his converts who asked him how they should worship that they were 'to dance as they had for the indigenous spirits and to sing their own songs adding the name "God"'.[71]

Harris's message not only allowed for certain continuity – religious, moral, social and cultural – with the past but also inspired people with confidence in the present and the future. Making prosperity in the here and now dependent on faith, people were told that if they lived a 'Christian life' and believed in the power and efficacy of baptism and prayer they would experience greater happiness and contentment, greater success in their undertakings whether they were farming or fishing, greater prosperity in general, and protection from harm. On the other hand, failure to believe would result in greater poverty, ill health and misfortune. This highly pragmatic approach to conversion has its obvious drawbacks, for people tend to assess the plausibility and even necessity of a particular belief system according to tangible, concrete results. And belief systems, like the Harris one, that are presented as being highly relevant to the immediate concerns of everyday life can prove to be highly fragile, more fragile for example than those more vague, diffuse, general belief systems which are so difficult to disprove or refute on the basis of experience. This does not mean that people will necessarily completely abandon a highly relevant, pragmatic belief system once they discover that it does not appear to be working for them, but it does mean that they will be very inclined to adapt and modify it in an attempt to ensure that it serves their purposes.

On the other hand, pragmatic belief systems, like all belief systems, have their own way of protecting themselves from disconfirmation. For example, when a fisherman prays in faith in the hope of catching more fish to enable him to care for his family and prosper, and in fact catches a smaller quantity of fish and becomes poorer, that person does not necessarily conclude that prayers said with faith are ineffective. Such a person might well accept the explanation of a prophet or spiritual guide which might attribute the apparent failure of prayer to the fact that it was said with insufficient faith.

The disciples of Harris might well be forgiven for believing that after accepting baptism they would no longer experience misfortune and suffering. Yet, while many followers claimed to have had their faith in the teachings of Harris confirmed in a concrete, visible way, attributing such things as the improvement in their living standards or the birth of a child to the acceptance and practice of these teachings, others continued to experience adversity and misfortune. The most common explanation given for the persistence of misfortune and 'evil' in all its forms is that people continue to sin and therefore suffer. This explanation is in some respects inadequate, since among other things it does not explain why wrongdoers often prosper. However, from all accounts Harris was a charismatic figure, whose authority and credibility rested not so much on the consistency and logic of his teachings but more on the acceptance and faith in his claim to have been sent by God to give the Ivorians a second chance to worship, and be protected by the true and only God whom they had not worshipped since that time in the distant past when their ancestors had alienated themselves from Him.

Among the Aladura, for example in the Cherubim and Seraphim Society discussed earlier on in this chapter where faith healing through prayer and holy water is a fundamental, unanswered prayers were attributed by the founder Orimolade to three causes – praying without faith, praying for something which will not be totally favourable to the petitioner, praying without first having repented for a serious sin.[72]

Although, the French colonial administration approved of much of the content of Harris's message, in particular his emphasis on hard work, obedience to authority and the need for restraint and temperance where alcohol was concerned, it nevertheless took the decision in December 1914 to expel him. Aware of the very large following acquired by Harris in such a short time the French were doubtless afraid that the authority and influence of one who did not recognise any authority except that of God might become a focus of discontent and overt opposition to colonial rule in the Ivory Coast. Moreover Harris's conversion campaign coincided with the final build-up for the First World War which began in August 1914 and involved West African soldiers and carriers in campaigns in West Africa itself, East Africa, and Europe.[73]

In this situation the French administration in the Ivory Coast, still involved in 'pacifying' the colony and anxious to recruit soldiers and carriers for the war effort probably reached the conclusion that Harris was too great a risk. Furthermore, the French Catholic missionaries in the Ivory Coast had grown suspicious of the prophet and had come to regard him as the instigator of a plot to undermine Catholicism. This was clearly not so for Harris had been responsible for vast numbers joining the Catholic Church. And later the Protestant Church was also to benefit from Harris's preaching (see Chapter 5, pp. 145 ff.). In fact, the prophet at first advised his followers to join the Catholic Church. However some years after his return to Liberia where he worked as an itinerant preacher until his death in 1929, Harris seems to have changed his mind and began to tell his disciples that if they wished to remain loyal to him they must not join any other Church but the Methodist Church.

Despite this recommendation the Harris movement in the Ivory Coast became a Church in its own right. After Harris's expulsion from the Ivory Coast numerous disciples, some of whom claimed to be 'prophets' in their own right, carried their leader's message into distant and remote areas where there were no existing churches, either Catholic or Protestant. In this situation followers of Harris began to build a Harris Church. This development occurred not only in the remote, rural areas but also eventually in towns such as Abidjan, the present-day capital of the Ivory Coast. By 1940 there were three Harris Churches in Abidjan, and the number had increased to twenty-one by 1946.

Similar in many respects in its beginnings and early development to the Aladura Churches and societies the Harris movement has also, with the passage of time, tended to take on more of the character of a highly organised Church with a wide range of social and educational as well as spiritual interests.

Once a village-based movement – and in this it was unlike most of the Aladura Churches – the movement began to develop under John Ahui as a national Church. In the 1950s attempts were made to establish greater unity and cohesion between the different communities and churches that had emerged out of the Harris movement and to reach agreement on a standard doctrine and liturgy. Moreover considerable care was taken to point out that the founder of the different communities or churches, the Prophet Harris, was an African and chosen by God as His prophet for Africa, since God sends each people its own prophet to reveal His message to them.

The Church was organised in such a way that each branch had its own apostles, ministers and elders, the process of appointment being based on that used for choosing officials in a village or ward. The ministers and apostles would normally be appointed from among the group which supplied the administrators of the village or ward. For their part the elders would come from the oldest or most senior of the age-grades or sets. The youth were in theory given a place in the Church hierarchy, but in practice authority and responsibility were confined to adults and in particular to the old. This prompted many of the youth to leave the Church, which came to be known for a short time as the 'religion of old men' in contrast to those mission Churches referred to as 'Churches of children'.

Over time a number of rival Churches emerged in the Ivory Coast. In 1949, for example, followers of Harris in the Grand Lahou region united under a certain Gaston N'Drin and refused to acknowledge the authority and leadership of John Ahui. According to N'Drin Ahui did not place nearly enough emphasis on the importance of reading the Bible and was therefore going against the teaching of Harris. This neglect of the Bible by Ahui may well have stemmed from the fact that unlike N'Drin he was illiterate, and perhaps also from the fact that he was strongly opposed – again unlike N'Drin – to mission-run schools, and therefore did not encourage people to send their children there to learn to read. Others, like Bodjo Ake who claimed to be Harris's successor and established his own Church, were also opposed to mission schools which they believed undermined the status and authority of the elders and senior members of society.

All opposition to education had been dropped by the mid 1960s and the Harris Church under the leadership of John Ahui with its estimated 100,000 members was connected with a number of development projects. It was officially recognised as one of the four 'national', religious organisations in the country, the others being Protestantism with about 200,000 members, Catholicism with around 500,000 members and Islam with close on one million members. Before concluding this section on independent Churches in the Ivory Coast it is worth considering one of the largest and most influential of these Churches: the Deima Church, founded by the prophetess Marie Lalou, who claimed to be Harris's successor.

The Deima Church of Marie Lalou

After the Harris Church the Deima Church is perhaps the largest of the more than thirty independent Churches active in the Ivory Coast. The Deima movement was begun by Marie Lalou in 1922. A Godié woman from north of the lagoons it is not certain whether Marie Lalou was baptised a Protestant or a Catholic, though at one time or another she was probably a member of both Churches.[74] Though married for some time Marie Lalou had no children and one day, allegedly in obedience to instructions received in a dream, she put an end to sexual relations with her husband. After her husband's death and that of her husband's brother whom according to custom she should have married on the death of the former but refused, Marie Lalou, held in great suspicion by many, began to preach in her own area that God opposed anyone who wished evil of others. Furthermore, she offered holy water to people maintaining that if they drank it with a pure heart they would be protected from any evil that others wished upon them.

Regarded by many as a witch Marie Lalou was forced to leave the village and take refuge in the bush, until befriended by a hunter who persuaded his chief to let her settle in his village. Insisting that God had forbidden her to associate with men, she refused her family's request to remarry and was reported to the colonial administration in 1949. The latter felt that she was acting in good faith and so took no action against her, and this in itself won her a number of new followers.

Some of Marie Lalou's ideas on religion, revelation and prophecy resemble those expressed by Ishola, Oke, Lijadu and other Nigerian founders and advocates of African Churches. She maintained, for example, that God chose a prophet from among each nation to reveal His message to that nation, and therefore there were African prophets for the different peoples of Africa, and so on. Marie Lalou wanted an African Church led by Africans for Africans, believing that the mission Churches were concerned above all else with 'foreign' issues. She believed that while the Creator God ruled over all He nevertheless provided each nation or people with its own god, and concluded from this that the gods brought by the missionaries to Africa were ineffective and powerless because 'foreign'. She maintained further that the missionary presence had led to an increase rather than a decrease in the number of evil spirits and had therefore failed the African.[75] Missionary forms of ritual and worship, missionary teaching and the missionary's Bible, were all dismissed as ineffective and inappropriate for the protection of African people against misfortune and evil spirits.

Marie Lalou claimed that she had been called upon by God to protect people from such spirits by means of holy water and ashes derived from special plants and which traditionally symbolise longevity and provide protection against poisoning, witches, and all sources of harm. Like Harris whose successor she claimed to be Marie Lalou launched a strong attack on the indigenous religion, ordering the destruction of all those material objects associated with it.

Deima Church services take place on Fridays and Sundays and are presided over by a 'prophet', the title given to the local religious leader. On Friday the prophet wears a black robe and shawl to remind people that Christ died on that day, and on Sunday he wears white to symbolise the day of Christ's resurrection. Services are simple, consisting of songs, prayers and a short exhortation, and the principal religious objects found in the church are a bottle of holy water, a cross said to contain a strong spirit and a container of holy ashes. Prophetess Marie Lalou was head of the Church until her death in 1951 when she was succeeded by Princess Jeniss. The prophetess appoints the Church leaders at the local level and 'ordains' them by bestowing on them a cross, a bell and holy water and holy ashes.

There are certain similarities between the Deima and Harris movements. Both emphasised the powerlessness of the rituals, images and spirits of traditional religion and the need to destroy the material objects of that religion. Baptism was regarded as the central, most important sacrament and was offered as the most effective means of fending off misfortune and evil. And both movements stressed the positive material benefits to be derived from the acceptance of baptism and the practice of a 'Christian life'. They also sought to combat the widespread use of witchcraft especially for the purpose of acquiring wealth and power at the expense of one's neighbour. People were constantly exhorted to love their neighbour and to renounce witchcraft or be punished by God. Both movements to some extent came into existence to protect people from the effects of witchcraft.

In addition to these similarities the Deima Church, like the Harris Church and offshoots of that Church, strictly forbids adultery, sexual relations on the ground and the use of alcohol. But overall the Deima movement probably owes more to traditional religion than the Harris Church which has much closer links with Protestantism.

Ghana

The Harris legacy. The Church of William Wade Harris and His Twelve Apostles

The Prophet Harris spent three months in south-western Ghana in 1914, making numerous converts among the Nzima people in particular. Many of these converts joined the Methodist Church, while one of them called Grace Thannie, once a priestess, after accepting baptism from Harris accompanied him to the Ivory Coast as Madam Harris.[76] On returning to Ghana Grace Thannie founded the Church of William Wade Harris and His Twelve Apostles, more widely known simply as the Church of the Twelve Apostles, and so named because Harris supposedly told people to choose twelve apostles to administer their Churches.

This Church established by Grace Thannie was multi-ethnic and was one of the first of the so-called 'spiritualist' Churches in Ghana in which great emphasis is placed on the activity of the Holy Spirit.[77] Each day the prophet or local religious leader raises a bowl of water three times before a cross and invokes the blessing of the Holy Spirit upon it. Then the sick, with holy water on their heads, dance to the accompaniment of music, pray and hope that the Holy Spirit will deign to use the holy water that spills over their body as a cure. Then, dressed in the same way and using the same approach to healing as the Prophet Harris, the local prophet or religious leader will place the Bible on the head of those who are to be healed.

Membership of the Church of the Twelve Apostles is acquired through a form of baptism which involves being bathed by a person of the same sex who also makes the sign of the cross over the one who is being baptised. Several times a year there are public confessions of sins followed by communion services, and once a year by an *agape* or feast at which members share food and drink with each other.

Of the many other 'spiritualist', or 'spiritist' or 'spiritual' Churches in present-day Ghana the Musamo Christo Disco Church (Army of the Cross of Christ Church) is among the best known.[78]

The Musamo Christo Disco Church

The similarities between this movement, founded in the 1920s by the Ghanaian Joseph William Egyanka Appiah, and some of the Aladura Churches in Nigeria are striking. When Appiah first established his prayer group known as the Faith Society in the Winneba district of Central Ghana in 1919 he appears to have had little or no intention of breaking away from the Methodist Church.

In August 1919 Appiah claimed to be the recipient of a revelation from God which was followed by the descent upon him of the Holy Spirit. Other extraordinary things were also to happen to him such as the 'three baptisms', which he believed gave him power to heal and to protect people from evil spirits. Believing that he was chosen by God to be a great king *(Akaboha)* Appiah decided to appoint his companion Abena Baawa, whom he named Hannah Barnes, the queen *(Akatitibi)* of his society.

In 1922 the Methodist Church ordered Appiah to put an end to what it described as his occult practices or to leave the Church. Convinced that he had been called to be a prophet Appiah refused to comply with this order and in 1923 left the Methodist Church. Appiah was very soon in conflict with many of the local people because of his fierce attacks on traditional religious rituals and customs. As the opposition to him mounted Appiah decided to make what he regarded as an 'Exodus', on the biblical pattern of the Exodus of the Israelites from Egypt, from Onyaawonsu to Gomoa Fomena. The Exodus took place in October 1925 and on his arrival at Gomoa Fomena Appiah, known from this time as Prophet Jemisimiham Jehu-Appiah, began to establish the Holy City of Mozano (My Town) which was moved to Gomoa Echiem in 1951.

In his preaching Appiah spoke out strongly against traditional religion and warned that the end of the world was close at hand. In the development of the ritual and worship of the Church he made very great use of the customs of the old Fante court, and in particular of the Old

Testament as did the founders of the Aladura Churches. For example Appiah, borrowing from the Old Testament account of the Exodus smeared the blood of a sacrificial animal on the entrances to the homes of his followers in Mozano. And like the Aladura Churches the Musamo Christo Disco Church prohibited, at least at the outset, the use of medicine, relying exclusively on faith healing. The Church does not prohibit polygamy, and insists on the use of the local language and music during worship. Nevertheless this Church, which has a branch in London, stresses that it is not an African Church in the sense of being solely for Africans, but a Church with a universal mission to convert all to Christ.

In practice the majority of adherents have been Fante. Other independent Churches also, like the predominantly Ewe Apostolic Revelation Society founded by Prophet Wovenu in 1939 and centred on its holy city of Tadzewu, seem to attract most of their members from one particular ethnic group only. Appiah died in 1948 and was succeeded by his son Matapoly. By the 1950s, though still rather small in size, the Musamo Christo Disco Church continued to expand at a relatively steady pace. Like the Harris Church and many Aladura Churches, in insisting on the abandonment of traditional religion it did not at the same time reject all traditional belief, values, customs and norms. It upheld many, offering what it regarded as a new perspective and new solutions to problems of a traditional as well as a contemporary nature.

Independency in West Africa – the situation in 1960

Between 1860 and 1960 some 5,000 independent Churches had emerged in Africa and of them, 90 per cent were still in existence in the 1960s.[79] The majority of West Africa's independent Churches were and are to be found in the former British colonies and in particular in Nigeria and Ghana. In former French West Africa where the Catholic Church was the main, established Christian body, independency was not as widespread although, as we have seen, there were a considerable number of these Churches in the Ivory Coast, and several others in the republics of Benin, Cameroon, Togo and Upper Volta. Perhaps the fact that the Catholic Church when instructing converts may have placed less emphasis than the Protestant Churches on the need for converts to know the Bible and regard it as the sole, authentic voice of God explains in part why independent Churches have been less numerous in Catholic than in Protestant areas.[80] In emphasising that the Bible was the sole source of authority and guidance the Protestant Churches were in fact providing people with a blueprint for the establishment of a new religion. This was however not the only 'cause' of independency. Furthermore, as the next chapter shows, the character of independency has undergone considerable change over time.

Conclusions

The African or Ethiopian Churches discussed earlier on in this chapter were movements of protest against the increasingly negative assessment of African capabilities made by many European and American missionaries both black and white from the 1880s onwards. These Churches were also a direct, conscious attempt to assert the cultural and spiritual values and rights of Africans which missions were either unaware of or chose to ignore.

On the other hand the rise of the Harris movement and the Aladura Churches do not appear to have been so directly linked to the tensions generated by the racial intolerance of many European and American churchmen. While Harris recommended his converts to join the Catholic and later the Protestant Church in the Ivory Coast, the Faith Tabernacle movement in Nigeria sought on a number of occasions to establish links on the basis of equality with North American and British based Churches. Most of these Churches were in some way a reaction to the colonial situation. Born out of disasters in the form of influenza epidemics and war, the Aladura and 'spritual' Churches were a response to what many perceived as the cultural and spiritual breakdown of their society due to the impact and influence of the West. Moreover they were and continue to be one form of response to the religious and moral problems posed by 'modernisation', seen on the one hand as a challenge to create new or different values and meanings and on the other was feared as a threat to the existing pattern of values and meanings. The fact that many of the more serious problems posed by 'modernisation' have not as yet been overcome may well explain, in part, the continuing emergence of independent, Aladura-type Churches.

These Churches presented, in an idiom and manner that many could understand and apply, an answer to numerous popular anxieties and problems such as the above-mentioned epidemic and other health, social, political, economic, and cultural problems. Furthermore – and this would seem to be of the utmost importance in explaining why people turned to the Aladura Churches – the First World War and the 1918 influenza epidemic, which was followed by the bubonic plague and other epidemics in the 1920s, completely destroyed the confidence of many people in traditional medicine and many of the rituals, symbols and spirits associated with it.

According to Nigerians who remembered both the First World War and the influenza epidemic, the latter was caused by the former, and both were caused by the gods. As one contemporary expressed it, 'That [1918] was a very horrible time . . . caused according to many of us by the great death of many soldiers on the battlefield during World War I'.[81] This informant continued: 'When we went back to consult Ifa we were told that angels were waging war in heaven and that when this happens there will be war and disease on earth . . . . We must make sacrifices . . . so sacrifices were made'. But even those who prepared and offered sacrifice died in the epidemic. According to this same eye witness:

Some of the Egungun masquerades [were] made to carry the sacrifices away to the [Iwo] city gates and one of them died . . . . It was a horrible year [1918] . . . . That was the first year I touched a dead person . . . . I was sick, my father was sick, his wife was sick, about 10 of us were sick in the same long room . . . . We resort to only sucking oranges and then we don't die again. That was the worst year.

In the circumstances of the time it was very difficult if not impossible for people to obtain either traditional or modern medicines. The same informant stated:

We in Iwo did not take medicine for even if you wanted to take medicine you could not go to the farm to gather leaves and roots otherwise you return to meet people dead on the road. People believed that the power of medicine was entirely unhelpful while there was a war in heaven causing them this suffering . . . therefore we avoid using medicine and we retire to concentrate on God, the Oba, the Supreme God, Olodomare. When Egungun, one of the lesser gods, died carrying sacrifice to the city gate everyone knows that there is no one that cannot die but the Almighty.[82]

So people prayed, '"May Olodomare keep us safe, may He keep those who have taken water safe" . . . . We concluded that God was the only invincible, that no medicine would act, that we must take water and boil it. There were many things smelling in the localities, people dying, animals dying, and so we concentrate on God only.'[83]

This loss of confidence in the healing power of gods and spirits of the 'old order', with the exception of the Supreme Being, was certainly a factor in predisposing many traditional religionists and members of the mission Churches to join the Aladura Churches. But, as this chapter has attempted to show, there were also numerous social, political, economic, cultural and religious factors that contributed to the rise of independent Churches. And through these Churches, whose principal aim was to demonstrate the power and relevance of faith for a world in the process of being turned upside down by forces beyond the control of ordinary people, Christianity became as much an 'African' as a 'European' religion. Therein lies their significance.

Notes

1   On the meaning of the term Ethiopianism in the Southern African context, see B.G.M. Sundkler: *Bantu Prophets in South Africa* (2nd edn),. London: Oxford University Press, for the International African Institute (IAI), 1961. For its meaning in the West African context, see E.A. Ayandele *The Missionary Impact on Modern Nigeria 1842–1914*, op. cit., pp. 177 ff.

2   E.A.A. Adegbola, Ifa and Christianity Among the Yoruba. Ph.D. thesis. University of Bristol, 1976, p. 133.

3   ibid., pp. 136–7.

4   National Archives Ibadan (henceforth NAI) Oke Papers. 3/1/6.

5   ibid.

6   ibid.

7   ibid.

8   ibid.
9   ibid.
10   ibid.
11   P.B. Clarke, Islam and Change in Nigeria c. 1918–c. 1960. In R. Willis and A. Ross (eds), Religion and Change in African Societies, Centre of African Studies, University of Edinburgh, 1979, pp. 97 ff.
12   J.J. Martin, The Dual Legacy: Government Authority and Mission Influence among the Glebo of Eastern Liberia, 1834–1910. Ph.D. thesis, Boston, Ann Arbor University Microfilms, Michigan, 1968: 206.
13   NAI Oyo Prof 1/662 Commissioner of Policies copy of 'Awon Asotele . . . 1931'.
14   *Yoruba News* 20/10/1929.
15   J.B. Webster, *The African Churches among the Yoruba 1888–1922*. Oxford: Oxford University Press, 1964.
16   M.J.C. Echeruo, *Victorian Lagos*. London and Basingstoke: Macmillan, 1977: 93.
17   NAI, op. cit.
18   E.A. Ayandele, *The Missionary Impact on Modern Nigeria 1842–1914*, op.cit., chapters 7, 8 and *passim*, and the same author's *Holy Johnson*. London: Frank Cass 1970.
19   G.O.M. Tasie, The Prophetic Calling: Garrick Sokari Braide of Bakana (d. 1918). In E. Isichei (ed.) *Varieties of Christian Experience in Nigeria*, op.cit., pp. 99–115.
20   ibid., p. 107.
21   Citation from A. Osuntokun, *Nigeria in the First World War*. London: Longman 1979: 117.
22   ibid., pp. 117–18.
23   ibid., p. 118.
24   Interview with Pastor Shadare Sesebe, Superintendent of The Precious Stone Church and son of Pastor Shadare, 7/4/78.
25   E.A.A. Adegbola, Ifa and Christianity among the Yoruba. Ph.D. thesis, op.cit., 1976: 236.
26   ibid., p. 256.
27   Interview with Shadare Sesebe, op. cit.
28   Church Records, Precious Stone Church, Ijebu Ode.
29   ibid.
30   ibid.
31   ibid.
32   National Archives Ibadan (henceforth NAI) Oyo Prof 1/662 Faith Healer Babalola and Aladuras. Operations in Oyo Province, Nov. 1931.
33   H. Callaway: Women in Yoruba tradition and in the Cherubim and Seraphim Society. In O.U. Kalu (ed.), op. cit., p. 329.
34   ibid.
35   Blue Book, Colony and Protectorate of Nigeria, 1919.
36   See, for example, Blue Books for 1924 and 1926.
37   NAI Ije Prof 4.J.655.
38   ibid.
39   D.B. Barrett, *Schism and Renewal in Africa*. Oxford: Oxford University Press, 1968: 147.
40   NAI *Yoruba News*, 16–23 Sept. 1930.
41   ibid. *Yoruba News*, 2–9 Sept. 1930.
42   ibid. Oyo Prof 1/662. Senior Resident Oyo Province to District Officer, Ife,

14/3/1931.
43   ibid. Assistant Commissioner of Police Oyo-Ondo Province to the Resident Oyo, 5/9/1931.
44   ibid.
45   J. Akinyele Omoyajowo, *Cherubim and Seraphim. The History of an African Independent Church*. New York and Lagos: Nok Publishers, 1982.
46   ibid., pp. 143–4.
47   Interview with the Archbishop of the Cherubim and Seraphim, Ibadan, 26/7/78.
48   J.D.Y. Peel, *Aladura: A Religious Movement among the Yoruba*. Oxford: Oxford University Press, 1968.
49   H.J. Fisher, Independency and Islam: The Nigerian Aladuras And Some Muslim Comparisons. Review Article. *Journal of African History* **XI** (2), 1970: 269–77.
50   Interview with member of Cherubim and Seraphim Society, Ibadan, 15/5/1978.
51   For a full account of the development and teachings of this Church see H.W. Turner's *History of an Independent Church*, Vols I and II, Oxford: Oxford University Press, 1967.
52   ibid., Vol. I, pp. 46 ff.
53   Oshitelu Papers, University of Ibadan Library.
54   ibid.
55   ibid.
56   ibid.
57   On traditional concepts of illness and its causes and the Yoruba Priest-healer, see T. Asuni: Socio-Medical Problems of Religious Converts. *Psychopathologie Africaine*, 1973, **IX** (2): 223–36.
58   ibid.
59   H.W. Turner, op. cit., Vol. 1, Chaps. 3 and 4.
60   ibid., p. 59.
61   ibid., pp. 164–5.
62   ibid., p. 165.
63   ibid.
64   ibid., pp. 108–9.
65   J.D.Y. Peel, *Aladura: A Religious Movement Among the Yoruba*. op.cit.
66   NAI. *Daily Service* newspaper, 27/7/1944.
67   Citation from S.S. Walker: *The Religious Revolution in The Ivory Coast*, North Carolina, 1983, p. 35.
68   ibid., p. 40.
69   G. MacKay Haliburton, *The Prophet Harris*, Harlow: Longman, 1971: pp. 126–8.
70   S.S. Walker, op. cit., p. 160.
71   ibid., p. 159.
72   J.A. Omoyajowo, op. cit., p. 154.
73   P.B. Clarke, *West Africans and World Wars I and II*. London: Ethnographica Publishers Ltd, forthcoming, Chapter 1.
74   B. Holas, *Le Séparatisme Religieux en Afrique Noire*. Paris: Presses Universitaires de France, 1965: 288–90.
75   D. Paulme, Une Religion Syncrétique en Côte d'Ivoire: Le Culte Deima. *Cahiers d'Etudes Africaines* Vol. 9, No. 3, 1972. Also B. Holas: Bref Aperçu sur les Principaux Cultes Syncrétiques de la Basse Côte d'Ivoire. *Africa*, 24, Jan. 1954. And Holas: *Le Séparatisme Religieux en Afrique Noire*, op. cit.
76   G.M. Haliburton, op. cit., p. 157.
77   C.G. Baëta, *Prophetism in Ghana. A Study of Some 'Spiritual' Churches*. London:

SCM Press, 1962, Chap. 2, pp. 9–28.
78   ibid., Chap. 3, pp. 28–68. And K.A. Opoku, Changes within Christianity: the Case of the Musamo Christo Disco Church. In O.U. Kalu, op. cit., pp. 309–21.
79   D.B. Barrett, *Schism and Renewal in Africa*, op. cit.
80   ibid., p. 138.
81   Interview with Pa Adeniyi. Ibadan, 30/5/1978.
82   Interviews with Pa Adeniyi and some of his contemporaries. Iwo, 5/6/1978.
83   ibid.

7
Christianity since independence: growth and change.

Anglophone West Africa

From whatever point of view one considers them it is clear that virtually all Christian Churches and societies in Anglophone West Africa, whether mission controlled or independent, have changed considerably since independence. In most instances the changes considered here began to take shape prior to independence such as the change in the relationship between the Christian Churches from one characterised – at least at the official, public level – by intolerance and rivalry to one of far greater mutual respect and co-operation. There has also been a pronounced change in the thinking, attitudes and approach of many of the Christian Churches and societies towards Islam and traditional religion (see Chapter 8, pp. 214–19). Further, although African leadership at the local level does not necessarily mean complete African control, the vast majority of Christian Churches, societies and institutions administered and directed by non-Africans at independence have since then appointed Africans to positions of the highest responsibility and authority. There have also been changes in the independent Churches, and while some of these have made for greater similarity in terms of ethos and organisational style with the older, mission-established Churches, the latter have also moved some way towards introducing a form and style of worship similar to that of the African and Aladura Churches and societies.

In a number of West African states such as Nigeria and Ghana these changes have been accompanied by steady growth. But with state control of education in many countries it has not been possible to use the school to anything like the same extent as in the past for the purpose of conversion. On the other hand the catechist with improved training and enhanced status within the Church continues to be, particularly in the rural areas, a principal agent of evangelisation.

Christianity has also experienced new beginnings in this period in the form of such Churches as the Nigerian Mennonite Church,[1] active since independence in south-eastern Nigeria, and the Eden Revival Church established in 1963 in Ghana by the former Presbyterian Charles Yeboa-Korie. Both of these Churches have links with North American Christian, evangelical-type movements and the latter's connections in this respect

illustrate, as Hastings points out, 'the tendency of independent Churches
to reacquire American or European links, to come very closer in ethos to
the smaller Protestant type of mission-found church'.[2] In fact, since
independence, North American evangelical, fundamentalist Christian
movements in particular have influenced the thinking and attitudes not
only of the leadership and members of the independent Churches in West
Africa but also of many other Christians who belong to the older, mission-
established Churches. They have also had a profound impact, not always
positive, on Christian-Muslim relations (see Chapter 8, pp. 217–18).
There have also been important changes in the way the older, historic
Churches understand their role and mission in West Africa. Before
discussing these and other developments it is necessary first to provide
some idea, at a general level and with specific reference to a number of
West African states, of the growth of Christianity since independence.

Growth: an overview

The growth rate of Christianity in West Africa since independence has
been uneven. In countries such as Cape Verde, and São Tomé e Principe,
which regained their independence in 1974 and 1975 respectively and
where the overwhelming majority of the population at that time was
Catholic, there has been little or no change. The same applies to most of
those countries – The Gambia, Mali, Niger, Chad, Guinea (Conakry),
Senegal, Mauritania – where there was a large majority of Muslims. If
anything, this majority in most cases has been increased. In other
countries – Benin, Cameroon, Ghana, the Ivory Coast, Liberia, Nigeria,
Sierra Leone, Togo, and Burkina Faso (Upper Volta) – Christianity has
continued to make headway, as has Islam, with the independent
Churches expanding at a somewhat faster rate than the historic or
mission-established Churches. It can, however, be misleading to
generalise here since the Catholic Church in Ghana, Benin and elsewhere
has continued to make rapid progress. By way of contrast its progress in
Guinea (Conakry), Senegal, the Ivory Coast and Burkina Faso has neither
been as sure or as steady due in part to the failure to train a sufficient
number of African clergy, to financial and political difficulties in certain
situations, and to the appeal and dynamism of Islam.

The charismatic and fundamentalist, evangelical movements, already
referred to, have increased their scope and influence in West Africa in
recent times, and this has been particularly noticeable in Nigeria and
Ghana. This can be attributed to outside influences in particular to
influences from evangelical Churches from North America, and to a loss
of confidence in 'secular', political theories and approaches to the
establishment of the 'good' society. So often one is told or hears it said
that security and hope lie in Jesus and not in politics. For an increasing
number of Christians faith in Christ is seen as the only hope for a society
faced with the mounting problems generated by industrialisation and
'modernisation'. It is possible to exaggerate the extent of the shift towards
Christian fundamentalism for there are also signs of increasing

secularisation, particularly among the western educated in urban centres such as Abidjan, Lagos and Dakar.

Case studies

Sierra Leone

Christianity, as we have seen, enjoyed its greatest success in the western area, formerly known as the Colony of Sierra Leone. In contemporary Sierra Leone, much more so than was the case in the past, Christian Churches are actively engaged in evangelisation not only in the western area but throughout the provinces (formerly the protectorate), with the possible exception of that part of the northern sector inhabited by the Susu, and the area of the south inhabited by the Vai. Among the older, longer established Christian bodies in Sierra Leone the United Methodist and the Roman Catholic Churches have made most headway, while membership of the Anglican Church has shown virtually no increase at all other than the increase due to 'natural' conversion since around 1900. Likewise independent Churches, with the possible exception of the Church of Salvation, established in 1946, appear to be making little progress.[3] Opposed, even persecuted by other Christians who regarded him as a false prophet, the founder of the Church of Salvation E.J. Fofana managed to acquire a site for a church or temple in the town of Bo in 1963, and by 1982 this Aladura-type Church had six other churches, seven prayer groups and a commercial secondary school, all self financed.[4]

In post-independence Sierra Leone some of the old difficulties which confronted the Christian Churches in the past and which they helped to create still persist. Limited by finances and manpower some Churches are confined to working in particular areas and consequently these Churches continue to be identified with one or a few language groups only. The tendency of the wealthier, western-educated Creoles to regard their membership of the Anglican Church in particular as a symbol of their higher status in society has the effect of making change and adaptation extremely slow and difficult and limiting participation in Church services and activities in general to their own community.

There has been an attempt on the part of the United Methodist Church, and many of the Churches, to place far less emphasis on the educating and training of a Christian middle-class élite and far more on tackling directly the acute social and economic problems arising from urbanisation and industrialisation, problems which affect most seriously the more deprived members of society. This became possible as the government began to take over more responsibility for education and health. The Christian Churches, of course, are still involved in both of these spheres. For example, in the 1970s the Catholic Church alone was responsible for 40,000 students in 35 per cent of the country's secondary schools.[5]

After over 180 years of Christian involvement, between 8 and 9 per cent of Sierra Leone's population of nearly three million is Christian, compared with about 38 per cent Muslim and over 50 per cent traditional religionists.[6]

Liberia

The Christian Churches in Liberia have expanded at a steady pace in recent times and today some 33 per cent of the population of one and a quarter million is Christian. Muslims make up about 20 per cent of the population, and the remaining 45 per cent are adherents of the traditional religion.[7]

Of the numerous Churches in Liberia the largest is the United Methodist Church which is strongest in and around Monrovia, the capital. The Lutheran Church on the other hand is by and large a rural Church. The Catholic Church, which had a difficult beginning in Liberia, has made a considerable impact in recent times on the Cape Palmas region and along with other Churches has made significant contributions in the fields of medicine and education.

There are no large independent African Churches of Liberian origin, although it was two black Americans, Lott Carey and Colin Teague, who built the first church in Liberia in 1822 (see Chapter 2, pp. 37 ff.). The African Methodist Episcopal Church, and the African Methodist Episcopal Zion Church, both active in Liberia are two other examples of Churches in which black Americans played a leading role. Apart from the Church of the Lord (Aladura) which, as we have seen, entered Liberia from Nigeria in 1947 there are no independent Churches of any size in the country. All these Churches have made little progress in recent times. Although not large the Roman Catholic Church has perhaps made the most headway since the 1950s and this has largely been because of its heavy involvement in education.[8] The Pentecostal Churches such as the Assemblies of God and Seventh Day Adventists, concentrating in the main on the interior, have also been expanding quite rapidly. The older Protestant Churches, for their part, while they have attracted some of the indigenous people, for example, some of the Bassa, Kru, Kpelle, Grebo and Vai peoples, are still strongest among the Americo-Liberians along the coast.

Ghana

Most of the Christian Churches in Ghana, with the possible exception of the Anglican Church, have expanded since independence in 1957, and this is particularly so in the case of the Roman Catholic and some of the 'spiritualist' or independent Churches. The Roman Catholic Church now has over one million members while the independent Churches can claim about one-third of the affiliated Christian community in the country.[10] The Eden Revival Church established in 1963 is but one of the independent Churches in Ghana that has attracted a considerable number of adherents in recent times, drawing its members from virtually all classes of society, including some of the new social élite. The late 1950s

VII   A woman Presbyterian minister in Ghana officiating at the communion service

and the 1960s appear to have been years of very rapid growth for faith-healing Churches in Ghana and other parts of West Africa.[11]

In parts of present-day Ghana a majority of Christians participate in one form or another in the life of the independent Churches. This is the case, for example, in the coastal Ga town of Labadi close to Accra where there are at least ten independent Churches, alongside the Presbyterian,

Anglican and Catholic Churches. According to one writer the largest of these independent Churches, the Church of the Messiah 'is in a general sense representative of all but the highest strata of the Labadi population (most of whom attended the 'orthodox' churches)'. The majority of the members are women but 'all age groups and most occupational categories are represented, with farmers, fishermen, wage workers, petty traders and clerks predominating'.[13] Moreover, the membership is multi-ethnic in composition, and most of the members see the Church as an important means of obtaining divine help in solving everyday problems of work, family relationships, health and so on. For them it is a practical, 'this worldly' form of Christianity which, like for example the Harris Church, strongly opposes any reliance upon or recourse to the traditional gods for protection, emphasising that the Christian God alone can protect and save. This Church, like many 'spiritualist' Churches, is an important means of upward social mobility for some people, founders in particular, in present-day Ghana, and it receives considerable financial support from those in the business world. It also endorses an individualism, a commitment to action and an approach to the wider society more in keeping with the new socio-economic order than with traditional socio-economic arrangements.

The older, historic Churches, now under Ghanaian leadership, continue to be involved in educational activities, in community development projects, and agricultural development programmes. Many of these initiatives are undertaken jointly by the Churches indicating the trend towards increasing co-operation between the various Christian denominations in Ghana, a trend that is in fact manifest throughout West Africa (see pp. 208 ff.).

Nigeria

All the Christian Churches in Nigeria have undergone important changes since independence in 1960. In the older Churches the leadership is now almost entirely Nigerian and the number of Nigerian clergy has increased dramatically in this period. Within the independent Churches there have also been a number of changes, particularly in the pattern of organisation. Attempts have also been made to forge greater cohesion and unity between these Churches but with little success. This failure is often attributed to the problem of reaching agreement on the question of leadership. Competition for leadership, however, may not be the real explanation for this but rather the fact that these Churches are not united internally, members preferring congregations that are small in size so that the close personal relationships established among themselves and between themselves and their local leader or prophet can be more easily maintained. It is often believed that where people can relate closely to each other and come to know each other the 'spirit' is stronger and thus the chances of achieving their spiritual goal much higher. This question of Church unity will be taken up again (see pp. 210–11) and meanwhile we can consider briefly aspects of the growth of Christianity in Nigeria in recent times.

Although there are no reliable statistics available most observers agree that the Aladura Churches have continued to expand at a rapid rate since independence. Furthermore, new Aladura Churches such as the True Church of God continue to emerge. Established in eastern Nigeria in 1953 this Church has over 120 branches in Nigeria and a small number in Cameroon, and it is the problem of ill health in the main which brings people, Roman Catholic, Anglicans and others, into this Bible-centred, faith-healing movement.[14]

One of the most popular of these new Churches is the Celestial Church of Christ established as the Heavenly Christianity Church in Porto Novo in the Republic of Benin, in 1947 by a former Methodist, Mr Oschaffa. Brought to Nigeria in the early 1950s by fishermen the Church spread throughout western Nigeria by the 1970s. Established in Ibadan in 1964 it now has twenty branches in that city alone and is also active in many of the main centres of northern Nigeria, in Europe and the United States. The Brotherhood of the Cross and Star from Cross River State, now widespread in the eastern region of Nigeria also has overseas branches in Britain and elsewhere. This Church places very great emphasis on what it sees as an inextricable connection between spiritual and material well-being. The two largest Aladura Churches in Nigeria, which continue to expand rapidly but not without encountering some opposition from members, are the Christ Apostolic Church and to a lesser extent the Cherubim and Seraphim Church.

Some of the older Churches, while continuing to spread, have also had difficulties, but of a different kind. During the Civil War in Nigeria (1967–70), the Roman Catholic and Anglican Churches in northern Nigeria were weakened by the return to the east of the country of many of their members. This, however, had a positive effect in that these Churches were now obliged to concern themselves increasingly with the creation of a 'local' Church, relying much more on local support and local initiative. In Borno State, as we have seen (see Chapter 4, pp. 114–15), the Catholic community was composed in the main of Ibos and with their departure the Church authorities had to extend their activities in a much more systematic way into the towns and rural areas of the state with a view to building a local Catholic community.

Shortage of clergy meant a heavy reliance on catechists which led in turn to a reassessment of the training schemes provided for catechists, and of their rank and status within the Church. The subsequent changes here, which among other things gave the better trained, more senior catechist public recognition as part of the Church hierarchy, contributed enormously to the growth of Catholicism in the rural areas of Bauchi and Gongola States and elsewhere.

Among the other Churches that have continued to expand in Nigeria are those that belong to TEKAN, the Fellowship of the Churches of Christ in Nigeria, and ECWA, the Evangelical Churches of West Africa. This last mentioned group of Churches, like a number of others in Nigeria, is now a missionary body in its own right, having sent over 100 missionaries to other parts of Africa.

Alongside a growing fundamentalism, the charismatic movement has had a strong influence on the Christian Churches in Nigeria. It features prominently in the NKST Church in Benue State, in Roman Catholicism in Kano, Jos, Warri and elsewhere, and in what are largely student Christian movements such as the Scripture Union, and explains to some extent the vitality, appeal and expansion of Christianity in Nigeria in the past decade or so. Fundamentalism, noted above as causing tension between Christian denominations and between Christianity and other religions also appears to appeal to students and young people in the main who see politics as corrupt and irrelevant.

Finally, while observers tend to concentrate on the phenomenal growth of independency in recent times it should be recognised that the Anglican, Catholic and older Churches in general not only continue to expand but also to show considerable vitality.

VIII   A modern-day missionary going about her work in northern Nigeria

Francophone West Africa

The growth of Christianity in Francophone West Africa since

independence has been much more uneven and much less evident than in Anglophone West Africa. While there has been expansion in the Republics of Benin, Togo, the Ivory Coast, the Cameroon, Senegal and Burkina Faso there has been either stagnation or decline in terms of numerical strength in Guinea (Conakry), Mali, and Niger. And even in certain areas of countries like Senegal and the Ivory Coast there is some evidence that considerable numbers of Christians have been turning towards Islam or have simply abandoned all forms of institutionalised, organised religion.[15] Research has shown that among students both at secondary and tertiary level in Burkina Faso (Upper Volta) there is considerable doubt about the content and relevance of the Christian faith as presented by the Church.[16] This response can also be found in Nigeria and other Anglophone West African countries.

Nevertheless, the Catholic Church which is both the largest and the oldest Christian body in Burkina Faso continues to expand its frontiers at a relatively rapid pace, converting on average 12,000 adherents of traditional religions each year.[17] The growth rate is even more impressive in the Republics of Benin, Togo and the southern region of Cameroon. Guinea (Conakry), as has been indicated, has presented special difficulties for Christian expansion which will be considered below, and direct evangelisation has also been a problem in Mali and Niger.

There are relatively few independent Churches in Francophone West Africa, with the exception of the Ivory Coast, and of those that exist most have entered from Nigeria or Ghana. Senegal appears to have no independent Churches, likewise Mali and Niger, while Burkina Faso has one. Some attempt has already been made at explaining why these Churches should be so thin on the ground in Francophone West Africa (see Chapter 6, pp. 159, 188). Although a minority almost everywhere in the region, Christians none the less have exercised and continue to exercise considerable influence over many spheres of life, an influence that has not gone unchallenged by Muslims either in the more distant past or in recent years (see Chapter 8, pp. 215–16). Attempts have been made, with some success, to establish better working relations between Christians and Muslims at all levels (see Chapter 8, pp. 217–19). This subject, alongside that of mission strategy and the indigenisation of the clergy, has absorbed a great deal of the attention of the older Churches in Francophone West Africa since independence.

The Ivory Coast

With well over one million members, the Roman Catholic Church is the largest Christian denomination in the Ivory Coast today. Next in size come the various Protestant Churches, followed by the Harris Churches which together have over 100,000 members.

The Christian Churches are strongest in the southern region as a whole and especially in urban centres such as Abidjan, where an estimated 50 per cent of the population is Roman Catholic. Once regarded by the western educated élite as the 'religion of old men' and somewhat unprogressive and backward-looking the Harris Church is now seen in a much more favourable light. Members of the élite have come to speak of it as 'authentic, African Christianity', and it is now regarded as one of the four national religions of the Ivory Coast.

Not only have people's attitudes to this Church changed but the Church itself has also undergone a process of change. It has gone out of its way to attract young people by establishing youth committees and by inviting the young to participate in the decision-making process of the Church. In order to meet the demands and interests of the younger generation who see some positive benefit in western education, the Harris Church has begun to encourage older members to send their children to school. It has also made a great deal of the fact that it is the only genuine African version of Christianity in the country. Some members have appealed to the spirit of independence and nationalism in the country by claiming that people who join other Churches allow themselves to be dictated to by outsiders.

While the Harris Church has come to resemble in many respects the mission-established Churches the latter have also come closer in form and style to the Harris Church. Led for the most part by Africans these Churches have now introduced African dance and rhythm into their services. Paradoxically the result has not always been greater co-operation between these different branches of Christianity but a determination by Harris Church people to assert their unique, distinctive character as an African Church. In fact, as far as organised dialogue between the Christian Churches is concerned, the Ivory Coast lags behind many other countries in West Africa.

Guinea (Conakry)

The history of the Christian Church in Guinea since independence in 1958 has been a stormy one. Beginning in the year of independence various Christian associations such as the Christian youth movement were banned by the government. In 1961 the government took control of mission-run schools and Qur'anic schools, and has throughout kept a close watch on religious broadcasts and sermons. Foreign missionaries were expelled, starting with Bishop Milleville in 1961 and reaching a climax in 1967 when all the remaining missionaries were told to leave the country.

While these actions created many difficulties for the Christian Church they do not appear to have unduly hindered its expansion. Under a Guinean leader, Bishop Tchidimbo, later to be imprisoned on a charge of plotting with others to overthrow the government, the number of people in Conakry under instruction to become Catholics increased considerably between 1961 and 1965.[18] Developing new methods of instruction and of necessity relying heavily on catechists and lay volunteers the bishop made considerable headway, until confronted with the government's decision of 1 May 1967 to expel all overseas missionaries, both Catholic and Protestant, with the exception of the Christian Missionary Alliance. It was officially announced that this was part of President Sekou Touré's policy of ensuring that in every sphere, both spiritual and temporal, Africans were in control. A number of African priests and nuns – many fewer than those expelled – from Senegal, Benin, Togo and Burkina Faso were allowed to enter Guinea. With a much smaller number of clergy Bishop Tchidimbo had to devote even more attention to the formation of lay assistants. Then in December 1970 he was arrested following an attempted invasion led by Portuguese mercenaries and sentenced to life imprisonment with hard labour 'for collaboration with the enemy'. The bishop, who denied any knowledge of or connection with the invaders, was released from prison in 1978.

In the last few years a number of foreign missionaries have been allowed to enter Guinea to work alongside the growing number of indigenous clergy, and although they constitute a very small proportion of the population, the Christian Churches are continuing to grow at a steady if very slow pace. Guinea, like Senegal, has no independent African Churches.

Senegal

Although very much a minority in Senegal, Christians none the less – and principally for historical reasons – exert considerable influence in the political, cultural, social and economic life of the country. This is something which some Muslims object to very strongly, arguing that as far as rights, privileges and influences are concerned, the situation of believers in Senegal is upside down (see Chapter 8, pp. 214 ff.).

While nowhere very thick on the ground Christians are to be found mainly in Dakar and among the Serer and Diola speaking peoples in the south-west. In Dakar in the mid 1960s Christians, the vast majority of whom were Roman Catholics, accounted for an estimated 14 per cent of the population and this in fact represented a slight decline when compared with the situation in 1900.[19] The problems further facing the Christian Churches in Dakar, problems arising from divorce and remarriage, are considerable.[20]

To the north of Dakar in the Diocese of St Louis there are about 8,000 Christians out of a predominantly Muslim population of close on one million while to the south in the region of Kaolack there are no more than 4,000 baptised Christians and another 1,000 receiving instruction out of a population of 600,000, of whom again the vast majority are Muslims. Further south in the Diocese of Ziquinchor in the Casamance region Christians are more numerous, about 40,000 while the total population is about 600,000. Here the trend seems to be on the whole towards Islam.

Among the Protestant Churches the Assemblies of God in particular appear to be making most headway, while the Paris-based Evangelical Mission Society, active in Senegal since 1863, appears to attract very few new members. It is worth noting, however, in partial explanation of this, that the society does not give top priority to either numerical or geographical expansion, regarding its role primarily as one of bearing witness to the Christian teachings and way of life. Some Roman Catholic missionaries have also suggested that this approach might be the right one for their Church to adopt, both theologically and practically, in a country where the overwhelming majority of people are Muslims (see pp. 219 ff.). The Catholic Church, however, has continued to play an important part in the field of education, and to extend its activities, especially in the less islamicised areas of the country.

Burkina Faso (Upper Volta)

By the 1970s some 5 per cent of the population of Burkina Faso (Upper Volta) was Christian, mainly Roman Catholic, a further 20 per cent Muslim, and the remainder – the majority – traditional religionist. The sense in which people are Christian, Muslim or traditional religionist can and does vary here as elsewhere in West Africa. To take the example of Christianity, the religion with which we are principally concerned, adults and young people, particularly students, tend to hold different views concerning the role and purpose of the Christian faith in their own life and in that of the nation: for young people its wider social, political and cultural implications are much more of an issue than they are for older people. While adults are more concerned with the solutions to life's problems which Christianity provides at a personal level, the young are much more inclined to ask what contribution it can make to national development.[21]

Many people attributed Christianity's development in the past to its involvement in education and medical welfare, and to the fact that it was well organised.[22] Today Christianity continues to expand with an estimated 12,000 converts each year from the traditional religions.[23] Again, this progress is attributable to Christian involvement in education, to well-organised missionary activity among traditional religionists, to the fact that Christianity is seen as a 'modern' religion and, of course, to natural conversion, children following the same religion as their parents. At the same time Christianity, with the increase in the number of African clergy, is no longer regarded to anything like the same extent as it was in the past as an 'imported religion'. But its strong links with the colonial regime have not been forgotten (see Chapter 5, pp. 134–35).

While many traditional religionists are converting to Christianity, and for that matter to Islam, a process facilitated by the fact that traditional leaders have converted to one or other of these two world religions, there is at the same time some evidence to suggest that a growing number of people in the urban areas, and in particular the younger generation, are moving away from institutionalised, established religion. Some of them know little and care less about the Catholic Church's teachings and rarely attend services.[24] Consequently, when one discusses numerical growth or expansion it is important to keep in mind this tendency, which often comes with increasing prosperity or higher standards of educational attainment, to move out of the Churches or at least to limit active participation in Church life to a minimum. This trend has also been observed in other urban centres in West Africa, for example in Dakar and Abidjan.

The competition between Christianity and Islam for the allegiance of traditional religionists continues, albeit on a much more tolerant and friendly basis than in the past (see Chapter 8, pp. 220 ff.). And it is the Muslims who appear to be making most headway. This is due in part to the fact that they are now better organised, more united and make effective use of all the available 'modern' means of communication to proclaim their message, often emphasising the positive contribution Islam can and does make to the progress of the nation.[25] Islam also appears to have a more acceptable solution to the problems of divorce and remarriage which is an issue of growing concern among Christians in the urban areas. Islam is not, however, without its critics, especially among the younger generation, many of whom maintain that it is much too slow in adapting itself to a rapidly changing world.[26]

The transfer of ecclesiastical authority and the Africanisation of the clergy

Wherever one looked in West Africa – and indeed Africa as a whole – in the 1950s there were few if any Africans in positions of leadership in the mission-established Churches. The goal of self-governing Churches discussed in Chapter 3 had nowhere been realised. But as political independence approached, there developed a greater awareness on the part of some of these Churches of the need to transfer ecclesiastical authority to Africans. Joseph Kiwanuka, made a Catholic bishop in 1939, was the only African Catholic bishop in sub-Saharan Africa until 1951.[27] As late as 1957 some missionary societies, for example, the Universities' Mission to Central Africa, did not have a single African bishop. According to Hastings, it was still rare in the 1950s 'to find a Church or diocese seriously planning the training of [African] clergy to take over the most senior, as also the most technical, of the posts held by missionaries'.[28]

Among the exceptions were the Evangelical Church of Togo (EET), already autonomous by this time, the Evangelical Churches of West Africa (ECWA) situated mainly in northern Nigeria, and the Evangelical Church of the Cameroon (EEC). In the second half of the 1950s a number of African bishops were ordained by the Catholic Church, but were not at that time given full responsibility for the local Church. The Ghanaian priest John Amissah, for example, was ordained a bishop in 1957, the year of Ghana's independence, but it was only 1960 that he was entrusted with full responsibility for the Diocese of Cape Coast. The 1960s then witnessed a whole series of African appointments to the most senior posts in the Churches, and today there are very few expatriate bishops anywhere in West Africa.

This transfer of ecclesiastical authority was prompted by and consistent with a political situation that demanded African leadership in all walks of life. However, the shortage of trained African clergy meant that it was not always possible to respond fully to this demand. In Guinea (Conakry), as we have seen, there were no more than a handful of African priests in 1967 when the expatriate missionaries were ordered to leave the country. And a similar situation developed in Nigeria when during the Civil War (1967–70) some 281 expatriate Catholic missionaries were withdrawn from the then eastern region to be followed by another 100 almost immediately after the war. At this time only about twenty Nigerian priests were being ordained each year. Since then the numbers have increased dramatically.

There has also been a relatively rapid increase in the number of indigenous Catholic priests in Cameroon where by 1970 they numbered nearly 200 and accounted for about 38 per cent of the Catholic clergy in the country. Togo, Benin and Burkina Faso (Upper Volta) have also made significant progress in the formation of an African clergy since independence, and the same is true of Ivory Coast, Senegal and Mali, though in the case of these last three mentioned countries the indigenisation process has gone ahead at a much slower rate.[29] A similar situation exists in the Catholic Church in Liberia where in 1961 there were only three indigenous priests.

While from the outset most of the mission Churches had accepted the need for self-governing African Churches little was done about it in practice until the 1940s, and even then there was often a marked lack of real enthusiasm for the idea. With the regaining of independence it became increasingly clear that continuing expatriate leadership of the Churches on a long-term basis was no longer viable or acceptable, and things began to change, resulting today in a fairly extensive African ministry at every level in these Churches. They are by no means self-propagating or self-supporting for they still employ considerable numbers of expatriate missionaries and rely heavily on financial assistance from abroad. However, although still present in strength, expatriate missionaries have been obliged by the above changes to examine their role and purpose in West Africa and elsewhere on the continent.

In the light of the changes that have taken place in recent times and in a situation in which great emphasis has been placed on the need to adapt the Christian gospel to the African condition, many expatriate missionaries have questioned the necessity of ministering in West Africa. Among other things they believe that their continued presence could well prevent the local Church from taking over full responsibility as long as it can continue to call on expatriate personnel. In the mid 1970s there were still an estimated 235 expatriate Roman Catholic bishops and 12,700 expatriate Roman Catholic priests for the whole of Africa, and this represents an increase rather than a decline in the total number of expatriate Roman Catholic clergy working in Africa since 1960.[30] On the other hand, the number of expatriate missionaries working in Africa from some other missionary societies has declined over the same period of time. This is true for example of the Baptist Missionary Society (BMS), the Church Missionary Society (CMS) and the Methodist Missionary Society (MMS). In the mid 1970s the vast majority of the 37,400 expatriate missionaries in Africa were Roman Catholics. These high figures prompted one writer to ask 'whether the Christian faith, if it is to continue to be within the mainstream of Africa's evolving life, can move forward to a virile African Christianity with this large expatriate element'.[31]

While some of those involved in this debate, both African and expatriate, have called for a moratorium on expatriate missionaries in Africa, others believe that if trained, or retrained where necessary, for the new, developing situation, there is no reason why both the younger and older expatriate missionary cannot continue to play an important role in building up the Christian Church in Africa for some time to come. The indigenisation of the Christian Church in Africa, of course, depends not only on finding a solution to the expatriate missionary question but also on the type of training given to African clergy. If the old methods are retained and the pursuit of higher and higher qualifications persists – the 'diploma disease' as it is sometimes called – then the presence or absence of expatriates may not make a great deal of difference.

In West Africa, and no doubt elsewhere in Africa, when all the discussion about training of African clergy and the role of the expatriate missionary is put to one side, it remains clear that much still depends on the catechists who are largely responsible for the ever-increasing numbers of rural parishes. In some parts of West Africa there is even a shortage of trained catechists let alone clergy and in this situation schemes have been developed to permit village communities interested in Christianity to choose one of their members, who may well be illiterate and polygamist, as well as unbaptised, 'to preside over prayers and teach Christian doctrine'.[32] In a sense, it is ministry at this village level that may well determine to a considerable extent the future of the Christian Churches in Africa.

Towards co-operation and unity: the growth of interdenominational organisations

Relationships between the various Christian denominations in West Africa were characterised more by rivalry, competition, and even outright opposition than by co-operation during much of the period covered in this study. Catholic missionaries in The Gambia in the 1890s found the Methodists even more objectionable than Muslims.[33] And as one writer comments with reference to western Nigeria 'there was cut-throat competition between Anglicans, Methodists and the Independent Churches'.[34] Even though the Anglican, Bishop Crowther, helped the Roman Catholic mission to establish itself in eastern Nigeria in the 1880s[35] relations between Anglicans and Catholics in the region were for a very long time grounded in the same sort of competition.[36] In former French West Africa, for example in the Ivory Coast, Catholic and Protestant spokesmen strongly opposed each other. In the Ivory Coast, once it had become clear that the Harris movement was going to be more influential and have a greater impact than had been anticipated, the Roman Catholic mission there began to attack it, arguing that it was 'promoted by a mysterious and malevolent international power [Protestantism]'.[37]

While the pages of history are filled with numerous other examples of competition, rivalry and opposition between the Christian Churches in West Africa there are also, from quite early on in the modern period of Christianity, examples of attempts to unite the various Protestant denominations. In theory and to some extent in practice both the London Missionary Society and the Qua Ibo mission were, as far as Protestant Churches were concerned, non-sectarian in character. In 1910 the Endinburgh Conference on Christian missionary activity emphasised the need for greater co-operation between Protestant missionary societies, pointing out that the main purpose of missionary endeavour in Africa was not the establishment of Methodism, Presbyterianism or any other 'ism', but the establishment of an indigenous Christian community.[38] The fact that the different mission societies even when prepared to co-operate had different spheres of influence often meant that in practice such co-operation was extremely difficult to achieve.

None the less, organisations such as the United Christian Council of Sierra Leone founded in 1924 were created with a view to encouraging increased co-operation between the Christian Churches. Today this council has twelve full members, and an affiliate member is the Church of the Lord, an Aladura Church. The Roman Catholic Church is not a member, and perhaps even if it decided to apply for membership it would not be admitted because of the opposition from some of the more fundamentalist Christian Churches that form part of the Council. Furthermore, despite the numerous joint activities in education, broadcasting, refugee schemes and in other fields for which this council is responsible, denominational differences, grounded in tradition, status and identity as much as anything else, remain strong in Sierra Leone.

The Catholic Church, for its part, emphasising the need for order, authority, dogma and cohesion among its own members made little or no attempt to forge closer ties with the Protestant Churches in the pre-colonial and colonial periods. From the Catholic standpoint Protestantism was in disarray. Writing in 1926 on Protestant methods of evangelisation one Catholic expert on missionary method commented: 'The profound weakness of Protestantism lies in the fact that despite the heroic efforts and undoubted dedication of its missionary personnel . . . there is no doctrinal certainty, but rather a groping about after the Truth and consequently dissipation of mental, emotional and physical effort'.[39] The official Roman Catholic position in those times was quite straightforward: unless other Christian 'sects' agreed to accept the authority and teaching of the Roman Catholic Church which was alone in possession of the full Truth, then there was no point in co-operation at any level. Some Protestant Churches were equally self-confident and self-righteous, seeing in Catholicism a complete distortion of the Christian faith. Thus, whatever co-operation existed at the official level between Christian denominations in the pre-colonial and colonial periods it rarely involved collaboration between Catholics and Protestants. One of the main reasons given by the Catholic Church for leaving Liberia in the 1880s was opposition from Protestants. In the Ivory Coast, Catholic and Protestant spokesmen argued bitterly over the converts made by Harris, both sides claiming that they had the sole right to instruct them further.

While many Churchmen continued to think in terms of what distinguished one Christian denomination from another, and in particular Catholics from Protestants, more and more African politicians, journalists and others involved in the independence movement began increasingly to emphasise the need for solidarity and unity. This had an effect on the relations between the different Christian Churches, and on the relationship between these Churches and Islam. Moreover the ecumenical movement, a response to some extent to the spread of Communism and increasing secularisation, was gaining momentum reaching a high point in the Roman Catholic Church's Second Vatican Council (1962–5). At this council the Catholic Church responded in a more positive manner than ever before in modern times to demands from its clergy and laity in Africa and elsewhere for closer co-operation between the Christian Churches and other religions (see Chapter 8, pp. 217 ff.).

The mistakes of the past – opposition, criticism and hostility – were admitted and from the 1960s Christian Churches pursued the cause of unity among themselves with a greater vigour than ever before. In Ghana a Christian Council embracing numerous Protestant denominations was established in 1929, but it was not until 1966 that the Catholic church established relations with this body. In Nigeria, likewise, a Christian Council was formed in 1930 and once again the Catholic Church was not a member. However, since the 1960s numerous ecumenical institutes and associations have been founded and ensure at least a minimum of co-operation between the Churches. Among them are the Catholic Church's Pastoral Commission, the National Institute for Religious Sciences, the Institute of Church and Society, the Christian Association of Nigeria, the Christian Health Association of Nigeria, the National Institute of Moral and Religious Education, the Association for Christian Higher Education, and the Community Development Group.

It has proved much easier, for obvious reasons, for Churches to co-operate on social and other issues than to unite and form one Church, as the failure in the 1960s of the proposed Church union among Protestants in Nigeria shows.[40] The Aladura Churches in Nigeria have also attempted, as we have seen, to form themselves into a single Church. The Nigeria Association of Aladura Churches was established in 1960 and the Spiritual Association in 1961. Both were created for the purpose of generating co-operation and eventual unity between all the Aladura Churches. And in 1967 proposals were advanced with a view to establishing dialogue between the three major Aladura Churches in Nigeria, the Cherubim and Seraphim, the Church of the Lord and the Christ Apostolic Church. To date nothing of real substance has emerged out of these proposals. Often, in the case of the Aladura and indeed other Churches large, highly centralised organisations do not attract the support of the people. For the latter, membership of a smaller unit makes possible strong personal commitment to their beliefs and practices and to each other, something that is much more difficult to achieve in larger, more bureaucratic, institutions.

One of the principal aims of the independent Church movement is, as we have seen, to provide a practical, relevant form of Christianity, and in the modern context this has meant providing solutions not only for problems of health but also for the problems created by urbanisation and industrialisation such as unemployment, homelessness and so on. They have also had to cope with the growing demand for education. By way of response a number of Aladura Churches in Nigeria in an effort to demonstrate that they are relevant and in touch have established their own schools, their own employment and accommodation schemes, and have begun to make use of all the latest, most up-to-date techniques in broadcasting and journalism to spread their message. They are now run much more on the lines of established Churches than was the case in the past, and this in the minds of some members has tended to weaken their 'spiritual' impact. These Churches do after all claim that while the western view of the world lacks a spiritual dimension and is predominantly a 'materialist' one, by way of contrast they have a more profound understanding of reality grounded in spiritual awareness.[41] What we are perhaps seeing at present in a number of Aladura Churches is what Weber describes as the transition from prophet movement to established Church.

While the Aladura Churches, then, have gone to considerable lengths to make changes, for example, in the way they are organised and administered in order to promote themselves and also in order to gain admission to the various ecumenical bodies, the older Churches have been slow to engage in dialogue with them. There are none the less a number of ecumenical associations which have admitted Aladura Churches to full membership, the Ghana Evangelical Fellowship established in 1969 being a case in point.

On the growth of interdenominational organisations, it is worth noting that in some countries, among them the Republics of Benin and the Ivory Coast, there are still no formally constituted interdenominational organisations to co-ordinate activity between the Catholic and the Protestant Churches, or even between the Protestant Churches themselves. Nevertheless, even in these countries, as is the case throughout West Africa, there is at present greater tolerance and co-operation between the Christian Churches at the official level than there ever was in the past, while at grass roots level there always has been a high degree of tolerance and respect. Moreover, the Christian Churches have also attempted to co-operate more closely and to enter into dialogue with Muslims, and to approach traditional religions with greater sensitivity.

Conclusions

Many of the Christian Churches in West Africa have not only expanded since independence but have also undergone considerable change. They are now, for the most part, under African leadership and although the progress here has been uneven, there has been some attempt to view Christianity from an African perspective, to express it through the medium of African symbols and rituals, and to adapt it to the interests, spiritual and material, of African society.

Of course, for many the progress has neither been fast enough nor has it gone far enough. Some still maintain, as did the founders of the African Churches (see Chapter 6, pp. 156 ff.) that if the process of indigenisation does not go faster and deeper African culture will be irreparably undermined. To 'de-westernise' African Christianity and present an African perspective it is not sufficient, though many would appear to believe that it is, to change the appearance of some of the symbols of Christianity and introduce a number of African rituals. There must also be an African interpretation of the underlying meaning of those symbols and rituals based on African historical, cultural and religious experience. This is what the independent Church movement was, and is, all about. What is being suggested is that the West African interpretation and expression of Christianity as found in many of the older Churches in particular needs to be much more inductive and empirical in approach. This would not necessarily be a barrier to closer co-operation between the various branches of the Christian Church both in Africa and elsewhere, especially if it were recognised that no interpretation was final and definitive but that all, being only partial and particularistic expressions derived from different societies, could complement each other.[42]

There is a movement, however gradual and faltering, towards greater co-operation between the Christian Churches in West Africa, and as we shall see in the following chapter a similar change is taking place in the relations between the Christian Churches, Islam and traditional religions in West Africa.

Notes

1 E. and I. Weaver, *The Uyo Story*. Elkhart, USA: Mennonite Board of Missions, 1970.
2 A. Hastings, *A History of African Christianity, 1950–1975*. Cambridge: Cambridge University Press, 1979: p. 179.
3 A. Espitalie. The Importance of the Old Testament in the Life and Worship of Independent Churches in West Africa with special reference to the Church of Salvation (Sierra Leone). B.A. Dissertation, School of Oriental and African Studies (SOAS), University of London, April 1983.
4 ibid., pp. 2–3.
5 A.J. Gittins, *The Mende and the Missionary*, Vol. 2, Ph.D. thesis, Edinburgh, 1977: 534.
6 D.B. Barrett, *World Christian Encyclopaedia*. Oxford: Oxford University Press, 1982: 610.
7 ibid., p. 456.
8 E.M. Hogan, *Catholic Missions and Liberia*, op.cit., Appendix 3.
9 D.B. Barrett, op. cit., p. 323.
10 ibid., p. 324.

11   A. Hastings, op. cit., p. 251 and *passim*. And R.W. Wyllie. *Spiritism in Ghana: A Study of New Religious Movements*. Montana: Scholars Press, 1980.
12   L. Mullings, Religious Change and Social Stratification in Labadi, Ghana . . . The Church of the Messiah. In G. Bond, W. Johnson and S. Walker (eds) *African Christianity. Patterns of Religious Continuity*. New York and London: Academic Press, 1979: p. 72.
13   ibid.
14   R.T. Curley, Dreams of Power: Social Process in a West African Religious Movement. *Africa* **53** (3), 1983: 22 ff.
15   This observation is based on my field work in Senegal in April-May, 1981.
16   R. Deniel, Croyances Religieuses et Vie Quotidienne. Islam et Christianisme à Ouagadougou. *Recherches Voltaïques* **14**, CNRS Paris-Ouagadougou, 1970.
17   D.B. Barrett, op. cit., p. 731.
18   C. Rivière, *Mutations Sociales en Guinée*. op.cit.: 368.
19   V. Martin, *La Chrétienté Africaine de Dakar*. Dakar: IFAN, 1964, p. 39.
20   Interviews with parish clergy, Dakar, April-May, 1981.
21   R. Deniel, Croyances Religieuses et Vie Quotidienne. op.cit., 1970: 36–7, and p. 132.
22   ibid., p. 118.
23   D.B. Barrett, op. cit., p. 731.
24   R. Deniel, op. cit., p. 125.
25   P.B. Clarke, 'West Africa and Islam . . .', pp. 241–2.
26   R. Deniel, op. cit., pp. 206–8.
27   A. Hastings, op. cit., p. 113.
28   ibid.
29   P. Guillaume, L'Eglise Catholique en Afrique Francophone. *Année Africaine 1970*, p. 254.
30   E. Kendall, *The End of An Era. Africa and the Missionary*. London: SPCK, 1978: 79.
31   ibid., p. 81.
32   Bauchi, Roman Catholic Mission, Memorandum on the Training and Deployment of Catechists.
33   HGF Archives, Paris, Boîte 264. Dos. B. Sénégambie. Lettres-Divers.
34   O.U. Kalu, The Shattered Cross: The Church Union Movement in Nigeria 1905–1966. In O.U. Kalu (ed.) op. cit., p. 341.
35   P.B. Clarke, Methods and Ideology of the Holy Ghost Fathers in Eastern Nigeria 1885–1904. In O.U. Kalu, op. cit., p. 38.
36   F.K. Ekechi, *Missionary Enterprise and Rivalry in Igboland 1857–1914*. London: F. Cass, 1972.
37   S.S. Walker, *The Religious Revolution in the Ivory Coast*. op.cit., 51.
38   C.P. Groves, *The Planting of Christianity in Africa*. Vol. III, London: Lutterworth, 1948–1958: 292.
39   Revd R.P. Charles, *Les Méthodes Protestantes de Pénétration de L'Islam*. Paris: Institut Catholique, 1927.
40   O.U. Kalu, *The Shattered Cross: The Church Union Movement in Nigeria 1905–1966*. In O.U. Kalu (ed.) op. cit.
41   The Archbishop of the Cherubim and Seraphim Church, Ibadan, among others made this point in interviews held in June 1978.
42   M. Wiles, Theology and Unity. *Theology* **77** (643), January 1974.

8
Developments in Christian relations with Islam and African traditional religions.

Islam

Not only has there been a move towards greater toleration, co-operation and unity between the various Christian denominations in West Africa, but there has also been a profound change at the 'official level' in Christian-Muslim relations in the region in recent times. At the grass roots level relations have almost always been characterised by such tolerance and co-operation.

A good deal has already been said in previous parts of this study, beginning with Chapter 1, concerning Christian views, attitudes and approaches to Islam in the pre-colonial and colonial periods. One of the aims of the Portuguese in the fifteenth century was to establish Christian kingdoms in West Africa for the purpose of counteracting the growth and influence of Islam. And the missionaries of the first era of Christian evangelisation in West Africa for their own reasons, which often tended to overlap with those of their respective governments, were likewise determined to halt the spread of Islam (see Chapter 1, pp. 12–13).

Believing that Muslims in West Africa were only very loosely attached to their faith, these missionaries were fully convinced that their task would be relatively easy. On the other hand some of their lay contemporaries who knew West Africa saw things differently. One, Coelho, who visited the Senegambia in the second half of the seventeenth century wrote 'The Jolofs are all Muslims and by that very fact are extremely difficult to convert'.[1] Another seventeenth century European visitor to the Senegambia, while observing that a good deal of mixing of African traditional religion with Islam took place, was nevertheless convinced that the Senegalese were *in principle* Muslims and obeyed the main precepts of the Qur'an.[2] This observer noted, moreover, and somewhat ironically, that more expatriate Christians converted to traditional religion than traditional religionists to Christianity. He wrote 'It is more frequent to see the French embrace the cult of the indigenous than to see the latter convert to the religion of the French'.[3]

Islam, though not as widespread as the above quotations might suggest, was much more deeply rooted in Senegambian society than the Christian missionaries imagined. Having arrived in Takrur in northern Senegal in the eleventh century, Islam was slowly but steadily becoming an integral part of the religious, intellectual and cultural life of the society.[4] And this was much more so the case by the 1840s when the modern period of Christian missionary activity in the region began in earnest.

Like their predecessors, the missionaries who arrived in West Africa in the early nineteenth century, and for a long time afterwards, had probably never heard or read anything positive about Islam. Made aware through their worship and liturgy, papal pronouncements, the writings of Christian theologians and historians, popular literature, and political rhetoric of the so-called Islamic threat to Christianity and European civilisation these missionaries, to whom Islam was a post Christian heresy, once again set out to halt and even reverse the progress of Islam in West Africa. And at the outset they were also full of confidence that this could be accomplished with little difficulty. As we have seen they were greatly mistaken (see Chapters 3, 4 and 5).

By the last quarter of the nineteenth century most missionaries on the ground in the Senegambia and elsewhere had been forced by their lack of success to abandon the idea of converting Muslims and of Christianising Muslim territories. From this period onwards the concentration was more on 'stemming the tide' of Islam rather than on attempting to roll back its frontiers. The race was on to build a barrier against further Islamic penetration into non-Muslim areas (see Chapters 4 and 5). Of course, there were those who never relaxed their efforts or gave up hope that Islam could be overcome. Believing that Christianity and western civilisation were superior to anything that Islam had to offer, these missionaries were convinced that once Muslims had reached a higher level of intellectual awareness they would be able to appreciate these facts and would then make the decision to become Christians.[5]

The view was fairly widespread in missionary circles in the late nineteenth and early part of this century that the survival of Islam depended on the continuation of slavery, and that once this was undermined the whole edifice would come tumbling down. In the opinion of many missionaries no one became a Muslim out of conviction or for religious reasons, but simply out of material considerations, because Islam was an easy option or because force had been used to convert people.

Among the Christian clergy who presented a much more positive view of Islam were Mojola Agbebi and Edward Wilmot Blyden, and a number of Christian journalists in southern Nigeria. Agbebi spoke of Islam as 'Christianity's older brother and more experienced rival', as 'a demonstrative and attractive religion', and of the African Muslim as 'our co-religionist'.[6] Similar views were expressed by Blyden in his *Christianity, Islam and the Negro Race*, written in 1888.[7] Southern Nigerian journalists supported the positive, tolerant, more objective approach to Islam adopted by Agbebi and Blyden and condemned the negative, hostile attitude of Christian missionaries towards Muslims in northern Nigeria, arguing that they should be left alone since they were already 'religiously civilised' and that more attention should be paid to the moral and spiritual well-being of Christians in the south.[8]

This positive response to Islam did not, it should be noted, indicate a preference for Islam on the part of those who adopted it. It was to an extent a genuine, sincere appraisal, based on observation and experience, of the merits of Islam in the West African setting. There were other considerations involved as well. Blyden, for instance, attempted to move away from the negative, stereotypical view of Islam found in a great deal of the literature on Islam produced by non-Muslims. On the other hand, he was aware of and was influenced by the writings of Nöldeke, Muir, Spanger and Deutsch which he felt provided a much more objective, balanced presentation of Islam.

There were many other reasons, of a theoretical, practical and personal nature, as to why Islam appealed to Blyden. He saw Islam as carrying out what he termed as a 'civilising mission' in West Africa by providing, among other things, a thorough, systematic education, leading to a form of development which did not involve European cultural domination. According to Blyden – and this was of great significance given his experience of racial prejudice against black people like himself – Islam did not discriminate on grounds of race or colour, while Christianity sometimes failed to uphold the dignity of the African.

The response to Islam shown by Blyden, Mojola Agbebi and others was also as much a criticism of the Christian Church's attitude to the norms and values of African society as it was a positive statement about Islam. Blyden was writing at a time when Africans in Sierra Leone and elsewhere were being superseded or downgraded and in some cases even dismissed from the colonial administration by Europeans who were in some instances less well qualified than those they took over from or replaced. He wrote, moreover, at a time when pressure groups composed of European missionaries were attempting to oust Africans from positions of leadership in the Church (see Chapter 3).

Blyden and other like-minded Africans highlighted the positive side of Islam not only because they were genuinely convinced that Islam did contain an indisputably positive dimension, but also for the purpose of persuading Christian leaders and spokesmen of the need for a change in the 'form' and presentation of Christianity if it was to compete successfully with its main rival in Africa.

At the outset, therefore, Christian missionaries in West Africa were not only optimistic about the prospects of holding back the advance of their main rival Islam, but also about converting large numbers of Muslims to Christianity. By the last two decades of the nineteenth century this optimism, on both counts, had begun to give way among missionaries in the Senegambia to dejection and despondency. The next response of the missionaries consisted of attempts to build barriers with a view to blocking any further advance of Islam. Some of the African and Aladura Churches were also strongly opposed to the progress of Islam. To the National Church of Africa (founded as the Unitarian Brotherhood Church) Islam, as much as Christianity, was a foreign religion. And while the Aladura Churches shared a number of rituals in common with

Muslims, they were often as determined as the mission Churches used to be to convert Muslim to Christ (see Chapter 6).

The post-independence era

Since the early 1960s many Christian Churches in West Africa have been involved with Muslims in attempts to create a climate for better understanding and closer co-operation between Christians and Muslims. The Catholic Church in West Africa was greatly encouraged to pursue better relations with Islam and other non-Christian religions by the Second Vatican Council (1962–1965). On the question of Islam the Catholic Church acknowledged the mistakes of the past, stressed the need for mutual understanding and presented for the first time a positive, if cautious and minimalistic view, of Islam. Catholics, it was stated, looked with esteem upon Muslims 'who adore one God, living and enduring, merciful and all powerful, Maker of heaven and earth and Speaker to men'.[9]

Despite the fact that the Catholic Church had been somewhat cautious in its approach, omitting in its official statements on Islam many points that Muslims would have liked to have seen incorporated – for example a clear recognition of the prophetic mission of Muhammed – the Declaration, nevertheless, marked a breakthrough in Catholic-Muslim relations at the official level. It also went some way to vindicating the work of a small group of Catholics and Muslims who for a long time had been advocating closer co-operation and dialogue. On the Catholic side there was the French intellectual Massignon who many years previously had asked Christians to embark on a 'spiritual Copernican revolution', and return to the origins of Islamic teaching, 'to that point of virgin truth that is found at its centre and makes it live'.[10] As for Muslims, in both Nigeria and Senegal, they had already been meeting in association with Christians in the late 1950s and early 1960s for the purpose of improving relations and generating a better understanding of each other's faith. And in 1962 the 'Society for African Culture' in Senegal, composed of both Christians and Muslims, had sent a letter to Rome requesting the bishops of the Catholic Church to consider ways and means of initiating dialogue between Christians and Muslims in Africa.[11]

In Nigeria in October 1962 Christians from different denominations met Muslims in Kano and established a Christian-Muslim Committee to explore ways of enhancing co-operation and mutual understanding. Then in 1963 students at Ahmadu Bello University in Zaria, in Northern Nigeria, met to discuss the question of 'Ecumenism and the Undergraduate'. In 1964 the then Premier of Northern Nigeria Ahmadu Bello said in his capacity as Chancellor of Ahmadu Bello University that the task of the university was 'to bring about a dialogue between the Islamic culture from the East, the Christian culture from the West and a third culture, that of the Ancient States and Empires of Africa'.[12]

All of this was, both in tone and substance, a long way from the negative and provocative statement made in 1959 by the former French

Archbishop of Dakar when he declared that the marks of the Islamic tradition were 'fanaticism, collectivism, and enslavement of the weak', all of which made it very similar in method to Communism.[13] But from the 1960s and especially from 1969 with the appearance of the document 'Guidelines for a Dialogue between Muslims and Christians', Catholic Church leaders in Francophone West Africa have made dialogue with Muslims a top priority. They have established various Commissions on Islam and held numerous conferences such as the one at Niamey, capital of Niger, in 1975. At this conference the Catholic Bishop of Niamey invited the Muslim mystic, scholar and disciple of Cerno Bokar Taal,[14] Ahmadu Hampaté Bâ, to address the conference. The latter emphasised the need for religions to unite in order to arrest the growing trend towards atheism and expressed the hope that both Christians and Muslims would meditate more frequently on chapter (sura) 29, v. 46 of the Qur'an which he interpreted as being a direct challenge to both to get to know and understand one another better. Ignorance of each others' faith was, he suggested, the greatest obstacle to closer co-operation and dialogue.[15]

In Nigeria, though informal dialogue between Muslims and Christians has a long history, and despite the coming together of students in the early 1960s, it was not until November 1974 that the first official Muslim-Christian dialogue in Nigeria took place in Ibadan on the intitiative of the Catholic Church. The dialogue concentrated on 'areas of agreement' between the two religions and on how both religions could combat materialism. In addition, the modernisation of religious concepts and of religious language was considered with a view to making religion more intelligible to contemporary Nigerians. The common problems which Christianity and Islam should face together were listed as secularisation in education, nepotism, abortion, materialism and bribery and corruption.

Some Muslims emphasised that the real unity of Islam and Christianity consisted in the fact that they are 'united at source': God created them both and both professed entire submission to one God.[16] Muslims and Christians, however, approached God in different ways, and the main difference arose from the fact that Christians emphasised and believed in the divinity of Christ. Muslims throughout West Africa, whatever their level of education or socio-economic background, express this same point of view. Interestingly enough, recent research indicates that some Christian groups, think that even the divinity of Christ need no longer prove to be an obstacle to Christian-Muslim unity. An archbishop of the Cherubim and Seraphim Church in Western Nigeria pointed out that Muslims do not, in his opinion, regard Christ with any less esteem and reverence than the Christians. It is, he maintains, a question of understanding correctly the Muslim position.[17] There is in Nigeria a Dialogue Committee and a journal, the *Nigerian Dialogue*, for the purpose of furthering unity and understanding between Muslims and Christians.

Despite these attempts to create understanding among Muslims and Christians in Nigeria and Senegal there is the view that dialogue/ecumenism is simply a front for proselytisation. Others, particularly

Christian missionaries, fear that dialogue may result in destructive self-criticism, and further undermine the work of the Christian missions. There have also been temporary setbacks to dialogue between Muslims and Christians in Nigeria occasioned by the Civil War and the Shar'ia and 'secular state' debates.[18]

Christian-Muslim relations and changing views on missionary activity

The impact of recent developments in the field of Christian-Muslim relations on Christian thinking about missionary activity has been considerable. Some Christian missionaries actively engaged in this dialogue in Senegal have called for a radical rethink in the way the Catholic Church and the Christian Churches in general approach the whole question of mission. They believe that in the past too much emphasis was placed on geographical and numerical expansion.

As one Catholic missionary expressed it, 'The entire history of mission until very recently . . . confirms to some extent that attitude [of competition], capable of giving rise to conflict, that mentality more or less guided by the desire to gain ground'.[19] This has led to, among other things, an emphasis on quantity rather than quality, on the necessity to propagate the Christian gospel in a spatial sense and consequently to ignorance of and hostility towards Islam and traditional African religions, which have always been regarded simply as obstacles to expansion.[20] The role of the missionary was not primarily to extend the visible limits of a visible Church but to be a sign of and point people to the future Kingdom of God in accordance with the capacity of each individual to accept and understand this sign. If this view of the role of the Christian missionary were widely endorsed then, it is maintained, missionaries would realise that there was no contradiction between dialogue with Islam and Christian mission.[21]

This approach to missionary activity is by no means accepted by all Christians and many Muslims are doubtful that it will ever be generally accepted. For the latter, papal visits to Africa and elsewhere are but one clear indication that the Catholic Church pursues a universalistic, expansionist policy. It is widely believed that every major world religion is of necessity universalistic. Nevertheless, many Christians and Muslims in West Africa are clear that through co-operation they can dispel the inauthentic and false image of themselves as 'brothers at war', and contribute much in the struggle against underdevelopment and materialism. Doctrinal differences, it is worth noting, are not seen as the biggest obstacle to closer co-operation, but rather unfair competition and discrimintion in such areas as education, employment and politics, especially where these are used as instruments of conversion. And here, though the situation varies from one area of West Africa to another, and even within the same country, neither Christianity nor Islam can claim that history is entirely on its side.

African traditional religions

In the Republic of Togo there exists the South Togo Cultural and Religious Research Group, established in 1967 with headquarters at the monastery of Dzoghégan near Palimé, and here Christians have been engaged in ecumenical activities which so far have included the study of the ancestor cult. This is but one instance of the changing Christian approach to African traditional religions in recent times. For most of the period under review in this study missionaries, though there were always exceptions, viewed African traditional religions as a morass of bizarre beliefs and practices. Missionaries, of course, were not alone in this. Sociologists, including Comte who is the acknowledged founding father of the discipline and nineteenth century travellers like Richard Burton, were hard pressed to acknowledge that even a modicum of 'real' religion existed in Africa. According to Burton the African had 'barely advanced to idolatry', and had 'never grasped the ideas of a personal Deity, a duty in life, a moral code'.[22]

Not all missionaries were in entire agreement with this. For example, the American missionary Thomas Jefferson Bowen who compiled a dictionary of the Yoruba language pointed, albeit a little paternalistically, to the 'higher aspects' of Yoruba religion. He wrote, 'In Yoruba many of the notions which the people entertain of God are remarkably correct . . . . They have some notion of his justice and holiness . . . . They may extol the power and defend the worship of their idols whom they regard as mighty beings, but they will not compare the greatest idol to God'.[23] In Bowen's view, however, these 'higher aspects' of Yoruba religion had very little to do with the Yoruba but were at source the product of European influence, a clear example of the application to African society of the Hamitic hypothesis.[24]

Since they were in West Africa primarily to establish Christianity and therefore to suppress all contrary beliefs and rituals, most missionaries gave little thought to providing an objective, balanced view of African traditional religion. But one can detect a slight change in perspective with the publications of such scholars as William Schmidt, a Catholic priest. Schmidt argued that African religions were at the outset monotheistic, fetishism and animism being later developments. The Supreme Being, he claimed, and not lesser gods and idols, was at the heart of African traditional religion.[25] This was not the first time such a view had been expressed by a Christian cleric. Writing in the early eighteenth century Loyer, another Catholic priest, stated 'They (Africans on the West Coast) believe in one Supreme God, the Creator and sustainer of all things'.[26]

Other writings to appear in the 1920–1950 period, among them those of Basden,[27] Williams[28] and Smith,[29] advanced the idea of the existence in African traditional religions of the belief in a Supreme Being. The origins of this belief, however, were still not clear to everyone interested, nor was the place of God in African religious life. While some maintained that the existence of the belief was the result of contact with Christians others, like those just mentioned above, were convinced that the belief was of African origin. As to the place of the Supreme Being or High God in African religious life most observers claimed that people paid little or no attention to Him, seeing Him as remote, withdrawn, and unconcerned with everyday life.[30]

This was a view that did not fit in with the belief and practice of a number of West African traditional religionists including many in Nigeria, and it is a view that more and more students of African traditional religions, among them some who once endorsed it, are now inclined to reject. Parrinder is among those who over time have come to alter their view of the place of the Supreme Being in African traditional religions. He writes that while he once endorsed the view that 'the African's God is uncertain and remote', he had come to think of that God as being 'closer to ordinary people than this suggests'.[31] Awolalu is much more precise and definite. He says with reference to the Yoruba belief in the Supreme Being, Olódùmarè, that 'though his abode is said to be in the heavens above, He is not removed from the people and is not inaccessible'.[32] And Idowu maintains that 'the whole superstructure of Yoruba belief' rests upon the 'basic fact' that 'The existence of Olódùmarè eternally has, for all practical purposes, been taken for granted as a fact beyond question'.[33]

From the 1940s missionary writing on African traditional religions became much more objective. Works like Temple's on the Bantu were attempts to deepen Christian and western understanding in general of African religious and philosophical thought,[34] while Parrinder with the same end in view provided a number of interesting analyses of African rituals and beliefs.[35] Other research carried out by anthropologists, such as that on the Dogon of Mali,[36] also treated African religious systems with a great deal more empathy than had been the case in the nineteenth century.[37]

Practice often lagged behind theory. While in some missionary circles views on the nature of African traditional religions were altering, becoming less ethnocentric and less influenced by evolutionary theories of religious development, many other missionaries continued with vigour their offensive against these religions. Of course, there were always the exceptions like Bishop Shanahan in eastern Nigeria who, as Ayandele points out, 'saw that what Ibo religion wanted was not "destruction", but "transformation"'.[38] Others – Catholics, Protestants, members of the African and Aladura Churches – took a much more hostile, aggressive approach than this to African traditional religion.

Prophet Harris in the Ivory Coast, as we have seen, regarded adherents of the traditional religions to be non-believers who, if they did not convert to Christianity, would be destroyed. Agbebi, while holding views similar to those held by Shanahan referred to 'the rubbish of idolatry' in Yoruba religion, and James Johnson was even more abusive and critical.[39] In the Aladura Churches and among the black American missionaries in Liberia (see Chapter 3) traditional African religions were strongly opposed. As one writer comments with regard to the Cherubim and Seraphim Society, this Society like the foreign observer . . . has failed to see the traditional religion from an objective standpoint and has, therefore, strongly advocated a radical break with it and a profession of absolute faith in God. But interestingly enough, the same feature which is partly responsible for the misrepresentation of the traditional religion (viz: the veneration of divinities) has been observable in the Cherubim and Seraphim in the near veneration of angels and heavenly bodies.[40]

Determined to establish a new and distinctive religious tradition missionaries likewise were not prepared for alternative ways as found in African traditional religions of praying, thinking, believing and behaving in religious matters. Commenting on this aspect of the missionary enterprise in Sierra Leone one scholar suggests that the missionaries were perhaps even less prepared to have their basic convictions challenged than 'the Mende – who had learned to live and survive alongside outside influences and different cultures'.[41] It is too readily assumed that the European layman or missionary came from a more 'open' society and culture than the African and was therefore inclined to be more open minded, and more flexible in thought and behaviour. It is this line of thinking that in part explains why anthropologists and others conclude that African systems of thought, such as that of the Dogon are essentially 'closed', hieratic sets of formulations placed outside the realm of experimentation.[42] There is evidence to suggest that the Mende, among other African people, displayed an 'open-ness' to other world views and religious perspectives not often found in European circles. No one tradition of thought, of course, is in itself, of necessity, more open than another, all being to a large extent socially imposed, and therefore subject to the constraints of the dominant world view of the particular society in which they emerged. But if Dogon, Mende or other African systems of thought were as 'closed' as some scholars would have us believe then it is difficult to explain the existence in these societies of, for example, alternative belief systems and of religious pluralism.

Many Christian missionaries in the pre-colonial and colonial eras (and today, though to a much lesser extent) wanted total conversion. They wanted converts to Christianity to abandon all contact with African traditional religions and culture. They also sought to transform African societies and regulate affairs, including the law, so that the Christian view of the world as they interpreted it, prevailed unchallenged. In their view Christianity and African traditional religion were diametrically opposed systems of belief and practice. In northern Ghana, for instance, in the late 1930s a Catholic bishop sought the amendement of laws which, as he saw it, offended against the Christian code of ethics.

As Chapter 4 discussed (pp. 98–9) there was something of a mass movement to Catholicism in the Lawra and Wa districts in Ghana in the late 1930s. According to one account the movement began when, following on the failure of the intercession of the traditional priests to bring rain to the region which was suffering desperately from drought, a missionary came on the scene, prayed in public for rain, and within a few days the heavy rains came and saved the crops.[43] The missionary was also able to help suppress an epidemic of dysentery with medicaments provided by the medical officer, and this apparently also had a great impact on many people turning them in the direction of Christianity.[44]

The local chiefs and traditional priests viewed this mass movement with alarm, believing that the new Christians would no longer respect their authority or perform their communal obligations. While strain and tension came to characterise relations between the chiefs and the Christians the missionaries, or rather the bishop of the area, sought from the colonial authorities 'the complete condemnation' of local law and custom, and showed 'an entire disregard for the chiefs' side of the question'.[45] Explaining his case to the authorities the bishop wrote, 'The African who becomes a Christian abandons the beliefs and customs that make up Pagan worship and submits himself to the Christian law'.[46]

Although the situation could and did vary from one region to another and from one Christian missionary or prophet to another, the approach to African traditional religion was for a very long time one of confrontation. There was a demand for total renunciation. Indeed it was almost taken for granted by Christian leaders that confrontation between the 'new' and the 'old' religion was not only necessary but inevitable.[47]

In the ensuing encounter African traditional beliefs and practices were not eradicated; rather, they tended to domesticate Christianity.[48] Indeed, there has been considerable debate in recent times as to whether these belief systems were in any way radically altered or displaced by either Christianity, or Islam.[49] An outline of this important debate is presented in the Conclusion to this study.

At the beginning of this chapter it was noted that in recent times the Christian Churches in Togo, and the same is true elswhere, have begun to consider with tolerance and respect the beliefs and practices and religious values contained in African traditional religions. This represents a change in approach from one of confrontation to dialogue. It has now been publicly recognised by many of the Christian Churches that Africa has, and has always had, a rich spiritual heritage. It does not of course mean that there has been any relaxation in the effort to convert traditional religionists to Christianity, but simply a change in attitude and approach.

Since independence then, there has been a noticeable change in the attitude and approach of the Christian Churches towards Islam and African traditional religions, a change brought on by both religious and political developments such as the Second Vatican Council and the regaining of independence.

Notes

1   N.I. de Moraes. La Petite Côte d'Après Francisco de Lemos Coelho (XVII siecle), Bulletin de l'Institut Fondamental d'Afrique Noire (henceforth BIFAN) sér B, No. 2, 1973, p. 251.
2   Carson, I.A. Ritchie. Deux Textes sur le Sénégal, BIFAN. T. XXX, sér B, No. 1, 1968, p. 313.

3   ibid., p. 318.
4   See P.B. Clarke, *West Africa and Islam*, London: Edward Arnold, 1982, for an overview of the development of Islam in West Africa.
5   Citations from M. Echeruo, *Victorian Lagos*. London and Basingstoke: Macmillan, 1977: 83–4.
6   For a full account of Blyden's views on Islam see E.D.A. Hulmes, Christian Attitudes to Islam: A Comparative Study of the Work of S.A. Crowther, E.W. Blyden and W.R.S. Miller in West Africa, D. Phil., Oxon. 1980.
7   M. Echeruo, op. cit., p. 83.
8   N.A.I. Oke Papers 3/1/6. The African Religion: Neither Christianity Nor Muhammedanism, by Adeniran.
9   G. Anawati. Excursus on Islam. In H. Vorgrimmler (ed.) *Commentary on the Documents of Vatican II*, Vol. III. London: Burns and Oats, 1969, pp. 151 ff.
10   ibid., p. 152.
11   V. Monteil, *L'Islam Noir*. Paris: Editions du Seuil, 1971: 112.
12   Citation from Revd V. Chukuwulozie 'Christian-Muslim Relations in Nigeria', unpublished paper presented at Jos University, 1976.
13   Monteil, op. cit., p. 129.
14   L. Brenner. *West African Sufi, The Religious Heritage and Spiritual Search of Cerno Boker Saalif Taal*. London: C. Hurst and Coy Ltd, 1984.
15   A. Hampaté Bâ, Jesus en Islam. In Compte-Rendu de la Session de Niamey, Catholic Commission for Muslim Relations, Dakar, April 1976.
16   Chukuwulozie, op. cit.
17   Interview, Ibadan, July 1978.
18   See P.B. Clarke, *West Africa and Islam*, op.cit., Chapter 8.
19   Revd P. Hollande, La Dynamique Missionaire de l'Islam. Mémoire de Maîtrise en Théologie, Institut Catholique de Paris, 1975, pp. 95 ff.
20   ibid.
21   ibid.
22   R.F. Burton, *A Mission to Gelele, King of Dahome*, 3rd edition. 2 Vols, London, 1864. Vol. 2, p. 199.
23   T.J. Bowen, *Adventures and Missionary Labours*, 1857 (1968 reprint edition, Cass, London), p. 310.
24   E.R. Sanders, 'The Hamitic Hypothesis: Its Origins and Functions in Time Perspective', *Journal of African History* 10 (4), 1969.
25   For a brief summary of Schmidt's work *Der Ursprung der Gottesidee*, in which these ideas are contained see William Schmidt, *The Origin and Growth of Religion: Facts and Theories*, trans. H.J. Rose, London: Methuen and Coy Ltd, 1931.
26   Revd G. Loyer, OP *An Account of a Voyage to the Kingdom of Assinie* (Relations du Voyage d'Issinie). Paris, 1914: 138.
27   G.T. Basden, *Among the Ibos of Nigeria*, and *Niger Ibos*. London: Seeley, 1938.
28   J.J. Williams, *Africa's God*. Anthropology series of the Boston College Graduate School, 1, 1–81, 1936.
29   E.W. Smith, *African Ideas of God*. London: Edinburgh House Press, 1950.
30   D. Westermann, *Die Glidiyi-Ewe in Togo*, Berlin, 1935.
31   G. Parrinder, *West African Religion* (2nd ed.) London: Epworth Press, 1969: 24–5.
32   A. Awolalu, *Yoruba Beliefs and Sacrificial Rites*. London: Longman, 1979: 12.
33   E.B. Ìdòwu, Olódùmarè. *God in Yoruba Belief*. London: Longman, 1962: 18.
34   P. Tempels, *Bantu Philosophy*. Paris: Présence Africaine, 1959.
35   G. Parrinder, *West African Religion*, op.cit., chap. 10 and passim.

36 M. Griaule, *Conversations with Ogotemmëli*. Oxford: Oxford University Press, 1965.
37 E.E. Evans-Pritchard, *Theories of Primitive Religion*. Oxford: Oxford University Press, 1965.
38 E.A. Ayandele, *The Missionary Impact on Modern Nigeria, 1842–1914*, London: Longman, 1966: 265.
39 ibid.
40 J.A. Omoyajowo, *Cherubim and Seraphim*. New York and Lagos: Nok Publishers, 1982: 95.
41 A.J. Gittins, The Mende and The Missionary. op.cit., Vol. II, p. 551.
42 M. Douglas, *Natural Symbols*. Harmondsworth: Penguin 1968. See also R. Horton, African Traditional Thought and Western Science. *Africa* **XXXVII** (2), April 1967.
43 Rhodes House, Oxford, Mss. Africa s. 454, Three Memoranda, Chief Commissioner's Office, Tamale, 9th March 1937.
44 ibid.
45 ibid.
46 ibid.
47 For an example of this confrontational approach in the first period of Christian missionary activity in Africa, see R. Gray's, Come Vero Principe Catolico: The Capuchins and the Rulers of Soyo in the late Seventeenth Century, *Africa*, **53** (3), 1983: 39 ff.
48 L. Sanneh, *West African Christianity. The Religious Impact*, London: C. Hurst and Coy Ltd, 1983: Chaps. 8 and 9.
49 R. Horton, African Conversion, *Africa* **XLI** (2), April 1971, pp. 85–108. See also the reply by H.J. Fisher, Conversion Reconsidered: Some Historical Aspects of Religious Conversion in Black Africa, *Africa* **XLIII** (1), January 1973.

9
Christianity, nation building, nationalism and the State.

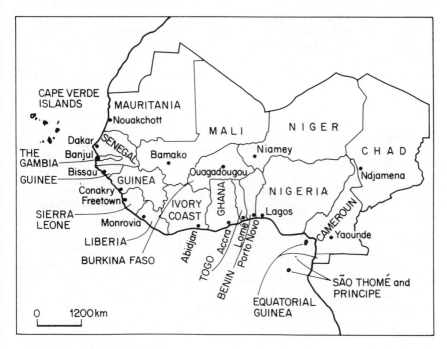

IV   Contemporary West Africa

Some reference has already been made in previous chapters to the contribution of Christianity to the closely interrelated processes of nation building and nationalism and to its relations with the state in West Africa. Here we propose to consider these questions in a more systematic way and in more detail.

Nation building and nationalism

The process of nation building and nationalism, as has already been suggested, are closely interrelated. There are many definitions of nation, some very broad, others more precise and specific. Some writers take the view that a nation is, quite simply, any group which demands to be treated as such. For others this is too broad and general a definition and they would prefer to define a nation as 'any cohesive group possessing

independence within the confines of an international order as provided
by the United Nations, which provides a constituency for a government
effectively ruling such a group and receiving from that group acclamation
which legitimises the government as part of the world order'.[1]

The degree of group cohesion required cannot, of course, be measured
with any precision and does in practice vary from one country to another.
While countries like the United States have been described as a 'nation of
nations', and the same may be said of the Soviet Union and other
countries including Canada, one can find examples on the other hand of
smaller, more highly integrated, less diverse nations such as Denmark. It
would seem that a high level of cohesion and integration is much less
important than a widespread identification with and acceptance of the
collectivity as a reality. And external contact often plays an important part
in generating such acceptance among diverse peoples living within the
same territorial boundaries.

Countries where there is great diversity and where the political
boundaries have been arbitrarily determined by others, which is the case
for the most part in West Africa, seek to develop greater unity and
cohesion at the national level, while at the same time strengthening ties of
a cultural, political and economic nature at the sub-regional and
continental level. Although their boundaries were determined by
European colonial powers West African states, as historians have shown,
do not consist of totally arbitrary amalgamations of peoples. In the
Nigerian case, to take but one example, there are links between the
peoples who compose the federation of a cultural, linguistic and
economic kind, which have a long history.[2] Nevertheless, events such as
the Civil War (1967–70) emphasise the need for greater unity while
respecting and allowing for genuine diversity in cultural and religious
matters, and this is part of the ongoing process of *nation building*.

Nation building, while it involves such activities as the preservation
and development of a common national heritage, the maintenance of an
acceptable level of cultural, political and economic independence, and the
pursuit of the means necessary to control a nation's destiny in an
interdependent world, does not entail uniformity. It is, according to some
political scientists, 'that process of generating among a collectivity a
community of culture, economics and politics which is designed to enable
most of its members to maximise their potentialities'.[3] While others
would substitute *all* for *most* here, few if any would deny that there is any
necessary conflict between a certain level of cultural diversity and the
requirements of nation building.

At this point we can move on to discuss the role of Christianity in the
twin processes of nation building and nationalism. A number of
historians and social scientists, and perhaps none more so than Ibn
Khaldun and Émile Durkheim, have stressed the cohesive role of religion
in society. The former wrote of how religion strengthened group feeling
and solidarity, both of which however were based ultimately on bonds of
kinship.[4] Durkheim, the sociologist, maintained that religion cemented
social relations, made and remade 'the soul of the collectivity and of

individuals' and strengthened the bonds attaching the individual to the society of which he is a member. What he terms commemorative rites 'revivify the most essential elements of the collective conscience' so that 'the group periodically renews the sentiments which it has of itself and its unity'.[5] Religion brings people together in society and by uniting together in society people 'become conscious of the groups they form, from the simplest to the most elevated, and thus those sentiments which the state expresses, defines and regulates, but which it assumes to exist, come spontaneously into being'.[6]

Much of the contemporary discussion concerning civil religion is based on Durkheim's view of the role of religion as a form of social cement. The American Way of Life which is said to stand for the Constitution, democracy and individual freedom, personal activism and laissez-faire economics has been described as a civil religion which serves to unite Americans.[7] There are many examples of where religion, not always necessarily of itself, but on occasion as a result of the use made of it for this purpose has become the focus of group, community or national identity. Further, in many parts of the world religion has played an important role in nationalist movements, for example in Burma, where nationalism during the colonial era was often referred to as Buddhist rather than Burmese nationalism. And in India Aurobindo Ghose emphasised that 'religion', Sanatan Dharma (eternal religion, Hinduism), and nationalism were the same thing. Gandhi derived much of his theory of non-violent resistance *(satyagraha)* to colonialism from Hinduism. Almost everywhere one cares to look in the so-called developed and developing worlds religions have helped provide some if not all of the leaders, symbols, rituals and cohesion found in nationalist movements.[8] And since we are dealing with Africa, and in case it should be overlooked, African traditional religion has also contributed to nationalism in these ways.[9]

While religion can contribute and has contributed to the cohesion, unity and integration of societies it can be used, and this has also happened, to reinforce division within the same community or between different states. This is something Durkheim did not consider. Religion, like education, can be used both to unite and divide, to assist positively in the process of nation building and nationalism, or to act against them.

Nation building and nationalism are, as we have already suggested, complex processes with a 'physical' as well as a moral and cultural side to them, both of which are often closely interlinked. In examining these processes from the 'physical' angle one would, if space allowed, consider in detail such matters as economic development, health, education, communications and social welfare, while on the moral and cultural side consideration would be given to values, norms, symbols, and questions of language, art, history, equality, identity and so forth.

These various aspects of nation building and nationalism can only be touched upon in a short study such as this. It is important to bear in mind, since people hold different views on the questions of the means and goals of nation building and nationalism, that what is being considered here is what has happened and not necessarily what should have happened. In other words, there is no attempt to suggest that there is only one model of nation building or that the model of nation building which the Christian missionaries had in mind – the contemporary European model – was either the best or the most appropriate for West Africa.

According to Ajayi the Christian missionaries played a prominent role in introducing into Nigeria – and one could extend this comment to cover West Africa as a whole – 'the ideas of nation building of contemporary Europe'.[10] Ajayi maintains that by training 'a group of Nigerians who accepted these ideas and hoped to see them carried out . . . the Christian movement sowed the seeds of Nigerian Nationalism'.[11] Ajayi makes it clear that he is referring to contemporary European ideas of nation building and nationalism, and that both of these concepts are relative and refer to ongoing processes. He also refers to the significant contribution made by Islam in the nineteenth century when it introduced into Nigeria 'the concept of a state transcending the bounds of personal loyalty to a clan, a traditional ruler or a particular locality'[12]

Ajayi maintains that Christian missionary spokesmen and policy makers such as Henry Venn, the General Secretary of the CMS (from 1841 to 1871) do not appear to have interested themselves in or envisaged a formal, European political involvement in Africa. They looked to Africans themselves first as agents of the missionaries and later as fully responsible for the building up and governing of one or several independent West African states. Venn wrote in 1857,

> We hope that with God's blessing on our plans a large body of 'Native' growers of cotton and traders may spring up who may form an intelligent and influential class of society and become founders of a kingdom which shall render incalculable benefits to Africa and hold a position among the states of Europe.[13]

The missionary plan Venn wrote about and attempted to implement consisted in developing agriculture, substituting 'legitimate' trade for slave trading, extending 'civilisation' through the school – all of which would facilitate the spread of Christianity – and the emergence of a self-governing, self-supporting, self-propagating African Christian Church (see Chapter 3) and self-governing African states. An integral part of this plan was the creation of an African middle class who would eventually have the responsibility for seeing that the plan was carried through. Such a class did emerge under mission tutelage and according to Ajayi this 'was the greatest contribution of the Christian missions to Nigerian Nationalism'.[14]

Through their schools and various educational institutions the Christian missions trained a new African élite,[15] some of whom, as Ayandele notes became 'enchanted by European ideas'.[16] It was this new élite that came to figure prominently in the processes of nation building and nationalism.

Not all of the new African élite accepted passively and uncritically missionary ideas and methods of nation building. Some were scathing of the educational provisions made available by the missions while others rejected the attacks on African culture and ethical and moral norms (see Chapter 6).

It is difficult to measure the extent to which mission influence was indispensable to these developments in Nigeria or elsewhere in West Africa. It is possible that the changes introduced by the missionaries may well have come about through African initiative alone. There are those historians who maintain that Africa in the nineteenth century contained the seeds of its own 'modernisation'.[17] It is pointed out, for example, that 'the change over from a subsistence economy to one geared to production for the export market', and undertaken 'autonomously' is but one piece of evidence in support of this view.[18] Furthermore, the creation of large-scale, centralised states in both Muslim and non-Muslim areas of West Africa long pre-dates the arrival of the nineteenth century missionary from Europe and America.

The Christian missionary contribution to nation building and nationalism in West Africa in the nineteenth century was double-edged. While making a contribution to these processes in the medical, social, agricultural, linguistic and religious fields the nineteenth century missionary was also one of the principle 'pathfinders' of European political influence in West Africa. In Ayandele's words the missionary in Nigeria 'African or European was the bearer of British influence in a subtle but sure manner', since 'unlike the administrator and the trader he lived among the people from the first, professed interest in their wellbeing and spoke their language'.[19]

But it was not the intention of the missionary, at least until the 1880s, to prepare for the formal British colonisation of Nigeria or anywhere else in West Africa for that matter. This is not to suggest that they did not at times work hand in hand with European traders and British government officials, for they certainly did. Missionaries and traders, though they often disagreed, were instrumental in the establishment of a British Consul in Lagos in 1853, to cite but one example. The political role of some missionaries even at this time was not always as subtle as Ayandele suggests, for some like Henry Townsend of the CMS saw, as Ajayi points out, their 'work in Africa very largely in political terms'.[20] Although not always in agreement with the details of British policy Townsend had little hesitation in calling on Britain to increase its influence in Nigeria for the purpose, as he saw it, of spreading the Gospel. As Ajayi comments: 'he was the sponsor of the policy of setting up Abeokuta rather than Lagos or anywhere else as the main centre of both missionary and British influence'.[21]

While missionaries involved European traders and administrators – more deeply than otherwise might have been the case – in African affairs and came in some instances to rely upon them for financial and military support, there could also be strong disagreement especially where these traders and administrators were not of the same nationality as the missionaries themselves. We have already discussed the conflicts that emerged between the Portuguese authorities and Spanish missionaries on the West Coast of Africa in the seventeenth century (see Chapter 1, pp.

12–13) and in the late nineteenth century in Nigeria relations were at times strained between the French Roman Catholic missionaries and the Royal Niger Company. The missionaries went so far as to participate in armed uprisings against the Company in 1887 and 1890.[22] These same missionaries were none the less very much in favour of spreading *French* influence in the region and opposed the whole idea of self-governing African Churches.[23]

Later, with the formal establishment of British rule in northern Nigeria missionaries, both Catholic and Protestant and of French, Irish and British nationality once again opposed in no uncertain terms the British policy of indirect rule in northern Nigeria on the grounds that it protected Islam and frustrated their attempts to convert the Muslim population of the region.[24] In former French West Africa the attitude of the missionary to the French authorities in the second half of the nineteenth century and the early part of this century was much the same as in Nigeria. Many approved of the French military conquest of the western Soudan in the 1880s and 1890s since this would, it was wrongly believed, undermine Islam and prepare the way for Christianity. It was generally accepted that missionaries, where possible, should assist in the spread of French civilisation which was somehow regarded as a necessary preparation for becoming a thoroughgoing Christian. There were, of course, exceptions. For example, the missionaries in Timbuktu in the early years of this century were reluctant to teach the French language, while others believed that educational work was not part of the missionary task.

In former French West Africa missionaries as a rule only rarely criticised the colonial authorities except when they felt that the latter were impeding their progress by protecting or favouring Islam. There was also at different times a degree of anti-clericalism in the admininstration and a fairly constant element of freemasonry, both of which displayed a certain antipathy towards the missionary and this gave rise to criticism of the administration. However it was in general the personality of the governor of a particular territory that very often determined as much as anything else the actual state of relations between missionary and colonial administration.

Few clergy, whether they were African, American or European directly opposed, as far as is known, the colonial occupation of West Africa which began in earnest in the 1880s. This is not to suggest that they all gave it their full approval or that all those who approved of it did so in the same way and for the same reasons. Nor is it to suggest that the missionary was indispensable to the colonial occupation. It would most probably have occurred without him. Colonial society was more than anything else the product of economic and political forces, and while missionaries tended to share many of the ideas current in Europe and America at the time on the development, transformation and 'modernisation' of other societies, it was above all the search for markets, trade routes and for enhanced national status and prestige that led to late nineteenth century European imperialism in Africa.

Granted that they did not all come to approve of it in the same way or for the same reasons it was nevertheless the case that many missionaries believed that colonialisation would assist in the essential task of destroying the existing socio-economic and political structures in Africa, thereby facilitating the work of planting the Gospel in new and more propitious soil. For the missionary, virtually all things African – marriage customs, traditional rituals, as well as forms of domestic slavery, secret societies, and virtually all that was associated with traditional African religion – had eventually to be replaced, and the quicker the better before Christianity could flourish (see Chapter 8, pp. 220 ff.). This, of course, is to generalise and to single out the missionary as if he were the only one who thought along these lines. Others in Europe, including theorists and practitioners of both capitalism and socialism, while pursuing different aims, held similar views to the missionary concerning the need to demolish the existing cultural and socio-economic systems in pre-industrial societies such as Africa.

Even cultural nationalists like Blyden opposed any hasty or premature challenge to European rule in West Africa and, according to his biographer, 'actually dubbed as ingratitude African agitation and their protests over growing discrimination in the administration of the colonies'[25] (see Chapter 3, pp. 54 ff.). Blyden, as Lynch points out, was not prepared to countenance strong opposition to the decision to exclude African doctors from the African Medical Service after 1902, or to the decision taken in the late 1890s not to appoint them to the highest medical positions, or to the fact that African doctors were paid at a lower rate than Europeans.[26]

One of Blyden's primary objectives was the establishment of an independent West African state that would be internationally recognised and able to play an active part in world affairs. And he believed that a temporary period of European rule was necessary if this goal was to be achieved. It is against this background that his acceptance of discrimination and foreign rule needs to be assessed. While this rather optimistic if not naive approach lost him many friends in the 1890s and early years of this century among the West African-educated élite in Lagos, Freetown and elsewhere, other clergymen of African descent like Alexander Crummell in Liberia thought along the same lines and supported Blyden. According to Crummell, who would have liked to have seen the whole of West Africa under British authority, western rule in Africa was necessary for 'progress', and 'the European drive to open Africa' was the 'highest philanthropy of the most zealous religionism'.[27] The idea of exporting their own civilisation and life style to what were regarded as culturally backward peoples was a central aspect of late nineteenth century imperialist thinking and one which many missionaries from North America and Europe shared.

While Blyden looked forward to a day in the not-too-distant future when West Africa would be independent, most European missionaries from the 1890s onwards did not speculate a great deal on such matters, expecting colonial rule to continue for a very long time. Even as late as the 1940s missionary leaders in the section of their mission reports dealing with politics made no reference to self-government but simply described the existing situation, giving no hint of a change to self-government.[28]

During the colonial era the mission-established Churches, while continuing to provide educational, medical, social and religious services seldom seriously questioned the right of Europeans to rule Africa,[29] and this did not go unnoticed by African nationalists themselves. Some nationalists demanded that Christianity should address itself much more to the ongoing, mundane affairs, political and otherwise, of this world rather than urge Africans to look to another, future world, for the fulfilment of their aspirations and ambitions.

The *Daily Service* newspaper, organ of the Nigerian Youth Movement, a nationalist party established in the 1930s, commenting in July 1942 on the implications of fifty years of 'Christian Education in Ijebuland' in present-day Ogun State, Nigeria, commented that in themselves the implications of Christian education were 'revolutionary'. Among other things,

> Christian education inspired man with a spiritual force which enabled him to extricate himself from the shackles of ignorance, fear and superstition, [and] brought hopes of a better life. [But] 'Christian educationalists by emphasising the 'other worldly' dimension of Christianity at the expense of the 'this worldly' are failing. Africa is no longer the 'Dark Continent' where people can be carried away with obsolete theories of heaven in some geographical region to which they may proceed after impoverishing themselves below by selling all that he has.[30]

To these nationalists 'slavery' and 'injustice' would never disappear as long as colonial rule continued, for in itself it was a form of both, and the task of the Christian Church was to apply its teaching directly to that issue and to educate people to that end, something which they appeared not to be doing.[31]

So far we have focused on the role of the mission-established Churches, sometimes referred to as the older or historic Churches, in the processes of nation building and nationalism. The independent Churches and societies also need to be considered. It is clear from Chapter 6 that issues related to nation building and nationalism were partly responsible for the rise of a number of independent Churches. Some of these Churches were established for the purpose of providing Africans with a forum for exercising responsibility and managing their own affairs and as a means of defending and preserving African religious and cultural values (see Chapter 6, pp. 156–59). They were, in part, a response to increasing European control and dominance in Church life, and to some extent in the political sphere also. Some of these Churches such as the National Church of Nigeria and the Cameroon (NCNC) founded by the former Nigerian president, Nnamdi Azikiwe, were in all but name political movements. It was of course often necessary, given the restrictions on political parties, political protest and the absence of channels for the expression of political opinion to establish a religious movement for purposes of political self-expression, and as a way of establishing the principle of 'Africa for the Africans' in opposition to foreign rule in

Church and State.[32]

Not all independent Churches were equally political nor can their emergence always be seen as a form of direct opposition to colonialism and foreign influences generally. Although his ultimate political objectives were different, the Prophet Harris encouraged the people of the Ivory Coast and Ghana to participate actively with the administration in the development of the country along western lines. Later, after his expulsion from the Ivory Coast, he was to change his position and advise the Ivorians not to assist further in the French imperial scheme for the Ivory Coast.[33] By way of contrast other African prophets (e.g. Josiah Oshitelu), while never explicitly confronting the colonial authorities, made pronouncements almost from the outset that were regarded as 'subversive' by the regime. The prophecies already quoted in Chapter 6 such as the one that predicted that 'all white men who live in the land will perish', and others by other prophets opposing taxation were all seen by the authorities as 'subversive', and as a way of galvanising potential opposition to colonial rule.

The independent Church movement contributed to nation building and African nationalism by emphasising and spreading widely among ordinary people the idea that there was an African alternative to European values and European control.[34] They have also made a significant contribution to the indigenisation of Christianity itself in West Africa. Some of these Churches enabled many people to cope with the disturbing influences of the 'modern', which was often felt to be strange, without meaning and unattractive. The new religions that have emerged in Japan in the past 100 years or so have in some respects fulfilled a similar function.[35] It can be argued that the independent Churches simply provided an escape route from reality and generally held back the process of development in the fields of medicine and science by their emphasis on an allegedly non-scientific – some might term it an 'irrational' – approach to healing, and even by their opposition to customary or traditional medicine which an increasing number of experts now see as highly valuable and relevant.

The term 'irrational' seems misapplied here for there was, as Chapter 6 shows, a 'situational logic' and consistency to faith healing as practised and encouraged by the leaders of the independent Churches: given the scarcity and difficulties of access to modern medicine and the failure of traditional medicine during the epidemic of 1918 for example, the religious healers performed a valuable and useful role in society. As one scholar points out 'They carried and continue to carry a considerable load of the health service'.[36] And this writer continues, 'While they may condone paranoid ideas they do not tend to enhance them nor even create them like the traditional healers do. They alleviate rather than create anxiety as the traditional healers do'.[37]

In more recent times the independent Churches have tended to become much more like the 'older' Churches in organisational form and in other ways, and have also become much more involved in education, socio-economic development and other fields. They promote literacy through their Sunday Schools and Bible study groups, are responsible for schools, healing centres, printing presses, guest houses,[38] hospitals, co-operatives, and trade training.[39] Other independent Churches, such as the Holy Apostles, a branch of the Cherubim and Seraphim, have been largely responsible for the economic development of whole, local communities.[40] In the Ivory Coast the Harris Church is now involved in the same type of activities, and like the Holy Apostles of western Nigeria and the Church of the Messiah, Labadi, Ghana and many other independent Churches, encourages members to work hard for the benefits of themselves and the wider society.

The Christian Churches, then, contributed in different ways to the twin processes of nation building and nationalism in West Africa. And while the mission-established Churches in particular operated at times as vehicles for the spread of colonialism, they also helped the cause of national building and nationalism by providing a considerable amount of the necessary infrastructure. This is not to suggest that other forces were not involved, or that the course taken by nation building and nationalism were the only ones or the right ones. It is simply to describe what happened and not what might or should have happened. There is, given the nature of the issues involved, a considerable amount of overlap between what has just been discussed and what follows.

Church – State relations

Religious institutions can relate to the State in different ways, depending both on the type of religion and the type of society in question. In the centralised societies of pre-colonial Africa, there tended to be a close identity and interaction between the religious and political sphere and a strong sense of common purpose between the two. The religious authorities were often the political authorities, and this made for a strong sense of common purpose and an emphasis on common values. (An illustration of this has already been provided in Chapter 1). It would be incorrect to assume that where such a relationship exists societies are free of all conflict, or that such a relationship is indispensable to the harmony, stability and progress of a society.

During the colonial era and in most West African countries today there was and is (at least in principle) a separation between Church and State, between the religious and the political spheres. Moreover as far as world religions such as Christianity and Islam are concerned, they can encourage loyalties that are wider than the local society or nation in which they exist: they preach universal brotherhood and require faith in a God who is the God of all men. This does not necessarily mean that their preaching contradicts the requirements of citizenship, although this sometimes can happen.

During the first phase of missionary activity in West Africa the Christian missions were heavily dependent upon their respective European governments and were to all intents and purposes State controlled. In the nineteenth century many of them were much more financially independent, and the Roman Catholic missions were of course much more directly under the control of the Vatican.[41] This situation varied, the Catholic missions in former French and Portuguese West Africa being much more subject to and dependent on government financial assistance and government approval when appointing and deploying personnel than was the case in former British West Africa. Nevertheless, it was the case that missionaries in general enjoyed more freedom from secular control than in the earlier period. However, certain restrictions were placed on their movements and on what they could do, especially where it was a question of mission work in Muslim territories. This – it has recently been suggested in the case of northern Nigeria – was a policy designed more to protect government interests rather than one based on Muslim objections to Christian missions and western education.[42]

Christian missionaries did not have things all their own way in non-Muslim areas either. Colonial governments, on occasion, gave support to the local ruler where there was a dispute between the latter and the missionary. In the dispute already referred to between the head of the Catholic mission in the Lawra and Wa districts of Ghana the colonial authorities informed the bishop, who wanted to see the powers of the chiefs limited and the traditional courts adapted to conform more to Christian interests, that this could not be done. The bishop was informed that the courts were 'under the paternal guidance of Administrative Officers who are placed in the most favourable position to appreciate the points of view of the Pagan and the Christian. And I would add that the Pagan Chiefs are not lacking in the qualities which are necessary to enable them to rule their people of whatever religious beliefs with justice and tolerance'.[43]

Ayandele's analysis of the attitude of traditional rulers to missionaries with special reference to the pre-colonial period has already been mentioned (see Chapter 1, pp. 12–13). He writes of the very real fear felt by some of these rulers that missionaries might undermine their authority and indeed the whole social structure. Therefore they rejected missionary overtures. A classic instance of this response came from the Awujale, Ademiyewo of Ijebu-Ode, Nigeria.[44] Rulers such as Ademiyewo feared the disrupture, political, economic and cultural, that they believed would inevitably come about as a result of a foreign presence in their kingdom. They also entertained, as Ayandele points out, a certain contempt for the white man whom they regarded as 'a harbinger of evil'.[45]

The greatest problem facing the missionaries in many parts of West Africa in the pre-colonial era was that they were regarded by the rulers of the more established, better organised, more self-sufficient kingdoms in particular as agents of a foreign power, and as the first step on the way to foreign political intervention. This was certainly the case, not only in Ijebuland but also in many other areas of West Africa. In the 1840s the missionaries in Senegal were never able to convince the rulers of Serer that they were not agents of French military power, and this proved to be a serious obstacle to Christian expansion.[46] As Ayandele notes, this reaction of the traditional rulers was one important reason why some missionaries were favourably disposed to European military expeditions in West Africa.[47] Later generations of West African clergymen were also to place the blame for these expeditions on the shoulders of the traditional rulers. In his address in 1942 on the occasion of the fiftieth anniversary of the British military expedition against the Ijebu a clergyman said that it was 'the mistakes (among them the opposition to missionaries) made by our forefathers which made the expedition necessary, inevitable and justifiable'.[48] There were also a number of traditional rulers like Sodoke of the Egba of Abeokuta, who welcomed missionaries and expected that the latter would in return obtain for them military assistance against their opponents, act as intermediaries between themselves and European officials and traders, and in some instances introduce western education if not necessarily Christianity.

With the onset of colonial rule and the application of the principle of religious freedom, never applied unconditionally, the hand of the missionary was strengthened, although as we have seen they were by no means free to do exactly as they liked. The 'older' Churches were taken more seriously and given more latitude by the State than the independent Churches which were regarded as much more of a threat to the *status quo*. Moreover, in the former Portuguese West African colonies the ties between the Catholic Church and the government were extremely close, especially from 1940 when Portugal and the Vatican signed a Concordat which included a missionary agreement. This was followed in 1941 by the Portuguese Government's Missionary Statute which provided for considerable government financial aid to the missions, mission control over education in return for a state veto over the appointment of bishops and support for Portuguese colonial policy. This agreement between the Catholic Church and the Portuguese government militated against the interests of the Protestant Churches (see Chapter 5, pp. 150–53).

In former French West Africa, though the links between the Catholic Church and State were by no means as close, there was a general tendency to favour Catholic missions to the disadvantage of Protestant missionary societies who were suspected of being agents of British interests. On the other hand in Liberia, there was for a long time a strong connection between the Protestant Church and the State which Catholic missionaries felt at one time was to their disadvantage (see Chapter 3, pp. 55–6).

Today all West African states, with one or two exceptions like Mauritania, describe themselves as secular and assure all their citizens of full equality before the law without making any distinction on religious grounds. As for traditional African religions these are given the same status in some countries, as for example in the Republic of Benin, as any other religion. There is, however, a tendency to be suspicious of certain religious organisations such as the Jehovah's Witnesses, and certain types of Pentecostalism. Togo banned the former and a number of Pentecostal churches in 1978.

In the preamble to a number of constitutions there is a pronounced religious emphasis and while this does not mean there is no separation between Church and State, it is often welcomed by both Christians and Muslims as the Shari's debate in Nigeria (1976–8) demonstrated.[49] Furthermore, although profoundly shaken by the total or partial takeover by the State of Church schools and hospitals in Ghana, Guinea (Conakry), Nigeria and elsewhere since independence and in some cases having fought to defend what they considered to be their legitimate interests, ecclesiastical authorities at national or regional level, notwithstanding what individuals may have said or done, have not as a body called into question the established political system of the day. The response in fact has been to become more deeply involved in economic and social development projects by starting co-operatives, credit unions, agricultural training schemes, industrial workshops and so on.[50]

While stressing that the mission of the Christian Church is at one level – the supernatural, spiritual level – of more significance and value than that of the State, and that while government has the greater competence in the political, economic and industrial spheres and religion in the moral and ethical realms, the Christian Churches have tended to stress the need for solidarity between Church and State. While emphasising the need for an opposition some Christian writers have expressed the view that the Christian need not in principle oppose the one party state system.[51] Leaders of the 'older' Churches, while encouraging Christians to participate in the political life of the nation, stress that the Church as a religious institution cannot become involved; its role consists simply in presenting its teachings 'on matters on which the Church is competent'.[52]

There have been instances, and some of these have already been mentioned, where individual churchmen and branches of Churches have in practice become involved in politics in the pre-colonial, colonial and post-colonial eras. Perhaps one of the best illustrations of such involvement in the colonial era was the involvement of members of the Catholic clergy in the nationalist struggle in Cameroon, where they opposed the nationalist movement, the Union of the Peoples of Cameroon (UPC), suspecting it of being Communist in inspiration and intent.[53] And for similar reasons, although on a smaller scale, the Church opposed nationalist developments in Guinea (Conakry) (see Chapter 5). Although some may see this as a form of casuistry Mfoulou suggests that such opposition was not necessarily opposition to nationalism *per se* but simply to a particular kind of nationalist movement.[54] In more recent times, aspects of the involvement of some of the Christian Churches in such events as the Nigerian Civil War (1967–70) have been seen as involvement in politics.[55]

On the question of Church-State relations the independent Churches take a similar line to the 'older' Churches. While emphasising the need for harmony these Churches claim that the spiritual welfare of the people is primarily their concern while the State has the right and duty to exercise temporal authority. And like the 'older' Churches these Churches also reserve the right to advise and direct the State on religious matters and condemn injustice.

The status of a number of the independent Churches has been enhanced since independence. For example, the Harrist Church in the Ivory Coast has not only received recognition from the State, but is also considered as one of the 'national' religions.[56] This concept of a 'national' Church is interesting and takes us back to previous attempts to establish this kind of Church in Nigeria and elsewhere (see Chapter 6, pp. 156–59). In the Ivory Coast the government political party, the Democratic Party of the Ivory Coast (PDCI), recognised the Harris Church as constituting the fourth national religion, along with Catholicism, Protestantism and Islam and actively encouraged these religions to engage in the process of nation building and to uphold Ivorian culture and traditions. The Harris Church for its part made a determined effort to show that it was the only authentic Ivorian religion and this was one of the main reasons why it was given government recognition.

Conclusions

This support for and endorsement of 'national' religions appears to reflect a growing tendency to measure the value of a religion in terms of the contribution it can make to national development. It also reflects a move in the direction of 'civil religion' where the justification for religion in itself is not to be found primarily in its doctrinal content, but perhaps even more so in the extent to which it can make a positive contribution to the nation, upholding and sustaining national values and interests and operating as a force for unity and integration.

This is not an entirely new departure. At the beginning of the section on Church-State relations we discussed the close identity of religion and politics, of traditional African religions and the State, and the strong sense of common purpose between the two in the pre-colonial period in West Africa. The Christian mission-established Churches moreover played an important role in introducing European ideas of national building and in spreading European civilisation, while adhering in principle to the position that Christianity had to be judged far more by the validity of its doctrinal content, its claim to be in possession of the Truth, than by its usefulness.

With some modifications this would appear to be the position of most Christian Churches in contemporary West Africa. They would not claim to be in sole possession of the truths of Christianity, nor would they deny that Islam and the traditional African religions contain important supernatural truths and insights (see Chapter 8). These Churches furthermore would not necessarily share the nineteenth century missionary ideas of nation building and nationalism. And while they believe they can and do make an important contribution to the kind of national building and nationalism that are now seen as more authentically African, they would not want to be judged solely by the relevance or the contribution they make to these and related processes. They continue, on the whole, to see themselves along with other religions as the guardians of spiritual truths and moral values with the right to educate and instruct people in these truths and values, while the State has responsibility for the material well-being of the people.

Of course, in practice, given their involvement in educational, social and economic activities, and their claim to be guardians of spiritual and moral values, the Churches cannot escape having a political dimension. This the State does not in general oppose, providing religions do not create dissension or mobilise people against the prevailing political and economic orthodoxy. Although the situation can vary enormously, what the state often looks for and in some instances demands in present-day West Africa is that the Christian Churches and other religions avoid polemics and demonstrate a strong sense of common purpose in the task of nation building, while not intervening directly in politics. This view of things in practice sees religion primarily not as an alternative system of authority and values, whose requirements contradict political requirements, but one which can help to legitimate existing political, social and economic arrangements, performing a role similar to that of traditional African religions in the past.

Notes

1 C. Friedrich and W. Foltz (eds), *Nation Building*. New York: Atherton Press, 1966, p. 31.
2 J.F.A. Ajayi and M. Crowder (eds), *A History of West Africa*, Vol. 1. Harlow: Longman, 1972, and E. Isichei, *A History of Nigeria*. London: Longman, 1983.
3 C. Friedrich and W. Foltz, op. cit., p. 31
4 Ibn Kahldun, *The Muqaddimah, An Introduction to History*, translated by F. Rosenthal, edited and abridged by N.J. Dawood, London: Routledge and Kegan Paul, 1967: 26 ff; 97 ff and *passim*.
5 E. Durkheim, *The Elementary Forms of Religious Life*, translated by J.W. Swain, London: George Allen and Unwin, 1971.
6 E. Durkheim, Germany Above. *The German Mental Attitude and War*. Paris: Colin, 1915: 30.
7 R.N. Bellah, *Beyond Belief. Essays on Religion in a Post Traditional World*. New York: Harper and Row, 1970.
8 D.E. Smith, *Religion and Political Development*. Boston: Little, Brown and Coy., 1970.
9 See, for examples, G.C.K. Gwassa, Kinjikitile and the Ideology of the Maji-Maji. In T.O. Ranger and I.N. Kimambo (eds) *The Historical Study of African Religions*. Berkeley: University of California Press, 1972.
10 J.F.A. Ajayi, Nineteenth Century Origins of Nigerian Nationalism, *Journal of the Historical Society of Nigeria* **2** (1), 1961.
11 ibid.
12 ibid.
13 Citation from J.F.A. Ajayi, Henry Venn and the Policy of Development, in O.U. Kalu (ed.) *The History of Christianity in West Africa*, p. 68.
14 J.F.A. Ajayi, Nineteenth Century Origins of Nigerian Nationalism, op. cit.
15 J.F.A. Ajayi, *Christian Missions in Nigeria 1841–1891, The Making of a New Elite*. London: Longman, 1965.
16 E.A. Ayandele, *The Missionary Impact on Modern Nigeria, 1842–1914*, London: Longman, 1966: 29.
17 H. Brunschwig, *L'Avènement de l'Afrique Noire*. Paris: 1963.

242   *West Africa and Christianity*

18 M. Crowder, *West Africa Under Colonial Rule*. London: Hutchinson, 1968, 8 ff.
19 E.A. Ayandele, *The Missionary Impact on Modern Nigeria, 1842–1914*, op.cit., p. 29.
20 J.F.A. Ajayi, *Christian Missions in Nigeria*, op.cit., p. 79.
21 ibid.
22 P.B. Clarke, Methods and Ideology of the Holy Ghost Fathers in Eastern Nigeria, 1885–1905. In O.U. Kalu (ed.), op. cit., p. 40.
23 ibid., p. 41.
24 J.H. Boer, *Missionary Messengers of Liberation in a Colonial Context*, op.cit., 104 ff.
25 H.R. Lynch, *Edward Wilmot Blyden, Pan-Negro Patriot, 1832–1912*, London: Oxford University Press, 1967: 242.
26 ibid., pp. 242–3.
27 W.L. Williams, *Black Americans and the Evangelization of Africa 1877–1900* op.cit., p.134.
28 See for example, H.G.F. Archives, Paris. Report on the Catholic Diocese of Guinea (Conakry), 1940. B. 265, Doss. B.
29 A.A. Mazrui, *Political Values and the Educated Class in Africa*. London: Heinemann, 1978: 153.
30 NAI Daily Service, 2/7/1942.
31 ibid., 27/7/1944.
32 T. Hodgkin, *Nationalism in Colonial Africa*. London: Muller, 1956: Chapter 3.
33 S.S. Walker, *The Religious Revolution in the Ivory Coast*, op.cit., 167.
34 T. Hodgkin, *Nationalism in Colonial Africa*, op.cit., p. 113. And G. Balandier, Messianismes et Nationalismes en Afrique Noire, *Cahiers Internationaux de Sociologie* **XIV**, 1963: 41 ff.
35 B.R. Wilson, *A Sociological Interpretation of Religion*, Oxford: Oxford University Press, 1983.
36 T. Asuni, Socio-Medical Problems of Religious Converts. *Psychopathologie Africaine* **IX** (2), 1973: 235.
37 ibid.
38 R.J. Hackett, Nigeria's Aladura Churches – Gateways or Barriers to Social Development, *Africana Marburgensia* **XIV** (1), 1981: pp. 9–26.
39 For example, the Mennonite Church Nigeria, Inc, Ikot Ada Idem, at Uyo has organised co-operatives which in turn have established hospitals, and offer people trade training in tent making. See E. and I. Weaver, *The Oyo Story*, op.cit., pp. 73 ff.
40 S.R. Barrett, All Things in Common: The Holy Apostles of Western Nigeria (1947 onwards), in E. Isichei (ed.), *Varieties of Christian Experience in Nigeria*, op.cit. pp. 149 ff.
41 R. Gray, The Origins and Organisation of the Nineteenth-Century Missionary Movement. *Tarikh* **3** (1), 1969: 19 ff.
42 P.K. Tibenderama, The Emirs and the Spread of Western Education in Northern Nigeria, 1900–1946. *JAH* **24**, No. 4, 1983.
43 MSS. Africa s. 454, Three Memoranda of the Gold Coast, 9th March 1937, op. cit., p., 13.
44 Ayandele, *The Missionary Impact on Modern Nigeria*, op. cit., p. 57 and *passim*.
45 E.A. Ayandele, Traditional Rulers and Missionaries in Pre-Colonial West Africa, in *Tarikh* **3** (1), 1969, pp. 23 ff.
46 M.A. Klein, *Islam and Imperialism in Senegal*, Edinburgh: Edinburgh University Press, 1968, chap. 3.
47 Ayandele, Traditional Rulers and Missionaries in Pre-Colonial West Africa.

op.cit.
48 NAI Daily Service, 3/6/1942.
49 P.B. Clarke, *West Africa and Islam*, op.cit., pp. 250 ff.
50 D. Diane, Le Catholicisme en Haute Guinée. Mémoire, University of Paris, I, June 1981.
51 Alfred de Soras, *Relations de l'Eglise et de l'Etat dans les Pays d'Afrique Francophone*. Paris: Mame 1963: 122–3.
52 F.A. Arinze, *The Christian and Politics*. Onitsha: Tabansi Press Ltd, 1982: 29 and *passim*.
53 J. Mfoulou, The Catholic Church and Cameroonian Nationalism: from misunderstanding to opposition. In E. Fashole-Luke *et al.* (eds), *Christianity in Independent Africa*, op.cit., pp. 216 ff. See also R. Joseph. *Radical Nationalism in Cameroon*. Oxford: Oxford University Press: 1977: 177 ff and *passim*.
54 J. Mfoulou, The Catholic Church and Cameroonian Nationalism. In E. Fashole-Luke *et al.* (eds), op.cit., p. 226.
55 A.F. Walls, Religion and the press in 'the Enclave' in the Nigerian Civil War. In E. Fashole-Luke *et al.* (eds.), *Christianity in Independent Africa*, op.cit., pp. 207 ff.
56 S.S. Walker, op. cit., p. 128.
57 ibid., pp. 126 ff.

10
Conclusions: Christianity and religious change in West Africa.

This study has focused on the methods used to spread Christianity, such as the school, the important role played by African and expatriate clergy and lay men and women, particularly that of the catechist in its extension over West Africa, African responses, Christianity and nation building, nationalism and the state, and Christian relations with Islam and the traditional religions of West Africa.

The impact Christianity has had on many aspects of life – education, politics, art, language, and economics – has also been discussed in some detail and so also, but in a more general and implicit way, has the specifically religious impact of Christianity.

This last point has given rise to a great deal of discussion in recent times in particular and it seems appropriate to return to it here in this conclusion. The central question at issue in this debate on the religious impact of Christianity is this: did Christianity add anything substantially new to indigenous, African ideas and beliefs about God and/or the Supreme Being, the afterlife and so on which both appealed and appeared relevant to West Africans and that might explain why they converted to Christianity? This is a thorny, complex and difficult question, and I will do no more here than summarise and comment briefly on the views of some of the principal participants in the debate. This question also prompts another similar type of question touched upon in the introduction to this study, and one which will also be considered briefly here: what has contemporary African Christianity to contribute to Christianity elsewhere?

With regard to the first question Professor Horton has put forward the theory that when it comes to a consideration of ideas and beliefs about the Supreme Being neither Christianity, nor Islam, introduced anything substantially new or different to Africa, and for our purposes West Africa. Moreover, the missionary activities of these world religions, this writer maintains, do not in themselves explain why people in West Africa came to focus more attention on the Supreme Being and less on the tutelary gods and spirits.[1]

The increasing emphasis given to belief in the Supreme Being in African society was not the direct consequence of the introduction and spread of Christian and Islamic teaching, but more the response of

African traditional religion itself to change in the political, economic and cultural spheres and in the sphere of communications. Prior to the widening of the political, economic and cultural frontiers of African societies from the nineteenth century onwards in particular, African peoples, although they recognised and believed in the existence of a Supreme Being, looked far more to the lesser gods for guidance, direction and assistance in the managing of everyday life. This was appropriate in small-scale societies where it was quite consistent and logical to single out the lesser gods for special attention and to regard them as the guardians and protectors of particular communities or groups.

Once the boundaries between societies began to be eroded by increasing levels of contact – political, social, economic and cultural – it was no longer possible to attribute the same role or the same importance to the lesser gods. This was because the significance and importance of these gods was in large measure determined by the fact that they were the gods and guardians of a particular, smaller, more 'closed' society and, therefore, could not be so easily assigned the same role and significance in a wider society. So what happened as a result of the change from small scale to much larger, more 'open' societies? The main proponent of this theory we are discussing, Professor Horton, suggests that Africans began to turn more and more to the worship of the Supreme Being whose existence they already recognised but who for all *practical purposes* they had largely ignored. Recognised and acknowledge by everyone, the Supreme Being became much more the focus of attention and worship. Non divisive, and not the property of any one particular community, the Supreme Being could be regarded as the God of the whole community which incorporated different peoples, speaking different languages and with different traditions.

What part did Christianity play in this change in religious orientation, the change from concentration and focus on the lesser gods to a much more thoroughgoing commitment to and belief in the Supreme Being? Horton examines the role of Islam as well as Christianity in this process and therefore, while concentrating on Christianity, we will occasionally refer to Islam as well. In Horton's view neither of these two world religions were at root responsible, or 'caused' this change in African religious perspectives. They certainly speeded it along, assisted and contributed to it, but they did not initiate it. It was a change that would have taken place, no doubt much more slowly, without them.

Horton's theory has been subjected to a considerable amount of criticism by historians, social scientists and theologians among others. It is important first of all to make a distinction between how those people who converted to Christianity actually saw matters and what might have been the case. Some, no doubt, were convinced that Christianity provided a very different interpretation of the Supreme Being and a different set of beliefs than the traditional religions. This was the case, for example, with the Prophet Harris (see Chapter 6, pp. 178–84).

On the other hand there were those – some of whom became Christians while others did not – who maintained that there was no substantial difference between traditional religions and Christianity on the question of the Supreme Being. The principal focus of the traditional religions, despite appearances to the contrary, was the Supreme Being. As one former traditional religionist, now a Christian, expressed it: 'When making sacrifice we used to say "Olodumare let it be active"; we did not bother in our minds with the lesser gods'.[3] As we have seen Parrinder, on reflection based on further investigation, modified his opinion concerning the attention paid to the Supreme Being in West African traditional religions. He no longer accepts that the ordinary traditional religionist looked upon the Supreme Being as 'uncertain and remote'. God, he suggests, was probably much closer to people than some writers make out, and 'has been believed in from time immemorial'.[4]

Granted, then, that some observers and active participants do not accept that the belief in a Supreme Being was introduced into West Africa by Christianity or Islam, is Horton therefore correct in suggesting that the change in emphasis was facilitated more by material factors – improvements in communications, increase in trade between societies, the widening of political boundaries, leading to the creation of larger and more diverse political, cultural and economic formations – than to Christianity and Islam? Does this change consist, in substance, of a development within African traditional religious thought which led away from emphasis on the lesser gods to giving greater significance and importance at the personal and community level to the Supreme Being, a development attributable primarily to the above mentioned 'material' factors rather than to Christianity or Islam?

Few would dispute the belief in the Supreme Being in African society 'from time immemorial', but it is by no means certain that Horton's view as to why the Supreme Being came to be placed at the centre of religious life in Africa is correct. Some writers appear to be suggesting that in some instances at least this was always the case.[5] Even if one accepts the development or change in religious perspectives as outlined by Horton, would one not expect to see in all societies that have been 'opened up' and that have had their political, economic, social and cultural boundaries 'widened', more significance and importance attached to the worship of the Supreme Being? However, as some writers have pointed out, this has not always happened. These writers provide examples of a number of societies which, although in close contact for considerable lengths of time with other societies and open to numerous outside influences, continue to focus as much if not more attention on the lesser gods as on the Supreme Being. In some small-scale societies, on the other hand, relatively uninfluenced by the wider world, belief in and worship of the Supreme Being is of paramount importance.[6]

There is other evidence which would appear to contradict Horton's theory of religious development. Horton seems to make the mistake of assuming that because certain familiar organisational patterns and forms of worship directed towards the Supreme Being were not present or highly visible the Supreme Being was largely ignored. There are various ways of expressing belief and of worshipping, and because in a particular society there are none, or only a very few temples dedicated to the Supreme Being, the conclusion should not be drawn that the Supreme Being is considered to be remote and uninvolved in the life of individuals and society. As one scholar says with regard to traditional Yoruba religion:

> It is not correct to say that people do not offer any cult to the Supreme Being. If cult is seen solely as putting up a temple or erecting a sanctuary for the worship of a Supreme Being it is true that this is not given prominence among the Yoruba. But if, in worship, prayer, adoration and invocation, are given prominence, we will maintain that the Yoruba worship Him. His name is on the people's lips at all times in prayer, spontaneous acts of thanksgiving for blessings received, in oaths and in proverbs.[7]

The same can be said with regard to the belief in and worship of the Supreme Being among the Ibo, and many other West African peoples.

Horton's point that the *opening up* and exposing of a society to other cultures, traditions, influences and the enlargement of its political and economic frontiers leads to the type of change in religious perspective that he suggests does not take into consideration the fact that people respond to this kind of opening up in a variety of different ways, as studies of millenarian movements show. Some individuals and societies when they are 'opened up', rather than changing their religious outlook and beliefs cling more tenaciously than ever to their traditional, customary beliefs and practices.[8]

Horton's discussion of the developments and changes in African religion has directed people's attention to the need to avoid seeing African traditional religions as static and unchanging, a point that was made in the introduction to this study. But it does tend to offer what amounts to a mono-causal, very general explanation of religious change which is a highly complex phenomenon. Moreover, it may well tend to obscure some of the contributions made by both Christianity and Islam to religious development in West Africa and Africa as a whole.

Certainly, when Christian and Muslim preachers spoke about the Supreme Being this was not necessarily a new idea in the West African context or elsewhere in Africa for that matter. However, the way the idea of the Supreme Being was presented, the content given to it and the cultural and linguistic form in which it was couched were often different. The Christian notion of a Saviour God whose death was the only one, valid, worthwhile sacrifice, cancelling out all other forms of sacrifice, may have had parallels in African traditional religions, but also seems to have offered a different notion of salvation from what was widespread.[9]

Thus, while they had much in common including the belief in the Supreme Being, something that a majority perhaps of Christian evangelists did not or were unprepared to recognise until quite recently (see Chapter 8, pp. 220 ff.), there were differences, sometimes far less significant than was imagined, in belief and practice between Christianity and traditional African religions. The same applies to Islam.[10]

Christianity and Islam were seen to offer – and to some extent were –

'alternatives' to traditional African religions, and this in some measure accounts for why people converted. This, as previous chapters discussed in the context of evangelisation through the school and other methods of evangelisation, is not the whole story. Moreover, in speaking of 'alternatives' in this way it is not being suggested that people accepted or totally commited themselves to one only of the several religions available. While some no doubt did this, others regarded all faiths as having much in common and as part of the total religious fabric of society.

The question of the contribution that West African and African Christianity as a whole might make to world Christianity, is perhaps just as important for many as the contribution Christianity has made to African traditional religions in West Africa and elsewhere on the continent of Africa. There has already been some discussion of African ideas on and approaches to Christianity which have more than local significance (see Chapters 6 and 7).

A point made in the introduction might be repeated here by way of a final comment: that the African experience of Christianity is one that has been acquired in the wider context of colonialism, nationalism, nation building, industrialisation and underdevelopment, and this fact must make that experience and the theological perspectives born of it of very great significance for Christian Churches beyond the frontiers of West Africa and the African continent as a whole. Not only are some of the 'crucial points of expansion, vigour and innovation' in the Christian Church to be found in West Africa and elsewhere in sub-Saharan Africa but so also, it might be argued, is much of the experience necessary to deal with some of the most relevant contemporary issues which are not only of concern to African Christians in Africa, but are of worldwide dimensions.[11]

Notes

1 See for example, R. Horton's views on African Conversion to Christianity and Islam, in Africa **XII** (1), April 1971, ibid. **45** (3), 1975, and **45** (4), 1975. See also H.J. Fisher's reply to Horton: Conversion Reconsidered: Some Historical Aspects of Religious Conversion in Black Africa, in *Africa* XLIII (1), 1973.
2 R. Horton, African Conversion, op. cit., 1971, pp. 101 ff.
3 Interview – Ibadan, 30/5/1978.
4 G. Parrinder, *West African Religion*, op.cit., p. 25.
5 J.O. Awolalu, *Yoruba Beliefs and Practices*. London: Longman, 1978: chap. 1, pp. 3 ff.
6 See for example H.J. Fisher, Conversion Reconsidered: Some Historical Aspects of Religious Conversion in Black Africa. In *Africa* **XLIII** (1), 1973. And A.J. Gittins, The Mende and Missionary, and R.W. Wyllie, Spiritism in Ghana: A Study of New Religious Movements, *Studies in Religion*, No. 21, Montana, 1980.
7 Awolalu, op.cit., p.17.
8 K. Burridge, *New Heaven New Earth*. Oxford: Oxford University Press, 1969.
9 Some Yoruba Christians, for example, believe that, as one expressed it 'Ifa is no other than Christ; he was saving others from death; he was slain with a

spear. This signifies Christ'. Interview, Ibadan, 6/6/1978.

10 P.B. Clarke, *West Africa and Islam*, op.cit., pp. 259 ff.

11 R. Gray, *Christianity and Religious Change in Africa*, African Affairs, 77 (306), January 1978: p.89 ff.

Select Bibliography.

Adegbola, E.A.A., Ifa and Christianity Among the Yoruba. Ph.D. thesis. University of Bristol, 1976.

Ajayi, J.F.A., *Christian Missions in Nigeria 1841–1891. The making of a new élite*, Longman, London, 1965.

Ajayi, J.F.A., Henry Venn and the Policy of Development. In Kalu, O.U. (ed.) *The History of Christianity in West Africa*, Longman, London, 1980.

Ajayi, J.F.A., Nineteenth Century Origins of Nigerian Nationalism. *Journal of the Historical Society of Nigeria* **2** (1), 1961.

Ajayi, J.F.A., and Crowder, M. (eds), *A History of West Africa*, Vols 1 and 2, Longman, London, 1972 and 1974 respectively.

Akiga, S., History of the Tiv. MSS, University of Ibadan, Africana Collection.

Audouin, J. and Deniel, R., *L'Islam en Haute Volta*, Editions Harmattan INADES Edition Abidjan and Paris, 1978.

Awolalu, J.O., *Yoruba Beliefs and Sacrificial Rites*, Longman, London, 1978.

Ayandele, E.A., *The Missionary Impact on Modern Nigeria 1842–1914. A political and social analysis*, Longman, London, 1966.

Ayandele, E.A., Traditional Rulers and Missionaries in Pre-Colonial West Africa, in *Tarikh* **3** (1), 1969.

Ayandele, E.A., *Holy Johnson*, Frank Cass, London, 1970.

Baeta, C.G., *Prophetism in Ghana: A study of some 'spiritual' Churches*, SCM Press, London, 1962.

Baeta, C.G. (ed.), Christianity in Tropical Africa, London, Oxford University Press (O.U.P.) for the International African Institute (I.A.I.), 1968.

Bane, M.J., The Catholic Story of Liberia, Declan MacMullen, New York, 1950.

Bane, M.J., *Catholic Pioneers in West Africa*, Dublin, Clonmore and Reynolds Ltd 1956.

Banton, M., *West African City*, Oxford University Press, Oxford, 1957.

Barrett, D.B., Schism and Renewal in Africa: an analysis of six thousand contemporary religious movements, Oxford University Press, Nairobi and London, 1968.

Barrett, D.B. (ed.), *World Christian Encyclopaedia. A Comparative Survey of Church and Religions in the Modern World*, A.D. 1900–2000. Oxford

University Press, Oxford, 1982.
Barrett, S.R., *The Rise and Fall of an African Utopia: A wealthy theocracy in comparative perspective*, Waterloo, Ontario, 1977.
Bartels, F.L., *The Roots of Ghana Methodism*, Cambridge University Press, Cambridge, 1965.
Bee, M., La Christianisation de La Basse Côte d'Ivoire, in *Revue Française d'Histoire d'Outre Mer*, No. 62, 1975.
Berman, E.H. (ed.), *African Reactions to Missionary Education*, Teachers College Press, New York and London, 1975.
Boer, J.H., *Missionary Messengers of Liberation in a Colonial Context. A Case Study of the Sudan United Mission*, 2 Vols. Amsterdam, 1979.
Bond, G., Johnson, W., Walker, S. (eds), *African Christianity. Patterns of Religious Continuity*, Academic Press, New York/London, 1979.
Bouche, D., La Participation des Missions au Développement de l'Enseignement dans les Colonies Francaises d'Afrique Occidentale de 1817 à 1940. *Etudes d'Histoire Africaine* **VIII**, 1976.
Bowen, T.J., *Adventures and Missionary Labours*, 1857 (1968 reprint edition Frank Cass, London).
Boxer, C.R., *The Church Militant and Iberian Expansion*, Johns Hopkins, Baltimore, 1978.
Brown, M.A.G., Education and National Development in Liberia. Ph.D. Thesis, Cornell, 1967. (University of Microfilm, Ann Arbor, Michigan, 1967).
Cabral, N.E., *Les Iles de Cap Vert. Cinq Siècles de Contacts Culturels, Mutation et Mélange Ethnique*, Doctoral Thesis, Sorbonne, Paris, 1979.
Callaway, H., Women in Yoruba Tradition and in the Cherubim and Seraphim Society, in Kalu, O.U. (ed.) *The History of Christianity in West Africa*, Longman, London and New York, 1980.
Chabert, R.P., L'Islam Chez les Sauvages et Les Cannibales de la Nigéria du Nord. Conference, Institut Catholique, Paris, 1927.
Christian Reformed Church, *The Coming of the Gospel into Tivland*. Christian Reformed Church Publication, n.d.
Clarke, P.B., Birom Woman Evangelist: Vo Gyang of Forum. In Isichei, E. *Varieties of Christian Experience in Nigeria*, Macmillan, London, 1982.
Clarke, P.B., Christian Approaches to Islam in Francophone Africa in the Post-Independence Era (*c*.1960–*c*.1983): From Confrontation to Dialogue, in *Bulletin on Islam and Christian-Muslim Relations in Africa* **I** (2), April 1983.
Clarke, P.B., *The Christian Encounter with Islam in Africa, c.1840–c.1982*, Forthcoming.
Clarke, P.B., Methods and Ideology of the Holy Ghost Fathers in Eastern Nigeria, 1885–1905, in Kalu, O.U. (ed.) *The History of Christianity in West Africa*, Longman, London and New York, 1980.
Clarke, P.B., *West Africa and Islam*, Edward Arnold, London, 1982.
Cornevin, R., *La République Populaire du Benin* (2nd edition), Editions G-P Maisoneuve et Larose Paris, 1981.
Crampton, E.P.T., *Christianity in Northern Nigeria*, Gaskiya Press, Zaria, 1975.
Crowder, M., *West Africa under Colonial Rule*, Hodder and Stoughton,

London, 1968.

Curley, R.T., Dreams of Power: Social Process in a West Africa Religious Movement, *Africa* **53** (3), 1983.

Cuoq, J.M., *Les Musulmans en Afrique*, Editions G-P Maisoneuve et Larose Paris, 1975.

Curtin, P., *The Atlantic Slave Trade: A Census*, University of Wisconsin Press, Wisconsin, 1969.

Debrunner, H.W., *A Church Between Colonial Powers: A Study of the Church in Togo*, Lutterworth, London, 1965.

Delcourt, J., *Histoire Religieuse du Sénégal*, Editions Clair Afrique, Dakar, 1975.

Deniel, R., *Croyances Religieuses et Vie Quotidienne. Islam et Christianisme à Ouagadougou*, CNRS-CURS Paris and Ouagadougou, 1970.

Diane, D., Le Catholicisme en Haute-Guinée de 1903 aux Années Cinquante, Mémoire (D.E.A.), University of Paris, I, June 1981.

Dubie, P., Christianisme, Islam et Animisme chez les Bamoun, Bulletin de l'Institut Français d'Afrique Noire, sér. B. Tom. XIX, nos. 3–4, Dakar (IFAN), 1957.

Echeruo, M.J.C., *Victorian Lagos*, Macmillan, London and Basingstoke, 1977.

Ejofodomi, L.E., The Missionary Career of Alexander Crummell in Liberia 1853–1873, Ph.D. Boston University 1974 (University Microfilm, Ann Arbor, Michigan, 1974).

Eketchi, F.K., *Missionary Enterprise and Rivalry in Igboland 1857–1914*, Frank Cass, London, 1972.

Erivwo, S., *A History of Christianity in Nigeria. The Urhobo, The Isoko, and The Itsekiri*, Ibadan University Press, Ibadan, 1979.

Evans-Pritchard, E.E., *Theories of Primitive Religion*, Oxford University Press, Oxford, 1965.

Fage, J.D., Slavery and the Slave Trade in the context of West African History, *Journal of African History* **X** (3), 1969: 393–404.

Fashole-Luke, E. *et al.* (eds), *Christianity in Independent Africa*, Rex Collings, London, 1978.

Faure, J., *Histoire Des Missions et Eglises Protestantes en Afrique Occidentale Des Origines à 1884*, Editions CCE, Yaoundé, 1978.

Fisher, H.J., *Ahmadiyyah: A Study in Contemporary Islam on the West African Coast*, Oxford University Press, Oxford, 1963.

Fisher, H.J., Conversion Reconsidered: Some Historical Aspects of Religious Conversion in Black Africa, in *Africa* **XLIII** (1), 1973.

Fisher, H.J., Independency and Islam: The Nigerian Aladuras and some Muslim Comparisons, *Journal of African History* **XI** (2), 1970.

Fisher, H.J., The Modernization of Islamic Education in Sierra Leone, Gambia and Liberia: Religion and Language. In Brown, G.N. and Hiskett, M. (eds) in *Conflict and Harmony in Education in Tropical Africa*, London, 1975.

Freeman, T.B., *Various Visits to Ashanti* (3rd edition), Frank Cass, London, 1968.

Fyfe, C., *A History of Sierra Leone*, Oxford University Press, Oxford, 1962.

Fyfe, C., *A Short History of Sierra Leone*, Longman, (new ed.), London, 1979.

Fyfe, C., *Sierra Leone Inheritance*, Oxford University Press, Oxford, 1964.

Gittins, A.J. The Mende and Missionary: Belief, Perception and Enterprise. Ph.D. thesis, Edinburgh, 1977.

Grau, E., Missionary Policies as seen in the Work of Missions with the Evangelical Presbyterian Church, Ghana. In Baeta, C.G. (ed.) *Christianity in Tropical Africa*, Oxford University Press, Oxford, 1968.

Gray, R., Christian Traces and a Franciscan Mission in the Central Sudan, *Journal of African History* **VII**, 1967: 392–3.

Gray, R., Come Cero Principe Catolico: The Capuchins and the Rulers of Soyo in the late Seventeenth Century, *Africa* **53** (3), 1983.

Gray, R., The Origins and Organization of the Nineteenth-Century Missionary Movement, *Tarikh* **3** (1) 1969.

Grimley, J.B., Robinson, G.E., Church Growth in Central and Southern Nigeria, Eerdmans, Michigan, 1966.

Groves, C.P., *The Planting of Christianity in Africa* (4 vols), Lutterworth, London, 1948–1958.

Gwassa, G.C.K., Kinjikitile and the Ideology of the Maji-Maji. In Ranger, T.O. and Kimambo, I.N. (eds) *The Historical Study of African Religions*, University of California Press, Berkeley 1972.

Hackett, R.J., Nigeria's Aladura Churches – Gateways or Barriers to Social Development, *Africana Marburgensia* **XIV** (1), 1981.

Haliburton, G.M., *The Prophet Harris. A Study of an African Prophet and his Mass-Movement in the Ivory Coast and the Gold Coast, 1913–1915*, Longman, London, 1971.

Harding, L., Les Ecoles des Pères Blancs au Soudan Français. In Cahiers d'Etudes Africaines (CEA) **3** (8), 1972.

Hargreaves, J.D., African Colonization in the 19th Century. In Butler, J., Boston University Papers in African History, Boston, 1966.

Hargreaves, J.D., *France and West Africa*, Macmillan, London and Basingstoke, 1969.

Hastings, A., *A History of African Christianity 1950–1975*, Cambridge University Press, Cambridge, 1979.

Hickey, R., *Heralds of Christ to Borno*, Augustinian Publications, Jos, 1978.

Hogan, E.M., *Catholic Missions and Liberia*, Cork University Press, Cork, 1981.

Holas, B., Bref Aperçu sur les Principaux Cultes Syncrétiques de la Basse Côte d'Ivoire, *Africa* **24**, Jan. 1954.

Holas, B., *Le Séparatisme Religieux en Afrique Noire*, Presses Universitaires de France, Paris, 1965.

Hollande, P., La Dynamique Missionaire de L'Islam. Mémoire de Maîtrise en Théologie, Insitut Catholique de Paris, 1975.

Horton, R., African Conversion, *Africa* **XLI** (2), April 1971.

Horton, R., African Traditional Thought and Western Science, *Africa* **XXXVII** (2), April 1967.

Hulmes, E.D.A., Christian Attitudes to Islam: A Comparative Study of the Work of S.A. Crowther, E.W. Blyden, and W.R.S. Miller in West

Africa, D. Phil, Oxford, 1980.

Idowu, E.B., *Olodumare, God in Yoruba Belief*, Longman, London, 1962.

Ikime, O., *The Isoko People*, Ibadan University Press, Ibadan, 1972.

Inikori, J.E. (ed.), *Forced Migration. The Impact of the Export Slave Trade on African Societies*, Hutchinson, London, 1982.

Isichei, E. (ed.), *Varieties of Christian Experience in Nigeria*, Macmillan, London and Basingstoke, 1982.

Isichei, E. (ed.), *A History of Nigeria*, Longman, London, 1983.

Jones, D., The Catholic Mission and Some Aspects of Assimilation in Senegal, 1817–1852, *Journal of African History* **21** (3), 1980.

Joseph, R., *Radical Nationalism in Cameroon*, Oxford University Press, Oxford, 1977.

Kalu, O.U., The Shattered Cross: The Church Union Movement in Nigeria 1905–1966, in Kalu, O.U., (ed.) *The History of Christianity in West Africa*, Longman, London and New York, 1980.

Kendall, R.E., *The End of an Era. Africa and the Missionary*, SPCK, London 1978.

Klein, M.A., *Islam and Imperialism in Senegal*. Edinburgh University Press, Edinburgh, 1968.

Kup, P., *The Story of Sierra Leone*. Cambridge University Press, Cambridge, 1964.

Lynch, H.R., *Edward Wilmot Blyden. Pan-Negro Patriot, 1832–1912*. Oxford University Press, London.

McKenzie, P.R., *Inter-Religious Encounters in West Africa*. Leicester University Press, Leicester, 1976.

Mahoney, F., Government and Opinion in The Gambia. Ph.D. thesis, University of London (School of Oriental and African Studies), 1963.

Martin, J.J., The Dual Legacy: Government Authority and Mission Influence among the Grebo of Eastern Liberia 1834–1910. Ph.D. Boston 1968 (University microfilm, Ann Arbor, Michigan 1968).

Mazrui, A.A., *Political Values and the Educated Class in Africa*, Heinemann, London, 1978.

Odamtten, S.K., *The Missionary Factor in Ghana's Development, 1820–1880*, Waterville Publishing House, Accra, 1978.

Oguntiyi, A., *A History of the Catholic Church in Ondo Diocese*, Ibadan University Press, Ibadan, 1970.

Oloruntinehin, B.O., *The Segu-Tokolor Empire*, Longman, London, 1972.

Omoyajowo, J.A., *Cherubim and Seraphim. The History of an African Independent Church*, Nok Publishers, New York and Lagos, 1982.

O'Neill, P., *The Catholic Faith in Ibadan Diocese, 1884–1974*,Daystar Press, Ibadan, 1981.

Parrinder, G., *Africa's Three Religions*, Sheldon Press, 1969.

Parrinder, G., *Religion in an African City*, Oxford University Press, Oxford, 1953.

Paulme, D., Une Religion Syncrétique en Côte d'Ivoire: Le Culte Deima, *Cahiers d'Etudes Africaines* **9** (3), 1972.

Peel, J.D.Y., *Aladura: a Religious Movement among the Yoruba*, Oxford University Press, Oxford, 1968.

Peterson, J., *Province of Freedom*, Evanston, Illinois, 1969.
Pirouet, M.L., East African Christians and World War I. In *Journal of African History* **XIX** (1), 1978.
Porter, A.T., *Creoledom*, Oxford University Press, Oxford, 1963.
Potter, S., The Making of Missionaries in the Nineteenth Century. In Hill, M. (ed.) *A Sociological Yearbook of Religion in Britain* **8**, SCM Press, London, 1975.
Rubingh, J., Sons of Tiv: A Study of the Rise of the Church among the Tiv of Central Nigeria, Baker, Michigan, 1969.
Ryder, A.F.C., *Benin and the Europeans*, Longman, London, 1969.
Ryder, A.F.C., Missionary Activity in the Kingdom of Warri to the Early Nineteenth Century, in *Journal of the Historical Society of Nigeria* **2** (1), 1960.
Ryder, A.F.C., Portuguese Missions in Western Africa, *Tarikh* **3** (1), 1969.
Sanders, E.R., The Hamitic Hypothesis: Its Origins and Functions in Time Perspective, *Journal of African History* **10** (4), 1969.
Sanders, A.C. de C.M., *A Social History of Black Slaves and Freedmen in Portugal, 1441–1555*, Cambridge University Press, Cambridge, 1982.
Sanneh, L., *West African Christianity. The Religious Impact*, C. Hurst, London, 1983.
Sundkler, B.G.M., *Bantu Prophets in South Africa* (2nd ed.), Oxford University Press, Oxford, 1961.
Suret-Canale, J. and Barry, B., The West Atlantic Coast to 1800. In Ade-Adjayi, J.F. and Crowder, M. (eds) *The History of West Africa*, Vol. 1, Longman, London, 1972.
Tasie, G., *Christian Missionary Enterprise in the Niger Delta*, E.J. Brill, Leiden, 1978.
Tasie, G.O.M., The Prophetic Calling: Garrick Sokari Braide of Bakana (d. 1918), in Isichei, E. *Varieties of Christian Experience in Nigeria*, op. cit.
Turner, H.W., *History of an Independent Church: The Church of the Lord*. 2 Vols, Oxford University Press, Oxford, 1967.
Walker, S.S., *The Religious Revolution in the Ivory Coast. The Prophet Harris and the Harrist Church*. University of North Carolina Press, Chapel Hill 1983.
Walls, A.F., The Nova Scotian Settlers and Their Religion, *Sierra Leone Bulletin of Religion* June 1959.
Webster, J.B., *The African Churches among the Yoruba 1888–1922*, Oxford University Press, Oxford, 1964.
Williams, W.L., *Black Americans and the Evangelization of Africa 1887–1900*, University of Wisconsin Press, Wisconsin, 1982.
Wiltgen, R.M., *A Gold Coast Mission History: 1471–1880*. Techny, Illinois, U.S.A., 1956.
Wold, J.C., *God's Impatience in Liberia*. Michigan University Press, Michigan, 1968.
Wyllie, R.W., Spiritism in Ghana: A Study of New Religious Movements, in *Studies in Religion* **21**, Scholars Press, Montana, 1980.

Essay Questions/Topics for discussion.

1 Account for the failure of Christian missionary activity in West Africa during the period 1445–1790 (Chapter 1).

2 What was the nature of the relationship between Church and State in the period 1445–1790, and what effect did it have on Christian missionary activity in West Africa? (Chapters 1 and 9).

3 Account for the revival of Christian missionary interest in Africa with special reference to West Africa in the late eighteenth century and the first half of the nineteenth century (Chapters 2 and 3).

4 How would you explain the slow growth of Christianity among the indigenous populations of Sierra Leone and Liberia during the nineteenth century? (Chapters 2 and 3).

5 Discuss the role of the emigrants in the spread of Christianity in West Africa, with particular reference to Nigeria from 1840–90 (Chapter 3).

6 Discuss the policy of establishing 'self-governing, self-supporting, self-propagating' African Churches and explain why it came to be opposed (Chapter 3).

7 Why was Bishop Crowther forced to resign and what consequences did this have for the Christian Church in Nigeria? (Chapters 3–6).

8 Explain why the Christian missionaries in the Senegambia had given up all hope of converting Muslims to Christianity by 1890 (Chapters 3 and 5).

9 Do you agree that the Christian missionaries were the 'pathfinders' of European imperial influence in West Africa? (Chapters 3, 4 and 9).

10 Compare and contrast the methods used to extend Christianity in West Africa during the period 1890–1960. (You should consider here both Anglophone and Francophone West Africa. Chapters 4 and 5).

11 What was the impact of both World Wars on the development of Christianity in West Africa? (Chapters 4 and 5).

12 Critically examine the role of the catechist in the spread of

Christianity in West Africa during the period 1890–1960 (Chapters 4 and 5).

13   Account for the slow progress made in forming an indigenous clergy in West Africa between 1850 and 1950 (Chapters 3–5).

14   What approach did the Christian Churches adopt towards Islam during the colonial era? (Chapters 4 and 5).

15   Explain the rise and assess the impact of the independent Church movement in West Africa between 1880 and 1960 (Chapters 3–6).

16   Why in your opinion did the Aladura Churches and societies place so much emphasis on prayer as a means of healing? (Chapter 6).

17   Account for the success of the Prophet Harris in the Ivory Coast (Chapter 6).

18   'Typical of his type'. Examine the activities of the Prophet Harris and any two other West African prophets in the light of this comment (Chapter 6).

19   'While much has changed, much remains the same'. Examine the development of Christianity in West Africa since independence in the light of this comment (Chapter 7).

20   Account for the improvement in relations between the Christian Churches in West Africa in recent times (Chapters 4, 5 and 7).

21   Account for the change in attitude and response of the Christian Churches to Islam and traditional African religions in recent times (Chapter 8).

22   Examine the role played by Christianity in nation building and nationalism in West Africa (Chapters 3–6 and 8).

23   In what sense if any can the independent Church movement be considered a nationalist movement? (Chapter 6).

24   Trace the developments in Church-State relations in West Africa from 1850 to the present (Chapter 9 and Chapters 3–6).

25   In what ways and to what extent if any has Christianity contributed to a change in African approaches to the Supreme Being? (Chapter 10).

26   What role have women played in the development of Christianity in West Africa? (Chapter 4 and *passim*).

27   'To see the development of Christianity in West Africa as due almost entirely to its influence in the field of education is to misunderstand the complex nature of that development'. *Discuss*. (Chapters 4–6 and *passim*).

Index

Abeokuta, 63–4, 79, 102, 104, 177, 238
Abidjan, 133, 184, 197, 203, 207
Abigail, 171
Abomey, 61
Abomey Mission, 138
Accra, 18, 23, 58, 98
Adamawa, 114
Adejobi, E.A., 177–8
Ademiyewo, Awujale of Ijebu-Ode, 237
Ademuyiwa, Haastrup, Prince, 102
Adikpo Mission, 106
Adjara, 61
Adjassi, 61
Ado Mission, 104
Ado, King of Akropong, 42
Adukoya, Joshua, 168
African Baptist Church, 160
African Church (Incorporated), 162
African Independent Churches, 4, 97, 103, 156–90
African Medical Service, 233
African Methodist Episcopal Church, 198
African Methodist Episcopal Zion Church, 98, 198
Agades, 23
Agbebi, Mojola (David Vincent), 160–61
Agoué, 61, 140
Agugu Society, 36
Ahmadiyya, 88
Ahmadu Bello, Sir, 218
Ahmadu Bello University 218
Ahmadu Hampaté Bâ, 219
Ahui, John, 185
Aina, John Ade, 168
Akan, 18
Akiga, 106
Akinsowon, Christiana Abiodun, 172, 173
Akintoye, 63
Ainyele, Isaac, 167–8
Akropong Mission, 42, 59
Aku, 79–80, 88, 125
Akure Mission, 104
Aladura Churches, 159–60, 166–78, 184, 188–91, 197–8, 201, 210–12, 217, 222
Alentejo, 7
Alexandria, 5
Algarve, 7
Algeria, 5
Al-Hajj Amadou, Dem, 72
Al-Hajj Umar, 72
Al-Hajj Umar Tall, 130
American Baptist Mission, 39
American Baptist Missionary Society, 160
American Board of Commissioners, 39
American Civil War, 161
American Episcopal Church, 53
American Methodist Episcopal Church (AME), 39, 53–4
American Methodist Episcopal Zion Church, (AMEZ), 54
American Presbyterian Mission, 39
American Society for the Colonization of Free People of Colour of the United States (ASC), 37–8
American War of Independence, 37
Amissah, John, 206
Anamaba, 58
Anderson, Isaac, 34
Anecho Mission, 61, 140
Anglican Church, 4, 23, 32, 35, 39, 48, 65, 97–8, 99, 101–3, 104–5, 152, 157, 161–6, 168, 172–3, 175, 197–202, 209

Angola, 14, 152
Annie Pepple House, 66
Antonio Domingos, Olu of Warri, 21
Anyanwu, Mr, 114
Anyi, 147
Appiah, Joseph William Egyanka, 188–9
Arabic, 132, 135
Archibong House, 68
Arda, 19
Arragon, Fr, 71–2
Asante, 42, 58–9, 97
Asantehini Prempeh I, 58
Asante War, 58
Ashanti, 1
Ashmun, Jehudi, 38
Askiya Muhammad I, 12
Assemblies of God, 125, 137, 139, 142, 198, 205
Assinie, 19, 179
Association for Christian Higher Education, 201
Atakpame Mission, 61, 138
Atar Mission, 126
Athiemé Mission, 138
Atsioupa, 61
Attoh Ahima, Rev. S., 62
Augustine, Bishop of Hippo, 5
Aurobindo Ghose, 229
Awolalu, 222
Axim, 18–9
Azaourisse, M, 138
Azikiwe, Nnamdi, 234

Baawa, Abena, 188
Babalola, Joseph 169, 171
Badagry, 61, 63
Bai Bure, 88
Bakana, 164
Bakan, 79
Balante, 151
Balentes, 73
Bamako Mission, 130, 133
Bambara, 1–2, 35, 76–7, 79, 130–4
Bambuk, 8
Bamoun, 148
Bangui, 150

Banikouara Mission, 139
Banjul (Bathurst), 44, 73, 79–80, 125
Bantu, 222
Banyun, 151
Baptist Church, 4, 31, 35–6, 51–3, 102, 151, 160–1
Baptist Missionary Society, 31, 64, 102, 148, 207
Barbot, 19
Bare Mission, 114
Bariba, 140
Barnes, Hannah, 188
Barra Mission, 44, 79
Barreira, Fr, 10–13
Barron, Fr Edward, 31, 55
Basden, 221
Basel Mission (Evangelical Missionary Society of Basel), 39, 41–2, 57, 59, 62, 96–7, 140, 148
Bassa, 39, 89, 198
Bassa Cove, 38–9
Bassam, 179
Bassari, 142
Bauchi, 109, 114, 174, 201
Baule, 1, 147
Bekwai, 58
Beledegu, 76
Belfast, 69
Belgium, 131
Bemoy, Prince, 11
Bena, King of, 12
Bendel State, 21, 100, 114
Benin, 2, 4, 9, 17, 19–20, 61, 69, 100, 114, 177
Benin, Republic of, 19, 48, 57, 60–2, 123, 129, 138–40, 142, 143, 145, 152, 160, 174, 189, 195, 205, 208, 212, 238
Benoit, 146
Benue State, 109, 202
Bethel Church, 162
Betu, 94
Biafada, 151
Bida, 66, 109
Bignona Mission, 75, 124
Bijago, 151
Bijagós Islands, 151

Bingerville, 146
Birom, 111–3
Bissau, 73
Blyden, Edward Wilmot, 51–6, 88, 162, 216, 233
Bo, 197
Bobo, 2, 133
Bobo-Dioulasso, 133, 137
Boffa, 126
Boghero Fr, 61
Bohicon Mission, 138
Boilat, 16, 43
Bolgatanga, 97
Bon Jesus da Redempçao, 61
Bonny, 65, 99
Borno State, 114, 201
Bot Dung, 112
Boukoumbé Mission, 139
Bour of Sine, 71–2, 76
Boutrous, 73
Bowen, Thomas Jefferson, 221
Boys' Brigade, 112
Braide, Prophet Garrick Sokari, 164–6, 179
Brass, 65
Brava, 151
Brazil, 22, 25, 48, 61, 69, 140, 160–1
Bremen Mission, 57, 60, 62, 87, 97, 140
Brewerville, 54
Bribrinae, 100
Bright, Bankole, 89
Bristol, 31
Britain in West Africa, 15–16, 30–5, 37, 43, 54, 56–8, 63-4, 66–7, 69–70, 87, 97, 113, 121–2, 131, 139–41, 148, 149, 152–3, 157–8, 162, 163, 166, 189, 195–202, 231–2, 237–8
British Anti-Slave Trade Act, 35
British Apostolic Church, 169
Brong, 147
Brotherhood of the Cross and Star, 201
Brothers of Ploërmel, 78, 123
Brouadou Mission, 126–7
Buchanan Thomas, 38
Bullom, 1, 51
Bundo Society, 36

Bure, 8
Burkina Faso, 12, 129, 133–7, 189, 196, 203, 205, 208
Burma, 229
Burns, Bishop Francis, 51
Burton, Sir Richard, 51, 221
Buxton, 67

Cacheo, 13, 73–5
Calabar, 68–9, 102
Calvin, John, 4
Cameroon, 1, 87, 114, 148–9, 152, 189, 196, 201, 203, 207, 234, 239
Cao, Gaspar, 21
Cape Coast, 23–4, 42, 58, 63, 98, 207
Cape of Good Hope, 7
Cape Palmas, 9, 38, 40–1, 55, 94, 179, 198
Cape Verde, 7–11, 13–17, 43, 81, 150–2, 196
Capitain, 23
Carabane, 73–5
Cardew, Governor, 49
Carey, Lott, 160, 198
Casamance, 75, 78, 122, 124, 205
Castile, 7
catechists, 69, 89–92, 104–5, 117, 136, 139, 142–3, 147, 153, 195, 201, 209, 244
Cayor, 77
Celestial Church of Christ, 201
Central African Republic, 150
Cerno Bokar Taal, 219
CGT (General Confederation of Workers), 129
Chad, 196
Chambonneau, 14
Chardonnier, 17
Cherubim and Seraphim Society, 170–5, 184, 201, 211, 219, 222–3, 236
Cheikh Kamara, 72
Christallier, Johann Gottlieb, 59
Christ Apostolic Church (CAC), 169–72, 201, 211
Christ Army Church, 166

Christian Association of Nigeria, 211
Christian Health Association of
    Nigeria, 211
Christian Missionary Alliance, 147, 204
Christian-Muslim Committee, 218
Christian Reformed Church, 108
Christiansborg, 41, 96
Church of Christ, 102, 108
Church of Christ in Tivland, 105
Church of the Lord, 175–78, 210–11
Church of the Messiah, 200, 236
Church Missionary Society (CMS), 31,
    34–7, 47–9, 62–8, 99–101, 103–4,
    108–10, 114–5, 131, 161–4, 208, 231
Church of Nazarene, 151
Church of William Wade Harris and his
    Twelve Apostles, 147, 187–8
Clapham Sect, 32
Clark, Pastor, 168
Clarkson, Thomas, 30
Coelho, 71, 215
Coker, Daniel, 53
Coker, David, 38
Combo Mission, 44
Communism, 211, 219
Community Development Group, 211
Compagnie des Indes, 14
Comte, 221
Condo, 39
Congo, 25
Congregation of the Holy Ghost, 16, 55
Congregation of the Holy Ghost and
    the Immaculate Heart of Mary,
    (see Holy Ghost Fathers), 31
Congregation of Our Lady of Apostles,
    103
Constantinople, 4
Copenhagen, 23
Cotonou Mission, 139
Counters of Huntingdon's
    Connection, 35
Cové Mission, 138
Cox, Melville, 39
Creek Town, 68
Creoles, 36, 48–51, 79, 88–9, 92, 177,
    197

Crocker, 39
Cross River State, 201
Crowther, Archdeacon Dandeson, 67,
    99
Crowther, Bishop Samuel Ajayi, 57,
    63–8, 99, 161–2, 209
Crummell, Alexander, 52–3, 233
Cuba, 48
Cudjo Cabos Leer, 24
Cult of St Anthony (Nana Ntona), 19
Cuttington College, 93, 95

Dagari, 98–9, 136
Dahomey, 63
Dakar, 9, 72–4, 78, 124, 133, 197, 205,
    207, 219
d'Almeida, Joaquim, 61
Dakar, Archbishop of, 219
Dan, 147
Dapango, 143
Dawson, James, 61
Dayepo, 94
d'Azambuja, Diego, 18
de Brito, Joao Rodrigues, 81
DEFAP, (French Evangelical
    Association for Apostolic Action),
    125
de Graft, William, 42, 63
Deima Church, 185–6
de Jesu, Venossa, 61
Démanet, Fr, 16
Democratic Party of the Ivory Coast,
    (PDCI), 240
de Muchins, 15
Dendi, 140
Denmark, 4, 19, 23, 41–2, 228
Dennis, Archdeacon, 101
Deutsch, 217
Dias, Joao, 151
Diola, 73–5, 79–80, 134, 151, 205
Divo, 147
Djefa Mission, 138
Djougou Mission, 139–40
Dogon, 2, 133, 222–3
Dogondoutchi, 138
Dohoua Mission, 138

Dolbel, 138
Domingos da Ascenão, Bishop, 18
Domingos, Antonio, 22
Dossa-Zoume Mission, 139
Douala, 149
Du Mission, 111
Duke Town, 68
Durkheim, Emile, 228–9
Dutch Reformed Church of South
 Africa, (DRCM), 105–8
Dzoghégau Monastery, 221

East Africa, 93
Eburi, 59
Ecumenical Centre for Mutual Aid
 (Service Oecuménique
 d'Entraide), 124
Edea, 148
Eden Revival Church, 195, 198
Edinburgh Conference, 210
Edo, 1
education and Christian Missions, 10,
 33, 35, 41–5, 48–53, 55–60, 68, 71,
 77–8, 81, 87–107, 113–5, 121–5,
 137–43, 146, 148–50, 153, 159, 195,
 197, 200, 210, 212, 217, 230, 238,
 241, 248
Efutu, 19
Egba, 64, 238
Egungun, 191
Egypt, 5, 66
Ekiti, 102, 104
Ekpé Mission, 138
Elmina, 18–9, 23
Emadu, Madam, 100
England, Bishop of Philadelphia, 31
England, Bishop of Charlestone, 55
Emugu, 106
Episcopal Church, 92
Eternal Sacred Order of the Cherubim
 and Seraphim Society, 174
Ethiopia, 5, 7
Ethiopian Churches, 157–9, 190
Evangelical Church of Cameroon
 (EEC), 207
Evangelical Churches of Chad, 150

Evangelical Church of Guinea, 151
Evangelical Church of Mali, 133
Evangelical Church of Togo, (EET),
 142, 207
Evangelical Churches of West Africa,
 (ECWA), 113, 140, 201, 207
Evangelical Lutheran Church, 95
Evangelical Missionary Society of
 Basel, (see Basel Mission)
Evangelical Society, 205
Evangelical United Brethren, 91
Ewe, 60, 140–3
Ewe Apostolic Revelation Society, 189
Ewe Presbyterian Church, 141
Eyamba House, 68–9

Fada N'Gourma Mission, 138
Fadiouth Mission, 76
Faidherbe, Governor, 75
Faith Society, 188
Faith Tabernacle movement, 190
Fante, 23, 58, 97, 189
Fante Society, 98
Farrington Mission, 39
Fellowship of the Churches of Christ in
 Sudan, 108
Fernandez, Fr, 61
Fernando Po, 69
First World War, 86, 88, 93, 96–7,
 101–3, 123–4, 131–3, 135, 138,
 140–1, 143, 146, 148–9, 184, 190–1
Fofana, E.J., 197
Fon, 1
Forum Mission, 111–2
Foumban Mission, 148
Fourah Bay, 36
Fourah Bay Christian Institute, 36
France in West Africa, 4, 9, 14, 17, 19,
 31, 34, 43–4, 55, 69–71, 74, 79, 87,
 93, 111, 121–53, 157, 162, 179–82,
 184, 189, 203–7, 209, 215, 218–9,
 232, 237–8
Franco-Prussian War, 78
Fraser, 32
Freeman, Thomas Birch, 42, 57, 60–1,
 63, 98

freemasonary, 129
Freetown, 32–4, 36, 48–51, 55, 89
French Congregation of the Holy
   Ghost, 31
French Evangelical Association for
   Apostolic Action (DEFAP), 125
French Holy Ghost Fathers, 69–70
Fridoil, 43
Frobisher, 19
Fulani, 1, 50, 134, 140, 151
Fulle Mission, 112
fundamentalism, 202, 210
Futa Toro, 15

Ga, 23, 199
Gabon, 55
Gagu, 147
Gallais, Fr, 43, 71–2
Gambia, The, 9, 13, 16, 43–4, 55, 74,
   79–80, 86, 110, 125–6, 152, 175, 196,
   209, 215–6
Ganawuri, 112
Gandhi, 229
Gao, 130
Garrison, W.L., 38
Gashua, 114
Gaspar Cão, Bishop, 17
Gbileh, 51
Gboko, 107
General Confederation of Workers
   (CGT), 129
George, David, 35
Georgetown, 44, 79, 125
Georgia, 38
Germany in West Africa, 4, 59–60, 87,
   97, 106, 131, 140–1, 148, 157
Ghana,
   ancient Empire of, 1, 8
   Republic of, 18, 35, 41–3, 48, 57–60,
   62, 86, 94, 97–9, 140, 159, 175, 177,
   179, 187–9, 195–6, 198–9, 203, 207,
   211–2, 223, 234, 236, 239
Ghana Evangelical Fellowship, 212
Ghey, Pastor, 112
Ghezo, King of Dahomey, 60
Gindiri, 112

GMA (Protestant Gospel Missionary
   Union), 133
Gnankoï, Samoe, 129
Godié, 186
Gold Coast, 58–9, 70, 96–9
Gomoa Echiem, 187
Gomoa Fomena, 187
Gongola State, 114, 201
Gorée, 14, 16–17, 31, 43–4, 55, 70, 74, 78
Gouroansi, 136
Grand Bassam, 143
Grand Cess, 93
Grand Popo, 61
Granville Town Mission, 14, 32–3
Grebo, 40–1, 51, 198
Greenville, 38
Grivard Lieu, 134
Guan, 1
Guerze, 127
Guilongou, 136
Guinea (Conakry), 126–30, 137, 196,
   203–4, 207, 239
Guinea Bissau, 9, 13, 79–81, 150–2
Guinea Democratic Party (PDG), 129
Gula, 51
Gwato, 20
Gwom Chai Mang, 112
Gyel, 112

Hacquard, Bishop, 134
Haddington, 39
Harris Church, 160, 183–4, 200, 203–4,
   209, 236, 240
Harris, William Wade, 94, 143–7, 160,
   166, 167, 179–87, 209, 211, 222, 235,
   245
Hastings, 36
Hausa, 1, 106, 108, 110, 112, 115, 134,
   138
Hayford Casely, 62
healing and Christian missions, 188,
   190, 201, 206, 224, 234, 235–6
Heavenly Christianity Church, 201
Heinze, 41
Henry the Navigator, 7–8
Hinduism, 229

Hippo, 5
Holland, 4, 13, 16, 17, 19, 23
Holy Apostles, 235
Holy City of Mozano, 187
Holy Ghost Fathers, 31, 44, 47, 50, 55,
    69–70, 78–9, 100, 106, 152
Holy Ghost Society, 107, 126
Holy Trinity Mission, 69
Hut Tax Rebellion, 88

Ibadan, 64, 102–3, 105, 159, 168–9, 173,
    177, 201, 219
Ibadan Catholic Mission, 103
Ibn Khaldun, 228
Ibo, 1, 65, 100, 114, 222
Ibrahim, Mallam, 115
Idah, 20
Idikan, 103
Idoma, 1, 107
Ifa, 190
Ife, 64, 104
Igbebe, 65
Igbide, 100
Ijaw, 1
Ijaye, 64
Ijebu, 102–4, 175, 177, 178, 234
Ijebu-Ode, 166, 170, 237
Ijebu-Remo, 102
Ikot Ekpene, 102
Ilesha, 102, 169
Illue-Ologbo, 100
Immaculate Heart of Mary (see Holy
    Ghost Fathers), 55
Imperi, 49
Indénié, 179
Independent Baptist Church, 102
India, 88, 229
Institute of Church and Society, 211
Iressi, 102
Isawa (the Jesus People), 115
Ishola, Adedeji, 156, 185
Islam, 3, 7, 10, 12–15, 18, 36–7, 43–4, 51,
    61, 65–6, 70–80, 82, 87–9, 91,
    108–17, 121–41, 148–9, 151, 159,
    161, 174, 175, 185, 195–6, 197–8,
    203, 205–7, 209, 210–2, 215–20, 224,

    230–31, 236,240–1, 244–8
Isokoland, 100
Italy, 22
Itsekiri, (see Warri)
Ivory Coast, 23, 35, 55, 94, 123, 127,
    143–8, 153, 160, 179–87, 190, 196,
    203–4, 208–9, 211–2, 222, 235, 236,
    240

Jaja of Opobo, 66
Jalabert, Bishop, 74, 122, 123
Jamaica, 34, 107
Japan, 235
Jehovah's Witnesses, 137, 238
Jeniss, Princess, 187
Jesuits, 16
Jimmy, King, 34
Jirapa, 98–9
Joal, 14–16, 43, 70, 71, 75
Johnson, Henry, 67
Johnson, Bishop James, 49, 64, 100,
    162–6, 222
Jolof, 50, 215
Jones, E.N., 89
Jos, 177, 202
Joseph, Fr, 14
Jos Plateau, 107, 109, 111–4, 132
Judaism, 18, 72–3
Jukun, 105

Kabre, 142
Kaduna, 114, 177
Kaedi Mission, 126
Kalabari, 65
Kaleo, 98–9
Kandi Mission, 139, 140
Kankan Mission, 127–8
Kano, 109, 114, 174, 177, 202, 218
Kanuri, 1
Kaolack, 72, 205
Kassena, 98
Katsina, 23, 109, 114
Katsina Ala Mission, 106
Keta Mission, 61, 138
Khartoum, 5
Khassonke, 77

Kilham, Hannah, 79
King, Mr, 114
Kissi, 89, 126–7
Kissy Mission, 14
Kita, 76
Kiwanuka, Bishop Joseph, 207
Komenda, 19
Kono, 89
Kontagora, 114
Korhogo Mission, 143
Korinya Mission, 107
Kosoko, 63
Kouandé Mission, 138, 139
Koupéla, 134
Kouroussa Mission, 127
Kpelle, 198
Kpolo Kpele Mission, 95
Krio, 79
Kru, 1, 50, 93–4, 198
Kru Bay, 11
Krutown, 56
Kulango, 147
Kumasi, 42, 58, 97–8, 177
Kumm, Karl, 109–10
Kunar Mission, 106
Kuru Mission, 112
Kwaia, 51

Labadi, 199, 236
Lagos, 61, 63–4, 69, 103–4, 140, 160–3, 172–4, 177, 197, 231, 233
Lahou, 145, 147, 179, 185
Lalou, Marie, 185–7
Lama-Kara, 142
Lawra, 223, 237
League of Nations, 148
Leicester Village, 35
Lejeune, Fr, 100
Lele, 135
Le Rouge, Bishop, 127–9
Leyden University, 23
Liberia, 1, 9, 31, 37–41, 44, 48, 51–7, 86, 92–6, 117, 143, 152, 175, 177, 182, 196–8, 222, 238
Liberia College, 93
Liberian Frontier Force, 94

Libermann, François, 31, 55
Lijadu, 186
Limba, 49–50, 89
Liokard, Governor, 138
Lisbon, 7, 13, 81
Liverpool, 31
Lobi, 147
Lodagaa, 2
Loko, 50
Lokoja, 65
Lokoja Mission, 109
Lomé, 140, 142
London Missionary Society (LMS), 31, 56
Lopes, Domasio, 81
Lot, Pastor, 112
Louisiana, 38
Louis XIV of France, 15
Lourenço, Gregorio, 20
Luanda, Bishop of, 151
Ludlam, Thomas, 34
Lugard, Lord, 131
Lutheran Church, 4, 51, 57, 92, 95, 157, 198
Lutz, Fr, 69

Ma Ba Diakhou Ba, 76
Mabanta, 49
Macaulay, Zachary, 31
MacCarthy, Governor, 35
MacCarthy Island, 44
Macenta, 129
Maclean, President, 42
Mahdi of Ijebu-Ode, 159
Maiduguri, 109, 113–4
Makurdi Mission, 106–7
Mali,
    ancient Empire of, 1, 8
    Republic of, (Soudan), 2, 76–7, 130–3, 137, 146, 196, 203, 208, 222–3, 232
Malinke, 1, 127
Mande, 1
Mandinka, 1, 50–1, 73, 79
Mango, 143
Manjaco-Papel, 151

Manjaks, 79
Mano Bagru, 49
Manon, 127
Marabouts, 71
Maradi Mission, 137
Maroons, 34–5, 48
Marshall, Thomas, 61
Maryland Colonisation Society, 38
Masabu of Bida, 66
Massignon, 218
Matapoly, 189
Mauritania, 1, 126, 196, 238
Mawu, 143
Mecca, 72
Medina, 72
Mende, 1, 36, 49–50, 88–90, 97, 177, 223
Mennonites, 150
Mensah Sarba, John, 62, 98
Merrick, Joseph, 148
Methodist Church, 4, 30, 35–8, 49, 68,
    92, 95, 97–8, 101, 105, 124–5,
    137–41, 145–7, 163, 179, 184, 187–8,
    197–8, 210, 208–10
Methodist Episcopal Mission, 51
Methodist Missionary Society, 208
Mfantispim, 98
Michel, 43
Mikpon, 61
Miller, Walter, 110–4
Milleville, Bishop, 204
Mina, 61
Mingo, 41
Mongo Mission, 126–7
Monrovia, 39, 51, 56, 93–4, 160, 197–8
Moore, Hannah, 30
Mopti, 130, 133
Moravian Church, (see United
    Brethren)
Môre, 136
Moro Naba, 12
Mossi, 12, 134–7
Moussa, 43
Mozano, 189
Muir, 217
Mulattoes, 23–4, 75
Musamo Christo Disco Church, 188–9

Mutilerberg, 57
Nago Yoruba, 140
Naimbaña King, 33–4
Nakana, 98
Nana Ntona (Cult of St. Anthony), 19
Nana Sasaxy, King, 19
Nandom, 98–9
Nasr-al-Din, 15
Natitingou, M, 139, 142
National Church of Africa, 157, 217
National Council of Nigeria and
    Cameroons (NCNC), 101, 234
National Institute of Moral and
    Religious Education, 211
National Institute for Religious
    Sciences, 211
Native Baptist Church, 64
Native Pastorate Church (Sierra Leone
    Church), 49
Navrongo, 98
N'drim, Gaston, 185
Netherlands Missionary Society, 31
New Sasstown, 93–4
Ngasobil, 75, 78
Nguru, 114
Nhô-Nacho (Lopes Domasio), 81
Niamey Mission, 138, 219
Niffu, 94
Niger, 23, 137–8, 160, 196, 203
Niger mission, 62–8, 99–101, 162–3
Nigeria, 1, 3, 9, 17, 21–4, 36, 48, 55, 57,
    59–69, 86–7, 99–115, 123, 131, 152,
    157, 178–9, 186, 188–90, 195–6,
    200–4, 216–8, 219, 222, 228, 230–1,
    236–40
Nigeria Association of Aladura
    Churches, 211
Nigerian Civil War, 201, 208, 220, 228,
    239
Nigerian Youth Movement, 234
Niki Mission, 140
Nkissi, 69
Njoya, 148
NKST Church, 202
Nöldeke, 217
North America, 9, 14, 30–1, 33, 37–41,

51, 55, 70, 95, 98, 102, 110, 125, 128,
147, 151, 160–1, 163, 190, 195–6,
198, 201, 228–9, 232–3
Norway, 4
Nouadhibou Mission, 126
Nouakchott Mission, 126
Nouna, 136
Nova Scotians, 33–6, 48, 160
Nupeland, 109
Nyam, 147
Nyangka, 147
Nzérékore, 127
Nzi-Comoë, 179
Nzima, 187

Oba, 191
Obuna, Mr, 114
Odubanjo, 168
Oduduwa, 4
Odunlami, Sophia Adefobe, 167–8
Ogbomoso, 102
Ogoja, 102
Ogunpa, 103
Ogun State, 166, 234
Oke, 186
Oke-Are Mission, 103–4
Oke-Ofa, 103
Oke-Padre, 103
Old Sasstown, 93
Old Town, 68
Olodomare, 191
Oloja of Shagamu, 102
Olorunkole Hill, 173
Olu Antonio Domingos of Warri, 21
Olu Sebastian of Warri, 21
Ondo State, 104
Oni of Ife, 170
Onitsha, 65, 69, 100–1, 108
Ongaawonsu, 187
Order of St Augustine, 114
Order of St Joseph of Cluny, 43, 50
Orekoya, Daniel, 168, 171
Organisation of Catholic Youth, 139
Orimolade, 184
Oschaffa, Mr, 201

Oshitelu, Josiah Olunowa
(Arrabablahhubab), 171, 175–7, 235
Ossu, 41
Oturkpo Mission, 107
Oussouye Mission, 124
Owa of Ilesha, 170
Owerri, 101, 107–8
Oyo, 2, 64, 102
Oyo Province, 171

Pa Antonio, 69
Pabre Mission, 136
Padri di Terra, 9
Pakédou Mission, 127
Palimé, 142
Papaille, 43
Parakou Mission, 139, 140
Paris Evangelical Mission Society, 78,
145, 147
Pastoral Commission, 211
Patani, 100
Pategi Mission, 109
Patyana Mission, 132
PDG (see Guinea Democratic Party)
Pennsylvania, 38
Pentecostal churches, 125, 198
Perkins, Cato, 35
Peru, 11
Peters, Thomas, 33
Phillip II, King of Spain, 21
Pinto, Joao, 15
Pires, Duarte, 20
Plateau State, 100
Platt, 145
politics and Christianity, 2, 3, 8–11,
15–16, 25–6, 30, 35, 40–1, 44, 66, 71,
81, 87, 97, 108, 112, 128–9, 134–5,
143–4, 147, 152–3, 157–8, 163, 166,
171, 178, 181, 184–9, 196, 205–6,
216, 227–41, 244–6
Ponty, Governor-General, 135
Poro Society, 36, 91, 96
Port Loko, 49
Porto Novo, 61, 69, 96, 138, 139, 201
Porto Seguro, 61

Portudal, 14–16, 70
Portugal in West Africa, 7–19, 25, 43, 61, 69, 74–5, 81, 87, 122, 150–3, 205, 215, 231, 237–8
Portuguese Missionary Statute, 238
Potiskum Mission, 114
Precious Stone-Faith Tabernacle Movement, 166–9, 175
Prempeh, Princess Victoria, 177
Prempeh II, 177
Presbyterian Church, 4, 51, 68, 149, 195, 199, 210
Presbyterian Church of Eastern Nigeria, 102
Presbyterian Church of the Gold Coast, 97
Primitive Methodist Mission, 69, 101
Protestant churches, 4, 13, 23–6, 39–41, 52, 55–6, 70–1, 78–9, 87, 91, 95, 100, 110, 114, 122, 126, 128, 133, 137, 139–42, 144–6, 148–52, 160, 176, 184-5, 187, 189–90, 198, 204–5, 210–12, 222, 232, 238–9
Protestant Episcopal Mission, 39, 52, 95
Protestant Evangelical Missionary Society, 124
Protestant Gospel Missionary Union (GMA), 133
Protestant Missionary Society, 210
Protten, Christian, 23

Qua Ibo Mission, 69, 101, 115, 210
Quaker Church, 4, 30, 37, 79
Quaque, Philip, 23

Rafan Mission, 112
Rapu, Mr, 114
Reformation, 4
Reo Mission, 135
Ribeira Grande, 81
Riis, 41
Rivers State, 162
Roberts, Bishop, 51
Robertsville, 39
Robinson, Revd J.A., 67
Roman Catholic Church, 4, 8–11, 13, 25–6, 31, 43–4, 47, 50, 55–7, 59, 60–2, 72, 74–82, 88–94, 97–110, 112, 113–5, 121–53, 160, 176, 184, 186, 189, 197–213, 218–22, 232, 237
Ross, 69
Rotifunk, 36, 49
Royal Niger Company, 231
Rufisque, 14, 70, 74, 78

Sabtenga, 134
St Andrew's Church, Bakana, 165
St Anthony's Church, 22
St Louis, 14–7, 43, 70–1, 73–4, 76, 78–9, 126
St Mark, 5
St Patrick's College, 102
St Paul's Breadfruit Church, 64, 162–3
St Saviour's Anglican Church, 166
St Thomas' Training College, 102
Saker Mission, 148
Sakpata, 143
Saloum, 76
Samory, 76
San, 130, 133
Sanatan Dharma, 229
Sankoh, Laminah, 89
Santiago, 10, 17, 81, 151
Santo Agostino, 21
São Jorge da Mina, 18
São Tomé e Principe, 14, 17, 21–2, 61, 69, 81, 150–2, 196
São Vicente, 81
Sapele, 100, 177
Sattan Lahai Yansanneh, 51
Savé Mission, 138
Savé-Kilibo, 139
Schmidt, William, 221
Scottish Presbyterian Society, 31, 101–2
Scripture Union, 202
Sebastian, Olu of Warri, 21
Second Vatican Council, 211, 218, 224
Second World War, 90–1, 93–6, 98, 102, 104, 111, 113, 123, 125, 133, 136, 139, 142, 147–9
Secret Societies, 36, 91, 98, 115, 233
Sedhiou, 73–4, 78

Segou, 130–1
Segu, 130
Segu-Tokolor empire, 130, 132
Sekou Touré, President, 129, 205
Sene, Fr, 75
Senegal, 2, 8–9, 13, 16, 31, 35, 43, 47,
    50, 55, 70–80, 86–7, 122–4, 126, 129,
    137, 196, 203–6, 208, 215–6, 218,
    220, 237
Senegal Company, 15
Senufo, 147
Seraphim, Fr, 13
Serer, 1, 70, 72–3, 75, 79, 205, 237
Service Oecuménique d'Entraide, 124
Sevav Mission, 106
Seventh Day Adventists, 95, 128,
    151–2, 198
Seys, John, 39
Shadare, Joseph (Daddy Ali), 166–9
Shah of Iran, 66
Shama, 18–19
Shanahan, Bishop, 100–1, 222
Shango, 36
Sharp, Granville, 30–2
Shendam Mission, 109, 114
Shenge, 36
Sherbo, 1, 38
Sierra Leone, 2, 9–11, 13, 26, 32–7, 44,
    48–52, 55, 63, 65, 79, 86–92, 114,
    160, 161, 175–7, 196–7, 217, 223
Sierra Leone Church (Native Pastorate
    Church), 49, 62
Sierra Leone Company, 33–6
Siguiri Mission, 127
Sine, 76
Sinendé, 140
Sisters of the Holy Rosary, 101
Sisters of Our Lady of Apostles, 143
Sisters of Our Lady of Cluny, 31
Sisters of St Joseph of Cluny, 71, 77–9
slave trade, 7–11, 16, 20, 22, 25, 31–3,
    43–5, 61, 74–5, 125, 216, 233–4
Slessor, Mary, 68
Small, Bishop, 98
Smeathman, Dr H., 32
Smith, 221

So, 143
Society for African Culture, 218
Society of African Missions (SMA), 31,
    50, 57, 60–1, 69, 93, 98, 110, 114,
    138, 143
Society of the Divine Word, 140
Society of the Evangelical Missions of
    Paris, 71
Society of the Immaculate Heart of
    Mary, 31
Society of Missions in Paris, 142
Society for the Propagation of the
    Gospel, 23, 32
Sodoke, Chief, 63, 238
Sokodé, 143
Sokoto, 109, 113–4
Sokponta Mission, 138
Songhai, 1, 12
Soninke, 1, 151
Sosé, 73
Soudan (see Mali)
Souk-Arrhas (Thagaste), 5
South Africa, 54
South America, 62, 64
Southern American Baptist Mission, 64
Southern Baptists Convention of the
    United States, 52
South Togo Cultural and Religious
    Research Group, 221
Soviet Union, 228
Spain, 7, 13–15, 18, 21–2, 61
Spanger, 217
Speisser, Fr, 73
Spiritual Association, 211
Stone, Pastor Moses Ladejo, 161
Student Volunteer Movement, 52
Sudan, 5
Sudan Interior Mission (SIM), 31,
    105–6, 109–11
Sudan United Mission (SUM), 105, 150
Sugu, 114
Sunni, 88
Suronki, 94
Susu, 26, 50, 151
Svane, Frederick, 23
Sweden, 4

Switzerland, 4

Tadzewu, 189
Tahoss Mission, 112
Tanguieta Mission, 139
Taraku Mission, 107
Tarma, 36
Taylor, James, 65
Taylor, Pastor, 79
Tchaourou Mission, 138
Tchidimbo, Bishop, 204
Teaque, Colin, 160, 198
TEKAN (Fellowship of Churches of
    Christ in Nigeria), 201
TEKAS, 113
Temne, 1, 11, 32, 36, 49–50, 89
Thagaste (see Souk-Arrhas)
Thannie, Grace, 147, 187
Thiandoum, Mgr, 124
Thompson, Revd, 115
Thompson, Thomas, 23–5
Thornton, Henry, 30, 33
Timbucktu, 130, 134, 232
Tiv, 1–2, 105–7
Togo, 48, 57, 60–1, 87, 129, 138, 140–3,
    145–6, 152, 160, 174–5, 189, 196,
    203–5, 208, 221, 224, 238
Tokolor, 1, 73
Toma, 127–8
Tombalbaye, Ngarta, 150
Tom, King, 33
Topo, 94
Townsend, Henry, 63, 231
trade and Christian missions, 2, 7–8,
    15, 19, 22, 25, 33–5, 43–4, 47–9,
    58–9, 66–7, 96, 112, 166, 231–3,
    235–6, 246
trade union movement, 129
traditional religion, 3, 14, 22, 24–5,
    36–7, 43–4, 47–50, 60, 63, 65–6, 68,
    70, 77, 81–2, 89, 110, 111, 113,
    121–2, 134, 140, 143, 144, 147,
    150–1, 163, 166–7, 174–5, 179–83,
    186, 188–91, 195, 198, 206–7, 213,
    215, 220–4, 229, 233, 238, 240,
    244–8

Treaty of Berlin, 143
Treaty of Versailles, 148
Tripoli, 23
True Church of God, 201
Tubman, President, 95–6
Tugwell, Bishop, 99, 162
Tunisia, 5
Tunolase, Moses Orimolade, 172, 174
Turan, 106
Turkey, 66
Turner, Bishop Harold, 54
Twi, 59, 140

Umaru of Bida, 66
Union of the Peoples of Cameroon
    (UPC), 239
United African Methodist Church, 163
United Brethren (Moravian Church),
    23, 49
United Christian Council of Sierra
    Leone, 210
United Free Church of Scotland, 97,
    101
United Methodist Church, 197–8
United Nations, 148, 228
United Native African Church, 161, 178
Universities Mission to Central Africa,
    31, 207
University of Liberia, 93
Upper Guinea, 16
Upper Volta (see Burkina Faso)
Urhobo, 100
Utonkon Mission, 107
Uwangue, 20
Uzulua, Oba, 20

Vai, 51, 54, 197, 198
Vaughan, Mr, 114
Venn, Henry, 32, 62, 65, 67–70, 230
Vicariate of the Two Guineas, 55
Vila De Ribeira Brava, 81
Vincent, Pastor Nathaniel Claudius,
    168
Virginia, State, 37
Vo Gyang, 112
Vom Mission, 112

Wa, 223, 237
Waddell, Hope, 68
Wagadugu, 134–7
Wala, 133
Wappi, 94
Warri (Itsekiri), 9–10, 20, 22, 25, 100,
   177, 202
Wase Mission, 109, 111
Weaver, Richard, 33
Weber, 212
Wesleyan Methodist Missionary
   Society, 31, 35, 42, 44, 57–8, 60, 62,
   79, 96–7, 102
Wesley, John, 30
Wessa, 79
West African Methodist Church, 160
Western Church, 4
West Indies, 16, 52, 62, 115, 148, 160–1
White Fathers, 31, 98, 130–1, 134, 137,
   152
Whydah, 19, 61, 69
Wiagha, 98
Wilberforce, William, 30, 32
Williams, 221
Winneba, 188
Wolof, 1, 15, 35, 71, 74, 77–9
World Missionary Conferences, 109
Worldwide Evangelical Crusade, 125,
   151–2

Wukari, 107
Wuli Mission, 79
Wusasa, 115

Xerele, 19

Yagba, 105
Yaoundé, 149
Yeboa-Korie, Charles, 195
Yelwa, 114
Yevogan of Abomey, 61
Yola Mission, 114
Yoruba, 1–2, 4, 36, 49, 62–4, 70, 79, 88,
   100, 102, 161–2, 167, 176–7, 221–3,
   247
Young Christian Workers (JOC), 143

Zagnanado Mission, 138
Zahn, Dr, 60
Zaire, 35
Zaki-Biam Mission, 106
Zaria, 109–11, 114–5
Zerma-Songhai, 138
Zinder, 138
Zinzendorf, Nikolaus, 23
Ziquinchor, 74–5, 78, 205
Zouerate Mission, 126
Zra, 147